Leathered Mercuries, goggled,
Diminishing into their own dis...
Riders snarl away, to ballet in t...
A dancing mirage,
Far up the desert of the shore.

Yammer-yammer incessant –
Raucous-raucous echoing reports –
Shout back from the cliffs.
Surf, with oily breath,
Ozones the crowd
Strung out, a tide-wrack,
So much detritus
Along the dunes.

Withdrawn, shifting somewhere
Beyond the headland,
The sea idled at its turning,
A distantly-glittering zone of water, far
From the rippling dimples of the sand.

Not long after the last
Castroled sirocco
Had roared its metallic anger
A tide, skimming across the beach,
Swiftly erased snaking tyre-ladders;
Bawling exhausts overtaken –
Drowned by the waves' roar.

Lynn Hughes

(After Douglas Phillips)

PENDINE RACES

PENDINE RACES

Motor Racing over Fifty Years

Lynn Hughes

GOMER

First impresion – 2000

© Lynn Hughes, 2000

ISBN 1 85902 830 6

Lynn Hughes has asserted his right under the Copyright, Designs and Patents Act, 1988, to be identified as author of this work

All rights reserved. No part of this publication may be reproduced, saved in a retrieval system, or retransmitted in any form or by any means: electronic, electrostatic, the Internet, magnetic tape, mechanical, photocopying, recording or otherwise, without permission in writing from the publishers, Gomer Press, Llandysul, Ceredigion, Wales

Produced and printed in Wales at
Gomer Press
Llandysul
Ceredigion
Wales

In tribute to Eddie Stephens and all the 'helpers'.
Also in rememberance of Ernie and Mostyn, with thanks.

CONTENTS

End-papers poem *Pendine Races* by Lynn Hughes after Douglas Phillips

Foreword: Denis Parkinson   ix

Chapter	*page*
1. Veteran Days	1
2. Motor Union Tour	7
3. Pembroke & Pendine	13
4. Vintage Years	21
5. The Golden Era begins	35
6. The First Welsh TT	61
7. Brough Superiority	85
8. Glory days	93
9. Tommy Thomas & Babs	117
10. Fall from Grace	177
11. The Man in White & the Skipton Butcher	187
12. Stanley Wood	213
13. The First Welsh Grand Prix	219
14. The Fife Flyer	227
15. Post-war Enthusiasm	239
16. Mr Manx Grand Prix	255
17. Pendine Hundred again	261
18. World Motor Cycle Land Speed Record	265
19. Fabulous Fred	275
20. Rex is King	287
21. A Glory that has passed	303
Postscript	307
Afterword	311
Acknowledgments	313
Appendix I Pembrokeshire Automobile Club, 1910 meeting: key	315
II 1922 Motorcycles	316
III Kings of Pendine	318
Index	321

Foreword: Denis Parkinson

I WELL remember my first experience of Pendine. It was late on a Sunday night at Easter, 1947. The journey from Wakefield to this remote corner of west Wales had taken far longer than I had ever imagined, and it was very dark and late when we arrived. I had been invited by the Swansea Motor Cycle Club to appear at their opening meeting of the season – and well briefed about etiquette at the Beach Hotel. All was quiet except for the drawing and sighing of the tide beyond the sea wall. There was a certain code knock that I had been given to gain access at the door. I knocked: boom-buddy-boom-boom. Silence. This was Sunday, in holy Wales, during Prohibition. The door eased open and an amazing sight greeted our eyes. The corridor and the bar were jammed with silent boozers. When they saw it was us all hell broke loose and soon they were roaring like lions!

My memories of the racing on the following day are now, after fifty years, hazy. The beach, when you first see it, especially, is astounding. One of the wonders of the world. It seems to stretch away into infinity when there's a haze. You can just imagine the trepidation those record-breakers must have felt, venturing as they were beyond man's experience into the unknown.

The sand on Pendine beach is generally firm, but invariably wet. Curiously enough, the wet parts often were the firmest, much like a road surface, whereas the yellow parts could induce those worrying slaloms that have put many a rider off sand-racing. We had to devise all manner of ingenious protective patents to keep water off electrics and sand out of the carburettor and brakes. But it was a losing battle, a damage-limitation exercise. Sand and water got everywhere eventually; and so luck played her part. After every meeting the bike had to be stripped: and it was surprising where the sand had got in to – every blessed nook and cranny! It played hell with the bikes, really – an expensive indulgence. In later days the 'Featherbed' Norton certainly did not like it. But it was great fun at the time and very quick, with mile-long straights in between hazardous turns.

It was entertaining and instructive to observe at first hand the differing cornering techniques of the competitors. Fred Rist was always pretty to watch, but not necessarily the quickest. There were some local boys down there who gave a very good account of themselves. One in particular, I remember, who wound up this nineteen-twenty-four Dance-era 350 Sunbeam Sprint running on dope and was practically uncatchable over the mile. That was a very fast little machine indeed. I think it annoyed Francis Beart who could not quite figure it out!

There was always such a welcome at Pendine and good, clean sportsmanship. Eddie Stephens and the Carmarthen club had a clear idea of how things should be run. (They'd been at it long enough!). They also understood hospitality of a kind I shall always associate with Wales. Some of the riders I met were also unforgettable. Les Griffiths, a wily old tactician, on an immaculately turned-out Manx. DR Griffith, an accountant and something of a loner, who had made his own sand-racer out of Norton bits and a JAP speedway engine back in the thirties – still going like stink! There was a clever rider, (Cliff) Edwards from Aberkenfig, who always impressed me, and thought he could have gone places – in a different context. Though sand racers did not always translate to road-racing, or vice-versa.

I was very lucky in my 14, 000 miles racing career in that I never really hurt myself or came off. Except once at Pendine, I dropped the bike, and got a telling-off from my father who was probably thinking of selling it on the following week! I always raced within my capabilities and never took any unnecessary chances. Of course I took some risks occasionally. But if someone passed me on a circuit that suited his ability better than mine, I'd let him go, because before long we'd meet again on another track and I'd probably do the same to him.

People always imagined that I was a 'works' rider, or that my machines were 'specials' from the Norton factory, but it was not the case. We had a thriving motor cycle agency in Wakefield selling Ariel, Excelsior, Norton, OK Supreme and Rex-Acme, and my bikes, like everyone else's, came 'over the counter'. My father, Bill, was my tuner, manager, racing mechanic and mentor. He always stressed to me the importance of learning the course before going flat-out. This applied as much to arenas such as Southport and Pendine as it did to Esholt Park or the Isle of Man. There were always soft places to avoid on Pendine which, if you hit them on braking, turning or acceleration, could prove disastrous.

Francis Beart was with me mostly during my hey-days at Pendine. I was very lucky to have him prepare my machines, as he was that rarity – not so unusual in Wales, of course – a wizard! A shy and somewhat preoccupied character, he hated any kind of attention, as he, with single-mindedness, addressed himself to his purpose – which was quite simply that of making motor cycles go faster, without losing out on all-essential reliability. Looking back, I realise now that I was in the presence of genius. So I was deeply privileged.

That same sense of privilege I feel about my whole career in motor cycle racing. To do in this life for a living something that you love doing best and which is so exciting as to be thrilling even in hindsight is a tremendous good fortune. And what survives is the joy of having worked with like-minded people, and the grand fellowship of motor cycle. Nowhere were they more enthusiastic than on Pendine, and like many another, I will leave part of my heart there.

November, 1998.

Denis Parkinson & Francis Beart, 1948.   [*Crown ©*]

Humber 3½ hp, Walter Davies with brother, Mansel, Llanfyrnach, Carmarthen Park, Bank Holiday Monday, 7th August, 1905. [JF Lloyd photo: © Carmarthen County Museum]

'Demonstration motor race against time'. L>R: Walter Davies, 3½ hp Humber; (?) 2¾hp Excelsior; (?) 2¾hp BAT; (AM Schreyer ?) 2¾hp Riley. Carmarthen Park, August 7th, 1909. (Inset: Mansel Davies, racing cyclist). [JF Lloyd photo: © Carmarthen County Museum]

1. Veteran Days

The First Motor Race

The first motor cycle race officially run on the beach at Pendine was on Friday, 18th August, 1905, a half-wet day. The race over four miles, sanctioned by the 'Motorists Society', was the inspirational idea of Mr Fred J Renfrey, proprietor of the Beach Hotel. He saw it as a novel attraction in the annual sporting event, known as 'Pendine Races' *Rasus Pendein*, whose classes - foot, bicycle and horse racing - divided between the grassy acre above the cliff and, when the tide was out, the beach. The £3 prize for first motor bicycle past the post on the sand was won by Mansel Davies, Llanfyrnach, on a Humber,[1] in evening sunshine. Second was A Evans, (3½ hp Olympic [BX 31]: entrant H Evans, Butcher's Arms, St Clears), and Benjamin Donald Richards, Whitland, (3½ hp Rex [BX 69]), was third. Llanstephan Brass Band were in attendance and played appropriate music between the running, the trotting, the gallops and the motor racing.

We can assume that racing with horses on the beach has a very long history. So much so, that Pendine Races had grown, in the 19th century, into an annual event in the sporting calendar. *Rasus Pendein*, though not advertised, were usually held in the early days of August, between hay and corn harvests, as dictated by the tides.

> Once a year (Pendine) tempts guests by horse races on the sands. A grand day that for Pendine, a distracting one for the well-intentioned landlady (of the Spring Well Inn). The sand burrows lend themselves kindly to grand stand purposes, though the umpire must perforce appear more dignified and take his position in a farm cart. The race is known, but not advertised, to begin at twelve - for by that time the tide having obligingly gone out - as everyone knew it would - the sand presents an unrestricted appearance. Some five hundred visitors have arrived - every one seems to know the other and shaking hands and mutual enquiries occupy all attention. After many appeals from the weigher who has, perhaps, been chosen for his good-tempered patience, if not his mathematical power, and racers are weighed, saddled - mounted *and started* had almost slipped from the pen - but that was not so soon done. The signal word had to be spoken and spoken it was too often by a mischievous boy, sometimes heard by an impatient jockey only. But false starters rebuked, order restored, impatience curbed, the right word given, and they are off. A

---

[1] The motor bicycle was borrowed from his brother, an apprentice at the Humber works, home on holiday. Mansel, an athlete, was an enthusiastic competition bicyclist.

pretty race to see, a mile and three-quarters, the farmers mainly riding their own horses, with slight use of the whip and spur, and very little else but the glory of winning as a reward. The five races took seven hours, so there was no unseemly hurry! There is plenty to do between races.

(Reproduced in *The Carmarthen Journal* July 25th, 1884, from the *Pall Mall Gazette.*)

The Journal , in August, 1904, reports that 'Pendine Races (foot and horse) were that year to be held at Great House Farm', adjacent to the beach.

At the turn of the century, places where motor-engined vehicles could securely try their speed in these, the veteran days of motoring, were few indeed.[2] A motoring note in *The Western Mail* of the 16th March, 1905, complained that 'motorists find it difficult to get suitable tracks where the speed of motor cars etc. may be tested'. It was in response to this that Mr Fred J Renfrey of the Beach Hotel Pendine wrote an historic letter, published the following day, suggesting that motors be invited to compete in that summer's annual races. *The Western Mail* enthusiastically takes up his cause and needs no convincing that Pendine is well-suited to the purpose.

> That the place is well adapted for this there is not the slightest doubt, so I am informed by several motorists, and the wonder is that the spot was not thought of before. So in addition to the contemplated horse, foot and bicycle races on the sands, there will be motor races which will be a monstre [sic] attraction to the place.
> As has been pointed out over and over in *The Welshman,* Pendine only requires to be advertised to be known etc., etc. It behoves the inhabitants therefore to fall into line (and) with a united effort they would speedily make the place the most frequented by visitors. By doing so they would have nothing to lose and everything to gain.

Whether in response to this exhortation or not, 'motorists', proud possessors of early examples of the novel mechanised transports - autocars and motorised bicycles, termed 'autocycles' (there was no distinction) - did make their way to open spaces such as Pendine to put them through their paces and there informally contest one vehicle against another - though some were, rightly, apprehensive about the corrosive effects of salt water and sand.

Straight, mile-or-more-long sections of highway, locally, like Pembrey Flats near Kidwelly, Nantycaws Hill, Carmarthen, and Arnold's Hill, on the A40 east of Haverfordwest, were to become synonymous with speeding and, *ipso facto,* police traps. There had been a legal requirement (seldom complied with) until 1896 for motorists to be accompanied by three running men, one of whom was to precede the vehicle, brandishing a red flag. The Motor Car Act of that year, abolished this custom and raised the speed limit from 4 mph to 12. After 1903, this was raised to a blanket official 20 mph speed limit on open roads which remained in force until 1930. Roads

---

[2]'There are 34,700 motor cycles registered in the UK in 1905': F Straight, Sec Auto Cycle Union. 'This shows how popular they have become'.

were generally narrow, crooked, stone- and nail-strewn, pot-holed, rutted - and mainly used by pedestrians, livestock, riders of horses and bicycles, as well as horse-drawn traffic. Charabancs, steam lorries and traction engines were becoming a common sight. The approaching sound of a petrol-driven motor vehicle was occasion for a mixture of excitement and the dread of calamity.

In dry weather, speeding motorised vehicles raised trailing clouds of dust which settled like a shroud over everything. One Cardiganshire author's[3] phrase, 'the white lanes of summer', conjures the scene; but any romance faded when the acrid taste of pulverised animal dung met nostrils and tongue. In winter and wet weather, the roads were axle-deep in mud, puddled and running in rivulets. Bridges were still a luxury in many out-of-the-way places. A wide-open space such as a beach, provided it was firm and dry between high and low water marks, was an opportunity free of all hazards and legal encumbrances, and the obvious best bet for fast runs. After all, where else would you find an arena which was free of charge, free of nails - and smoothly re-surfaced twice daily?

In this regard, Pendine beach was far and away the firmest and best-drained level space available in Wales. England had Southport and Scotland St Andrews, but Pendine was outstanding and to prove the best motor speed-trial beach in Britain. With between five and seven miles of good hard going, its full potential was yet to be recognised. As *The Carmarthen Journal* says in an early race report:

> A visit to the spot is really necessary to realise the magnificent and apparently illimitable stretch of sands about these parts, most of it as hard and flat as a billiard table; a place indeed for motor cars, even flying machines, to 'run riot'. Such a natural racing ground is rare in these islands ...

Pendine Sands were to provide, over a fifty-year period, the proscenium for thirty-eight years of motor cycle racing (allowing for interruptions occasioned by German political miscalculations), including the first 'Welsh TT' in 1922, 'The Welsh Hundred' and 'The Welsh Grand Prix' in later years. Elsewhere in South Wales, Oxwich, Cefn Sidan, Aberavon and Porthcawl were to facilitate shorter, sprint (even triangular) competitions. Pendine, however, had the capacity for hosting long-distance events, of fifty and a hundred miles - providing a two-and-a-half-miles-in-one-direction, five-mile-round-trip (lap) course, if needs be - with the possibility for adjustment up or down the beach if the corners became 'over-ploughed'.

The Carmarthen Journal, reporting the Pendine Races in 1907, is able to tell us of an expanded programme:

> The annual horse, bicycle and foot races were held at the Queen of watering places ... where athletic events, including the bicycle races, proceeded on a nearby grass track.

---

[3]Tom MacDonald: *The White Lanes of Summer*, (Macmillan,1975).

However, we learn that:

> a new feature of the athletic section of Pendine Races [had been] a motor bicycle race. The horse races and motor cycle races were held on the extensive sands and the beach was lined with people.

Whether or not the highly-strung race-horses were frightened by the roars and snarls, the pops and bangs of the exhausts of the autocycles, is a reflection one can ponder. Reading between the lines, they were! It must surely have been an unhappy mix, and there is no further mention of the two classes of event ever being held in conjunction again.

The Welshman report states that the winner of this new class of athletic event was Dr Phillips of St Clears; J Evans of Carmarthen coming second. Third was Mr Bowdon of Castell Gorfod, Meidrim. What machines they were riding and what their times and speeds were over what distance we shall, most likely, never know.

In 1908, running, bicycling and horse races only were held in a field near 'The Star'. In 1909, we learn from a report of the Pendine Races (*Journal*, August 20th) that 'the inferior bicycle and foot events were dispensed with and the meeting confined entirely to horse racing'. The motor races had in fact begun to take on a life of their own, having been run independently in July, though there is no account of them.

It is odd that bicycle races should be referred to as 'inferior'. For twenty years they had been the rage and were an accepted part of the athletic canon. From the bicycle craze of the 1890s many a good motor cyclist had been born.

In the years preceding the Great War, course- or circuit-racing for motors was largely unknown, mainly because of the scarcity of suitable venues, places of a sufficient hard, level surface. Cycle-tracks were called into service for racing motor bicycles, but found wanting. American-style board-circuits never caught on. The Brooklands asphalt circuit, near Weybridge in Surrey, which opened in 1909, was purpose-built to test the performance of the motor to its ultimate. The trouble was that it was inaccessible to the majority of enthusiast-motorists, and the 'Brooklands set' exuded an aura of exclusivity - a league apart - to the amateur competitor and bystander. The Weybridge circuit was criticised anyway for its poor spectator facility. Watching a race at Brooklands, a contemporary said, was reminiscent of watching 'two ruddy flies walking round the rim of a ruddy saucer'. For the motorist anxious to participate in competition, the local and 'point-to-point' notion of a hill-climb event seemed at the time more palatable and convenient. A comparatively short, uphill sprint - usually involving a tight curve - challenged machine and driver in terms of time-over-terrain. It allowed for crude handicapping and brought to account driver-skill within the limits of mechanical stamina. In addition, it provided a spectacle for local people, interested to compare the performance of different machines, and to support or deride the efforts of local heroes.

Looking back, it must be remembered that motor engineering was only a short-step away from the blacksmith shop. The transition from the horse to the motor was by far the greatest cultural revolution the world had ever seen. Those with real mechanical/electrical engineering ability were few and far between, as it was a completely new discipline. There were no training courses, apprenticeships were hard to come by and workshop manuals lay in the future. An unsurprisingly high proportion of blacksmiths' sons, therefore, number among racing motorists of the veteran era, some of whose future businesses would lie in supplying and repairing cycles, motorcycles and motor cars. As metal-workers, they at least had some tradition of mechanical repair and improvisation in connection with agricultural and industrial machinery.

In early competition, the general unreliability of machines was a factor always to be taken into account; and one which often marred spectator satisfaction.

One can surmise that the growing 'speed craze' activities on hills and on any comparatively straight stretches of road did not always find favour with the local populace. Closing public roads for competitions was inconvenient enough, but as nothing compared to the sheer danger experienced by pedestrians, cyclists and horse-driven road-users encountering tyros[4] and determined competitors on 'unofficial' practice sessions. Even on an off-road arena as remote from road traffic as Pendine Sands, prudence was advised. All Pendine race programmes from the earliest times prominently advise, in cautionary language, that the motor races are run by specific permission of private landowners who control access to the beach.[5] Consent that, abused, could by implication be withdrawn.

A Pembroke club Hill-climb

Modesty was not uppermost in the minds of S&F Green of the Motor Cycle Depot, High Street, Haverfordwest, when they took a quarter page advertisement in *The Haverfordwest & Milford Telegraph* on September, 30th, 1908, to shout about the success of their machines in the recent hill-climb event, staged on Arnold's Hill. In a run-down of the winners in the motor cycle event – a virtual Triumph benefit – they lay claim to having supplied six of them as well as two Vindecs. Their announcement,

---

[4] Pers. comm. T Ernest Hughes. Dulais Bridge, then a hump-backed bridge intersecting the mile-straight between Rhosmaen and Manordilo on the A40 was a favourite spectator vantage-point for observing riders 'practising' jumps. Also pers. letter from Emlyn Evans, Teignmouth (late of Llandeilo), recalls 'Motor cycle trials (or races) were held on the hill going up past Golden Grove Church and the Dulais flats in Rhosmaen - from the Tannery past Closglas Farm and as far as Glanrwyth, Talley Road (Station). These races would have been 'preliminaries' for the Pendine races. There was very little traffic in those days. Among some of the riders were Mostyn Griffiths, not sure of his machine (Triumph, Sunbeam), Dr Lindsay of Nantgaredig (Norton) Gerwyn Rees, Green Hall, New Road (Llandeilo) - he had an ABC - he was a first class mechanic as well - even helping the others; and your father took part as well ... It was a great thrill for us as youngsters to see those machines moving at about 60 or maybe 70 mph - pretty fast in those days.'

[5] The Stepney family of Llanelly were the ground landlords.

in 16-point type, clarions: 'Nine of these thirteen motor cycles were sold by S&F Green!' The only other makes in the running were others' Triumphs, a Minerva and a Rex.

The Chief Constable who sanctioned the event, and James, his Deputy Chief, were in attendance 'in addition to a number of interested spectators'. It is in every way typical of many such competitions that took place all round the country in the Indian summer of Edward V11's reign. What transpired is described in *The Haverfordwest & Milford Telegraph*:

MOTOR CARS:

HA Jones-Lloyd (12/16 Talbot) – Best formula car.
Dr Williams (14/16 Darracq)
Dr Griffith (8hp Rover)
J Thomas (18/25 Siddeley) – Fastest car
SJ Rees (10/12 Humber)
Hugh Thomas (12/14 Humber)
J Gaskell (8hp Rover)

MOTOR CYCLES – SINGLE CYLINDER

E Allen (TT Triumph) – Best formula motor cycle and best on time.
Eric Green (Triumph)
LH Higgon (Triumph)
AJ Gwilliam (Rex)
GA Hill (Triumph)
Hugh James (Triumph)
George Carrow (Triumph)
E Lipscombe (Triumph)
SD Pugh (Vindec)
D Evans (Triumph)

MOTOR CYCLES – TWIN CYLINDER

Ralph Green (5hp twin Vindec) – Best 2-cylinder

A special prize was awarded to GF Owen who, it was pointed out, rode his own machine.

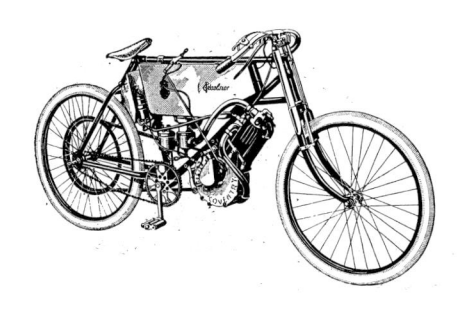

2. The Motor Union Tour

When, in 1909, the Motor Union of Great Britain and Ireland and the League International des Associations Touristes elected to hold speed tests on Pendine as part of their tour of the principality – centred on Swansea – there was great anticipation in the area. We learn from a report in *The Autocar* of May 29th, 1909, that

> Captain Hind Howell, Chairman of the Sports Committee of the Motor Union, recently visited South Wales at the request of the Executive Committee and inspected the Pendine Sands on which the speed trials are to be held on July 16th. He reports very favourably as regards the suitability of the sands for the proposed events. He finds there is a stretch of about five miles available, of which the last 2½ will be used. The sands enable a course of 150 yards wide to be marked out, with ample room for pulling up after finishing the event and for parking the cars after passing the winning post. The sands are very smooth, and they will support the weight of the heaviest cars for the time required without any appreciable impression being made, and no artificial platforms of any kind will be needed. Great local interest is being taken in the events.

The Welsh Automobile Club, as hosts, took it upon themselves to make the arrangements. Construction of a new causeway on the front at Pendine took place, paid for by public subscription, 'to enable cars to be taken from the road direct to the beach'. This was a lasting solution to a local access problem. *The Welshman* tells us (June 18th, 1909) that 'The residents are preparing for what will undoubtedly be a day of much excitement in the quiet hamlet'. On the day, *The Carmarthen Journal* is impressed with the turnout:

> The attendance of the public was astonishing, considering the sparse population of the neighbourhood. From Carmarthen, St Clears, Laugharne, Saundersfoot, Tenby and all the small hamlets between, a regular stream of people coursed along the narrow roads leading to the little village, on foot, on bicycles or in brakes. The club had gone to no little expense in making their arrangements. The Secretary, Mr Schimmell Andrews and his able co-adjudicator, Mr Harvey, had carefully marked out the whole course and, for a whole mile of it, had put up a rough, single-wire fence, intended to keep back the public. The course lay eastwards from the little village of Pendine for at least two miles. The public, perhaps, thought this arrangement anything but convenient, as to see the finishers entailed a walk of four miles (there & back), but it enabled the cars to travel with the prevailing winds, and was a precaution for the safety of the public insisted on by the Motorists Union.

Motor Union Tour, 1909.

Motor Union Tour, 1909. Cupelle [DE 178] owned by William O'Donnell, Castle Hill, Fishguard. Motor cycle [CY 44? No 12] (right) is a 550cc side-valve Triumph, ridden by Mr JS Andrews, H'west.

The Welshman brought out a commemorative issue, carrying the full race programme. The first 'test' was to begin at 11am, and the list of events was as follows:

MOTOR BICYCLES

11.30am: Bicycles not exceeding 300cc (cubic centimetres – engine swept capacity)
11.40am: 300cc > 601cc
11.50am: Bicycles of unrestricted capacity
12 noon: Passenger Cycles of unrestricted capacity.

TOURING PETROL CARS

12.00 noon TPCs not above 10 hp (horse-power)
12.10 pm: 10 > 12 hp
12.20 pm: 12 > 14 hp
12.30 pm: 14 > 16 hp
12.40 pm: 16 > 24 hp
12.50 pm: 24 > 30 hp
1.00 pm: 30 > 40 hp
1.10 pm; 40 > 55 hp
1.20 pm: 55hp >

STEAM MOTOR CARS

1.30pm: with any power engine to be run on a distance handicap.

It appears that the length of the course chosen was indeed two miles – perhaps 2½ – and the 'tests' were a sprint in one direction. It was a misty day (no 'prevailing winds'), and a frustrating one for the spectators, as the coastguard signalling system (presumably semaphores) engaged for the day to relay information from finish to start stations was unable to function. It is worth quoting from the follow-up report that appeared in *The Welshman* (23rd July), if only for its completely uninformative flippancy. This 'cheeky chappie' correspondent was no motor-racing enthusiast!

> Our St Clears correspondent writes: 'Seaside Surprises: Visiting the salubrious, health-yielding spot of Pendine, to our great surprise our smiling friend Mr Ben Jones, contractor, of St Clears, with his brilliant staff carrying out a stupendous contract on behalf of the Welsh Automobile Club: the construction of a mile of fencing up the sands. A man of versatile qualities, we also watched him, aided by his assistants, unearth a couple of motor cars which had got stranded and were making slow but steady progress in the direction of Australia.
>
> The Motor race did not command any special commendation from the 3 – 4000 that were present. An old sporting friend from Carmarthen observed that in his younger days he would have shown his heels to all the motors, as far as appearances went... Even the officials of the Automobile Club could not on that day persuade Old Sol to dissolve the mist so as to allow the coastguard officer to carry on the signalling operations. The gentleman whose duty it was to fix up the winning numbers failed to obtain the necessary information to record the winning cars and had to disestablish his

place of operation and like the writer, had to give up the hopeless task of ascertaining the numbers of all the winning cars.

It was pleasing to find clergy of the establishment as well as the disestablishment in line at Mr B Jones fence, in full enjoyment of the sport. Fortunately the races ended without experiencing any accidents. The police, under Inspector Evans, St Clears, carried out their duties admirably. Young Mr Samlet Jones of the Mermaid Hotel, took charge of the many preservers of the peace on the way to and from Pendine, all returning to St Clears hilarious and happy in his conveyances. The appearance of the RSPCA officer, in uniform, in the vicinity of the horseless conveyances bore with it a sense of incongruity.

It sounds suspiciously as if young Samlet Jones, charabanc driver of the Mermaid, may also have plied the St Clears correspondent – in addition to the several 'preservers of the peace' – with some 'entertainment', so 'hilarious and happy' is the scribe's recollection of events!

The day was, perhaps, not such a disappointment to the many distinguished 'visiting firemen' from the higher echelons of the motor-sporting organisations. Present were W Joynson-Hicks, MP (President of the Motor Union), CH Dodd (Vice President, MU), B Hinde (Treasurer, MU), Rees Jeffrys (Sec, MU) Capt Hinds Howell (Judge), Captain Hughes-Morgan (President, Welsh Automobile Club), as can be gleaned from *The Carmarthen Journal,* in a much more helpful story: 'Large Crowds Watch Speed Trials'. This provides a plausible explanation of why the pace of competition was comparatively tame:

> The number of fast cars in these trials was somewhat limited. There was scarcely the support that was expected from the English section. The Committee stated in the programme the trials were intended as a friendly sporting event between members of

Motor Union Tour, 1909. [CY 14] De Dion registered to DG Thomas, 34, Eaton Crescent, Swansea and later W Heath, esq, Bryn-y-mor Road.

the Motor Union driving vehicles that they have in daily use against cars and motor cycles of the same type in the hands of amateurs, and not against those specially-built and 'tuned-up' by manufacturers. Anyone connected with the industry could only run the vehicle he privately owned and used in his personal service. The competitions were all scratch races, from standing-starts.

There was, nevertheless, some good motor racing – besides one or two walkovers. The last race of the day for petrol engines of unlimited capacity, was a hard-fought contest between the Weigel of Capt Hughes-Morgan and the Daimler of Mr TJ Williams. The Weigel got off to a poor start, occasioned by a 'choke in its petrol' but, despite this set-back, managed a second place in front of Mr H Spence-Thomas's 'very fine Mercedes'.

The ('high Tory') *Journal* is at variance with its rival paper as to why there were no advertised results – in the somewhat priggish, but characteristically Edwardian phrasing:

> The course lay from the village eastwards for about two miles, enabling the cars to travel with the prevailing winds. No times or speeds were taken and therefore could not be published and the element of advertisement was thus, as far as possible, eliminated.

The *Journal* man is professional enough (or was it sufficiently sober?) to endure the four- or five-mile walk to enquire out the results of the motor car and motor cycle tests for posterity:

MOTOR BICYCLES

300cc > 601cc:
Mr WC (Cox) Pollard (Quadrant)
Mr WE James (Oxford)
Mr ET Strick (NSU)
Mr JS Andrew (Triumph)

Mr Strick was not to know that he was making an unique record as far as Pendine was concerned. His NSU is the only instance of a 'Continental foreign' motor cycle, either competing in or winning a place in an event on Pendine – in almost forty years of racing history.

Unlimited cc
Mr WC Pollard (Quadrant)
(walkover- only starter!)

MOTOR CARS

> 10 hp
Mr Bertie Perkins (De Dion 7.4hp)
Mr JS Andrew (De Dion 7.4hp)
Mr FD Hindley (Rover 9.8hp)

10 > 16 hp
Mr ET Strick (Darracq 11.9hp)
Mr H Spence-Thomas (Argyll 12.28hp)

Won eventually by 75 yards, after each had led in turn.

16 > 24 hp
Mr WP Thomas (Clement-Talbot 19.03hp)
Mr TJ Williams (De Dion 23.86hp)
Mr LW Francis (Belsize 23.32hp)
Mr HA Jones-Lloyd (Clement-Talbot)

24 > 30 hp
Mr CD Makepeace (Enfield 26hp)
Mr Evan Lewis (Vulcan 25hp)
Dr JL Lock MA (Britannia 26hp)
Mr J Jenkins (Gladiator)

> 40 hp
Capt D Hughes-Morgan (Humber 30hp)
Mr James Thomas (Humber 32hp)
Mr M Whittingdon (Mercedes)
Mr WT Farr (Beeston Humber 36hp)

40 > 55 hp
Mr TJ Williams (Daimler 45hp)
Capt D Hughes-Morgan (Weigel 52hp)
Mr H Spence-Thomas (Mercedes 45hp)

Mr JL Kirk (Talbot), who was first past the post, was disqualified for using an open exhaust.

The engine outputs, as published, require to be taken with a pinch of salt. They seldom match manufacturers' estimates – usually exceeding them by the rate of a few horse-power. Human frailty! No result of the race for steam cars was given. As an uninteresting postscript we learn that, on his way home, Capt Hughes-Morgan's Weigel caught fire outside Swansea High Street station, causing a crowd to gather. Nothing happened. There was no explosion. The fire was put out and everyone went home.

So much for the Motor Union and, for that matter, the involvement of the Welsh Automobile Club in Pendine Races.

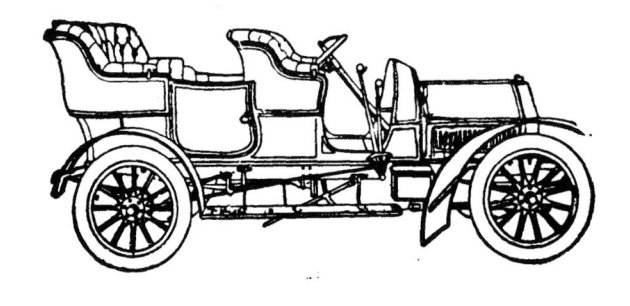

3. Pembroke and Pendine

FOUR years before the foundation of the Carmarthen Motor Cycle & Light Car Club, the Pembrokeshire Automobile Club was founded and became active on Pendine.[6] The club, one of the oldest, was an uneasy mix of 'gentry' and 'trade', chauffeurs and hired men in some cases doing the operating of levers while their 'owners' spectated. A fine photograph of the club's first meeting in 1910, at Williamston, near Burton – seat of the Scourfield family, is graphically descriptive of the club's demeanour. The motor cyclists are relegated to one side. Perhaps the photograph was taken before their departure to Pendine sands; some of the 'casting' fits[7].

On the 22nd of June, 1910, a Thursday, speed trials for autocars and motor bicycles were held on that fine stretch of beach which had, after all, once notionally belonged in Pembrokeshire.[8] We read in the *Haverfordwest & Milford Telegraph* that

> A good muster of the members were present. All the races were well contested, and an excellent day's sport enjoyed. Telephone lines were laid for the entire distance and Mr Martin Phillips again proved of great assistance.

A cup was awarded for first place, silver and bronze medals for second and third. They were awarded as follows:

SCRATCH RACE FOR CARS	HANDICAP RACE FOR CARS
Two miles >	Mr WH Greenish (20hp Humber)
Mr JV Colby (16/20 Sunbeam)	Mr Hugh Thomas (12hp Humber)
Mr Hugh Thomas (12hp Humber)	Mr JV Colby (16/20 Sunbeam)
Mr V Lange (14/16 Darracq)	Mr HA Jones-Lloyd (16hp Talbot)
Mr James Thomas (18/25 Siddeley)	Mr James Thomas (18/25 Siddeley)
Mr HA Jones-Lloyd (16hp Talbot)	Mr V Langue (14/16 Darracq)
Mr WH Greenish (20hp Humber)	

---

[6] An account book for 1908 is in the County Record Office, Haverfordwest. But the first meeting (ie. event) appears to have been 'run out' in 1910.

[7] There is a good print of this historic photograph in the Pembrokeshire archive at the Record Office in Haverfordwest Castle.

[8] In 1543 'the machinations in Parliament of Thomas Johnes of Abermarlais who was a Carmarthenshire man first and a member of parliament for county Pembroke second' resulted in the Lordships of Laugharne, Llanstephan and Llanddowror being excluded from the new shire of Pembroke by the 1536 Act of Union. (BG Charles *George Owen of Henllys*: Nat Lib Wales Press, 1973).

Pembrokeshire Automobile Club, first meet, Williamston 1910. For key: see Appendix 1 (p 315).

SCRATCH RACE FOR MOTOR CYCLES WITH PEDALS
Two miles >

D Pantall (3½ Triumph) Eric Green (TT Triumph)
Francis Phillips (3½ Triumph) Francis Phillips (3½ Triumph)
R Green (Rex Speed King) Stanley Williams (Rex Speed King)

SLOW RACE FOR MOTOR CYCLES
AJ Gwilliam (3½ Triumph) D Pantall (3½ Triumph)

Silver and bronze medals were awarded to first and second home.

In 1911, a separate Pembroke Motor Cycle Club was formed, more oriented towards the owner-rider.

Under the auspices of the older organisation, according to the *Haverfordwest & Milford Telegraph,* a meeting took place on the sands at Pendine on Monday, August 14th, 1911

> in the presence of a large gathering. The races for cars were very well supported, and though the sands were not in quite as good condition as in previous years, yet some exciting racing was witnessed, the finishes being very close. It was a little disappointing that the motor cyclists did not give better support to the extensive programme provided by the club. The general arrangements were carried out in a highly satisfactory manner by Hugh JP Thomas who kindly undertook the duties.

SCRATCH RACE FOR MOTOR CYCLES WITH PEDALS

Two miles >

E Green – rider Abraham (3½ Triumph)
Francis Phillips (3½ Triumph)
E George – rider McLean (3½ Triumph)

HANDICAP RACE FOR MOTOR CYCLES

Francis Phillips (3½ Triumph)
E George (3½ Triumph)
R Green (3½ Triumph)

FASTEST CAR

Two miles >

JV Colby (16/25 Sunbeam)
HJP Thomas (12/20 Humber)
W O'Donnell (16hp Humber)

Also ran:
J Bland (15 hp Rover)
HJP Thomas (28/26 Daimler)
P Christie (12hp Talbot)
E Green (14/20 Renault)
J Lewis (14/16 Alldays)

HANDICAP RACE FOR CARS

Two miles >

J Lewis (14/16 Alldays)
J Bland (15 hp Rover)
HJP Thomas (12hp Humber)

Also ran:
JV Colby (16/25 Sunbeam)
E Green (14/20 Renault)
W O'Donnell (16hp Humber)

OPEN SCRATCH RACE FOR CARS

Two miles >

P Christie (12/16 Talbot)

Also ran:
JV Colby (16/25 Sunbeam)
HJP Thomas (12hp Humber)
J Lewis (14/16 Alldays)
W O'Donnell (12/20 Humber)
J Bland (15 hp Rover)
E Green (14/20 Renault)

The prizes were awarded at the Annual Dinner on September 25th.

Handel Davies (3hp ABC), at 'Tro'r Gwcw' (Cuckoo Bend), 'Black Mountain Open Hill Climb', Sept 8th, 1921. [© *Handel Davies collection*]

Hill-climbs on the Black Mountain

From 1910 to 1914, those weekly papers *The Welshman, The Carmarthen Journal* and *The Haverfordwest & Milford Telegraph* carry notices for hill-climb events: at Penylan Hill in Carmarthen town; Philadelphia Hill (after the chapel at Nantycaws); Crwbin, above Llangendeirne in the Gwendraeth Fach valley; Pentre Cwrt – outside Llandysul; and at Talog, north of Carmarthen. There are occasional speed trials at Arnold's Hill, on the present A40 trunk road, three miles or so east of Haverfordwest. The hill-climb for cars and bicycles held on Sat 17th September, 1910, on the Black Mountain road out of Llangadog to Brynaman, ended abruptly for the Daimler of Mr TJ Williams of Maesygwernen, when his chauffeur, T Bowles ('whose skill as a careful and competent motorist is freely acknowledged by all who have ridden behind him'), skidded into a bank.

> He had as passengers WC Jenkins and Mr Thomas Rees, and he made a perfectly splendid pace, rounding two hairpin curves with wonderful precision and covering ground as though he were on the flat. He had raced over four-fifths of the distance in record pace, and looked like being an easy first in point of time, when – what happened no one quite knows. By some means the car got out of control. It swayed, and for an instant seemed as if it were passing over the face of the mountain, when Bowles, with fine presence of mind, clapped on all his brake-power, and using his wheel with skill, changed the course and ran into a bank. The impact was so great that the front axle and driving rod [steering-arm?] buckled like a cane, whilst the driving wheels lay flat upon the side of their rims. Strangely enough, the only hurt sustained was by Mr Jenkins,

who cut and wrenched his knee and struck his head against the back of the car. It was a great disappointment, but Mr Williams, who was watching the performance from the top of the hill, took it like the good sportsman he is, and met condolences freely offered upon his bad luck with the most cheerful complacency. There seemed prospects of a long stay in the mountains, but by great good fortune in one of the cars competing were a company of engineers ... [who] managed with much trouble to get the axle off, and took it to the smithy at Llangadock. There it was straightened out, and between two and three in the morning they bade the Black Mountain adieu!'[9]

The results were published on Sept 24th. There had been thirteen entries, and the Hughes-Morgan Challenge Cup was won by Mr WD Davies in a 16-20 Singer. The Cory Yeo Challenge Cup for motor cycles was carried off by Mr Donald Burnie, riding a 2¾ Douglas.[10]

When the Swansea branch of the Welsh Automobile Club held a hill-climb meeting at Golden Grove, on 3rd July, 1913, the venue location was posted on the club notice-board on the morning of the event, to prevent unscheduled practising and to keep spectators to a minimum. The start-line was on the flat straight between Golden Grove railway station and the B3400, Ffairfach-to-Carmarthen, cross-road. The course crossed that fairly busy artery, rose steeply through the picturesque village of Golden Grove, and ended a mile away, just beyond Penrhiw.

The hill-climb at Brechfa, up a rough road through the woods, was known, jocularly, as 'Dunlop's Dividend'- being hard on tyres.

Clubs were formed at Pembroke, Amman Valley and Aberavon (East Talbot) in 1911. The Swansea branch of the WAC closed as a 'Motor' club in 1913 to continue as a motor-cycle club. Neath, Ystalyfera, Cardigan, Llandovery and Hirwaun were to form MC clubs in following years. Motor racing on the public roads (with special permission) would not become outlawed until 1925.

On July 13th, 1911, Amman Valley & District Motor Club held a hill-climb meeting, 'in ideal weather', on the Black Mountain. 'The hill is a difficult one with some exceptionally bad corners', *The Motor Cycle* reports. It was referring in particular to an uphill right-hander, Tro Tir-y-Gât (Turn of the Land belonging to the Tollgate), over a hump-backed bridge over the little Clydach, and 'Tro'r Gwcw' (Cuckoo Bend), a very interesting steep, left-hand, hairpin. There was a good attendance and the results were:

> L (Luther) Davies (3½ James)
> H (Handel) Davies (3½ Rex) 3 mins 32½ secs
> DJ Llewelyn (3½ Triumph)
> JA Morgan (Rex)
> L (Lewi) M Davies (Rex)
> Winner's time: 3 mins 58.66secs.

---

[9] *Cambrian Daily Leader,* Mon, Sept 17, 1910.
[10] Father of RJD Burnie, Swansea, the most successful local private entrant/competitor in the history of motor cycle racing on Pendine.

An 'All-comers' Handicap', which included motor-cycle classes, was run off at Porthcawl on the 20th of July, 1912. A photograph in *The Motor Cycle* shows the lengths to which the organisers were obliged to go to keep the competing machines above water, with a sturdy-enough framework of duckboards to support a schooner.

> Owing to the wetness of the sand and the protest of the competitors, a start could not be made in the motor cycle events until 6pm. Some very good times were made considering the heavy state of the track. The distance was one mile. Before the competition could be finished the sea came up again, and the last race was won in about 9in of water. In the Sidecar Class two machines (Barnes's and Wade's) stuck in the soft sand. Newsome was the most successful rider, annexing two firsts. His speed was upwards of 50 mph.

Porthcawl did not share Pendine's very shallow draught at tide level!

Among the competitors were Kickham (Douglas), Weatherilt (Zenith), Britton (Douglas), Newsome (Triumph), Lewis (Premier), Barnes (Zenith), JJ Mathias (Humber), JC Moore (Rudge), E Chapman (5-6 Zenith – sidecar), AB Wade (Imperial-JAP), S Crawley (Triumph), A James (Indian), WC Pollard (Stevens-Precision), RB Rooke (Wright-Precision) LE Sawyer (7-9 Indian), J Clarke (Rudge) and P Mathews (Rudge). HFS Morgan was first in the Cycle Car class (Not exceeding

Sand racing at Porthcawl, 1913.

1100cc), followed by GW Hands in a Calthorpe and JF Buckingham in a 4.91 Chota. Not one of them names familiar on Pendine, past or future.

The Carmarthen Journal of the 5th June, 1914, under 'Motor Cycling Notes', carries a reference to the establishment of a new motor cycle club at Carmarthen. A hill-climb is to be held at Crwbin. It is the 17th of July before the Crwbin hill-climb is reported but, in an aside, the article tells us that 'The next meeting is to be held at Pendine on the 6th of August when speed trials will be held on the sands'. No report of this event is ever published, as the papers in the weeks that follow are crowded out with news of war preparations.

Post-war Revival

Motor cycles played an important role in First World War communications. Dispatch-riders and officers who had experienced the fearful danger of exposure to the machine-gun, the sniper's bullet, the air-burst shell and the land-mine, carried messages and command on such trusty mounts as the Triumph 550cc side-valve 'H' Model or the 2¾ hp Douglas. The Royal Flying Corps favoured the P&M (Phelan & Moore – later Panther). Experiences of these machines brought back from the Front, made the marques themselves revered war heroes. Their riders, across the social spectrum, and all who had undergone a baptism-by-fire of mechanical and electrical wisdom – were the 'new men'. They had become receptive to a world of innovation and technology. This was to result in a burgeoning of inventiveness and a vast output and variety of motors to satisfy taste and demand.

The Western Mail, in a piece anticipating the Six Days' Trial out of Llandrindod Wells, observes:

> There can be no question of the great revival of interest in motor cycling that the return of peace has brought. Before the war the ranks of the motor cyclists were gradually expanding. The good service of the motor cycle in the various war zones and the experience of our soldiers who used it in the Allied cause have added a new zest to pleasure riding, and the motor cycle is now assured of a very widespread popularity in its peaceful vocation.

The war had done little to hasten the development of motor vehicles in terms of engineering sophistication. Robust reliability was by far the most important virtue in a military vehicle, apart from easy maintenance and cheapness of manufacture. Mass-production methods learned in armament factories were a valuable asset to an industry-in-waiting. Motors had proved themselves in the war arena feasible replacements for the horse. (The early popularity of the motor bicycle was very much bound up in the horse analogy). The question was whether motor car or motor cycle was to prove the more practical candidate as personal transport. America, by 1919, seemed to have decided, with the exception of the Indian, Excelsior and Harley-Davidson, on the motor car rather than the motor cycle – so cheaply were mass-produced cars available. This left British manufacturers with an open door to a world market. Within a short period following the Armistice, there were over a hundred British motor cycle manufacturers offering two hundred or more different models to an eager public. Only a few were to flourish in the long term.

4. Vintage Years

It is July, 1919, when petrol restrictions are lifted after the war, before any motor sport activity is mentioned again.

In *The Carmarthen Journal*, readers are advised that another hill-climb is to be held at Crwbin on August 4th. The first Welsh Speed Trials to be staged on Pendine after the Armistice, took place on August 25th, 1919 – a Friday. And then, under the headline 'Motor Cycle Competition at Pendine', the *Journal* of August 29th, comments:

> Motorists will be interested to note that another motor cycle competition is to be held under the auspices of the Carmarthen and District Motor Cycle and Car Club, this time on Pendine Sands … on Thursday afternoon, 4th September. Connected with the speed competition is a run out by the club. Anybody can compete, provided he is a member of the club.

Two results of this meeting were duly published in *The Journal* on 12th September. Charles Sgonina, son of a Cardiff engineer/industrialist of German extraction,[11] was noted as having made a very promising debut on his belt-drive BRS Norton [BO 2328]. The machine was certified as having done 70mph at Brooklands. It appears that the course marked out on Pendine beach was approximately 1¼ miles long. 'Wm Edwards (BSA), Bridge Street Garage, failed to finish the second race despite having made a very fine show against higher-powered machines'; and in the first event – for machines not exceeding engine capacity of 557cc – the declared winners were:

One lap > 557cc
C (Charles) Sgonina, Penarth (Norton)
A (Albert) Lewis, Meiros Hall, Henllan (Rover)
Winner's time: 1min 4.5 secs: (no distance given)

A one-line notice appears in *The Motor Cycle* to the effect that there had been 'Capital sport at Pendine'. It records just one result, perhaps another class, but at variance with *The Carmarthen Journal*:

---

[11] Sgonina (Snr) owned the Flotsam Works, Allensbank Road, Llanishen, Cardiff, which made the 'sharp ends' of pneumatic road drills. The family lived at Melbourne Road, Llanishen. (WF Boothby).

Handel Davies (Brough Superior, '90-bore'), Whitsun, 1921. [© *Handel Davies collection*]

557cc class
C Sgonina (3½ Norton)
J (Jack) Thomas, Neath (6hp James)

For the sidecar result we are indebted to *The Carmarthen Journal* :

GENERAL CLASS
H (Harry) Church, Neath (Velocette)   J (Jack) Davies, Carmarthen (Verus)

EXPERT CLASS
2½ -mile sprint > 350cc
Wm (Billy) Edwards, Carmarthen (Verus)   S Horsell, Pyle (Coulson B)

Combinations: unlimited
T Thomas, Brynaman (James 5/6 hp)   A Lewis (Rover)
Winner's time: 1min 22.3 sec: (54.67mph).

And the Committee of the Carmarthen club are listed in *The Journal* as:

Judges: Starters:
WVH Thomas (Auctioneer)   J Conwil Evans
WE Williams (Jeweller)   T Jones (Pratt's)
T Jenkins (Queen's Hotel)   W David Thomas (Auctioneer).

Harry Church's little Velocette [NY 1437] was a two-stroke. Machine and rider had gained a considerable reputation in hill-climbs and at speed trials in south east Wales. We note from a snippet in *The Motor Cycle* in May, 1920, that 'Captain Lindsay's Team, entered for the Isle of Man Senior TT, consists of A Lindsay (Norton), J Thomas and Norman Black'. In the event, Dr Lindsay did not finish; Black came in 11th and Jack Thomas was 14th and last, coming in half an hour after the race had finished!

August 1920

Commenting on the August Bank Holiday, 1920, meeting at Pendine, *The Motor Cycle* is very complimentary:

> Pendine Sands form the finest natural speedway imaginable inasmuch as a machine can be steered 'hands off' on them, and there are few places of which this can be said.

As to whether this recommendation was prudent, much less true, was left to the judgement of the reader. There was an extraordinary field of 83 single entries for the Bank Holiday meeting. There would not be as many again. In the 500cc 'Open', the machine everyone had been agog to see perform was the ABC of Toms, being widely publicised as 'The best motor cycle in the world' – a little prematurely, as it turned out. The little ABC had some bad luck on the start-line when another machine fell on it and broke the 'vulcanite cover of the high tension magneto terminal'. The Edmund motor bicycles of Morris Isaac and Tom Hopkins were Villiers side-valvers – with 'sprung frames' (half leaf-spring, front and rear, undamped). Considered 'a gentleman's machine', they were light-weight bicycles at 200 lbs, but heavy as compared with Billy Edwards's ultra-light (100 lbs) three-port two-stroke Omega. He succeeded in blowing a cylinder head to pieces 'like a hand-grenade' on this fast little racer while leading the Closed race for 300s. Had he been experimenting with compression ratios or 'hot' fuel-mixes, one wonders?

Making his debut at Pendine was the doyen of all sprint racing motor cyclists, Marston Sunbeam's racing manager, George Dance. Howard Raymond Davies, 'crack' TT rider with some Welsh credentials and AJS competitions chief, was also on Pendine for the first time. The crowd were privileged to see a battle royal between these two legendary characters in action on the world's fastest racing machines in their class. Their presence was also an early indicator of the importance to be placed on Pendine by the manufacturers as a testing ground for their high-performance products. Any resulting publicity was useful in a highly competitive market.

Indians

There were red Indians on the beach – dazzling fire-engine red, with bold gold lettering on the tank. One [L 3537] was registered in the name of HH Bush of Neath, brother of FP Bush, the aviator and noted rider. In 1920, these popular and exotic imports from Springfield, Massachusetts, were among the very finest motor cycles in the world, with a hugely successful competition record behind them in both motordrome and long-distance events in the USA, and many Brooklands records and European race wins on this side of the Atlantic. Indians had come home 1 – 2 – 3 in the 1911 IoM Senior TT.

A great deal of misplaced snobbery persists in Great Britain about American motors and engineering, some of it justified when related to mass-produced articles. But the brilliant motor cycles that came out of Springfield and Milwaukee in the early days, and even today, are very much to be admired. Indians had been the world's best-selling motor cycle, with a network of over 2,000 dealerships.[12] Bush's wonderful (1915) Big Twin was the object of considerable interest and deference. Alongside some of the hub-geared British belt-drivers with puny little engines, its long-stroke IOE V-twin powerhouse boasted 61 cubic inches (994cc) of effortless 'grunt' directed through a three-speed gearbox by chain drive. It had leaf-sprung suspension and a mechanical oil-pump that force-lubricated its robust 7hp (15bhp) engine. To gain a little extra power a 'Frisco cut-out' (a pedal-operated exhaust-silencer by-pass) was often featured on the Indian which, in true 'Yankee' fashion, had foot-boards and a

---

[12] The great Freddie Dixon began as an apprentice to an Indian agency in Stockton-upon-Tees. Around 1909 he began demonstrating them and his prowesss in local sprints and hill-climbs. He was 12th in the 1920 IoM Senior TT on a 500 Indian V-twin and second to HR Davies on the little AJS, in the 1922 Senior.

Dr A Lindsay (Norton), FP Bush (Indian). [©: *Lindsay collection*]

left-hand, twist-grip throttle – not to mention an 'Oo-haa' bulb-horn hooter! Top speed was in excess of 70mph, which was hot-rod in 1920. The unlimited mile sprint, a V-twin line-up, where the Indian led Handel Davies's big James and King Smith's Harley-Davidson to the flag, must have provided spectacle indeed.

It is difficult, even for historians of motor racing, to imagine a time when the Norton legend was not taken for granted. In 1920 it was thirteen years since Rem Fowler had won the Tourist Trophy with the Peugeot-engined Norton, and it would be 1924 before they would re-open their TT racing account. Though Nortons were valued for sturdy build-quality and a sporting air, their side-valve engines were hardly electrifying. Sunbeam and AJS were the front-runners in road and track racing. AJS in particular stirred young men's pulses with their light-weight 349cc overhead-valve machine that was to win the Junior TT three times in succession, in 1920, 1921 and 1922. And when, in 1921, their top rider, Howard R Davies, was to win the Senior on the little Junior bicycle he had brought home to second place in the 350cc class a couple of days previously, there was nothing more desirable to 'speedmen' the world over than to own an ohv 350 AJS. They would have to wait until the Olympia Show of December 1922 before parting with a considerable £87 0s 0d. to buy the first 'TT', advertised as the '2¾hp, Overhead-valve TT Model', the original 'Over-the-counter boy-racer', better known to history as the 'Big-port'.

The brief summary of results was

OPEN

4 miles > 300cc
Wm Edwards (Omega)
T Hopkins (Edmund)
M (Morris) Isaac (Edmund)
Winner's time: 6mins 45 secs.

10 miles > 350cc
G (George) Dance, Wolverhampton
　(2¾ Sunbeam)
H (Howard) R Davies (2¾ AJS)
Wm Edwards (Verus)

10 miles > 500cc
G Dance (3½ Sunbeam)
C Sgonina (3½ Norton)
HR Davies (2¾ AJS)

10 miles: unlimited
G Dance (3½ Sunbeam)
A (Capt, Dr Alexander) Lindsay,
　Cwmllynfell (3½ Norton)
C Sgonina (Norton)
G (Graham) Ace, Tenby (Rudge Multi)

CLOSED

4 miles > 300cc
M Isaac (Edmund)
T Hopkins (Edmund)

4 miles > 350cc
S Jones (Verus)
S Pitman (Douglas)
D Price (Coulson B)
Winner's time: 6mins 8.6 secs.

4 miles > 500cc
A Lindsay (Norton)
C Sgonina (Norton)
J (Jack) Thomas (Norton)

4 miles: unlimited
A Lindsay (Norton)
C Sgonina (Norton)
RE Toms (ABC)

SIDECARS

One mile sprint > 750cc
H (Handel) Davies (James 5-6hp)
J Thomas (Norton)

one mile sprint > 1,000cc
ER Mitchell (Indian 7-9hp)
H Davies (James 5-6hp)
A King Smith (Harley-Davidson)

From 1920 on, the newly-formed Clubs, organised within regional 'Sections' of the Auto Cycle Union (ACU) and under its competition rules, took on the responsibility for arranging an annual programme of individual and collective events and competitions for their memberships. These would take the form of 'Open' or 'Closed' meetings: long-distance road trials, hill-climbs, grass-track or speed-trials. Pendine was a speed-trial or sand-racing venue. A Closed meeting was one where only members of a specific club (or clubs within a Section) would be eligible to compete. Often a meeting would be 'Open', but contain certain classes of event (eg. 'Novices') which were 'Closed' to outsiders. Such a meeting was arranged for Pendine Sands, under ACU rules, for August 19th, 1920, a Thursday.

The Carmarthen, Neath, Ystalyfera, Swansea and Cardigan clubs got together to organise an ambitious competitive event, 'The Welsh Open Speed Championships', for motor cycles and motorcycle-and-sidecars. The programme for the day, which attracted full entries for eleven classes and entertained a large crowd, estimated at over 2,000 people, was not a record, but good going for a week-day.

The judges were: Mr Perkins, Swansea; Dr Lloyd, Newcastle Emlyn; Mr Selby-Clare and Mr Ben Jones. Clerk-of-the-Course was Mr John Jenkins, Carmarthen; and Mr William Williams was Time-keeper. The Starter was Mr DJ Davies, Carmarthen.

A Triumph silver cup was awarded to Capt A Lindsay, as winner of the 'Unlimited cc' event – and a special prize of five guineas (donated by Messrs Bradbury Jones, West Wales Garage, Carmarthen) was awarded to George Dance for best performance in the Championship classes. It is interesting that remote Pendine should already be attracting stars of the calibre of George Dance who had made his name before the war as undisputed 'Sprint king'. He was always fastest man at the Isle of Man, at Brooklands and at any hill-climb, sprint or speed trial he chose to enter.

H. R. Davies

Howard Raymond Davies, the rider-manufacturer, was later to achieve stardom with an unique personal performance at the TT races on the Isle of Man[13]. Riding for AJS, in 1921, he was the first and only man ever to win the Senior Tourist Trophy (for machines with engines not exceeding 500cc) on a Junior 350 – and at record speed! He was to found the legendary HRD motorcycle-manufacturing firm whose avowed emphasis was upon sports and racing machines. In fact, it held as its ideal something of George Brough's philosophy that there was a market out there for the discriminating speedman who was prepared to pay that bit extra for something better made and of superior quality, proven, tried and tested on the severest public arenas.[14] The HRD, like the Brough Superior, was always perceived as a machine apart.

Perhaps Davies's ideals were too high-minded. He was not the consummate businessman and publicist found in George Brough, with the result that his little concern went into liquidation in 1927. When its assets were eventually[15] acquired for a derisory £400 by Phil Vincent, Cambridge University engineering graduate, sprung-frame believer and JAP iconoclast, Vincent knew that those initials spelt some ideal that was at once indefinable – and undeniable. That vision, with the aid of Australian, Phil Irving, was to result in the prestigious Vincent-HRD marque. The best-loved of these was to be the 998cc V-twin, first brought out in 1937 as the 'Rapide' and re-launched in 1949 as the Series D, 125 mph Black Shadow, later to be perfected in the fabulous Black Lightning and the less visually-appealing, all-enveloped, Black Knight.

---

[13]HR Davies, according to the author's late father (TE Hughes), who raced (AJS) on Pendine in the early '20s, conceived a prototype foot gear-change idea at Pendine (crude and non-positive-stop), to overcome the hazard of removing the right hand from the bar-grip and throttle for gear-changes – a manoeuvre that often led to 'speed wobbles' on sand!

[14]It would be fair to say that others also held these tenets: New Hudson, New Imperial, among others.

[15]Following liquidation, the assets were first acquired by E Humphries, of OK Supreme (who later took over Hughes Sidecars), 'Black Ernie' - because of his temper. Was that the origin of Vincent's 'Black' series?

Charles Sgonina

It is of interest that Charles Sgonina was placed in the 350cc class on a Verus, a machine not often associated with this rider, though he raced one with success at Margam Park, in 1922, winning the Evans-Bevan Cup at a record speed (for South Wales) of 72.29 mph. The Verus was made in Birmingham from 1919 – 25 by Wiseman, who also assembled Weaver and Sirrah motor cycles. The 350 would have had an ohv Blackburne engine. This little machine was incredibly light, with a dry weight of not much more than 100lbs. Sgonina, the engineer, took a close interest in either JAP or Blackburne overhead valve-operating systems – not yet available on his BRS or any Norton – a shortcoming he was soon to prove himself capable of remedying. It is fortunate that the text of a talk given by Charles Sgonina to an unnamed gathering has survived to tell us at first hand of his early motor cycle racing experience.[16]

> In 1918 I bought my first motor cycle, a belt-driven 500cc Triumph on which I blinded round the countryside. My next was an Enfield which gave me my first taste of chain drive, followed by a BRS Norton, belt drive, with a certificate that it had done 70mph at Brooklands.
>
> About this time I wanted to enter in competitions and converted the engine of this bike into an overhead valve, using a steel cylinder with detachable ports. I raced this bike at Weston Speed Trials and won a few events.
>
> Next at the first Pendine.[17]
>
> Next at Style Kop, where I was up against Graham Walker in the novices class and managed to beat him.
>
> This engine had a very short life, the piston cracking around the gudgeon pin. The only parts of any use after this smash were the cam wheels.
>
> As the speed bug had by now really got hold of me I decided to build something good. So I started building an inclined overhead valve engine and Nortons very kindly sold me one of their actual TT frames and gearboxes.
>
> This engine was not as good as my previous effort but with many alterations it did eventually get a move on. I rode this machine in quite a number of events with moderate success.
>
> During the winter of (1921) I built the Sgonina Special, a 500cc inclined overhead valve and one early morning I tried it out down Allenbank Road and clocked 86mph. I raced this machine in many events successfully and later altered it to overhead camshafts. After this it was the equal of any trade machine.

So great was the interest in Sgonina's overhead valve conversions that Nortons were obliged to publish a notice in the press, by way of disclaimer:

---

[16] He is known to have been Guest-of-honour at a Carmarthen MC & LCC Annual Dinner. If this was not his selected audience, in the nature of things, the detail and substance would not have been very different!

[17] The first meeting after the 1914-18 War, i.e. 1919.

The Sgonina Special. Shaft-driven single, then double overhead camshafts evolved from this perilous, exposed, chain-drive. *[photos courtesy AB Demaus]*

Sir, – We are very much interested in a Norton engine with overhead valves ridden by a private owner at Weston Super Mare.

Although we commenced on experiments with this type of engine something like fifteen years or more ago, we are not at present supplying an overhead valve engine, the one in question being made entirely on the owner's initiative, and by himself. We can congratulate him on a very workmanlike and sound job.

We mention this, as, from our experience in the past, any reference to an alteration of design in your pages has caused us to be inundated with enquiries, and many of the writers take it as a personal slight if we are unable to supply.

We might here mention that we have never made a departure from our standard engine in the shape of special cams, cylinders and such like for competition purposes, machines always being to catalogue specifications.
NORTON MOTORS LTD.

Whitsun 1921

A Whitsun 'Motor Championships' meeting was held at Pendine in May, 1921. The programme, according to *The Carmarthen Journal,* was 'a very attractive one'.

> There was a large entry, including crack riders from all over south Wales. It is the first time in history that 25-mile and 50-mile races have taken place, and the splendid times registered in both races will be difficult to surpass. Beautiful weather prevailed and a crowd of about 5,000-6,000 people turned out as spectators. The routes from Carmarthen and elsewhere were very congested with motor vehicles. Mansel Davies, Llanfyrnach, and RE Thomas, Gloag, collided and were concussed.

Alexander Lindsay, MD, stopped his 16H BRS-engined, side-valve, Norton during the race to attend to them and then resumed racing!

Handel Davies's Brough Superior

The sensation of the meeting was Handel Davies's shining new Brough Superior. The lean, low-slung sports-racer had a distinctive, polished chrome, bulbous-nosed saddle tank. Handel was already a leading figure in motor cycle sport in south and west Wales. His name had become a by-word in fast, powerful machinery. Handel and his brother, Luther, had come a long way from their little 'Cycle Works and Repairing Shop' in Garnant, in the Aman valley, in the early years of the century. Brooklands Garage, Handel's main dealership, was a Mecca for 'speed-men'. Luther, who described himself as an 'ironmonger', had gone into business in Newport after the war. Between them, the Davies brothers won an array of cups and medals in championships throughout the country.

WHITSUN, 1921

Brooklands Garage, Garnant. L>R Jowett car; AJS twin (c 1923); Sunbeam (c 1924); AJS sv (c 1924); Raleigh; Handel, standing, right. *[© Handel Davies collection]*

**EXPERT CLASS
WELSH CHAMPIONSHIP**

(Norton Motors Cup)

50 miles: unlimited
O (Ogwyn) Lewis, Neath (Norton)
FP (Fredrick Percy) Bush (Harley-Davidson)
Winner's time: 54 mins 49 secs.
(Both were novices, but took the Expert Class).

25 miles > 350cc
Wm Edwards, (Verus)
Ll Davies, Newport (Coulson B)
Winner's time: 32 mins 19secs.

2½ mile-sprint: unlimited
H Davies, (Brough Superior)
A Lindsay, (Norton)

OPEN

2½ mile-sprint > 350cc
H Church, Neath (Velocette)
TJ Stephens, Neath (Velocette)

It seems most likely that the Norton Motors Cup for the long-distance race was the largess of Harley-Davidson and Norton exponent, FP Bush, whose Blackpill, Swansea, garage business was so-named. The tragic story of this talented, but doomed, rider's fate is told below.

August 1921

The Pembroke Automobile Club ran an event for motors of two and four wheels on the beach on 18th August, 1921 (again a Thursday). Few cars were entered but, according to a report in *The Pembrokeshire Telegraph,* there was 'a large number of entries for the motor cycle races'. From a race programme that survives, we note that 'top people' were still involved. The club's President was Sir W Howell Walters, with vice-presidents Sir Ivor Phillips, KJB, Major Hugh JP Thomas, OBE, Capt FD Llewellyn and JB Gushal, esq; and the Rev EL Jones was included on the committee.

Whether 'Archie' Cocks, 'Aberdovery', on his genteel 3 hp Beardmore Precision (an early and well-made sprung-frame machine with an in-house engine) made it past the chequered flag or not, and if so in what position, is lost to history. The Beardmore, which cost '£95 Complete' was a more comfortable machine than the ordinary, being suspended by two half leaf-springs. Handel Davies entered a Coulson B for the closed event under 300cc. A rare machine also, the Coulson was another of the very few spring-frame motor cycles on the market in 1921. The power-plant was a 60 x 61mm V-twin single-carburettor JAP engine. Pembroke club men HGK Palmer and S Green entered 2¾hp Douglas and 2¾ AJS machines respectively in the closed event for 350cc solo motor cycles. Silver and bronze medals were awarded to first and second in each class. JLG Jenkins rode over from Cross Hands on his Norton. VR McKenzie, of Monti & McKenzie, Automobile engineers of New Road Garage, Haverfordwest, and JR Thomas both sported 4hp Triumphs. Garage proprietor Graham Ace and EJ Jeremy came over from Tenby; and the Davies brothers, Mansel and Walter, hauliers and garage proprietors (Sunbeam agents) of Llanfyrnach, turned up. All four entered 3½hp Sunbeams. Mansel was, perhaps, on the 'TT' model.[18]

Carmarthen cycle-shop/garage-owner, William 'Billy' Edwards arrived with Omega [BX 2716)] and James bicycles. Chauffeur and salesman Morris Isaac, a brilliant local rider, had an uncharacteristically bad day. Thirty-eight-year-old Isaac, employed by Messrs Bradbury Jones & Co, West Wales Garage, was a driver of professional standing.[19] He was soon to gain high honours in the Six Days' Trial and rode in both Senior and Lightweight Isle of Man TTs. In addition to his Coulson B, Handel Davies fielded a 3½ hp Rover and, making its first and very significant appearance at Pendine, a brand new 8hp Brough Superior, powered by a V-twin JAP-engine, '90-bore' (90 x 77.5mm). This famous Brough [DW 1921] was to carry Handel to victory on many a track. Pendine, with its long straights, seemed its natural arena. One day, a Brough model, the 100mph SS100 sports-special, was to be named 'The Pendine'. George Brough, its creator, was to become so enamoured of that place of wind, sand and sea that he and his wife, Connie, were to name their home in Redhill, Nottingham, 'Pendine'![20]

---

[18]This machine [DE 1614] still survives in 'near-original' condition. It was exhibited at the Museum of Speed, Pendine, in the summer of 1999.

[19]Morris drove Lord and Lady Kilsant in the Coronation procession of King George V, in 1910. Comparison can be made with the horse-racing circus where riders are employed by owners as jockeys. In the early days of motor racing private-owners and 'Trade' engaged drivers to 'jockey' their entries. Percy Rogers, 'Our Mechanic', rode New Imperial and Sunbeam machines for Fryer Bros, Brecon, much as Isaac drove those identical makes for Bradbury Jones, Carmarthen.

[20]The house, 269, Mansfield Road, Redhill, just past the cemetery, on the A 60, has been renamed 'Dale Mount' (V Short pers. letter 30-vi-99). Many (M Raven, E Hamilton) have assumed it demolished in favour of a modern development.

There was only one entry for the 'closed' side-car event, that of DF Ingleton with an elegant 750cc (6 hp) Martinsyde, designed and built by the Kingston-upon-Thames aircraft manufacturers. The race seems not to have been run. There were no entries either for the light cars up to 2300cc. Over that engine size, besides the two 12 hp Rovers of Messrs JB Gaskell and FD Phillips, there was a 10 hp Ford driven by EL Green, a 17/14 Dodge piloted by JW Hammond and the 45/50 Rolls Royce of Major HJP Thomas. The results were published as follows:

CLOSED

> 350cc
S Green (2¾ AJS
HGK Palmer (2¾ Douglas)

>550cc
M (Mansel) Davies, Llanfyrnach
   (3½ Sunbeam)
VR McKenzie, H'west (4½ Triumph)

OPEN

> 350cc
Wm Edwards, Carmarthen
   (2½ Omega-JAP)
H Davies, Garnant (2¾ Coulson)

>550
M Davies (3½ Sunbeam)
VR McKenzie (4hp Triumph)

> Unlimited
H Davies (8hp Brough Superior)
Wm Edwards (Omega-JAP)

CARS – VISITORS OPEN HANDICAP

L (Luther) J Davies (8hp Morgan)
JT Williams (17/24 Dodge)

No distances or times were published.

It was a day when trade entrants ruled the roost. It would not always be so. 'M Davies and (EJ) Jeremy (Tenby) collided after passing the winning post. There was a bad smash. The riders fortunately escaped serious injury, but their machines were badly damaged'.[21]

---

[21] *The Pembrokeshire Telegraph*, Aug 24 1921.

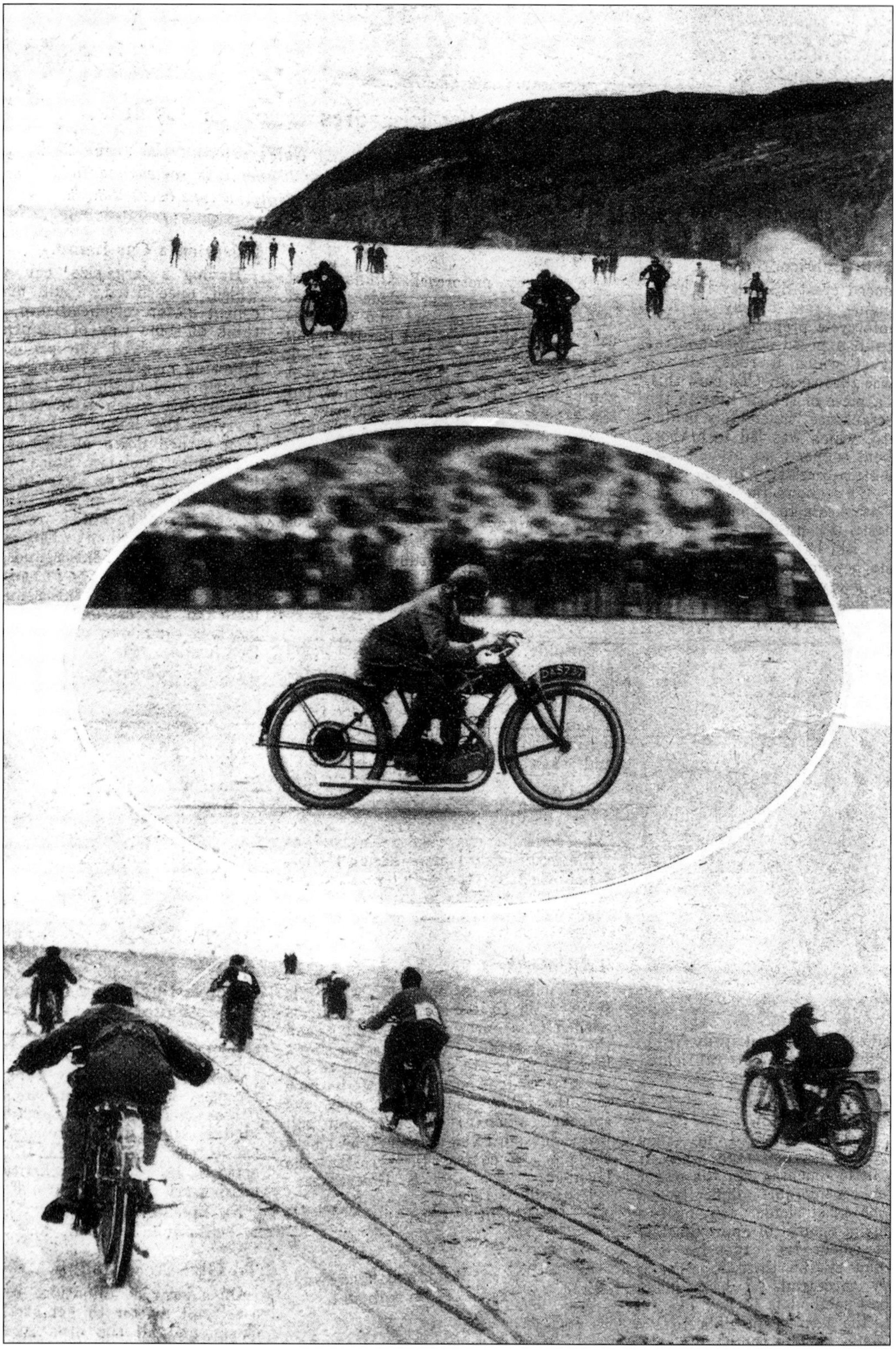

5. The Golden Era Begins

THE Pembroke club outing served as a practice-session for some of the local boys who, a week later, on August 25th, competed in the West Wales Open Speed Championship at Pendine. The meeting, held under the auspices of the West Wales Centre ACU, was run very efficiently by the combined local clubs. *The Motor Cycle* reports (not quite accurately) on September 1st, 1921, 'Motor cycle races have been staged at Pendine for nearly 20 years but not until last week has there been an officially open meeting on that fine natural speedway'. *Motor Cycling*, in a much more fulsome account,[22] declares that:

> The course is described as being the finest sand track in England and Wales and is undoubtedly so . . . and ideal for motorcycle racing. Owing to the inclement weather of the morning, the start was delayed an hour to allow the 'track' to become firm.

The weather did not deter the crowd of some 3,000 who turned out for the spectacle which eventually got off to a start at 1.30 pm and finished promptly at four-thirty. Several TT riders appeared, to add a splash of glamour to the day, among them George Dance and Charles Sgonina. Undisputed Star of this occasion, though, was Howard R Davies, fresh from winning the IoM Senior TT on a 350cc AJS – a feat never before or since equalled.

A couple of light aeroplanes had landed on the sands, offering scenic flights to willing subscribers 'to fill in the time'. People wandered round the paddock, staring at the machinery, *Motor Cycling's* correspondent among them.

> Among the 'gadgets' fitted to machines, Boshier-Jones had an Atmos carburettor fitted to each opposing cylinder of his 3½hp Douglas, while Jack Thomas, to reduce the weight of his Massey-Arran, had fitted a very tiny tank which would hold no more than a couple of pints of the necessary fluid. The event was likened unto a Brooklands affair, inasmuch that several bookies arrived on the scene and started shouting the odds.

It is reassuring to learn that the two mounted police sent from Carmarthen to keep the course clear were hardly needed as the crowd were thoroughly well-behaved.

Local men were prominent leaders in the Open Championship 300cc lightweight event. *The Western Mail* publishes a full account of the proceedings – including the prize-giving which took place at the Nelson Hotel that evening. This is one of the

---

[22](August 31, 1921).

few occasions in the history of racing at Pendine – Welsh Speed Championships, Welsh TTs, Welsh Hundreds and Welsh Grands Prix, when 'The National Newspaper of Wales' accords Pendine Races a little more space than just necessary for racing results. Considering the vast following that these events were to attract throughout the twenties and thirties, this is both surprising and disappointing.

> A crowd estimated at about 5,000 people was present at very successful motor cycle trials held at Pendine Sands, on the Carmarthenshire coast, in connection with the West Wales Centre Motor-cycle Clubs. In addition to the seven races confined to the West Wales Centre of Allied Clubs there were five events for the open speed championships held under the open competition rules of the ACU.
>
> South Wales riders did well in the open championship classes. The principal event of the day was the ten miles speed championship for solo machines up to 560cc. After an exciting race, George Dance of Wolverhampton was the winner, his time being 9 mins 18⅝ secs.
>
> **OPEN**
>
> **2½ mile-sprint > 300cc**
> M Isaac (2¼ hp New Imperial)
> Wm Edwards (2¼ hp Omega)
> I (Ivor) Thomas (New Imperial)
> Winner's time: 4mins 37secs.

And in the Club class under 300cc, it was the same story, only that H Church's two-stroke, 250cc, Velocette took the honours behind the two local heroes, coming in third ahead of Ivor Thomas's pleasing-to-look-at, but still not very competitive, Massey-Arran.

> **CLOSED**
>
> **2½ mile-sprint > 300cc**
> M Isaac (2¼ hp New Imperial)
> Wm Edwards (2¼ hp Omega)
> H Church (Velocette)
> I Thomas (Massey Arran)

HR Davies took the 350 'Open' event with certainty on the very fast 2¾ hp 'TT' AJS, winning the £2/2/- Special Prize. It had begun as a thrilling race. For the first three laps of the 10-miler he had ridden neck-and-neck with the Sunbeam of George Dance, which then, cussedly, developed trouble. So unassailable did the AJS's headway then become that the *Motor Cycling* race result baldly records:

> **OPEN**
>
> **10 miles > 350cc**
> HR Davies (AJS)
> Winner's time: 9mins 34 secs
> ('No one else worried about finishing')

The official verdict on George Dance's Sunbeam was – 'oiled'. Water or wet sand deposition on the plugs or electrical leads was the most frequent Pendine mechanical hazard. Consequent arcing would cause misfiring, leading to an oiled-up plug.

The *Western Mail* was a little more patient than the *Motor Cycling* observer. Some considerable way in retard, HF Brockbank, a rider/manufacturer, on the 2¾ hp Brock-Blackburne, is officially recorded as having crossed the line in second position!

10 miles > 350cc
HR Davies (AJS)
HF Brockbank, Southport (Brock-Blackburne)
Winner's time: 9mins 34secs.

The 'Big Port' AJS

AJS in 1921 were many steps ahead of the competition in terms of engine design and technology. To begin with, AJS went very early and successfully for overhead valves – which other manufacturers were nervous about in terms of reliability. AJ Stevens had been closely involved in aero-engine development during the war, and had concluded that ohv systems were the way ahead for the internal combustion engine. It was a question of metallurgy. They experimented with nickel-chrome steel as valve material, alloy cylinder heads, hardened steel rings around the connecting-rods and steel rollers around the big-end. Bronze bearings were generally used. AJS pistons were ultra-light and these, combined with a heavy, 7-inch diameter fly-wheel, gave for a very free-revving engine. The TT and model G sports machines (of 349cc capacity) were also very light, weighing no more than 190lbs, which was a good deal lighter even than a Douglas. A road-going model G was good for 70 – 75 mph in 1921. Developments, such as the 'Big-port' exhaust (2¼ ins), high compression and different carburettors and settings, increased this potential by 1922-3, to around 80 mph. The 'Big port' (a term only used retrospectively, when ports were normal-size again!) exhaust concept, though, is often dismissed as little more than cosmetic. It is doubtful whether it contributed anything very much in terms of efficiency or speed, 'but it sure frightened the enemy'!

The remaining results for the day were as follows:

CHAMPIONSHIP CLASSES

10 miles > 560cc
G Dance (Sunbeam)
C Sgonina (Norton)
HR Davies (AJS)
Winner's time: 9 mins 18.8secs.

10 miles: unlimited
G Dance (Sunbeam)
HR Davies (AJS)
FP Bush (Harley-Davidson)
Winner's time: 9 mins 24 secs.

one mile sprint: unlimited
G Dance (Sunbeam)
FP Bush (Harley-Davidson)
I Thomas (Sunbeam)
Not timed

Crowds at Pendine Races, August 1921.

The favourites kept the bookies happy in the Club classes, even though there was some manoeuvring between the 'works' riders and the local boys. Jack Thomas appeared for the 4-mile race for 350s mounted on HR Davies's AJS, while Morris Isaac had George Dance's Sunbeam. There was nothing so unusual in this, as trusted local 'crack-riders' were often given 'a go' on the works machines to prove the machines' worth. There were those who would believe George Dance could win riding a nail!

> 'It was a very close race for the best part of the 10 miles. On the last lap Isaac forged ahead and would probably have won had he not looked round. In doing so, he apparently slowed down. Thomas then came pounding along at enormous speed, and finished first'.

Third came in the guise of the Brock-Blackburne of TJ Stevens.

That was not an end to the contest. There followed an unconventional challenge from Isaac to Thomas to ride the same mounts again for four miles at the end of the programme. Was Isaac a bad loser? Not really. It was that people were as much as anything interested in the machines' respective performances with 'familiar' riders, men they could question at a later date. In the re-run event he won an unsatisfactory victory as Jack Thomas, embarrassingly, broke the gear lever on the works AJS at the start-line.

CLOSED

4 miles > 300cc
M Isaac (2¼hp New Imperial-JAP)
Wm Edwards (2¼hp Omega)
H Church (Velocette)
Winner's time: 4 mins 37secs.

Morris Isaac won a special award silver cup in this category and Harry Church also took a special award for the best performance by a two-stroke-engined machine.

4 miles > 350cc
J Thomas, (AJS)
M Isaac (Sunbeam)
TJ Stephens, Neath (Brock-Blackburne)
Winner's time: 4 mins 2 secs.

4 miles: unlimited
FP Bush (Harley-Davidson)
F Boshier-Jones, Neath (Douglas)
HH (Henry) Bush, Neath (Norton)
Winner's time: 3 mins 48⅖ secs.

JACK THOMAS Ltd.
Motor Cycle Experts,
15, Queen Street, Neath.

District Agents:

A·J·S Motor Cycles

New Hudson.   Chater-Lea.   Rudge.
Douglas.   Norton.   Rex Acme.
Sunbeam.

OR ANY OTHER MAKE.

Cash or Deferred Terms.   Assurances.
Personal Supervision.
Official Repairers to A.C.U.

Jack & Ivor Thomas, Neath

Jack Thomas, the Neath motor cycle dealer, noted for AJS, was one of the most popular local riders of the time, having won over 80 awards in speed trials. He was not especially successful on Pendine, though he was a consistent entrant as a competitor over many years. His finest achievement, apart from winning the Welsh Sidecar championship and the Grace Challenge Cup in 1921, was his third place in the 1922 Junior TT at the Isle of Man, riding a Sheffield Henderson. Ivor Thomas, also of Neath, is thought to be no relation. He (Ivor) was a first-class rider, destined to turn professional and ride works Scotts with Harry Langman, Jimmie Simpson and CP Wood. He was founder Chairman of Neath & District Motor Cycle Club, who were responsible for the organisation of the Welsh TT, between 1922 and 1927.[23] Ivor Thomas won the 500cc class in the first Welsh TT (run as part of the '100-mile', in 1922). He was regional representative for a major oil company.[24]

The Bush Brothers, Neath

The Bush brothers of Neath, Percy and Henry (FP & HH), were very competitive on Harley-Davidson and Norton machines.[25] The two racing brothers were sons of a well-known family of glue- and rope-makers. They were also 'rubber merchants' – presumably tyre suppliers. Both were tall, dark, athletic men with a penchant for American 'heavy-irons'. Henry, the elder, had a 1915 Indian Big Twin which he raced in local sprints and hill-climbs, and Percy was a Harley-Davidson disciple. 'FP' was the rider who, everyone predicted, looked as if he was 'going places'. For his performance on the Harley in the 4-mile Unlimited race he walked off with the Pendine Challenge Cup. AG Bush, a third brother, does not appear to have shared their enthusiasm for speed.

The crowd must also have been thrilled to see the big Harley and the sports Sunbeam beaten by the little ABC in the club-category for unlimited capacity engines, later on.

One-mile sprint: unlimited	**4 miles > 560cc**
LI Davies, Newport (3hp ABC)	I Thomas (Sunbeam)
H Davies, (Sunbeam)	FP Bush (Norton)
FP Bush (Harley-Davidson)	F Boshier-Jones (Douglas)
	Winner's time: 3 mins 56⅕ secs.

---

[23] Carmarthen Motor Cycle & Light Car Club assisted in a 3-day programme
[24] Hence 'Ivor the Oil'.
[25] For some reason Henry, 'HH' or 'Hy' is reported in all the press results as 'FJ'. A possible programme misprint.

SIDE-CARS

One mile sprint > 750cc	one mile sprint: unlimited
RW Hill (Veriot-Precision)	H Davies (Brough Superior)
- Griffiths (James)	RW Hill (Veriot-Precision)

The Veriot-Precision is a name to conjure with. A whimsically-named special, a 'spoof' perhaps? The 'Very 'ot-Precision' was hot enough to out-gun the big V-twins, the James and Brough Superior, in the sidecar event. It's possible it was a special 3-wheeler. No-one now remembers. It does not rear its head anywhere else in the entry, or feature in any of the standard works on the history of motor cycle racing or manufacture!

George Dance won 3 out of the 4 races he had entered, and Morris Isaac may have felt that he had won back his spurs.

Morris Isaac

Morris Isaac was typical of many a blacksmith's son born at the turn of the century who, seeing the decline of horse transport and the increase in motorised vehicles, chose not to follow directly in the family tradition. He was equally at home on horseback as on a motor cycle and had, before the Great War, made a name for himself as a jockey. Morris was to continue as a point-to-pointer and breeder of bloodstock for many years after he hung up his helmet and goggles. His father, John Isaac, was a Llanllawddog Master Blacksmith. He plied his trade, in a manner typical of the era just passing, as 'publican and blacksmith' at the Stag and Pheasant. John's brother Joe was official farrier to Cheltenham race course. One of thirteen children, by Margaret Isaac, all five boys had been apprenticed to the farrier's trade. Morris, a reasonably accomplished mechanic, had served an even more telling apprenticeship in France as a despatch rider from December 1915 until August 1919. When he won an ACU Gold medal and the fifteen-guinea silver cup, donated by Tom Norton of Llandrindod Wells for the best performance by a Welsh rider at the Six Days Trial, in September, 1919, *The Carmarthen Journal* ran a feature on his achievement:

> ... severe tests they were too. Speed tests are alright in their way, but the tests contested by the ACU were based on the reliability of the machines combined, of course, with the judgement and (ability) of the riders. It goes without saying that those who had experience as despatch riders out in France had the best chance, as their hard training out there amid the worst conditions befitted them for the trials. Even professional riders sent by the various makers were beaten by the boys who had done their bit . . . Mr Isaac rode a 3½hp Rover (solo). When asked what he thought of the roads he humorously replied that in some cases they were almost as bad as in France, but there were no shells whistling about. His machine came through the ordeal meritoriously, in fact, with a liberal application of water and a good sponge, could be offered for sale as new.

Morris Isaac was sponsored by the Carmarthen Motor Cycle and Light Car Club to compete in the 1923 IoM Lightweight TT on a 249cc New Imperial and in the Senior on a 492cc long-stroke Sunbeam. He was later to open a garage in Llandovery, specialising latterly in agricultural machinery and Massey-Fergusson tractor sales. The business until recently bore his once famous name.

The ABC

Luther Davies's little machine attracted a great deal of interest; and not only for its giant-slaying performance against two machines more than twice its size. The smooth and refined ABC was the most talked-about motor cycle of the day. It was the brainchild of aircraft engine designer Granville Bradshaw, and much ahead of its time. In a duplex cradle frame of modern concept it carried a 400cc ohv flat-twin engine, mounted transversely. Transmission was via an enclosed fly-wheel and a multi-plate clutch, married to a gate-selector 4-speed gearbox, like a motor car. It had electric lights. Brakes were internal expanding drum, front and rear. The bicycle had sprung suspension (front and rear) and even a degree of weather protection around the knees – all of which meant it was not such a feat of physical endurance to handle and pilot. The manufacture of Bradshaw's concept for the All British (Engine) Company was entrusted to the Sopwith aircraft company: the little engine, as it happens, was set to forge a career more in avionics than cycling. It was used as power-plant of, among others, the 'Flying Flea'. A good production ABC motor cycle was good for at least 60 mph, and could in all probability have taken all before it, were it not for its escalating purchase price (£130) and questionable reliability.

Luther's ABC. [Bob Thomas photo]

When ABC found themselves in difficulty in 1922, the French Gnome & Rhone aircraft-engine and motor manufacturing company licensed their design and continued to develop and perfect the concept. The tendency for cylinder heads to burst, push-rods suddenly to shoot off into the herbiage and for the foot-start to stop, were dealt with to a degree. In racing guise, in the hands of Naas and Captain Bartlett, the G&R ABC had some real success in continental Grands Prix, frequently beating the hide off the vertical parallel twins of Peugeot and Griffon.

It was still possible to buy a British ABC motorcycle in 1923, but it had no connection with Bradshaw's design. In retrospect, it is obvious that ABC went into production without sufficient testing and development of a quite brilliant concept. BMW were the main benefactors of Granville Bradshaw's inspiration. Appreciating the efficiency of the concept, they developed it (having, no doubt, also looked carefully at what Douglas were about with the boxer engine) and, in 1923, built it properly, adding shaft drive.

1922: Motor Cycle Cross-roads

That the motor cycle industry and the sport of motor racing stood at a cross-roads in 1922 was the result of what might today be termed 'socio-economic' considerations. Now that petrol-engined motor transport had become accepted as a serious alternative to horse-drawn means, the arrival on the scene of the Model 'T' Ford and, shortly after, the Austin 'Seven' at, admittedly, more than motor cycle prices, posed a problem for motor cycle manufacturers and the motoring public alike. As long ago as 1902, in its first issue editorial, *The Motor Cycle* questioned whether the subject on which it pinned its future existence was anything but transient – a rite of passage for its young male proponents between the safety bicycle and the autocar. Bracketed together as 'motors', in their infant and adolescent days, the car and the motor cycle, as they matured, came to assume separate identities. That this transitoriness was becoming generally understood is borne out by later issues of *The Motor Cycle* which carried 'flyers' for its sister publication, *The Autocar,* under the banner '**The Next Stage**'.

The popular debate by 1922 was what social role was the motor cycle to play? The railway network, supplemented by motor charabancs and tram cars, provided a very efficient public transport system. A better integrated system than we know today. As personal transportation, the motor cycle represented a somewhat raffish alternative even to horseback or horse-drawn travel. Punctures, mechanical break-downs and skirmishes with the police were the norm. The discomfort and dirt, the oil-stains and the physical strain involved in riding the early, virtually unsprung, 'bone-shaker' machines was considerable. High-pitched pillion seats, lack of weather protection and flimsy sidecars did not provide for safe or comfortable family conveyance: nor was the notion really socially-acceptable among the newly-emancipated middle classes. The motor cycle to most people represented a health hazard and a life-threat. A dirty, noisy one at that. It was necessary to wear weather- and dirt-protective clothing to arrive at journey's end even half-presentable; and, vitally, the customer at whom the product was aimed principally to appeal, the unmarried male, discovered that all but the most politically precocious female passengers were unimpressed. The era of the emancipated woman had not yet arrived, and modesty and the motor cycle were irreconcilable.

The Motor Cycle's dog-collared columnist, Ixion, speaks from the heart when he writes of the early days of motor cycling:

> Our weird hobby seemed without excuse or justification; it veneered us with a permanent grime which exceeded every known form of filth alike in squalor and in adhesiveness. The uncertainty of being able to start on a journey was only exceeded by the improbability of our ever our reaching our destination in the saddle. There were no garages; the longest push could only bring us to the door of some ambitious cycle repairer, more ignorant and less cautious than ourselves.

At the beginning of the century, 'motoring' had found favour as a pastime of the gentry. The 'leaders of society' seized upon it as a somewhat heroic ideal and a novel relief from boredom. In some circles, among the intelligentsia and those of a more liberal political persuasion, motors provided a 'progressive' talking-point. George Bernard Shaw and several of his fellow Fabian Society members were early motor cyclists, as were the novelists, Arnold Bennett, Rudyard Kipling and the young Evelyn Waugh. Motor cycle competition appealed to the gentry for a while. It looked as if it might, one day, usurp the sport of horse-racing. Certainly, in its early days, the sports motor cycle signalled an independence and freedom, a virility and excitement more akin to horse-riding, than did the pioneer motor car. General Sir James Hills-Johnes, Dolaucothi, Col Delme Davies-Evans, Penlan, Llanfynydd, and Sir Grismond Philipps, Glangwili, were among the earliest motor cycle enthusiasts in Carmarthenshire.

The modern-day concept of the 'sports car' was not to take hold in any popular sense until the mid-to-late twenties. We see motor cycle manufacturers from 1919 setting their sights on young men, monied bloods – officers and NCOs – returning from France with swollen pay-books and alive with the heroic-adventurist spirit. Possession of a Sunbeam, an AJS, a Norton, Douglas or a Scott was a goal in life. When the ABC and Brough Superior were announced at the Olympia Shows of 1919 and 1920, respectively, there followed a surge of orders for them. For the really well-off, a Beardmore-Precision or an Edmund motor cycle, an Indian, Ariel, Matchless, Harley-Davidson or Zenith meant, by 1920, high-placing in the ascendancy game.

It was still early days for the mass of the working classes to look even to the least expensive motor cycle as personal transport. The early twenties was a time of austerity, inflation and high unemployment. Considerations such as the scant availability of spirit and spares or the 'stabling' of oil-and-petrol leaking machines in urban terraced housing were problematic. Though ingenious manufacturers advertised accommodating features such as 'collapsible' side-cars, there were other considerations. Household insurance was invalidated by the storing indoors of a motor cycle. Motor cycles as a consequence were, to begin with, sold mainly as luxury goods to a middle-class market. They were soon to lose ground as the 'hobby' transport of the gentry and the more affluent, who would turn their attention more to the powerful 'grande touring' motors – Napier, Humber, Prince Henry Vauxhall, Lagonda or Bentley. The day was fast coming when the motor cycle manufacturing industry would have to define its objectives and reconcile itself to two distinct sectors of the market: the very basic level motor transport and the sports-racing image. The motor cycle was to become a niche market, and all but a handful of manufacturers would fail, sooner or later – long before the unthinkable occurred in the1970s.

A trawl of the motor cycling press for the 1922 Motor Cycle Show reveals that there were 213 manufacturers offering a plethora of models. (See p. 316 Appendix 2).

At Bridge Street Garage, Carmarthen, (proprietor Wm 'Billy' Edwards), in 1919, there was a main agency for Excelsior, Humber, Omega and Verus motor cycles and Blackburne engines – and a district agency for BSA, Enfield, James, Bradbury, Alldays, and Allen & Hobart. By 1925 Billy, now of Towy Garage on the Swansea Road, and a Ford main agent, had taken on agencies for AJS, Norton, Raleigh, Ariel, OK and Scott. The AJS main agent was Jack Thomas of Cimla Road, Neath, who also supplied Douglas, Sunbeam, Norton, Rex Acme and Chater-Lea. Alex Thom would supply you with a Triumph or Royal Enfield, if you went to his City Road, Cardiff, showroom. For Rudge and Francis Barnett, Ivor Roberts of Oxford Street, Swansea was your man. If your taste was somewhat discerning, you went to Colburn's at Forge Garage, Neath, for Coventry Eagle or Calthorpe. But for Brough Superior, AJS, Sunbeam, Norton, Velocette, Matchless, James and other makes such as New Hudson, Precision, Cotton, Grindlay-Peerless, or Excelsior, it was down to Handel Davies at Brooklands Garage, Garnant, or the Oxford Street shop in Swansea. And in later years

Edwards Garage (old) Swansea Road, Carmarthen. Wm Edwards with 1923 Royal Enfield.

[© *Wm. Edwards collection*]

you might have gone over to Eddie Stephens, Water Street, Carmarthen, for your Norton, New Imperial, Matchless, Royal Enfield, Rudge, BSA or Triumph.

Whitsun 1922

The Whit Monday Welsh Speed Trials at Pendine in 1922 were again organised by Carmarthen and District MC and Light Car Club. *The Motor Cycle* comments that there was 'a discernible improvement in mechanical reliability over previous years, very few having fallen out'. This was to be the exception rather than the rule for many years to come, as the motor cycle engine, especially when highly tuned for racing, had a long road ahead of it in development terms.

Lubrication was a major problem, with vegetable oils breaking down under high temperatures, and moving parts – like camshafts and rockers – often reliant on grease, rather than pressure-pumped oil – seizing or breaking. Even main bearings on some models were hand-pumped with oil; and total loss systems – where all oil pumped from the oil tank eventually went out via the exhaust – required precise judgement on the part of the driver, particularly in the heat of competition.

Gearboxes, clutches and brakes were often inadequate to deal with great surges of power or the retardation loads involved in changing down at racing speeds with a three-speed box. Brakes were rudimentary and inadequate, fading with the heat of sustained application. Tyres, even when they were wired or fastened on with studs, came off if they were distorted or lost some pressure. The 'beaded edge' variety represented an advance, but were not to be relied upon. Water – of which there was always plenty at Pendine – when it got onto electrical components was a constant cause of trouble. It played hell, too, with clutches and brakes.

Vibration was another enemy of the early racing motor cycle, bereft as it was of the sprung frame. Any rider who failed to check that every nut and bolt was double-secured, would pay the penalty. When the beach was dry and hard at Pendine, and corrugated with tide ripples, it could result in machines literally shaking to pieces.

High-temperature materials technology was several paces behind engineering innovation in the early twenties. The metals employed expanded at different rates, warping cylinder heads or seizing bearings.[26] As a consequence of low-grade or inappropriate fuel, exhaust valves over-heated and became red-hot, and under the hammer-and-anvil effect of the cams and valve-springs, they sometimes stuck – as though welded – or they distorted or stretched, so that compression was lost or the valve stem broke. This was not so serious on a side-valve engine – indeed it happened less frequently – but, as Billy Edwards, RE Thomas, Glogue, and LF Griffiths, among many others were to discover on the beach, with overhead valves, it could mean the piston, connecting rod, crankshaft and the cylinder wall – all went bang. When this happened at high speed, it was seriously life-threatening. In any case, it represented another, and expensive, type of 'total loss'!

---

[26] See references to Charles Sgonina's 'Special', which in terms of hard-metal technology and valve-innovation was ahead of its time. A 'first' for Wales, developed on Pendine.

Mostyn Griffiths's Triumph Ricardo

Interest was focused in the paddock, that Whit Monday, on a machine owned by the novice, Mostyn Griffiths of Llandilo, reflecting the upsurge in innovation. The bicycle in question was a four-valve-head Triumph, an advanced piece of design-engineering from Harry Ricardo's London design office. It was rumoured to have cost £120. Known as the Triumph Ricardo or 'Riccy', it had gained a reputation on the Isle of Man and in other arenas as a powerful contender. Though it bore Ricardo's name, we should not underestimate Frank Halford's detail input.[27] The sports 'Riccy' was reckoned to have a power output of 20+ bhp at 5,000rpm from its single-cylinder 499cc (80.9 x 85mm) ohv engine. Although a Ricardo did enjoy some success at Brooklands in 1921, it had not 'brought home the bacon' at the Isle of Man. Only one of its three-man team, which included Charles Sgonina, finished – in a lowly 16th position, while one of the backup team's old side-valvers finished fifth.[28]

The four valves of the Triumph Ricardo's engine were arranged in 'pent-roof' configuration, to facilitate optimum 'scouring' gas-flow effect, in accordance with Ricardo's theories. The cylinder barrel was of 45% carbon steel, spiggotted to a cast-iron head, held down by five studs on a metal-to-metal join. The piston was of light alloy, slipper-type. The 1922 racing model had dry-sump lubrication, whereas the super sports roadster retained the old hand-pump total-loss system and had more robust Druid forks. Engine breakages persisted, and Triumphs were discouraged to the extent that the concept was abandoned in 1924 in favour of Vic Horsman's two-valve Model TT. With everything to gain from this imaginative beginning, the truth is that Triumph's heart was not in racing in these early days. The story of the vintage period in motor cycle racing might have been different had they stuck with it. Comparatively few Triumphs are seen again or mentioned in dispatches on Pendine until the late thirties. With the arrival of the Tigers there is, of course, a predictable pre- and post-war upsurge.

A garage-proprietor's son, from a family of long-established and respected blacksmiths in the Towy and Cothi valleys, Mostyn Griffiths was a consistent and good rider who could have made the grade had luck been more on his side. Like many another, he had come up through that hard school of riding, as a Great War DR.[29]

TT Triumph works rider Charles Sgonina, son of a wealthy Cardiff industrialist, had converted his 490 Norton side-valver with his own patent overhead valves. In the 350 class a new AJS [NY 1299] replaced his lightweight Omega. The day was perhaps best remembered as the day when the American big V-twin gave the top British V-twin a run for its money.

---

[27] See Bob Currie: 'Halford's 1922 Works Job', letter H Ricardo/Bob Thomas (12 x 70) *Classic Motor Cycle*, Oct 1985.
[28] Charles Sgonina was in 7th place in the 1921 Senior (Start No 3) on one of the three works 'Riccies' when he went out with a broken valve on lap 2.
[29] Pers. reminiscences: TE Hughes (author's late father).

CLOSED CLASSES
2½-mile sprint > 350cc
C Sgonina, (AJS)
J Thomas, (Sheffield-Henderson)
Ll Davies, Newport (Cotton-Blackburne)

2½-mile sprint: unlimited
FP Bush, (Harley-Davidson)
A Lindsay, (Norton)
C Sgonina, (Sgonina Special)

NOVICES
One mile sprint > 500cc
M (Mostyn) Griffiths, Llandilo (4-valve Triumph)

2½-mile sprint: unlimited
L (Leslie) Emanuel
M Griffiths (Triumph)

CHAMPIONSHIP CLASSES
25 miles > 275cc
M Isaac, (New Imperial)

25 miles > 350cc
Ll Davies, (Cotton)
J Thomas, (Sheffield-Henderson)
TG Thomas, Carmarthen (Sheffield-Henderson)

50 miles: unlimited cc
FP Bush, (Harley-Davidson)
A Lindsay, (Norton)
H Davies, (Brough-Superior)

Line-up for the 'Unlimited', Whit, 1922. 2nd left, Morris Isaac (New Imperial); Wm Edwards (Omega); C Sgonina (AJS); Harley-Davidson - FP Bush (v tall) standing, right.   [*Morton's Motor Cycle Media*]

FP Bush & Harley-Davidson

In the long-distance event, the Harley-Davidson led from the drop of the flag and won by over a mile. FP Bush, Neath, showed such a clean pair of heels to two very swift machines, Dr Lindsay's 'tweaked' 490cc Model 9 TT Norton[30] and Handel Davies's 976cc 90-bore Brough Superior, that you wonder what he had under him! Bush, a giant of a man – a tremendous character and 'a man to watch' (indeed you could hardly avoid it, as he towered over everyone) – was an exceptional rider, and he certainly had a useful power advantage on board his Model J Harley-Davidson 'Sport', even in standard form – 18bhp from 1207cc.[31]

A number of Sport models, shipped over from Milwaukee, found buyers in post-WW1 Britain among a certain category of 'speedmen' who had a taste for hairy-chested, out-and-out power. These men also provided homes for Indians – fast and reliable machines – as the era of the Big British Sports Twin was only just dawning.

---

[30] Model 9TT, prototype of the BS: 'Brooklands Special', converted to chain drive, basically, a 16H (costing £115 + £20 extra for specially-tuned engine with Binks' 'Rat Trap' carburettor - guaranteed 75 mph).

[31] A neat method of modifying the F-head Harley-Davidson engine was later discovered. Two four-valve Rudge heads miraculously fitted the 1922 Model J - effectively converting it into an 'Eight-valve Sport'!

Typically, these 'big-motor' aficionados – who needed to be strong and fit – were ex-Flying Corps men, NCO or officer-class, who had made friends with the Americans they had recently fought alongside and, thereby, become somewhat indoctrinated! The Bush brothers of Neath fitted this category to the T. Four cylinder Hendersons, Excelsiors and Clevelands had, by this time, been imported and sold in Britain in small numbers, but were mainly used as side-car traction engines. Frederick Percy Bush was a First World War aviator. Regrettably, too little personal detail is known about this cracker-jack rider whose career was soon to be cut dramatically and tragically short.

Harley-Davidson, with their FCA Racer, a tuned and stripped-down version of the Model J, were a major force in racing. They had cleaned up in long-distance events in the USA, winning at Dodge City and in the 200-mile race at Marion, Indiana. A Harley-Davidson was the first motor cycle to break the 100mph barrier in Britain – lapping Brooklands at a record 100.76mph, in 1921. So, the unlimited 'long race' at Pendine on that day in 1922 was for second place – between Norton and Brough (which had 500cc superiority over the Norton). Handel Davies was having an uncharacteristically bad day.

Now that out-of-the-showroom 75 mph machines were making their appearance in club racing, the competition between privateers, 'works' riders and rider-manufacturers became keen. While the innovative efforts of pioneers such as JL Norton, the Douglas, Stevens and Collier brothers, Granville Bradshaw, George Brough and HR Davies were actively unleashing the motor cycle from the technological moratorium of the Great War, local riders, some of them garage proprietors with their own workshop facilities, often 'souped-up' their 'sports' and brand racing machines to rev faster and handle better than the manufacturers considered prudent. Handel Davies and his brother Luther were well-known for engine-tuning. Charles Sgonina, of Penarth, 'the Welshman with an Italian name', built his own Special in a TT Norton frame supplied by the works. A highly inventive design and development engineer at a young age, he rebuilt the Norton engine from steel with his own-design overhead valve conversions.

Dr Alexander Lindsay, Norton

General medical practitioner Dr Alexander Lindsay (MB, CLB), of Cwmllynfell in the Swansea Valley (later Nantgaredig, Carmarthenshire), a native of Buchlyvie, Stirlingshire, whose career in motor cycle racing dates from the early years of the century as a medical student in Scotland, was a keen 'hobby' engineer. It was not unusual for a doctor to use a motor cycle on his round, especially in a country practice.[34] Lindsay, a dedicated Norton man, often used a 16H [MS 1206] as day-to-day transport. For racing he converted his belt-drive BS Norton [BX 1099] to chain-drive, and was known for being capable of tuning last year's 'works' machines to out-

---

[33] District nurses were issued with motor cycles in the early thirties.

perform this year's. He even pioneered some rakish streamline farings, learned from observations of motor car racing at Brooklands. Like Sgonina, Lindsay is said to have fitted his own patent overhead valves to his 490cc long-stroke side-valve 16H BS, several years before Bracebridge Street had theirs off the drawing-board. It was a case of the privateers being prepared to experiment and risk reliability for extra performance, whereas the manufacturers were conscious that the worst publicity for their machines was mechanical breakdown and the stigma of unreliability.

Something too easy for us to forget today in any discussion about internal combustion engines and their 'tuning' in the early days is – petrol. In the twenty-first century we take for granted seventy-five years and more of industrial chemistry, viewing the petrol engine, as we do, from an era where the terms 'decarbonisation' or 'de-coke' would need to be explained to the majority! Petrols in the early days were of low-grade, little better than paraffin, whose high flash-point combustion resulted in a sooty deposit of carbon inside the cylinder (the piston-crown, cylinder-head and the valves), that required cleaning (usually scraping) off every three to five thousand miles. In racing engines the octanage of fuel was increased by adding alcohol and cocktails of other volatile spirits to the basic 'red-can' fuel. These additives were obtainable from pharmacists, distillers and specialist suppliers. A science, an art – nay, an alchemy – arose from the mixing of these cocktails, appropriate to the machine, the occasion and purpose. A one-mile sprint where, say, the Brough never got out of second gear required a different formula from sustenance required for a long-stroke Sunbeam or water-cooled Scott entered for the Hundred Mile.

The way in which this related to appropriate mechanical adjustment of the engine is lucidly described by Charlie Sgonina. RJD Burnie, later to become one of Pendine's 'top men', in an article in *Motor Cycling* (May, 1949) quotes his friend:

> 'The road to success (according to Sgonina) consisted of working continuously on a good engine, until, without raising the compression ratio or changing the type of plug, you started to burn up plugs; you then raised the compression ratio, put in a harder plug and repeated the process – presumably until Death (or Destruction) called a halt!'
> I think that if this is not taken too literally, it contains a profound truth.

It also explains how the local boys, patiently developing their particular machines in this way – and often (not always!) pooling their knowledge, sharing their secrets, could steal-the-march on the 'works boys', with their new, often untried machines. It also, of course, proves the true worth of the professionals – George Dance, Freddie Dixon and Herbert 'Bert' Le Vack, in particular – real alchemists in this 'black art'.

This all contributed to motor cycle racing's name for excitement.

August 1922

In this climate of inquiry, where amateur and 'trade' were thus curiously evenly matched in rivalry, local events such as Pendine's August Bank Holiday Monday's meeting in 1922, attracted huge crowds. Young men in particular were interested to see the latest mechanical innovations as well as delighted to see 'local boys' give the works riders a run for their money and, often enough, beating them at their own game.

The *Motor Cycle*'s racing correspondent came away from the West Wales Centre's Open meet

> assured that motor cycle racing *is* the finest of all sports. Everything combined to make it one of the most enjoyable of events – sunshine, a vast expanse of not-too-wet sand, satisfactory fields, thrilling racing and – George Dance. On the day, each class resulted in a 'race'. There were no solitary processions, no handicapping and no split-second time-keeping.

The Western Mail, on August 9th, 1922, reports that:

> a large crowd, including motorists from over a wide area, visited Pendine on the Carmarthenshire coast, to witness the open speed championships for motor-cycles, combinations and three-wheel runabouts held under the auspices of the West Wales Centre Motor-cycle Clubs. The event was held on Pendine Sands and the numerous entries included some of the crack motor-cyclists in the country, including such as George Dance of Wolverhampton and CP Wood of Bradford. The Judges were: Messrs TD Phillips, T Jones, D Rees, Trevor Hopkins, F Heyne, C Bunt, Ben Jones, JE Jones and C Rees; Starter – Mr Conwil Evans; Time-keeper – Mr William Williams; Secretaries – Messrs A Henstock, J Jones and J James.

George Dance

It was a day notable for the fact that George Dance volunteered the statement that it was as good a speed course as he had ever performed on. Pronouncements veering towards the extravagant, indeed any statements at all, from this source were rare! According to *Motor Cycling*, George on the day also achieved the mile sprint at an average of 80mph, though no official sprint times were taken, which is a great pity, as this feat may never have been repeated. The 80mph race-average was to remain an elusive objective that haunted Pendine riders.

George was a 'Go or bust'[34] rider, who did not believe in finishing in any other position but first. Out of sixteen entries at Pendine when he was among the finishers, George was first fifteen times and once third. If there was to be a monument raised to a rider deserving of the title 'King of Pendine', it would be in the image of George Dance. He was himself and at home on Pendine. It was his lucky place.[35]

George had required some 'luck' a week or so previously. The story is well-known, but worth the re-telling. At a hill-climb meeting at Catash, near Newport in Monmouthshire, he found himself in a gooseberry bush! His foot had slipped off the brake on a T-junction at the end of his climb and he had gone through a hedge into

---

[34] "Go' is, of course a 1920s euphemism.
[35] It is curious and sad that among all George Dance's memorabilia - his photograph and cuttings album (in private hands) and among his trophies and medals (in the National Motor Cycle Museum), nothing survives to commemorate his achievement at Pendine.

George Dance (Sunbeam Sprint with Cubitt car). [IMI Marston Ltd]

an orchard below. But not before securing best time of day! Charlie Sgonina had gone through the same hedge earlier in the meeting, veering the other way at the junction, missing the ignominy of the thorns.

Dogged by a jinx that robbed him of deserved victories in Isle of Man TTs, eight of which he led, George Dance smashed lap records there time and time again only to be denied the trophy – usually from mechanical failure, sometimes falls – when it was all but in the bag. He was a sprint-specialist, seemingly not so adept at the marathon. Under his relentless charge, 'The Sunbeam' was hard-pressed to stand the pace, though its reputation was for reliability. George, unlike Jimmie Simpson, was not a congenital 'machine-breaker'. Quite the reverse, with his feeling for engineering. The best rider on the course, he never took TT honours, except once, when he did finish in eighth position. Not the George Dance style.

Despite this denial of honours, George Dance was in every respect a 'super-star' of his day, naturally stylish, and a tremendous attraction. Looking at photographs of him now, it is clear he had 'matinée-idol' good-looks – Sunbeamland's Rudolf Valentino. He was taciturn by nature, but nevertheless there was about him a charisma, more than just that relating to a 'strong, silent type'. It was, of course, 'star quality'. If George Dance was there, it made a difference – he was magnetic: you could not take your eyes off him. It is a gift bestowed on but a few people in a generation.

There is no doubt Dance was in possession of a special gift for tuning racing machines. Although there is still, to this day, some mystique attached to a 'George Dance Sprint Sunbeam' in terms of performance, its magic was largely a matter of careful preparation. George applied the pure engineer's method of achieving his object: 'simplicate and add lightness'. He was renowned, like Freddie Dixon, for a legendary physical strength. It was said he could lift a 300lb machine as if it was made of paper. He saw to it that his own wide-handle-barred sprinters were a lot lighter. One was said to weigh as little as 98 lbs,[36] drilled in every particular, until it resembled a Gruyere cheese. 'What holds it together, George?' someone asked. 'Air pressure!' was the reply.

For the other riders it was an intimidating experience to line up alongside him, though he was the best of sportsmen and a lovely fellow, by all accounts. 'If George couldn't do you any good, he certainly wouldn't do you any harm'[37].

The Welsh Championship events got off to a good start with representatives of three local motorcycle dealerships enjoying 'a ding-dong' on lightweight machines. Billy Edwards, Bridge Street Garage, Carmarthen, got his Blackburne-engined Rex-Acme off the line first, but was soon overtaken by Morris Isaac, on the JAP-powered 249cc New Imperial. Luther Davies's JAP-engined Diamond fought hard for honours, but could only manage third place. Luther lived and worked in Newport, but was always associated with his brother Handel's Brooklands Garage in Garnant.

---

[36]Hard to believe! 198 lbs would sound nearer the mark. See R Cordon Champ's *The Sunbeam Motor Cycle*, (p59). Foulis, 1980.
[37]TE Hughes: pers. comm.

C Sgonina (AJS).

Charles Sgonina (AJS) chats to George Dance (Sunbeam). [*Photos: courtesy AB Demaus/Mrs Sgonina*]

There was some 'lurid' (a favoured epithet of motor-racing correspondents of the time) cornering witnessed in the 350cc event: the exhibitionist-culprit being TJ 'Jack' Thomas of Neath on a 349cc Sheffield-Henderson. His 'more haste, less speed' efforts brought him only the consolation of third place, behind Billy Edwards (349 AJS) and second-placed A Bullock, on a rare ohv 349cc Blackburne-engined Weatherell.

George Dance faced formidable rivalry in the 560cc event: TT works men CP Wood (Scott), Hubert Hassall (490cc ohv Norton, soon to score outright victory in the Ulster Grand Prix), and privateer (1921 Triumph works rider) Charlie Sgonina on the intriguing ohv Sgonina-Special.[38] These men were not lined up to let him have it his own way. The Sunbeam rider's sprint-championship and TT experience showed right off the mark and again on the corners, where he was unbelievably neat and tight – though the Norton of Hassall stayed with him all the way to the last bend when Dance, typically, pulled a rabbit out of the hat and accelerated away to cross the finishing-line – 100 yards ahead. The crowd was thrilled. He usually held on to reserves, but this time it had looked as if he were fully extended. The winner's average speed over 10 miles was 63.27mph. The twin two-stroke Scott had flunked on the start-line. An oiled-up plug: which one? The Scott-rider's nightmare!

In the Unlimited Championship event, George Dance again showed his supremacy. Out-gunned on the start-line by the big V-twins – George Grinton, the 'heavyweight' champion Scot from Edinburgh, on a 998cc Harley-Davidson, Handel Davies on the 976cc Brough Superior and by CP Wood on the less powerful, but very quick, 596cc water-cooled, twin-cylinder two-stroke Scott, meant George had to hang on to fourth position on acceleration off the mark. His was the 85 x 88mm single cylinder side-valve Sunbeam with 499cc. Come the corner and Handel Davies lost his lead to Wood, whose wide cornering – true and steady – was fast. Wood held his advantage for two laps. Dance having built up momentum – which he maintained with uncanny brilliance through corners – crept into second place. However

> Entering the last lap Dance had dropped to third, but, sure enough, less than two minutes later, the craning spectators saw what they had half expected – the Sunbeam whizzing across the line at 80mph, with the Brough Superior and the Scott relegated to second and third. There was a storm of applause.

Dennis May, in his popular series on motor cycling-racing greats, 'Pastmasters of Speed', that ran in *Motor Cycling* during the 'fifties, vividly conjures 'GD's' sprint technique, in days before British bikes sported twist-grip throttles – and when crash-helmets were not obligatory:

> He is on the start-line, giving 'er rhythmic gulps of throttle as the starter stands motionless with the flag raised aloft. At each thumb-and-forefinger tweak on that stubby lever a great blast of exhaust noise hits your ears. There is a tension, a vibrancy, about the rider's stance that suggests a blue-steel spring in compression ...

---

[38] Charlie Sgonina was quietly resented by the local boys who referred to him as 'that old Sgonina'. Part xenophobia, directed at his Italian name and part-German ancestry, he seemed to have it all going for him: money, looks, charm and exceptional talent! (Pers. comm. TE Hughes/Mostyn Griffiths c. 1953/5)

The flag flutters down. Faster than you can think, George jerks his head round to eyes front, plays the clutch in and the throttle back in a faultlessly synchronised double motion, hoists a sprucely gaitered left leg onto its rest, flattens himself along the 'Beam's shallow tapered tank, and is away with a bound that brings the front wheel rearing off the ground.

Although the surface is loose and patchy, he picks his course so perfectly and pays out power so delicately that his back wheels spin scarcely at all. As he screams up through the gears his bare head goes lower and lower until his right cheek is snuggling the side of the tank and he is peering under the left half of those wide-splaying bars.

R>L: G Dance (Sunbeam) demonstrates the 'getaway' - with Handel Davies (Brough Superior) and Charles Sgonina (AJS), 1922. [*Morton's Motor Cycle Media*]

OPEN

10 miles: unlimited

G Dance (Sunbeam) CP Wood (Scott)
H Davies (Brough Superior)
Winner's time: 9 mins 1.8secs (65 mph).

'Chairs' were quickly 'tied' on to these hot machines for the next event, which provided opportunity for revenge. As the turns were all left-hand, CP Wood gained an advantage with the Scott's right-hand-mounted side-car. He beat Handel Davies's Brough into second place; Bush with the Harley-Davidson outfit having to be content with third.

SIDECARS – OPEN

4 miles: unlimited

CP Wood (Scott) FP Bush (Harley-Davidson)
H Davies (Brough Superior) G Grinton (Harley-Davidson)
Winner's Time: 4mins 18¾secs.

In the closed events, things went as follows:

CLOSED CLASSES

4 miles > 300cc
M Isaac (249 New Imperial) & LI Davies (249cc Diamond) tied
Wm Edwards (249 Rex-Acme)
Winners' time: 4 mins 52 secs.

4 miles: unlimited
H Davies (976 Brough Superior)
A Lindsay (490 Norton)
FP Bush (998 Harley-Davidson)
Winner's time: 4 mins 18.6 secs.

One-mile sprint > 300cc
H Harris (349 New Imperial)
LI Davies (249 Diamond)
Wm Edwards (249 Rex-Acme)

one-mile sprint > 350cc
C Sgonina (AJS)
Wm Edwards (349 AJS)
LI Davies (349 Cotton-Blackburne)

one-mile sprint > 600cc
A Lindsay (490 Norton)
AW Nicklin (492 Sunbeam)
I Parker (492 Sunbeam)

one-mile sprint: unlimited
H Davies (976 Brough Superior)
FP Bush (998 Harley-Davidson)
A Lindsay (490 Norton)

OPEN CHAMPIONSHIP

One-mile sprint: unlimited
G Dance (499 Sunbeam)
C Sgonina (498 Sgonina Special)
H Davies, Garnant (976 Brough Superior)

4 miles > 275cc
M Isaac (New Imperial)
Winner's time: 4 mins 40 secs.

10 miles > 350cc
Wm Edwards (AJS)
A Bullock, Carmarthen (Weatherell)
LI Davies, Newport (Blackburne)

10 miles > 560cc
G Dance (Sunbeam)
Winner's time: 9 mins 29 secs.

CLOSED EVENTS

SIDECARS

4 miles > 750cc
V Anstice, Bath (Douglas)
H Davies (Sunbeam)

4 miles: unlimited
H Davies (Brough Superior)
V Anstice (Douglas)

LIGHT CARS

2½ mile-sprint
FN Morgan, Newport (FIAT)
I Board, Bridgend (GN)
AE Gardner, Cwmllynfell (Campbell)

2½ mile-sprint: Ford cars
T Lewis, Carmarthen
R Thomas, Gloag

Three-wheelers
LI Davies, Newport (Morgan)

A 'grotesquely comic race for Ford cars concluded a meeting...that provided a win apiece for almost all the most popular entrants', observes the *Motor Cycle*.

Sgonina wittily recalls[39] that in a particular 'mile sprint race at Pendine' he achieved his fastest-ever speed:

> The fastest I have ever travelled, I think, was at Pendine. In a one-mile sprint race I was up against George Dance on the works Sunbeam. At the word 'go' he gained three feet on me and after that I was gaining at the rate of 2ft 9in per mile. In fact when we stopped he said: 'You just managed it'. But I contradicted him and said: 'You just had it by three inches'. In talking after the event he said he knew his machine would do 95mph any day of the week. But I do not think I have ever reached the 100mph mark.

Dr A Lindsay's aerodynamic 16H Brooklands Special (BS) Norton. [© *Lindsay collection*]

---

[39]From a typescript speech by Charles Sgonina, addressed to an unknown gathering. Courtesy, AB Demaus.

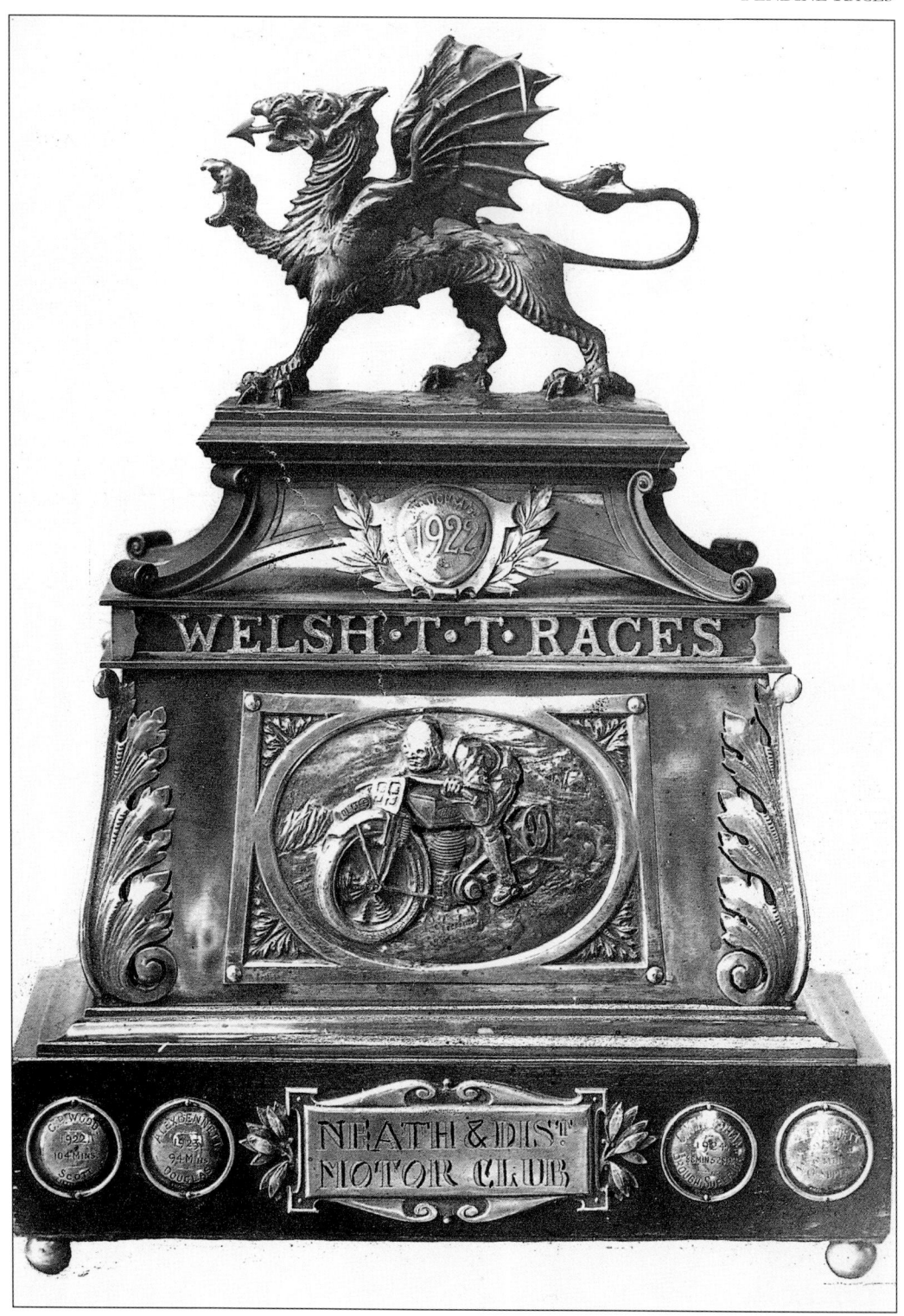

The Welsh TT trophy. [*Morton's Motor Cycle Media*]

6. The First Welsh TT

It was a shame that, after such a glorious meeting the day before, the first Welsh TT on August Bank Holiday Tuesday, 1922, had to take place on the sands in atrocious weather conditions. The Neath club had organised everything but the driving rain which kept up all morning, playing havoc with clutches, magnetos and plugs – not to mention long-suffering spectators and officials. Of a very large entry, very few were there at the finish of each class event: even the luminaries were extinguished. A young man from Bridgend who had won a series of novice class events at Porthcawl, was making his debut at Pendine: Leslie 'LF' Griffiths, son of a Bridgend solicitor, entered his long-stroke Sunbeam... 'but it wouldn't stand the strain. The piston gave up being a piston after I had covered 12 miles'.[40]

Scotts had the best of days, and not simply because of others' misfortunes. Clarence Wood, on the TT Squirrel [AA 4], took the initiative from the start, in the 100-mile TT, and held on to it throughout. One of those very smooth and deceptively fast riders, Wood was 'as one' with his machine. Ivor Thomas of Neath, on the second works entry (a smaller capacity machine), was riding a strategic race. The 536 and 431cc Scotts hummed round, setting up a plume of spray which threatened the electrics of close pursuants. Fifty yards behind, they were shadowed by Hassall on the experimental ohv works Norton and George Dance on the long-stroke side-valve 'TT' Sunbeam. Grinton, on the Harley-Davidson, too, was with, and after, them. The Harley, of necessity, having run only two laps of the 5-miles-in-each-direction course (20 miles) 'ran into the depot for replenishment at the bins'. Both Hassall and Dance's motors temporarily succumbed to the spray, and poor Morris Isaac, following on with the lightweight pack (who formed a 50-mile race-within-a-race), retired with 'eye trouble' while lying second to Billy Edwards's very fast ohv 350 AJS.

Dance, after some 'roadside repairs', restarted his machine and while Wood stopped for re-fuelling at 35 miles, he pounced, thinking to gain the advantage – but Wood had a lap in hand over him. Wood's refuelling was precisely handled, helped by the Scott's 3½-inch out-size fuel cap, enabling him come out in short order, yowling away, as he departed the 'depot'. He was only just maintaining his lead position. The Sunbeam works rider was obliged to continue in his wake, enduring the wet plume of sand-spray.

---

[40]Quoted from a type-written 'Notice' displayed at Leslie Griffiths Motors, 11, Ewenny Road, Bridgend. (Courtesy of Haydn Rees).

When Wood stopped for his second and final fuel-stop at 90 miles, he had opened a 4-mile lead over Dance and Grinton. His pit-stop this time took four minutes, allowing second and third – circulating neck-and-neck – to catch up with him. Wood was undeterred, knowing they would both need a fuel stop, and the downpour was at last easing. Dance's magneto finally 'packed up' at 98 miles when he was leading the 500cc class. This allowed the second works Scott, the 481cc Squirrel, to take the 500cc class ahead of Hassall's Norton. Grinton's Harley-Davidson is presumed to have fallen out, as had Handel Davies's Brough. A mistake had happened in refuelling. Luther's 600cc Precision had, according to reports, taken on some water with the petrol-mix, as, it was discovered, had the '90-bore'.

The final result of this, the first Welsh Tourist Trophy race for motor cycles, was as follows:

FIRST 'WELSH TT', 1922

100 miles: unlimited
CP Wood (Scott 596cc)

50 miles 500 > 532cc
I Thomas, Neath (Scott 481cc)
H Hassall (Norton 490cc)

50 miles 251 > 350cc
Wm Edwards (349 AJS)
TA Jones (349 Ivy)
LF West (349 Massey-Arran)

50 miles > 250cc
J (Jack) Evans (249 New Imperial)
JN Roberts (249 New Imperial)

Ivor Thomas came in victorious on the Scott in the 500cc class. The stratagem had worked: Scotts first in both classes. Ivor's accumulated successes in 1922 already included the Alex Thom and the Bevan and Evan William trophies. Throughout the war he had served with the Rifle Brigade, being twice wounded. Clarry Wood always accorded pride of place in his Harrogate home to the Welsh TT trophy he won that day.[41] It was a proud day for Wales as well, and an immensely popular result. The Scott riders, resplendent in their purple leathers, had gained their honours in the face of the most formidable opposition.

HW Hassall

Chief among the Scotts' antagonists had stood the person of Hubert Walter Hassall, who in the 'big time' road-racing circus was ranked as the most combative and successful inter-war rider. The 24-year-old Birmingham Norton man who, apart from winning at Dunrod, had chalked up victories in the French and Belgian Grands Prix two years running (1921- 22), and had accumulated 39 gold medals, 34 silver and 18 bronze at speed events all over the country.

At the annual dinner of the Carmarthen club in the Nelson Hotel in December, J Conwil Evans, who had been secretary since foundation in 1914, retired. His

---

[41] George Stevens: 'Scott Personalities' - *Yowl*, Nov 1962.

achievement in the cause of motor sport in Wales, together with that of his committee and considering the intervention of the Great War, had been significant. They had got an enterprise off the ground which enjoyed international standing. As Dr Alexander Lindsay said in his after-dinner speech

> Three years ago very few people knew of this quiet little seaside resort, but I am afraid that if the attendance on August Bank Holiday was a criterion of the gatherings of the future, then the GWR will have to run a special line for the two days' meeting.

He could not, of course, have anticipated the motorised transport revolution of the future which would not only serve to discard rail locomotion, but relegate the motor cycle.

Dr Lindsay brought the Carmarthen club's dinner guests to their feet for a silent tribute to a local and Pendine hero.

FP Bush

Tragedy had struck. In that year, the death of FP Bush, the Neath club's superbike 'crack', was one of South Wales's most notorious events. He had drowned in a sensational flying accident in Swansea Bay. Frederick Percy Bush was a larger-than-life character, 'one of the best-known racing motor cyclists in South Wales.'[42] After demobilisation from the RFC/RAF, where he had experienced three years in the skies over the trenches in France, he had gone into business for himself in the motor trade, at Norton Garage, Black Pill, and had only recently married. His young wife, the former Miss Boulton of Port Talbot, was an accomplished motorcyclist. Bush was also involved as a partner with Evan Williams, a 'commissioning agent', in a seasonal flying enterprise, The Welsh Aviation Co, centred on the Aeroplane Depot huts on the beach at Blackpill.

October 3rd, 1922, was one of those lovely sunny autumn days. Lloyd George was still exercised over the impasse concerning the Dardanelles. Marie Lloyd, doyen of the Music Halls, collapsed on stage. Percy Bush was called over in the afternoon to help start the engine of the Avro Biplane. His partner, Williams, had intended taking an army friend, Sergeant Major Biggins, up for an end-of-season 'flip around the bay'. The fuel tap was not switched on. Bush was persuaded to take the controls of a craft he had never flown before. It was only to be a short flight.

They did a circuit of Neath and a couple of aerobatic stunts over the bay. The pilot then made a pass at landing, came in a bit low and over-shot. In the second approach the engine cut out at about 300 feet, 'near Vivian's Stream on Swansea Sands'. The plane banked, nose-dived and spiralled from about 150 feet, crashing into the sea, 200 yards from the shore. The engine exploded on impact and the craft overturned, pinning the occupants in their seats. The disaster happened in full sight of the pilot's

---
[42] *South Wales Daily Post,* Oct 4th, 1922.

Avro wreck, Black Pill, Swansea Bay, *South Wales Daily Post.*

young wife, waiting-by in their motorcycle-and-side-car. Passengers on a L&NW train into Victoria station, and others travelling on the Oystermouth Railway, saw the pilot and his two passengers meet their death, drowned in shallow water before rescue could reach them.

Bush was 25. The snarling double-echo of his big Harley-Davidson, locked in combat with his brother's Indian, the Brough Superiors and all-comers, would, sadly, not be heard on the beach at Pendine again.

August 1923

'All South Wales', it appears, 'elderly people, boys and girls included – braved the super-dusty road to the scene of the racing' on August Bank Holiday Monday, 1923.[43] The West South Wales Centre was the sponsor of the first day of this two-day event. It was an occasion when mechanical failure once again marred otherwise well-organised proceedings. There is a cogent reason for this. Engine and chassis development were proceeding apace: lessons learned from Brooklands and the Isle of Man pointed to the superiority, in terms of power output and piston speed, of the overhead valve-operating system. But not in terms of reliability. Engineering ambition was ahead of metallurgy, ahead of fuel and lubrication technology. Dropped exhaust valves and burnt seatings were endemic.

George Dance was there with the new 493cc ohv Sunbeam. An experimental machine, it used inclined push-rods against triple coil-springs. Later, these were to be

---
[43] *The Motor Cycle,* Aug 15th.

abandoned in favour of vertical (parallel) push-rods and hairpin valve-springs. Reliability had been a hallmark of the old side-valve engines and, though George and Tommy de la Hay had enjoyed some successes with the prototype ohv bicycle in sprint outings during 1923, Sunbeam had not been not sufficiently confident to enter it for the IoM TT in June, sticking to the proven 'flat-head' 492cc long-strokes.

Norton

Nortons had, at last, for 1923, brought out their ohv racing engines. They were based on the bottom-end of the well-tried 79 x 100 mm 490cc side-valve engine, but with a DR O'Donovan-designed overhead-valve cylinder-head; the valves operated by adjustable push-rods. These engines, because of their basic sound design and durability, would be responsive to development and were, in time, to prove all-conquering: but for several years to come they would lack that all-important virtue - reliability.

Douglas

Douglas had put in a considerable amount of development-work on their familiar high-revving, horizontally-opposed, flat-twin engine, which had been available with inclined overhead valves since 1920, though it also had not gained a reputation for dependability. Based on a design conceived by Joseph Barter in 1907, the engines, redesigned by Les Bailey with help from Cyril Pullin, in 346cc and 494cc form, were given twin carburettors, revised induction and aluminium heads for 1923. The re-design included a shorter chassis (though they were still 'sweet and low'), and a superior RA (Research Association), Ferodo-based, braking system. The Douglas was a sleek, highly-desirable machine – and exceptionally light – the TT 350 'RA' model tipped the scales at 200lbs, the 'over-the-counter' sports 500cc weighing-in at just 250 lbs. This was 60lbs lighter than either an AJS or a Norton. The marque, though inherently fragile, was destined for great things in the hands of Vic Anstice, Len Parker, Cyril Pullin, Freddie Dixon, Clarry Wood and many a privateer.

Scott

Innovation or not, Scott was still the make to beat – proving beyond argument the inventive genius of Alfred Angas Scott who, incidentally, was shortly to die on August 23rd, 1923 at the age of 48. Pneumonia set in after getting wet, pot-holing. His highly-original concept, designed in 1907, was to go on competing in *grandes épreuves* through to 1929 and beyond. Scotts had won the Senior TT twice in succession in 1913 and 1914, and though these heights were denied them after the war, Scotts were always in high contention. The power plant was a parallel-twin water-cooled unit in cast-aluminium with iron liners. It was, for its time, a highly sophisticated two-stroke motor, offered in 481 or 532cc engine specification, and free-revving up to 3,000rpm and above. There were four forward speeds available: the two-speed gear-box transmitting power through a high- and low-ratio arrangement. 50mph was achievable in low ratio, and 80-plus in high.

The sound of the Scott twin-two-stroke engine in full-song was unique and thrilling to the ears in those days, compared to the 'chuff-chuff' and crackle of some other offerings. The aural effect of a tandem two-stroke is, of course, not unlike that of the compact four-cylinder four-strokes of more recent times and, indeed, similar to the Kawasaki KR 250/350s of the late seventies: the only other manufacturer to essay a water-cooled parallel-twin two-stroke, but with 'big bang' firing order. Anyone who has not heard the 'yowl', the mating call, of a race-tuned Scott at 'full chat', will have missed something – ear-ache.

CP Wood won two championship events on the day – the 'long' race and the unlimited sidecar competition, thrilling the crowds who sweltered on the beach. Clarry was developing into something of a sidecar specialist.

CP Wood

Captain Clarence Proctor Wood, MC, was a farmer's son by birth and upbringing, whose delight in speed and machinery had persuaded him to follow his brother, HO 'Tim' Wood, into engineering, and an apprenticeship with the Scott works in Shipley where he soon became a member of the trials team. Senior TT winner and lap-record-holder, Tim was the ideal 'big brother' for an aspiring racing driver. 'Clarry' had a precision brain and a coolness of temperament that had resulted in his war-time citation for bravery under fire.[44] He took a regular commission, as a Sapper, while somehow continuing racing and development on the competition machines. The 1919 Sports model, introduced before the famous Squirrel, bore the pared-down, drop-handle-bar features of CP Wood's racer. Like George Dance, he led, but never won a Senior IoM TT, but was twice placed. Clarry was a great favourite at Pendine.

---

[44]'Lt CP Wood, RE. He displayed the greatest coolness and energy in supervising the digging and wiring of points close to the enemy's lines under heavy shell and machine-gun fire. His fine example kept his men at work when other parties had been dispersed. Awarded Military Cross.' *The Times,* 3 v 1917.

CP Wood (Scott). Mostyn Griffiths 4th from left. [*Morton's Motor Cycle Media*]

A significant newcomer to the resort in August 1923 was JH 'Jimmie' Simpson, 25 years old and with a new contract to ride for AJS, a stable to which he was to remain faithful for the remaining ten years of his career. As a rider he was always in the first rank – but, either by bad luck or over-zealousness – was seldom able to stay there until the chequered flag. He rode in 26 Isle of Man TTs and won just one – his penultimate – and on a lightweight Rudge. Yet there were only two years of his 13-year motor racing career when he did not secure a placing or break a lap record on the island. Jimmie Simpson broke the barriers of 60, 70 and 80-mile-an-hour laps in the Senior TT. A good enough claim to fame!

Local men featured in the 300cc championship event. The smart money was on Morris Isaac who, to everyone's dismay, balked his ohv New Imperial virtually on the line. After that, it was the day of a promising newcomer, Percy Rogers of Brecon, on a similar machine. Rogers, on over-enthusiastic entry to the final turn before the flag, very nearly succeeded in losing the event to the pursuing Velocette of D Jones.

According to *The Motor Cycle*'s account of events:

> The 350cc championship was the first to go the full distance – five laps – and it was the first real race. George Dance (Sunbeam) established a commanding lead in the first lap with only Morris Isaac (Sunbeam) and JH Simpson (AJS) of the other nine runners looking at all dangerous. C Sgonina (AJS) who had gained 50 yards at the start, was well behind. Dance's acceleration after a magnificent turn should have made his position

even more secure on lap 2 – but no! Isaac was visibly closer next time round; and certainly the pace – 60 mph laps – was no slower. For the next two laps there were only yards between the duellists, and Simpson's best was only good enough for a somewhat poor third. There was a great cheer as the two Sunbeams entered their last lap neck and neck – whether for the local man or for the ever-popular Dance is hard to say – and as they appeared at the far end of the finishing straight the crowd thronged dangerously far forward to see who led. It was Dance, but only by a stirring final spurt did he gain a 0.8-second advantage over the finishing line.

Morris Isaac, given charge of a Dance-prepared factory Sunbeam, was highly competitive. It was a compliment he certainly deserved, as he was to prove in the teeth of the works riders. Jimmie Simpson, the AJS works man, was having his first baptism on sand. As we shall see, he was a fast learner!

It was Dance's turn to be left on the line in the 560cc event. The Scott of CP Wood hummed its song as it sped clear away from the field, to win this 10-mile event by some two miles in 9 mins 55 secs. Had Dance not pulled his throttle cable at the start, it would have been first-class entertainment to have witnessed the duel between these two past-masters of – quite different – cornering technique. Apart from appreciation of the 'magnificent' cornering of the TT Scott, the crowd was entertained to the spectacle of two local amateurs with IoM form – Charles Sgonina and Dr Alexander Lindsay – fight off the professional newcomer, AJS-man, JH Simpson from Leicester, with their modified Nortons. The 498cc 'Sgonina Special' was now fitted with a hazardous-looking, exposed, chain-drive overhead-camshaft valve operating system.[45] Simpson's cornering was also something to be seen. He beat the long-wheelbase Nortons every time on the bends, but the larger-capacity Nortons were just able to out-run the works AJS on top speed up the straights. Jimmie Simpson was already well up the Pendine learning curve.

The result:

CHAMPIONSHIP EVENTS OPEN

10 miles > 350cc
G Dance (Sunbeam)
M Isaac (Sunbeam)
JH Simpson (AJS)
Winner's time: 10 mins 26 secs.

10 miles > 560cc
CP Wood (Scott)
C Sgonina (Sgonina Special)
A Lindsay (Norton)
Winner's time: 9mins 55secs.

The Wood/Dance duel was set for a re-run in the Unlimited Championship event. Added excitement was provided, in the field of five which lined up, by the debut of two new, powerful (733cc), boxer-engined and light weight Douglases from the

---

[45] See John Griffith, *Motor Cycling* Aug 11th, 1955. 'Twenty Years Early': (Sgonina Special). Two ohv conversions were built before the more ambitious ohc engines, incorporating steel cylinders on Norton crank-cases. The first ohc was designed incorporating an exposed cam chain, the other - a dohc - was neater in appearance.

Bristol factory. They were driven by Anstice and Parker, both top-drawer riders. Douglas led Scott and Sunbeam up the shore-line into the noon haze. On the near-side (to the spectators) return run, the Douglas of Anstice was in the lead – a yard or two ahead of Dance's Sunbeam. No Scott. Wood had blown his front tyre on a rock or shell[46] at the Laugharne-end corner. It was now Douglas, Sunbeam, Sgonina, Douglas. Dance's clutch failed on lap three, leaving Sgonina to hold the second of the Bristol machines at bay: which he heroically did to the end.

10 miles: unlimited
V Anstice (733 Douglas)
C Sgonina (498 Sgonina Special)
L Parker (733 Douglas)
Winner's time: 9mins 20secs.

One-mile sprint: unlimited
G Dance (Sunbeam)
AW Nicklin (Sunbeam)
C Sgonina (498 Sgonina Special)
Won easily. Not timed.

Dance won the one-mile Open sprint in fine style on the prototype ohv 493cc Sunbeam. The rest of the meeting was confined to closed events for WSW Section club members. The 'works boys' did not pack up and go home. They made for the garages to prepare their machines for the Welsh TT, to be run the following day. What happened in the afternoon was as follows:

CLOSED

4 miles > 300cc
D Jones (Velocette)
P Rogers (New Imperial)
B Harris (New Imperial)
Winner's time: 5 mins 15 secs.
Won by 75 yds. A good third.

4 miles > 600cc
M Isaac (Sunbeam)
A Lindsay (Norton)
AW Nicklin (Sunbeam)
Winner's time: 4 mins 5 secs.
Won Easily; a good third.

4 miles > 350cc
M Isaac (Sunbeam)
F Rogers, Porthcawl (AJS)
I Parker (OK-Blackburne)
Winner's time: 4 mins 9 secs.
Won easily. Second man unplaced at half-distance.

One-mile sprint > 350cc
M Isaac (Sunbeam)
J Thomas (Rex-Acme)
FJ Redcliffe (AJS)
Not timed.

---

[46] Anyone who has walked the beach at Pendine will realise it abounds with shells of different types at certain times. E Donovan, writing in 1805, in *A Descriptive Excursion Through Wales,* observes: 'The sands were bestrewed with a greater variety of uncommon shells than I ever remember to have seen at any one time upon our most productive shores. There were several distinct parallel ridges of shells, that extended for miles along the beach, all of which had been apparently washed out of their native beds in the sands by the preceding tide. Shells of the *solen* genus were the most abundant of these species. *Siliqua* (razor) were most numerous, and of uncommon size. *Vagina,* another of the larger kinds, were scattered among the rest, and likewise *ensis*: that rare species, *legumen,* were plentiful here, beyond conception; and *pellucidus,* was sparingly sprinkled with the others. Many curious shells of the *Tellina* and other genera were also lying about the shore ...'

Carmarthen Motor Cycle & Light Car Club, 1923. L>R: Dr Lindsay? (Norton) [BX 2575]; Morris Isaac (Sunbeam); Luther Davies? [DW 2644]; Handel Davies [BX 2475]; Albert Lewis, Henllan [CY 5069]: (all Sunbeams).

one-mile sprint > 600cc
C Sgonina (Sgonina Special)
M Isaac (Sunbeam)
AW Nicklin (Sunbeam)
Not timed.

one-mile sprint: unlimited
C Sgonina (Sgonina Special)
M Isaac (Sunbeam)
AW Nicklin (Sunbeam)
Not timed. Won by two yards.

OPEN EVENTS SIDECARS

4 miles: unlimited
CP Wood (Scott)
AR Gardiner (Norton)
Winner's time: 4 mins 23 secs.
Anstice delayed at the start. Won by a mile.

JH Simpson

'Some of the most wildly exciting racing ever witnessed' is the enthusiastic verdict of *The Motor Cycle*'s correspondent reflecting on the second day's racing at Pendine, embracing the second 'Welsh TT', on August Bank Holiday Tuesday, 1923. The event, organised by the Neath club, was one that he and everyone present would best remember for the stylish performance of TT ace, Jimmie Simpson:

> The rider in question – JH Simpson (AJS), of Junior TT fame – gained second place in the 350cc (50-mile event). By lurid [that word again!] corner work, the like of which has never been seen outside of an American dirt track, he fought a first-class rider on a 3mph faster machine right into the last of 25 hectic laps up and down the sand.[47]

---

[47] *The Motor Cycle,* Aug 9th, 1923.

There were two outstanding racing motor cyclists making their first appearance before the crowd at Pendine over that Bank Holiday. Those present were privileged to have witnessed the contrasting styles of Jimmie Simpson and Alec Bennett who, and one can somehow always tell, were touched by that special gift – call it genius – that marks out one or two in a generation. You can see them coming a mile away: they are men who can take a racing motor cycle to the very edge of its capability, knowing the exact amount of power to apply or withdraw in a situation, and the precise limit of adhesion.

JH Simpson (AJS). *[Morton's Motor Cycle Media]*

James Hampson Simpson was a James Dean character in his early days – rebellious and a hell-raiser – with a reputation for wilfully exceeding sacred parameters: and a machine-breaker to boot. Being brought to book, following an incident at the 1922 Isle of Man Senior TT where he disregarded a marshal's instructions, he fortunately came to his senses and was rewarded with an AJS works ride. This was doubtless on the strength of his having broken the lap-record on the 'cold' lap, from a standing start, on a privately-entered AJS in the 1922 Junior, and leading the race – and the great Bert Le Vack – by a whole minute: till a dog crossed his path on Bray Hill. Simpson was twenty four.

Alec Bennett

Alec Bennett was a few years older. Often dubbed 'the Yank', he was in fact born in Ulster, flew with the Royal Flying Corps in the Great War, after which he emigrated to British Columbia. His motor cycle racing career began on the short-spurt dirt-tracks of Canada. He then returned and secured a place as tester/development engineer in John Marston's Sunbeamland, with George Dance, from which position a TT ride was axiomatic. Bennett led in the 1921 Senior, until he missed a gear and stretched a valve. The following year he won the Senior TT on the works Sunbeam by seven minutes, twenty one seconds, missing the 60 mph lap-record by 0.001 mph. He joined Douglas in 1923, but was never happy in Bristol.

Curiously enough, it was Simpson's cornering style that suggested dirt-track technique, rather than Bennett's. On the corners his boot went down and 'the arc of his rear wheel was fully two feet wider than that of his front wheel and always his near footrest ploughed the sand'. Bennett's style was quite different and distinctive:

> His aim was not principally to get through the turn itself on the limit, so much as placing himself precisely right for the exit, and so make it possible to bring full power back on at the earliest split-second. This method led him to develop an unusual cornering line, farther than normal from the inside of the apex. If he cut the shoulder dead fine it tended to take him too far out... in leaving the corner, which in turn forced him to delay a fraction longer in giving her full stick.[48]

The programme for the day comprised two events, somewhat complicated by the staging of 'races within races' – and 'the exigencies of the tide'. Previously, the 'Welsh TT' had been run over a five-mile-long return course (ie. a 10-mile lap). The pull of the moon on earth's waters on Bank Holiday Tuesday, 1923, however, had raised the water-table and necessitated truncating the course to a 1-mile return, so that there would be a significant difference in the times and average speeds recorded over these two long-distance events, when compared to the previous year's meeting. The 'Junior' race, over 50 miles was for two classes of machine – up to 250cc – and 250cc to 500cc. The 'Senior' was for 500 – 750cc machines, over 100 miles. There was no outing this time, therefore, for the heavyweights – Brough, Harley, Indian, Sheffield-Henderson or Zenith – which was a shame, as they added excitement, glamour, even *gravitas,* to the proceedings. This would be amended by popular demand in the future.

This Tuesday was the day when Morris Isaac of Carmarthen proved, if there was any doubt, that he had class. His brilliant showing in the 'Junior' was the essence of the appeal of Pendine. There was one difference though. On this occasion he, as an amateur, was driving an equal machine to the 'trade' riders. Usually he was taking mechanical risks with an off-the-shelf bicycle that had been super-tuned in a Carmarthen workshop. This time, he was astride a Marston-prepared Sunbeam [FK

---
[48] *Pastmasters of Speed:* Dennis May, Temple Press, 1958.

1470], something known to be very special. An Isle of Man TT competitor and International Six Days Trial Gold Medalist, Morris had evidently won the confidence of the Sunbeam people, George Dance in particular, to be allowed to 'demonstrate to the public' the virtues of one of their thoroughbreds, in his individual way.

As expected, Jimmie Simpson on the 'Big port' AJS, led the field of 18 competitors from the start. Morris Isaac, in second place, pulled well ahead of his friend and rival Billy Edwards on an AJS and ahead of J Parker (Sunbeam). The leaders held station in those positions (with frequent revisions!) for the first six laps, with Anstice (Douglas RA) tailing them at a distance – while a scrap between the AJSes of Jack Thomas and J Jones, and the Beardmore Precisions of ER Jacobs and G Thomas created a dust-storm in the background. Charlie Sgonina, poor fellow, had oiled up on the start-line. Quickly, he had changed a plug on his ohc 'Sgonina Special', and was soon valiantly in hot-pursuit of the 'big boys' – overtaking lightweight back-markers as if they were going in the opposite direction! Whenever Sgonina was around there was guaranteed excitement.

To the huge delight of the crowd, on lap seven, Isaac overtook Simpson. The marshals re-arranged the flags so as to provide 'virgin' sand for the turns. Simpson, having very quickly 'got the hang of it' on sand, came into the village-end 'new' bend in a sensational, overhauling skid that literally 'kicked sand in the eyes' of the local boy. Not for long: for the brilliant little Sunbeam had that 3 mph extra on the straight that the Carmarthen man was to make full use of from then on. At the end of the mile Carmarthen's advance on Leicester was about 30 yards. But on the exits, facing the straight again, it would be as little as five yards or three yards.

350cc line-up. L>R: C Sgonina (AJS); ER Jacobs (Beardmore-Precision); G Dance (Sunbeam), August, 1923. [*Morton's Motor Cycle Media*]

The onlookers were almost dazed and predicted a crash for the amazing AJS rider on each succeeding lap – and well they might – for he appeared to be defying all known laws of gravity and centrifugal force.[49]

Meanwhile, the heavy-breathing Sgonina had caught up and cheekily passed Anstice on the Douglas. He passed him on a wet patch – and drenched the Douglas's magneto with water. Out went a very cross Anstice on the 19th lap. Billy Edwards's engine had already seized on the 10th lap, leaving Sgonina – who knew when to treat his engines gently and when to ride like the devil on horseback – battling for the points with Parker's Sunbeam and the Beardmore Precision of Jacobs. With two miles to go to the flag, Simpson could be seen calling on his reserves, as the gap between him and Isaac visibly narrowed. He'd left it a bit late. With determined effort the Sunbeam, with its superior turn of speed, held it – crossing the line 200 yards ahead of the frustrated, yet elated, Simpson. There was scarcely a soft voice on the sands. The local man had beaten an idol, and created for himself a legend.

The scoreboard read:

CHAMPIONSHIP CLASS

50 miles > 350cc
M Isaac (Sunbeam)
JH Simpson (AJS)
ER Jacob (Beardmore-Precision)

With all the excitement of the 350cc gladiators, no-one had paid much attention to the lightweights. In fact, a tremendously exciting race had been fought out between the three leaders of the 250cc class, involving for a while real danger from D Jones (Velocette), who eventually fell out. It ended:

50 miles > 250cc
P Rogers (New Imperial)
G Smith (Rex-Acme)
M MacKenzie (New Imperial)

Welsh TT, 1923

Although there were two classes in the 100-mile 'Senior' event, it was regarded and fought as a single, matched contest. The performance difference between the 350 and 500cc machines was marginal anyway, as Howard Davies had proved in 1921 by winning the IoM Senior TT on a 350 AJS by two whole minutes.

CP Wood, on his trusty Scott, a favourite with the crowd, and last year's winner, was tipped at the start. He was unlikely to be the fastest among 'the cracks' – with rival TT super-stars like Dance, Simpson and Alec Bennett on hand – all spoiling for

---
[49] *The Motor Cycle*, August 9th, 1923..

Morris Isaac (Sunbeam), August, 1923. [*Morton's Motor Cycle Media*]

Morris Isaac with Alec Bennett (Douglas). [*Morton's Motor Cycle Media*]

the chase with their 'long-dog' entries. Very likely, the hare-hounds would eventually run themselves out, allowing the Squirrel to stroll it. Things seldom work out as predicted. This occasion was no exception: in fact, during the first five laps Wood was the hare.

Not on the first lap, as Irish-Canadian Bennett's very fast 600cc Douglas [DD 2602] was way away – round and up the straight like a rocket, towing Dance on his exhaust. Bennett was giving it his best. Even so, on lap two Wood had closed dramatically on the two Siamesed leaders out in front: and on lap three he astounded everyone by passing them and leading. The Scott was humming like a supercharged bumble-bee. It was a marvellous show!

But a man of Clarry Wood's experience and ability should have known that 'in order to finish first, first you must finish'. On the fourth lap he came trailing third again. On lap five the dark horse, WF Barker, piloting an ohv 350 Norton, had stolen past him and the Scott was audibly off-song. By lap seven Wood's machine was not there – missing. Radiator trouble. The Scott had over-heated, blown a head gasket and seized.

By this time, Bennett and Dance had lapped the whole field, except for Barker and AW Nicklin (Sunbeam). At the half-way mark they had recorded the remarkable time of fifty miles in 44 mins 50 secs (66.91mph). Edmunds (750 Rover-Blackburne), who had 'put up a very good show', running third in the 'brat pack', had gone out with a broken exhaust valve, as had the combative Sgonina. An incident involving HH Bush (Norton) and Jack David's Sunbeam put Bush out, though he was not seriously hurt in the tangle.

Dance and Bennett, the two finest riders in the world, were seemingly so evenly matched, both in performance and ability, that they were inseparable, even after fourteen laps:

> Every four minutes or so, the duellists would appear far down the straight; simultaneously they would brake for the corner and, as if coupled by some slightly elastic cord, they would disappear up the seaward side of the course. Probably never have two riders and two machines been more evenly matched. Both blended dash with caution so well in their corner work that their gains and losses were matters of inches or, at most, feet.

Their speeds must have been in the region of 90mph, as good riders on 80mph machines were simply nowhere in it. Among the local heroes young Leslie Griffiths of Bridgend was going well on his side-valve Norton until lap 16, the 80-mile mark, when he went down with magneto trouble. Calamity then struck the leaders. Dance dropped a valve and went out somewhere at the top end. Bennett, on the very next lap, failed to appear. Where was Barker? Then Bennett came into sight, having stopped, for no known reason. He crossed the line an easy winner. Barker had thought it was 'all over' and, foolishly, 'gone up the wrong way'. He should have been disqualified, but was awarded second place and, as Nicklin had stopped somewhere out on the course on the last lap, CC Hughes was admitted into third place on his Sunbeam. The result looked like this:

WELSH TT, 1923

100 miles: 500 > 750cc
A Bennett (Douglas)

100 miles: 350 > 500cc
WF Barker (Norton)
CC Hughes (Sunbeam)
A Jones (Douglas)
A Thom (Scott Squirrel)

Bennett had done what he set out to do. It was the only appearance at Pendine of a man who, as a freelance after a single 'works' ride for Nortons in 1924, picked and chose the events and mounts he rode in with great care. In a career that spanned the period 1921-1932, he rode in only 29 competitions, winning thirteen – eleven of them *grandes épreuves* – including five Isle of Man TTs. It is said that Alec Bennett derived very little satisfaction from his sojourn with the Douglas concern at Bristol. He had spent the best part of the year preparing this particular machine, above all attempting to instil some reliability into its wayward temperament. The Welsh TT victory at Pendine was his singular major achievement with Douglases. In his response speech at the presentation, Alec expressed his genuine regret at George Dance's misfortune, especially at his absence from the ceremony of the chequered flag – which would have answered a now unanswerable question!

Whitsun 1924

The 1924 'Welsh Speed Championships' were run off on Whit Monday, and there is no account of the event in the motor cycling press. *The Carmarthen Journal* and *The Welshman* were now visibly devoting less and less space to motor sport, despite the fact that an event on Pendine such as The Welsh TT was the only sporting event of international significance occurring on their patch. A summary of the results is all we have, under the heading 'Whit Monday Speed Trials'.

One-mile sprint > 275cc
J (Jim) Edwards, Carmarthen (Ariel)
P Rogers, Brecon (New Imperial)
W Evans, Llanpumsaint (Ariel)

one-mile sprint > 350cc
M Isaac (Sunbeam)
J Thomas, Neath (AJS)
VR McKenzie, H'west (AJS)

one mile sprint >
C Sgonina (Sgonina Special)
A Nicklin, Blaina (Sunbeam)
J Thomas (AJS)

4 miles > 175cc
ETM (Eddie) Stephens, Carmarthen (Ariel)
O (Oscar) Evans, Brynamman (Excelsior)

10 miles > 275cc
J Edwards, Carmarthen (Ariel)
P Rogers (New Imperial)
W Evans, Llanpumsaint (New Imperial)
Winner's time: 13 mins 59 secs

25 miles > 350cc
M Isaac (Sunbeam)
VR McKenzie (AJS)
T (Tudor) Williams, St Clears (AJS)

WELSH SPEED CHAMPIONSHIPS, 1924

50 miles >
JE Kettle, Newport (Scott Squirrel)
LF Griffiths, Cardiff (Norton)
C Sgonina (Norton)

JE Kettle turned in a magnificent result, after an immaculate ride. Leslie Griffiths records that he came in 7 seconds behind the leader, who covered the 50 miles in 50 minutes. A breathtaking pace for 1923! Kettle's record on Pendine, albeit brief, was destined to be top-notch. Les was set to become a Pendine faithful, and expert, for the rest of his very long racing career. His wasp-striped helmet, brown leathers and 'No 11' plate, a talisman for Pendine.

ETM Stephens

The four-mile, ultra-lightweight event was a first-appearance victory scored by a very youthful Eddie (ETM) Stephens. It was a significant event also for motor cycle racing at Pendine. Eddie, over the next twenty-five years, would compete in more events on Pendine than practically anyone. His name was to become synonymous with motorcycling and motor sport in Carmarthenshire and racing on Pendine in particular. He won countless trophies in all classes of competition, was inventive and tenacious as a racing driver, and immensely generous to up-and-coming young riders. As a leading light in the Carmarthen club, Hon Secretary for many years, Chairman and Clerk of the Course at different events, he worked tirelessly in his organisational efforts. Eddie was to become very influential in promoting other forms of motor sport in Wales. The grass-track events that customarily followed the Pendine meetings and road-racing at Eppynt in later years are just two examples. He was, quite simply, 'The guvnor'.

Apparently, Wynne Davies of Glantowy, Nantgaredig, in the 50-mile Championship race, 'met with a nasty mishap. In negotiating a corner he was thrown off his machine and had to be conveyed to the County Infirmary at Carmarthen where it was found he was suffering from a slight concussion and head injuries. They were not serious'.[50]

---
[50]*Carmarthen Journal.*

ETM Stephens, c1938.   [*ETM Stephens collection*]

August 1924

The 1924 August meeting was marred by dampness. A sea-mist that turned to drizzle held for most of the day, though it did not deter the crowds who turned up in their thousands. There was a tremendous entry, including riders of the highest calibre: Anstice, Dance, Grinton, Handley, Langman, Simpson and Wood, all world-class riders. Here they were mingling with the crowd in a remote little west Wales village and competing with the locals on equal terms. *The Motor Cycle* commented that the Pendine meeting usually:

> provided a spectacle full of concentrated excitement and a test of machines more severe than a Brooklands event over an equivalent distance; British racing men themselves are beginning to realise this... and agree that Pendine is one of the two finest racing tracks in Britain or Ireland.

We are left to guess that the other might be Brooklands itself.

> Picture a vast expanse of half-wet sand, hard enough for racing the heaviest machines and extending far enough to allow a five-mile lap – or, more correctly, two two-and-a-half-mile straights – to be flagged out without apparently making use of half the area available. Picture then, some sixteen well-matched machines hurtling forward at the fall of the flag and in an incredibly short time the leaders in clumps of three or four flying back down the other straight. See them jockey for position as they reach the corner. Some slow down and creep round within inches of the flags; others make great wide sweeps – perhaps misjudged braking, perhaps with intent to get round without braking at all; yet others plough great ruts with their footrests or feet as they follow a midway course in a series of well-controlled skids, miles an hour faster than you think the laws of centrifugal force or gravity would permit. An expert rider will corner faster on sand than on any unbanked road or track. See all this wonderful spectacle – if you can, for a single pair of eyes cannot follow in entirety some of the mad medleys which simultaneously start and within a short lap can bring about – and you will agree that sand racing in general, and a good meeting in Pendine in particular, ranks high among the half dozen sporting fixtures of the year.
>
> Only a good machine can survive the test successfully. Wet or dry sand absorbs power. The engines get very little rest, but the brakes must be good and the steering very good for full advantage to be taken on the forty or fifty corners between start and finish.

Drag & Fuel Handicap

No machine, it's true, escaped the handicap of the sand-drag – thought to sap as much as 15-20% of power in heavy going. Discrepancies in average speeds from year to year reflect, very often, the softness or hardness of the sand. A damp atmosphere influenced carburation and the spray thrown up by the front wheel and by other machines handicapped both rider and his ignition system. In dry, hard conditions, particularly if the tide had left corrugations, the vibration would shake loose any nut, bolt or screw that was not wired or 'double-bolted' on.

Another factor which handicapped riders was fuel. 'Can' petrol in the 1920s was of indifferent quality. By today's standards it was dirty, inconsistent and liable to leave copious deposits of carbon on plugs, pistons and valve seatings. In preparing engines for racing, decisions had to be made between tuner and rider in their choice of fuels. Most often these were the same person! Harry Ricardo (of Triumph 'Riccy' and diesel engine fame) in 1921 had patented 'Ricardo-Discol' fuels RD1 and RD2. The basis of these was ethanol, which was pure ethyl alcohol, and methanol – wood alcohol – together with acetone and up to 10% water. RD1 was sprint fuel and RD2 which was 'cooler' and gave greater economy, was for long distance events. The Hammersmith Distillery Co of London, which was a primary supplier, also supplied a blend of alcohol racing fuel, under the trade name 'Discol', consisting of 75% ethanol, 20% benzole, a 5% denaturant and other liquids, including water. In racing, the ideal would be to have several machines all set up in terms of timing, carburation and compression for different events over different distances but, most often, hurried adjustments had to be effected between events – which sorted out the (mechanical) men from the boys.

First off in the championship events was the Ultra-lightweight, 175cc class: won, on a Villiers-engined Diamond, as a virtual gift – unopposed – by Eddie Stephens.

The serious business of the day was the 350cc event. There were seven entries. According to the report in *The Motor Cycle*, Morris Isaac on a New Imperial led two Royal Enfields off the start-line, followed by another New Imperial. Dance had water-on-the-plug trouble, and was lying 'a bad fifth'. This cleared itself; and within the next two laps the Wolverhampton idol was back on song and the works Sunbeam was snapping at Isaac's heels. He was set to overtake the local rider – when water got on his plug again. The result was published as follows:

CHAMPIONSHIP EVENTS

10 miles > 350cc
M Isaac (New Imperial)
P Rogers (Royal Enfield)
Winner's time: 13mins 32secs. Won by 1.5 miles.

In the Lightweight, 250cc event, George Grinton broke his chain on the start-line. Such was his celebrity that the Clerk of the Course allowed for a replacement to be fitted. This caused a delay before the race got underway; and when the starter's flag fell, it led to a very close contest between the New Imperial of Grinton and the Rex-Acme of Brooklands record-breaker WL Handley. In the heat of the scrap Handley broke his gear lever and, as he put it, then 'had to go faster', as he was left with only top gear! He got into the lead by a particularly daring (or reckless) piece of corner-cutting, which won him the trophy, 50 yards ahead of Grinton and Handel Davies's borrowed (from Povey) IoM Velocette.

10 miles > 275cc

WL Handley (Rex-Acme)	H Davies (Velocette)
G Grinton (New Imperial)	Winner's time: 13m 34 secs. 4 starters:

Len Parker

The 560cc event was vintage Pendine stuff. Clarry Wood was at the start-line with the Scott, together with his brother-in-law Harry Langman, who had the other works Scott wound up[51]. Harry had recently come second in the Senior TT. Morris Isaac and C Hughes were astride Sunbeams. Len Parker, freelance quasi-works driver, was out on the customary Douglas. He was the man to watch – especially for his 'wheelies'. In 1924 he notched up eighty firsts and twenty-nine fastest times-of-day – the original daring young man on his flying machine:

> Parker, a past-master of take-off, who developed a deliberate technique for changing out of bottom gear into second (by hand of course, not foot) with the front wheel in mid-air, which augured a decent standard of controllability. It was Parker, too, toughest product of a tough era, who, to prevent himself cissily dethrottling when the plot showed signs of trampling him to death . . . mounted his throttle close in to the centre of the handlebars; once he'd slammed it in full open for his getaway he knew he'd never shift his stranglehold far enough from the grip to close it again; not until he was over the finish line, anyway.[52]

Parker was a wild and attractive character, 'with that high-voltage glint in his eye and a disordered jungle of hair'.[53] In another context he'd have carried Colt 44s, slung low, broken-in mustangs and brought back tethered outlaws to collect the bounty. Either that, or had a price on his head!

It was a really sensational first lap, with all five round into the Start/Finish corner 'in such a mad clump' that it was virtually impossible to tell what order they were in. 'Hughes', quipped *The Motor Cycle*, 'prevented what might have been a heap big or, rather, big heap, accident, by a clever swerve at the right moment'. The two Scotts circulated like clockwork, Langman preferring a tight line through the corners, Clarry taking his usual wide, but very fast, outer circumference, relying on acceleration to hold position. The other ding-dong battle was between Hughes and Parker, Isaac having succumbed to the spray. 'A thousand heads craned forward as the two Scotts entered the finishing straight, but the winner was only known when he crossed the line. It was Wood'. The Pendine crowd cheered and the Scotts yowled with delight.

10 miles > 560cc

CP Wood (Scott)	C Hughes (Sunbeam)
H Langman (Scott)	Winner's time: 10mins 38.20secs

---

[51] Harry and Clarry married two sisters.
[52] Dennis May 'Anniversary Stories': *Motor Cycling* May 28, 1958.
[53] Dennis May 'Pastmasters of Speed': *Motor Cycling* July 14, 1955.

August, 1924

H Langman [10] (Scott), Len Parker [37] (Douglas), August, 1924.

The big machines were sinking their rear wheels as the flag dropped for the Unlimited race. George Dance on the big-engined Sunbeam led on the first lap, away from the two Scotts of Wood and Langman, and AC Nicklin on another Sunbeam. Parker lay fourth on the Douglas, followed by two Brough Superiors. Nicklin, Wood and Dance were out by lap three with ignition failure, and Needham on the Brough was getting by on one cylinder. Conditions were very difficult, marring what would otherwise have been a finely-balanced contest.

10 miles: unlimited

| H Langman (Scott) | CM Needham (Brough Superior) |
| L Parker (Douglas) | |

The remaining races also proved disappointing as a spectacle, owing to the weather. The circuit was shortened for the 25-mile event to encompass the driest mile. But even then, out of a dozen starters, approximately four finished. Though there were five different leaders, the race was never really an exciting one, as engines succumbed left and right to the flying spray and the wet sand. The first lap order was: V Anstice (Douglas), CP Wood (Scott), CM Needham (Brough Superior), Mostyn Griffiths (Norton) and G Dance (Sunbeam). Anstice and Wood pulled in, leaving Needham in the lead, pursued by the Sunbeam of Hughes, whose headlong cornering was the only really memorable feature of what remained of Monday's meeting.

25 miles: unlimited

| H Langman (Scott) | CM Needham (Brough Superior) |
| C Hughes (Sunbeam) | Winner's time: 28m 5secs. |

In the closed events, confined to members of the South Wales Centre ACU, the results were as follows:

CLOSED EVENTS

4 miles > 175cc
ETM Stephens (Diamond)

4 miles > 275cc
M Isaac (New Imperial)
C Jones (Velocette)
P Rogers (Cotton)

4 miles > 350cc
M Isaac (Sunbeam)
J Clifford (AJS)
M Griffiths (Norton)

4 miles > 560cc
AW Nicklin (Sunbeam)
JC Ward (Norton)
M Isaac (Sunbeam)

1-mile sprint > 350cc
CF Edwards (New Imperial)
J Thomas (AJS Special)
M Isaac (Sunbeam)

H Langman

Fresh from having just been pipped to the post by 0.04 secs in the Senior IoM TT, by Alec Bennett on a Norton, this very fine and versatile cyclist had enjoyed a better day than he was used to. Harry Langman's own speed on the Scott around the Island had been a 61.23 mph average, which is just about equal to his best on sand.

On this, one of his last visits to Pendine, he would at last take away with him some mementos of his work. Langman was a dedicated Scott rider – as fast on tarmac, sprints, hill-climbs, as on sand, and a highly-decorated trialist. In the past this works-rider had been most often unlucky on his visits to Wales, though he was frequently in the money at Saltburn, Hest Bank, the Ulster Grand Prix and the Irish Speed Championships. He was sometimes over-shadowed by his team-mate brother-in-law, Clarry, who was cast in an heroic mould. Both were noted past-masters at the art of sidecar cornering.

Start of 100-mile Welsh TT, August, 1924. *[Morton's Motor Cycle Media]*

7. Brough Superiority

THE August Bank Holiday meeting at Pendine in 1924 was a two-day event. The main items on Tuesday's programme were the 50-mile race for 350cc machines, containing a 250cc class, and the 100-mile Welsh TT, with classes for 350cc, 500s and unlimited capacity engines.

In the Lightweight section Percy Rogers (riding for Fryer Bros, Brecon), TP Lewis, Ystalyfera and WA Aisbitt, Cheltenham, were on fast and very easy-handling ohv Cotton-Blackburne machines. They were marked by none other than Walter Handley – nineteen years old and destined as a future IoM TT and international road-racing ace – on a Blackburne-engined Rex-Acme works-entry. Oscar Evans of Brynaman was on a quick, and generally reliable, two-stroke Velocette. Ian Parker, Aberdare, on an oil-cooled OK Bradshaw found himself lined up with ER Jacobs, Birmingham, on a Beardmore-Precision. This bicycle's beautifully-made ohv engine, designed and produced by FE Baker, was capable of 6,000rpm. George Grinton, down from Edinburgh with the New Imperial, would give none of them quarter. North of the border he had amassed a shelf-full of trophies.

Welsh TT, 1924

There was a tremendous entry for the TT. Jimmie Simpson headed the list of favourites for the 350 class. He had the sole 'official' AJS works entry. His friend Jack Thomas, the Neath AJS main agent, was on a machine that the works had sent down as Simpson's 'spare'. Morris Isaac was on the only privately-entered 350 Sunbeam. The Marston had entered Jack David to back George Dance who was looking for outright victory on the big side-valve long-stroke. O Boulton of Redditch gave a Royal Enfield another of its rare outings at Pendine. There was a Chater-Lea entered by MR Edwards of Cowbridge, an OEC-Blackburne, ridden by AA Anderson of Port Talbot and a Beardmore-Precision in the hands of DL Hancock of Neath.

'Oil Boiler'

Probably the most unusual model entered was a Matador, driven by GL Werts, and attracting a lot of attention in the paddock. Matadors were 'assembled' in Preston, Lancashire, by Bert Holding's company. Bert was a renowned competition rider and

August 14th, 1924 L>R [3] AVCarter, B'ham (Norton); [14] V Anstice, Bristol (Douglas); [8] J David, W'hampton (Sunbeam); [27] M Griffiths, Llandilo (Norton); [28] ER Jacobs, B'ham (Beardmore-Precision). *[Morton's Motor Cycle Media]*

his machine had innovations such as double shoes operating on a rear drum brake. One brake was pedal-operated – expanding – and the other hand-activated – contracting – an early attempt at 'ABS'! Adjustable handlebars were optional. Fitted with an oil-cooled Bradshaw engine, affectionately known as 'the oil-boiler'[54], the Matador was held in high esteem by speedmen. A 350cc version, ridden by A Tinkler to third place in the 1923 IoM sidecar TT, and 4th in the Junior, had created a stir.

A muddle as to whether they were coursing the 5-mile or the 2-mile circuit resulted in an embarrassing 'false start'. When they got going, JH Simpson's blood was up, leaving no one in any doubt as to who was leading the way. Two local heroes, Morris Isaac (Sunbeam) and CF Edwards (New Imperial), exercising judicious restraint on the corners showed the fiery Jack David of Wolverhampton (Sunbeam) the way round. They were followed by AA Anderson (OEC Blackburne), Jack Thomas (AJS), G Grinton (New Imperial), WL Handley (Rex-Acme), J Clifford (AJS), O Evans (250 Velocette), DL Hancock (Beardmore Precision), JA Thorne (Cotton), GL Werts (Matador-Bradshaw), P Rogers (250 Cotton) and MR Edwards (Chater-Lea).

---

[54]Manufactured from Glanville Bradshaw's design by James Walmsley & Co of Preston, the engine's 5/6 pints of oil were rapidly pumped from the sump to an annular chamber surrounding the top of the cylinder barrel. Heat absorbed by the oil was dissipated as it drained back down via the aluminium cylinder- and (large) crank-case. The Bradshaw also powered New Scale, OK, Sparkbrook, Sirrah and Dot.

Jack David got his Sunbeam into third place, behind Morris Isaac, while Jimmie Simpson proceeded to lap all the rest of the field, with the exception of the two Sunbeam aces who were changing places corner by corner. With three-quarters-of-a-lap headway, Simpson slowed down and entered the 'depot' for a fairly lengthy refuelling. This gave David the lead, but only briefly, as he too had to stop for fuel. When Simpson and David came out they were evenly spaced: though Morris Isaac was holding first position. Not for long though, for Simpson was in business-mode, and he passed both Sunbeams:

> Cheers for the local man were diverted to the wonderful AJS rider who, because he refrained from doing anything lurid, gave everyone the impression that he now had the race in his pocket.

Isaac's motor fell sick and he dropped back. LF Griffiths's Norton broke a rocker on the 49th mile. The two leaders kept up the pace and J David had enough leeway over the field to stop for fuel a second time without losing second place. Simpson won a convincing victory and David held second place – although Isaac mistakenly had thought he had that honour when he took the flag a lap short. Third place went to P Rogers, Fryer Brothers of Brecon's 'mechanic', a clever local rider (thought to originate from Llanelly), on a 2¼ hp Cotton-Blackburne. Fryers were 'Motor cycle-specialists and ironmongers'. There was a large difference between the 'men' and the 'boys', Edwards coming in fourth a long while afterwards.

WL Handley

Another scrap was going on further down the field between Scots speed champion Grinton and Handley on the 250s. Handley, the TT winner, was the popular victor by 13 seconds. It had been an entertaining tussle, drawing the plaudits of the crowd. It was Wal Handley's last visit to Pendine. Before him lay a colourful career in international road racing on cycles and in cars. His 100mph lap round Brooklands in 1937, on the BSA 500 Empire Star, when effectively retired from motorcycle racing, was to merit a 'Gold Star'. And that is how the eponymous 'over-the-counter' Clubman's and cafe-racer of the late forties and fifties got its name!

In among the 'heavies' entered for the 100-mile Welsh TT, in the 500cc and unlimited categories were local Norton riders Alex Grey of Cardiff, Mostyn Griffiths of Llandilo and LF Griffiths of Bridgend. Other visiting Norton men were WF Barker and AV Carter, from Birmingham, and A Anthony of Hereford. Scotts had the full TT works team out in Harry Langman, Clarry Wood and Ivor Thomas of Neath. Douglas sent down Vic Anstice from Bristol, with Len Parker, privately-entered, but on a works-prepared machine. Jack Thomas, Neath, was also on a 'Hot Scott'. JE Kettle represented the sole Triumph in the entry-list. In the event – for the TT – he rode a Scott, a marque with which he is usually associated. Bert Lewis of Cardigan was on a 'Long-stroke' Sunbeam. George Dance had a 'secret weapon' – thought to have been a Long-stroke bored out to 597cc to compete in the 501-750cc category.[55] George Grinton, the Harley-Davidson exponent, had his angry-one groomed for the big show. Archie Jones of Bargoed was on a menacing 1,000cc Zenith. Brough Superior had A Greenwood up on the works machine and CM Needham had 'popped over' from a weekend's sport at Brooklands on his side-valve SS80.

CM Needham

The hundred-mile was a different style of race. The sand was in perfect condition: rock-solid and rippled. This was to cause trouble. Dance and Anstice, disappointingly, proved non-starters, for mechanical reasons. To everyone's surprise, a standard machine, privately-owned, was to prove the star of the day: an SS80 (988cc) side-valve Brough Superior, piloted by CM Needham. Manchester-based Charles Needham used what he called his own 'Spit-and-polish' as personal transport in the course of his work as a textile designer.

A cool-headed Needham led at the end of the first lap. A newcomer to Pendine , he was demonstrably a quick and experienced rider, founder of the 'Fast Motors Ltd' club.[56] His road-going Brough was followed by another 'cooking' entry, an ohv Norton with FA Grey of Cardiff in the saddle. In a long-distance event such as this, the crowd were not rushing to the bookies on this showing. The smart money was

---

[55] M Griffiths, TE Hughes pers. comm. Circa 1955.
[56] Manchester-based: entrance qualification required a sprint around the town hall while its clock chimed midnight!

AV Carter (Norton) and FW Dixon Douglas), August 1924.   [*Morton's Motor Cycle Media*]

still on works entries – WF Barker, whose Norton had won its class last year, or the Scotts of CP Wood, Harry Langman and Ivor Thomas which were circulating in close order, a purple blur, inches, feet, from Barker's mudguard. Jimmie Simpson was certainly in the running in the 350 cc class – and he was a clever, stylish rider: worth watching – especially for his cornering tactics. A long field was strung out behind the leaders: 'wild man' Len Parker on a TT Douglas – the fastest through the corners – Mostyn and Leslie Griffiths (Nortons), JE Kettle on a TT Scott Squirrel, B Lewis (Sunbeam), Jack David (ohv Sunbeam), A Anthony (Norton), trailed by a not-at-all-well 'official' Brough Superior, driven by A Greenwood.

The leading Brough was fairly loping along, Charles (the driver) verbally ordering oil with his fuel as he passed the depot, where the Georges – Patchett and Brough – were in attendance. Stalking in his shadow was the Norton of Grey, obviously giving his best first. Len Parker on the Douglas was really 'putting her to go' through the corners, he and Simpson vying for the most sensational and impossible poses. All the while Barker was moving in on him. Like two cruising sharks, the Scotts held station with Barker within their grasp. On lap three things changed: Grey pushed the Norton past the leading Brough. Two of the Scotts swam past Barker, Langman moving very quickly into a dangerous third place. The Brough kept to its easy, yet fast, 70 – 80 mph pace. Grey's spurt did him no good – as he dropped to sixth on the next lap. Calamity overtook Clarry Wood, too: a weld gave on the Scott frame, resulting in an unheard-of collapse. On the same lap, Langman's gearbox packed up, passing the baton of the official Scott challenge over to team-mate Ivor Thomas, the Welsh IoM TT man. He was making another of his rare appearances on the beach, to the delight of the crowd. The Brough Superior found itself back in the lead. Behind Needham, Parker's Douglas and the big works Norton were still involved in all manner of acrobatics with Simpson's AJS, cornering at 'lurid' angles, and joggling for position. 'Needham appeared the only man on the sands who was not madly excited', observed *The Motor Cycle*. Simpson was not far behind: fast and watchful.

It was time for Needham to collect his order from the depot and in and out he went in what was the fastest trick ever seen, to find himself sandwiched between Barker first and Parker second. Barker's moment of glory was short-lived. He slowed; at the same time Parker stopped, his Douglas chassis breaking up. That was not so unusual. But when Douglas frames came apart they did so always in a big way. 'The break usually occurred beneath the head, which had the disconcerting effect of jerking both throttles wide open and snapping the back brake pedal off'.[57] Alarming stuff! Barker's carburettor was falling off and, simultaneously, the same was happening to Grey's Norton. Ivor Thomas faded into the distance. If there was a challenger left to Needham's SS80 it was the private Scott of Kettle, still touring round smoothly: only that the Brough lapped him just as he achieved second place! Simpson was behind Kettle.

Needham had time for a leisurely pit-stop, involving a change of plugs. Despite this, he still managed to win the 'Hundred Mile' by a lap, and at a speed, incredibly, five minutes faster than the previous year's record – set by Alec Bennett on a very special 733cc Douglas. Kettle, a lap behind, was only a few seconds behind Bennett's 1923 time. Barker fitted a new carburettor and came in a creditable fourth behind AV Carter's Norton, and having covered sufficient laps to qualify for the 500cc trophy.

It had been an extraordinary race – as spectators had come to expect of Pendine at its best. A variant on the hare and the tortoise fable. No one had really guessed that the pace was so blisteringly hot. Several machines on the dry, wave-rippled dry beach had literally shaken themselves to pieces. Needham, it appears, had taken the side-valve Brough SS80 to Brooklands on the previous weekend with Patchett, where he had won a race for standard machines, and simply brought it down, without the usual engine overhaul and change of gear-ratios for the beach and had two days' enjoyable, even profitable sport. It was a truly remarkable performance. The following day he headed home for Hale.

The winner's time was 88mins 52secs.

CF Needham (Brough Superior) .
[*Morton's Motor Cycle Media*]

---

[57]Dennis May: *Motor Cycling* May 28, 1958.

THE WELSH TT, 1924

50 miles > 250cc
WL Handley (Rex-Acme)
G Grinton (New Imperial)
Winning time: 69 mins 50 secs.

50 miles: 251 > 350cc
JH Simpson (AJS)
J David (Sunbeam)
M Isaac (Sunbeam)
Winning time: 63 mins.

100 miles: 350 > 500cc
JE Kettle, Cardiff (Scott)
Winning time: 94 mins 12secs.

100 miles > 500cc
AV Carter (Norton)
Winning time: 96 mins 55 secs.

100 miles: unlimited
CM Needham (Brough Superior)
Winning speed: 67.54 mph.

Rex-Acme

The Rex company was one of the aboriginal motor bicycle manufacturers, and one of the first to produce motor cycles designed for racing. Credited to the Rex list of innovations are the V-belt drive, foot-operated brakes, two spark-plugs-per-cylinder and sprung front forks.

When the company 'came home from the war' in 1919, they combined with their neighbour Coventry-Acme, and under George Hemingway's direction, continued their engine-manufacturing and racing activity. The new tank-colophon bore the three-legged Manx insignia as a reminder of pre-war racing involvement.[58] It was not until the nineteen-year-old Wal Handley joined the firm, in 1923, that the newly-merged company enjoyed real sporting success. He began by winning the Lightweight class in the Belgian and Ulster Grands Prix. In the 1925 IoM TT he distinguished himself and the marque by becoming the first man to take the chequered flag first in two races in one week: the Ultra-lightweight and the Junior. His speed for the Junior was the much vaunted and debated mile-a-minute average, with a lap-average of 65.89mph – 10mph faster than the previous year. He even raised the Lightweight lap average to over 60mph. Rex-Acme went on to win another Lightweight TT and several high-placings, but their day was over – owing, more-than-likely, to their reliance on bought-in engines.

---

[58] This was not all that distinguished. Although Rex raced in all TTs from 1907 till 1912, they only once finished in the first three.

Sunbeam, Blue Bird. [*Hulton Getty Pic Lib*]

Malcolm Campbell, Villa and Blue Bird, 1924.

8. Glory Days

The World Land Speed Record

MUCH ink has been spilled over the Land Speed Record attempts on Pendine, particularly the occasion that involved the tragic death of John Godfrey Parry Thomas, in March, 1927. Strictly speaking, these events in motoring history do not fall within the definition of 'races', and could be said to be outwith the scope of this title, *Pendine Races*. But there is sufficient argument for their inclusion.

As will have been seen from the unfolding story, the motor races on Pendine had begun as 'speed trials' in somewhat abstract fashion, as handicap events 'against the clock'. This method of testing the capabilities of motor cars and motor cycles was a preoccupation of 'speedmen' in the early days of motoring. Most of this activity centred on Brooklands, near Weighbridge, in Surrey, where a purpose-built circuit had been built. It opened in 1907[59], two years after the first motor race was staged on Pendine. In the Veteran days of motoring it was generally the wealthier classes who indulged in motor sport – as they, obviously, had the means and the time. But after the First World War a new sub-culture of motor racing appeared – spear-headed by an emerging middle- and working-class engineering intelligentsia. These were young men who had served their time at the Front. They, as engineers of necessity, had learned to be innovators and were often fearless drivers into the bargain. Parry Thomas was one. And among the best.

The Flying Mile

The Land Speed Record was not a clearly-identified objective to begin with. It was one among a whole range of time-against-distance targets, many of them from a standing start. The Land Speed Record had formerly been known as 'the flying mile' and 'the flying kilometre'. Into the equation considerations of engine size and vehicle weight were thrown and, while there was no consensus between motoring organisations in Britain and those on the Continent and the USA, the notion of a 'world' land speed record was not in being.

At different times an electric- and then a steam-powered car had achieved increased recorded speeds over these defined distances. The two-mile-a-minute

---

[59] Motor racing only seriously got underway in 1908.

record was attained by Frank Marriott in 1906, in the Stanley Steamer, at 121.57 mph. In 1910, Barney Oldfield is said to have clocked 131.72 mph on Ormond Beach, Daytona, USA. All these records were claimed from single-directional runs and were largely disputed by one international organisation or another. It was resolved to try to co-ordinate the ground rules and, by 1914, heads of agreement had been drafted. But for the next five years there were other preoccupations.

When the 1914-18 War 'restrictions' were lifted in 1919, interest in record-breaking rose to new heights among the motor-racing classes. The consensus principle emerging was that 'flying' records, in order to be recognised internationally, (ie. be perceived as 'world' records), would in future have to be calculated as the result of the mean average of two runs in opposite directions – so there would accrue no advantage from wind or slope. The return run had to take place within thirty minutes. Tommy Milton's single-directional bid in the twin-engined Dusenberg, timed at 156.03 mph at Daytona in 1920, was not recognised in Europe.

Brooklands & Pendine

Under the new rules for the 'flying mile', Brooklands, on safety grounds, was deemed too small for the return, and thus the circuit became obsolete for very high speed work. So, the race was on to discover alternative places where there was sufficient space for a 150 mph flying mile to be achieved in both directions. In this contest, Pendine, as an arena, was a leading participant for the British record, and found itself, by default, a competitor in the wider 'world' race. For this purpose it became an extension of Brooklands.

The early twenties saw an upsurge in interest in motor racing. Speed demanded engine power. A ready-to-hand source was ex-Royal Flying Corps and other superannuated aero-engines. 'Heroes', like the Grand Prix drivers Count Louis Zborowski, Malcolm Campbell, Henry Segrave and Godfrey Parry Thomas, acquired a penchant for 'special' behemoth high-speed racing cars – of which Chitty-Chitty-Bang-Bang was the most famous. It occurred to them also that these were ideal vehicles for immediate World Land Speed honours. The contest was unofficially on to pass the 150 mph, 180 mph and, ultimately, the 200 mph WLSR milestones. Enough was known about aviation in 1920 for them to realise that land vehicles acquired 'lift-off' and became projectiles at speeds of 130+ mph[60]. Weight, they reasoned, would delay this tendency. But not indefinitely. Increased weight demanded ever-increasing power. This meant the heavier and more powerful the machine, theoretically, the faster one could hazard. But at what point would it lose stability? Would the tyres fail? Would the driver be able to breathe? Would he lose consciousness because of the air-pressure, or some effect of gravity? They were now venturing to travel faster than human beings had ever travelled, faster than aeroplanes flew.

---

[60] It is remarkable that basic avionics principles - stabilisers, ailerons, wind-tunnel streamlining - were not applied in racing-car design much before the 1970s.

First World Land Speed Record

Objectives such as these delved into the unknown, challenging man's ingenuity and courage in his continued exploration of the universe. They were perceived in much the same way as the ascent of Everest and, in later times, the breaking of the sound barrier and journeying to the moon. These were men 'who dared' to venture. Pendine was soon, for a short while, to provide the arena for acts of ultimate human endeavour. Between 1924 and 1927, the little village on Carmarthen Bay would be world-famous.

In an article specially written for *Motor Sport*,[61] Malcolm Campbell attempts to explain the lure of record breaking.

> The answer is simple and may be expressed in one word – Ambition. Motoring makes different appeals to different people, some finding their desires for achievement satisfied by long-distance records; others in gaining successes over difficult trials routes; whilst reliability trials, short hill climbs and other forms of the great pastime appeal to the sporting instincts of different classes of motorists.
>
> No one will deny that the joys of sheer speed possess an extraordinary fascination, but before taking the wheel of the Sunbeam, I had no idea of the wonderful sensation of driving at a really high velocity. The outstanding recollection of my first trip on this car was the time occupied in slowing down and even when the brakes were applied, it seemed at the moment as if it would never stop again. On becoming accustomed to the higher speeds and the manipulation of the car, this feeling, of course, disappeared, though at the time it was a most remarkable experience. One only has to sit behind the big engine and let the car go on a good stretch of sand to feel as if some supernatural force were at work; a force which, though controlled by the hand of man, is so terrific as to inspire awe …
>
> I cannot attempt to describe the fascination of sheer speed and will content myself by stating that every run I take on the big car makes me feel ten years younger. Perhaps that may be a personal justification of my hobby, though naturally there are many useful things to be learned as the result of abnormally high speeds. From my own point of view, any attack on the world's record is not a business proposition, there is little to be gained and a good deal to be risked financially, as it is practically impossible to insure one's car except at an exorbitant premium.

Agreement in principle between Europe and America in 1924 concentrated minds further, as the 'race' became elevated on to a global plane. Some racing drivers were already considering wastelands and beaches across the Atlantic. But, as yet, there was no need: and (some) money to be made in the short term with facilities closer to home.

In the course of the 1924 Six Days' Trial in Wales, the RAC conducted a survey of Pendine with a view to licensing Land Speed Record attempts. In their report the 5 – 6 miles x 150 yards of usable, flat, open surface available was 'considered ample' for speed-record attempts within 3 miles-a-minute.

The 'flying mile' (World) Land Speed Record, was established (under the new rules) at 129.17 mph by Kenelm Lee Guinness with the 12-cylinder, 18.322-litre

---
[61] December, 1925: 'Some Experiences with the World's Fastest Car'.

Sunbeam, at Brooklands, one afternoon in May, 1922 – quietly and without any fuss. It stood, until the Welshman, JGP Thomas, driving his Leyland-Thomas, also in a two-way run at Brooklands, was timed at 129.73 mph, on June 26th, 1924. These men were living dangerously, as there was hardly room for the return run.

After unsuccessful attempts at the 'flying kilo', during the summer of 1924, on Saltburn and Skegness sands, and later at the Danish Automobile Club's speed trials on the Fanoe Islands (where his car had lost a tyre at 150 mph, fatally injuring a boy spectator), Malcolm Campbell, in September, brought his 12-cylinder, 350 hp, Sunbeam car to Pendine, Carmarthenshire. There he captured the 'flying kilometre' record of 146 mph from the 300 hp FIAT of EAD Aldridge (at Brooklands) by a tenuous 00.14 mph. This was the first World Land Speed Record to be secured at Pendine.

Malcolm Campbell

Malcolm Campbell, born in 1885, was a charming, handsome, but often somewhat dour, Scot. His obsession with speed began, as with most of his motor racing contemporaries, in motor cycling. He competed in long-distance trials, winning three successive gold medals in the London – Edinburgh – London event, between 1906-8. Racing cars was the logical progression and Brooklands, the headquarters of speed, became his natural habitat. He was a romantic with a family fortune, not quite a playboy, but a young man who could indulge his whims. Flying, early in his career, became one of Campbell's interests, but he burnt his fingers in a business venture – aeroplane manufacturing. He made a name for himself at Brooklands, racing a whole variety of fast cars. After the fashion of the time, he gave his racing cars, as one does a boat, a name. The authorities at Brooklands kept a strict eye on these names, as the 'set' thought it very *chic* to be *risqué*. 'The Flapper', a succession named after a racehorse was just within bounds; but Campbell's friend, Count Zborowski, later managed to sneak 'Chitty-Chitty-Bang-Bang'[62] past them. The Flappers brought Campbell little success.

In the Great War, Campbell joined the Royal Flying Corps, where he attained the rank of Captain. When racing resumed afterwards, in 1921, he took to motor racing seriously, breaking records the while. He persuaded Sunbeams to part with the 12-cylinder machine in which KL Guinness had claimed the 'flying mile' that had come to be regarded as the first official World Land Speed Record (WLSR). He elected to call her 'Blue Bird', after a play of that name he had seen at the Haymarket Theatre in the West End.[63] The name seemed to be a lucky one, so Campbell christened each successive racing car/record breaker he owned in future after the same ideal.

---

[62] A complaisant young lady, the subject of a bawdy, RFC Officer's Mess song. (Via M Worthington-Williams and W Boddy).

[63] *The Blue Bird* by Maurice Maeterlinck. Its theme was the pursuit of the unattainable, the elusiveness of happiness: appropriate for a World Land Speed record contender.

The 350 hp 12 cyl. Sunbeam after creating a World Record for the Flying Kilometre at Pendine Carmarthenshire. Sept. 25th 1924. Average Speed 146.16 mph. Highest speed over the mile in one direction. 150.25 mph.

M. Campbell

Malcolm Campbell, September, 1924.

Sunbeam Blue Bird, 1924.

Seeing Pendine again with its large-scale vastness stretching away into the blue beyond, Captain Malcolm Campbell must have reassured himself that there was no need yet for the trouble of shipping cars and equipment to the Continent or over to America, at least not in the short-term. Listening to the locals, he would have gleaned that, caught right, the beach could be as hard as iron and as smooth as a billiard table (not often at the same time!) for five miles or more, ample space in which to unleash 350hp to a sustained maximum and haul it back in again. Two miles for the run-up; the measured mile; and two miles to slow down. About turn. And then the return.

Pendine was still regarded as a remote corner. As one writer in the *Referee* observed:

> The Pendine sands where Malcolm Campbell let loose his wonderful 360hp Sunbeam and broke the flying kilometre record by covering the distance at 146.16 mph, is perhaps the least known of Nature's race tracks. It lies in a hollow of Carmarthen Bay, between Saundersfoot and Kidwelly, and is not very accessible. The Pendine is so little known that it is not mentioned in the Guide Books[64], and yet it is unique in that it offers facilities for speed work that [are] only equalled by Ormond Beach, Daytona, USA, where all the greatest assaults against the clock by motor cars too fast for any roads have been made in the past. On the hard, smooth sands of Pendine any speed is possible for it has the advantage of immense length and width when the tide is out.
>
> The writer went 50 mph over it in a Dodge which felt like a snail's pace. To gain an impression you certainly want to be doing 100 mph and the family touring car is not yet built to do that.

Campbell's was the same car in which Kenelm Lee Guinness (of KLG plug fame) had taken the record at Brooklands at a speed of 133.75 mph in 1922. The sand was wet and he reckoned the wind and rain cost him 20 mph but, on the fifth attempt, he managed a return average of 146.16 mph.

The Motor's account of the event is prosaic enough:

> Capt Malcolm Campbell travelled up to Tenby on Saturday, September 20th, and his 12-cylinder Sunbeam made the journey on a lorry. Certain apparatus was also conveyed to the same place, and parties of officials, Press representatives and others also made their way to Carmarthenshire. There was only one inference to be drawn from these significant movements, and on Wednesday, everything being in order, except the condition of the Pendine sands, the anticipated speed carnival commenced. On that day Capt Campbell took his lone seat in the 350 hp Sunbeam and covered a mile and a kilometre one way from a flying start in 23.96 secs, a speed of 150.25 mph. The officials had measured a mile on the Pendine sands some miles south of Tenby. Col Lindsay Lloyd and Messrs Gregory and Sprague were present with other officials of the

---

[64]This is not entirely true, though references to Pendine in literature are few. As early as 1805, E Donovan in *A Descriptive Excursion Through Wales* traversing the beach 'descended into a frightful sandy desert' where he found no refreshment but an abundance of 'curious shells'. Mary Curtis, whose guide book, *Antiquities of Laugharne, Pendine and their Neighbourhoods*, is considered a minor masterpiece, in fact devotes less than a single page to Pendine!

Royal Automobile Club. There was a strong cross-wind, and the sand was very wet, so much so that the spray thrown up at times quite hid the racing car. Capt Campbell's object was to beat the existing world's record of 146.34 mph, but on the first attempt on Wednesday the big Sunbeam failed, the mean speed attained being 145.24 mph. On Thursday the attempts were renewed, and on this occasion with greater success, for Capt Campbell covered a kilometre with flying start in the mean time of 15.305 seconds, equal to a speed of 235.21 kilometres or 146.16 miles an hour. On the first run the kilometre was covered in 15.01 secs. Thus, although the kilometre speed was faster than on Wednesday, the mile speed was slower, this being caused by the patches of very wet sand. The car made its best time of 25.17 secs. On the eastward side of the course. The mean speed up and down the course was half of the two runs, and for the kilometre it worked out at 146.16 mph. Subject to confirmation by the official body, this constitutes a world's record. The equipment of the Sunbeam included Dunlop straight-sided cord tyres, Lodge sparking plugs, two BTH magnetos, two Claudel-Hobson carburettors, Rudge-Whitworth wire wheels, Smith's instruments, Elliott's engine revolution counter, while Shell oil and petrol were used in the attempts.

The Carmarthen Journal, in a more poetic editorial, is critical of the organisers, making a case for treating the sands with greater respect by applying local wisdom:

It is not easy to grasp the meaning of modern speed as demonstrated by the fastest motor car in the world, especially when it is viewed in such trackless and widely-flung leagues as Pendine Sands. Such landmarks and points of comparison that Nature strewed about this coast when she laid down this superb foreshore are far too distant to be immediately helpful – the faintly-discernible horns of the Bay and the still further blue wash of the Channel. A close-up examination of even 150mph is likely to lose some of its tremendous significance for want of some nearby stationary points of comparison. It was possible last week when Captain Malcolm Campbell drove his monster machine across those spacious reaches of sand to get the eye to take in much of the significance of what was passing before it, but only by exercise of close attention. Even after it was all over it was difficult to realise that this roaring vehicle had been covering ground at nearly 75 yards – nearly half the distance between two football posts – in one second of time!

The first glimpse of the car getting into its stride, so very far away – several miles – that it looked merely a small black blob against the blur of the Kidwelly coast; the almost dramatic swiftness with which it took definite shape and like a long-tailed, black, furious insect passed before the immediate view of the onlookers and was again swallowed by the spumey intricacies of the Tenby coastline.

The weather was not good; indeed, all the conditions for the trial were poor. It is unfortunate to begin with that the RAC could not have selected a week when the spring tides were on. This would have given the lighter and warmer part of the day to the work and also drier, harder sand. Heavy showers and a strong west wind contributed to make the sand sloppy: in fact, Pendine sands were at their worst.

Some of these discouragements could have been avoided had the promoters of the race consulted the Members of the Carmarthen Motor Club in selecting the course instead of choosing it themselves. That, at any rate, was the general opinion of the onlookers.

> The probability is that with the assistance of people who know the sands as intimately as several motor officials at Carmarthen do, a harder course could have been chosen and a straighter stretch for the flying start. It is an important point, in view of the fact that Captain Campbell in his Thursday's attempts to beat the world mile record only failed by about two yards.
>
> What he had to beat was a speed of 146.001 – only 1.75 yds short. (His own 70 mph Rolls Royce could only do 50mph. Blue Bird was recording 170 mph).
>
> It is to be hoped that in future big trials the utmost care will be taken by the promoters to secure the advantages that Pendine can offer. These of course are very considerable, probably greater than anything in the kingdom. Pendine ought to be the abiding home of world records.

The *Journal*, in fairness, was sensible of the celebrity and commercial potential that could derive from providing the arena for world-class speed record-breaking events. It was right to upbraid both Campbell and the RAC for compromising this opportunity for Pendine and Carmarthenshire with a slip-shod – and even arrogant – approach.

Sunbeam, 'Blue Bird'

It was one thing to be holder of the World's Land Speed Record, but Campbell was far from content with his performance on Pendine in the autumn of 1924. He knew the old Sunbeam was capable of raising the record by an appreciable margin, even though its limitations were apparent. Over the winter months he pondered the lessons learnt and modified the car. Different camshafts were fitted and a long exhaust pipe. He had nearly been asphyxiated by the lack of an exhaust system on his previous attempt. His exhaust outlets – all twelve of them – came forth without benefit of manifold direct, only just clearing the bodywork. Oil fumes had smothered his screen, face and goggles in a tarry slime, thrown up by the spray. Jarvis, the coachbuilders, designed an up-swept bulkhead, put on a radiator cowl and a revised tail to Campbell's design. The screen was dispensed with altogether and the car loaded ready for the journey back to Pendine in March, 1925.

The weather was again hostile, but after sampling the hospitality of the Beach Hotel for several days, Campbell finally got some runs in – and the magic figure of 150 mph was exceeded. The new record attributed to Blue Bird was 150.87 mph. The next target was three miles-a-minute; and though, incredibly, this represented a mere 3 seconds in time difference, Campbell and his team knew this was really stretching the aged Sunbeam's capability.

> One very remarkable point in connection with record attempts is the value of the unit of time. In a mile run three little seconds make all the difference between 150 mph and 180 mph ... To beat the watch by those three little ticks, one must be prepared to spend considerable sums of money, months of persistent effort and the technical resources of many sections of the motor industry have to be requisitioned. Perhaps it might seem rather futile to take so much trouble to cut down the time for such a short run by so limited an amount as three seconds, but the wealth of technical information

obtainable by such efforts cannot be over-estimated. One learns the real meaning of wind resistance, becomes familiar with the peculiar influence of gyroscopic action, whilst the effects of perfect balance and harmony in all parts of the machine are demonstrated in a remarkable way.'[65]

They were gracious, and spacious, times when *The Autocar* in June 1925 could indulge William Platt, 'the author of *A Popular Geology* etc.', in an essay on '**Pendine: its Sands and its Fossils**: A Carmarthenshire Beauty Spot Popular as a Venue for Motor Races'[66]. It was a matter of concern in motoring circles that shells on the beach were the cause of many casualties to racing aspirations: razor shells, in particular, slicing tyres – as their name implies.

> The little village of Pendine, in South Wales, at the western end of the rugged and broken Carmarthenshire coast, was known to but few people until someone discovered there one of the finest stretches of clean, firm sand that the world can boast. It then became famous at such times as it was selected for motor speed tests; but for the rest of the year it remains the same simple, undeveloped, insignificant village that it was before.
>
> From the point of view of the Nature lover, this choice little stretch of coast combines extreme beauty with considerable scientific interest. Motorists who intend visiting Pendine could do worse than devote a few minutes to considering what are its special features.
>
> Seawards stretches the magnificent plain of firm, bright, golden sand. Away to the west, if only we go far enough, there is a submerged forest[67], and this begins to tell us the tale which we are seeking to know. If you were to dig about at low tide in the sand that partly buries that forest, you would find the primitive stone weapons of prehistoric man[68]. Evidently prehistoric man lived in that forest before it was submerged by earth movements. Clearly, the sinking movement brought into play the cliff-line on the East of Pendine; while the action, since then, of persistent winds from west, piled up the fine sand-dunes; so that, since the time of primitive man, land has been lost by sinkage, and then partly regained by piling-up action of persistent winds.
>
> Now let us examine the bold mass of grey cliffs on the right hand or west side of Pendine Beach, and the broken rock masses at the foot of these cliffs. The formation is called by geologists 'carboniferous limestone', and to those readers who know a little geology, I would recommend a study of the conglomerate band about 10 feet up.

---

[65]'Some Experiences with the World's Fastest Car'. Malcolm Campbell in *Motor Sport,* Dec. 1925.

[66]Campbell may have taken note of this essay too late, as a sharp shell slashed one of his tyres, very nearly spelling disaster on one run. On a subsequent occasion he paid the children of Pendine to gather up any shells lying in Blue Bird's path.

[67]Marros/Amroth.

[68]There is no specific evidence for this assumption. Far more scientific would have been reference to the bone finds in the limestone quarry at Coygan, due east, towards Laugharne, where Edward Laws, in *Little England Beyond Wales* refers to the discovery in a cave of 'a hyena den' where, apart from the hyena excrement, 'as fresh as if they had been voided recently', there was a singular Neolithic artefact, a reindeer antler, shaped into an awl, alongside of two flint implements. In the cave, rhinoceros, wolf, horse, hippopotamus, red deer, wild boar, lion, Irish elk and aurox bones, from the Pleistocene period (30,000 years ago) were identified.

Limestone is extremely rich in fossils, and out of every dozen pebbles one or two will bear distinct traces of fossil contents. You will find chiefly corals of several sorts of shells.[69] The corals may be fine ones, some like vermicelli, or larger ones, the size of a little finger. Occasionally they are feathery in outer form.

The next (motor car) race meeting on these sands takes place on June 13th.

Whitsun 1925

There was a closed motor cycle race meeting, the Welsh Speed Championships, 'Confined to Welsh Motorists only', organised by the Carmarthen and District Motor Cycle and Light Car Club on Whit Monday, June 1st, 1925. A series of events for light cars was run off at the end of the motor cycle racing. It was the occasion of the debut appearance of the youthful Lionel 'LV' Thomas of Swansea, a first-class rider who had made a name for himself in sand races around the Swansea area and was soon to provide many thrills for the crowds at Pendine. He is, perhaps, best remembered for his exploits on a 1924, George Dance-designed, 'Sprint' Sunbeam which regularly, until the late 'forties, performed 'David and Goliath' feats on the 'Big Boys from the Midlands'. The Sunbeam was set aside for a while in the late twenties, in favour of a Model K (camshaft) 348cc Velocette. Then 'Elvy' got seriously to grips with Nortons, a marque with which he became principally identified during the thirties.

Jim Edwards of Towy Garage, Carmarthen, Billy's brother, on an Ariel, won the mile sprint for solo machines up to 275cc. Jim, a great Ariel adherent, was the general foreman, who ruled the workshop with a rod of iron. Eddie Stephens, also of Towy Garage (their apprentice), was second on a Rex-Acme (though *The Western Mail* reckons it was a Cotton), followed by Lewis Charles of 61, Sandy Road, Llanelly (Rex-Acme). The official record of the results is:

One-mile sprint > 275cc
J Edwards (Ariel)
ETM Stephens (Cotton)
Lewis Charles (Rex-Acme)

one-mile sprint > 350cc
L (Lionel) V Thomas, Swansea
  (Sunbeam)
AW Goode, Swansea (Cotton)
J Thomas (AJS)

one-mile sprint: unlimited
M Griffiths, Llandilo (Sunbeam)
CE Knott, Bridgend (Douglas)

10 miles > 275cc
ETM Stephens (Rex-Acme)
J Edwards (Ariel)

NOVICE CLASS

10 miles > 350cc
E (Ernie) Hughes, Llandilo (AJS)
L (Lionel) Flower, Llandysul (Rudge)

WELSH CHAMPIONSHIP

25 miles > 350cc
LV Thomas (Sunbeam)
J Thomas (AJS)

50 miles: unlimited
M Griffiths (Sunbeam)
A Grey, Cardiff (?)
(A protest was lodged)

---

[69]See Footnote 46, p. 69.

The one-mile sprint for solo 350s was particularly well subscribed. The list of entrants for the meeting provides us with a good cross-section of club racers from all over south and west Wales, and the variety of machines they based their faith upon. On Sunbeams, 'The Gentleman's Bicycle', were Morris Isaac and LV Thomas. The proprietor of the Nelson Hotel, the Carmarthen club's regular meeting place, A Henstock was out on a Rex-Acme, as was CL James of the Golden Lion, Llanelly. Bill Thomas of Pwll, Llanelly, and Jack Evans of the Midland Garage, Llanybyther, were astride New Hudsons. TJ Philips of Aberavon had driven over with a Zenith; AW Goode had come over from Swansea on a Cotton; Willie Tucker of Login was there on a Raleigh and David Davies of Arfryn, Pontyberem, had an OK Bradshaw. The two AJS riders were Jack Williams of 1, Middleton Street, Briton Ferry and Billy Edwards, Towy Garage, Carmarthen. Eddie Stephens was given a Rex-Acme and a BSA from the garage to demonstrate. Jack Thomas, Neath, and CE Knott, Bridgend, had not decided what they would ride when they returned their entry forms. Jack usually rode AJS machines.

For the present writer, there is particular interest and nostalgia in an entry for the '10-mile Novice Championship up to 350cc'. In the race programme it reads: 'Ernie Hughes, White Hart, Llandilo . . . AJS', the entrant being the present author's late father who, when he died in 1996, in his 95th year, was the oldest known surviving Pendine competitor. An inscribed silver flower-pot container is in existence that testifies to his having won his debut event, though he always maintained that his success was due in no small part to the way in which Handel Davies, Garnant, had prepared the machine, a 'Big-Port'. 'There was something very special about that AJS,' he often said, 'it was five-mile-an-hour faster than any other.' Among his rivals in the event were Rees Thomas, Gloag, who was destined for more than local fame on a Brough Superior; A Henstock; Lionel Flower, Llanfair, Llandysul; Lewis Charles, Llanelli; Jack Evans, Llanybyther; Willie Tucker, Login and David Davies, Pontyberem.

LV Thomas's Sunbeam Sprint

LV Thomas demonstrated right off what he had in store by winning the one-mile sprint for 350cc solo machines on the ohv Sunbeam 'Sprint', ahead of fellow Swansea club member, AW Goode, on his Cotton. That Sunbeam was, over the years, to become a celebrated machine. As his friend, Dudley Gershon, commented:

> Lionel was a great enthusiast and quite famous for his efforts, particularly at Pendine, with an incredibly fast 350cc 'Sprint' Sunbeam of '23 vintage, which surprised many professional riders in the 'thirties with its capabilities, beating 'works' Nortons in the mile sprints. He had altered the cams and converted it to alcohol with about the necessary 14 to 1 compression ratio, and he could get it up to 100 mph in faster time than anyone expected. The crankcase bolts would pull out, and his expedient was to drive a steel wedge between the rocker supports and the frame tube beneath the tank! But it then held.[70]

---

[70] *Motor Sport,* May, 1977.

It is one of only a few Pendine racing machines known to have survived. It now resides in private hands, in the Leeds area, *concours* restored.

The event for light cars revealed a fad for attributing names to cars more appropriate to sailing dinghies: 'Saucy Sue', 'Cockle Girl', 'Miss Gadabout', 'Manna', 'Bluebird' (another one) and 'Silver Streak'. AP Brown of Mumbles entered an Alvis; and there was a five-mile race for standard Ford cars that must have occasioned a stampede for the ice-cream carts.

Car Racing, 1925

Racing cars were seen on the beach a week after the Whitsun motor cycle competition. The South Wales AC held 'a very successful meeting on the sands', according to an editorial comment in *The Autocar*, on 19th June, 1925. There was a small but distinguished entry-list which included Malcolm Campbell, Raymond Mays and Jack Barclay. This meeting had, in previous years, been held on Porthcawl where the sand quality could prove troublesome. On this occasion the entry was under-subscribed

> Possibly because Pendine, which is about 18 miles from Tenby on the western end of the South Wales coast, is an awkward place to get at, being far from motoring centres . . . Nevertheless the relatively few cars there were of stout quality, and the finishes of the events were interesting. The wonderful stretch of sand was in good condition over the mile course chosen, the weather brilliant, and the wind abeam. Also the organisation was excellent, and there was no danger to the spectators.

ACs had a good outing, especially at the hand of JA Joyce. His was a small racing car, which enabled him to get off the mark more sharply than some of the heavier metal. Handicapping was the name of the game, when they were not attempting record-breaking against the clock. Malcolm Campbell just had the edge on Joyce at the line, with Jack Barclay a close third in the TT Vauxhall.

Car racing June, 1925. L>R: T Martin (Chrysler); R Mays (AC); M Campbell (Chrysler); T Barclay (Vauxhall).

An Austin 'Twenty' and Vauxhall 13/98 line up on duck-boards. [© *Lindsay collection*]

OPEN

One mile sprint > 1,500cc
JA Joyce (AC) 48.4 s
R Mays (AC) 53.0 s
FN Morgan (Fiat) 61.2 s

one mile > 2,000cc
JA Joyce (AC) 49.4 s
EA Mayner (Mercedes) 50.0 s
R Mays (AC) 58.8 s

one mile > 3,100cc
J Barclay (Vauxhall) 49.6 s
JA Joyce (AC) 49.8 s
EA Mayner (Mercedes) 51.2 s

one mile > unlimited
M Campbell (Sunbeam) 43.0 s
EA Mayner (Mercedes) 49.25 s
J Barclay (Vauxhall) 50.0 s

Winners' one mile handicap
M Campbell (Sunbeam) scr
JA Joyce (AC) 6 s
J Barclay (Vauxhall) 6 s

All-comers' one mile handicap
M Campbell (Chrysler)
N Martin (Chrysler)
T Barclay (Vauxhall)

CLOSED

One mile > 1,500cc
ES Harries (Salmson) 79.0 s
JA Joyce (AC) 101.60 s

one mile > 3,100cc
HR Wellstead (Morris Sports) 68.0 s
JA Mallins (Morris Sports) 68.4 s
Miss Cordery (Invicta) 70.4 s

one mile > unlimited
T Barclay (Vauxhall) 58.6
M Campbell (Chrysler) 67.8 s
HR Wellstead (Morris Sports) 71.4 s

Ladies one mile > unlimited
Miss Cordery (Invicta) 68.8 s
- (Chrysler) 74.0 s

Amateurs one mile > unlimited
CV Wood (Delage) (not timed)

Campbell was driving the 12-cylinder, ex-KL Guinness, Sunbeam racing car, Blue Bird, and, on the day, did a standing-start mile in 43 seconds: an average of 83.7 mph. He announced that he was awaiting favourable conditions to further attempt the Land Speed Record. A persistent on-shore wind was causing runnels in the beach at intervals which precluded a longer course for the run-up and wind-down necessary for an attempt at the record.

Malcolm Campbell (2): Achieves 150 mph

Not long after, on July 24th, 1925, *The Autocar* reported Malcolm Campbell's successful increment in the Land Speed Record stakes on Pendine.

> From the time when motoring first commenced and men began to discover the fascination of records, the kilometre has been the chosen distance on which to obtain the fastest possible speed, and since the early days, when the electric Jeantaud averaged 39.24 mph, twenty-two cars have broken this record.
>
> Last year Malcolm Campbell took the twelve-cylinder Sunbeam to Pendine Sands, in Wales, and, timed by the RAC official recorder, averaged 146.16 mph. On Tuesday last, Campbell again attacked the record and was successful in averaging 150.869 mph for the kilometre, and 150.766 mph for the mile, speeds determined by the average of two runs made in opposite directions.
>
> The mile record was previously held by the 300 hp Fiat, driven by EAD Eldridge, at an average of 145.92 mph. Pendine Sands when in good condition and free from ripples, allow the car three miles in which to get going, a measured mile for the record, and two miles in which to pull up afterwards. Owing to the width of the sand the driver has no idea of direction, and as a result it is most important that flags or other plainly visible signals be used to point out to him the exact line for the record.

The Carmarthen Journal observes that the condition of the course had not been good, the receding tide having 'rippled' the sand which was also patchy and uneven in certain parts. Campbell confirmed this and hinted at his future plans to the reporter:

> 'I could not let my machine go all out until I had reached the second half of the mile because the sand was so uneven and undulating that I was travelling as if on a switchback. Another difficulty was that at times I was blinded through my glasses being covered by sand and spray, and I had to wipe the sand off while travelling at top speed. The condition of the sand, particularly at the far end of the course was especially bad... I hope to come down to Pendine again with a bigger car'.

Malcolm Campbell knew when he pulled up that he had reached the old Sunbeam's limit, possibly over-reached it. In terms of out-and-out speed, his Grand Prix racing car was no longer up to the job. The era of the leviathan was at hand. Giant aero-engined racers like the Higham Special, privately-owned and raced by the glamorous Mercedes works driver, Count Louis Vorow Zborowski, were poised to

Sunbeam, Blue Bird, 1925. [*Hulton Getty Pic Lib*]

be the chief contenders for the Land Speed Record. (Though he could not have anticipated how this car's endeavour would come about, nor how it would tragically end). Fourth in a line of aeroplane-engined monsters that Zborowski had had built (one being Chitty-Chitty-Bang-Bang) the Higham (named after his estate in Kent) was powered by the fearsomely-potent, American, 27,059cc 'Liberty' engine, through a 1908 Benz four-speed gear-box and a chain final-drive.[71]

Campbell knew, too, that his friend, the flamboyant Italian racing driver, Guilio Foresti, was working with fellow-engineer, Edward Moglia, in building the 355 bhp Djelmo – from designs of the brilliant Breton, Louis Coatalen. He was an ex-Panhard, Humber, Hillman and Sunbeam automobilist, the Colin Chapman of his day. This project was backed, financially, by the Egyptian gambler (or 'sportsman', in the idiom of the day), Prince Djelaleddin, who had been impressed with Coatalen's concept for the present Sunbeam racing car whose days as a record-breaker appeared now at an end. It is rumoured that Djelaleddin had paid Coatalen an amazing £6,000 for the Djelmo drawings alone! Looking much like an over-grown Bugatti, an out-dated and inherently unstable concept, the Djelmo was specifically intended for the three-mile-a-minute barrier.

---

[71]This long-serving power-plant, producing 420 horse-power on the brake, had propelled several First World War fighters and bombers, mainly American-built 'Liberty' planes. It was to power British-designed fuselages, including the De Havilland DH 4 (B, L & M2s), the USD 9 reconnaissance/fighter, the Pomilio BVL 12 bomber and the Royal Flying Corps's De Havilland D9; and, at the outbreak of another World War, in modified guise, it was powering a forerunner to the Sherman tank.

Meanwhile, the Sunbeam company were also at work on a powerful LSR sprint machine for Henry Segrave. Against current thinking, it was to have a comparatively small, but supercharged, engine (V-12: 3,978cc, producing 305 bhp) – another derivative of the aviation industry. The car's weight was said to be under the ton. A man not given to indecision, Campbell set in motion a plan of his own. He had had at the back of his mind for some while an idea to purpose-build a car, based on the 450 hp Napier-Lion, a secret-list aero-engine that would certainly crack 180 mph. This concept, to be dubbed 'Blue Bird' (another one!), under the guidance of designer Amherst Villiers, would take a year at least to reach fruition.

August, 1925

The 1925 August Bank Holiday Monday Open Speed Championships at Pendine were staged in atrocious weather conditions. *The Motor Cycle* comments, with some feeling:

> It seems that rain and Pendine go hand-in-hand... If not quite as bad as it was last year, quite bad enough to spoil the meeting from the competitors' and spectators' points-of-view.
> Near the end the rain became so heavy that an abandonment seemed almost inevitable; the officials, however, decided to give his money's worth to any heroic competitor who cared to turn out, and the last three classes were run on a beach entirely devoid of spectators.
> The rain did not come in intermittent showers, but in a persistent fine drizzle driven like smoke by a strong wind across the great expanse of sand. The sand became thoroughly saturated, and it is not surprising that the number of retirements in each race was very large. In spite of this, however, some remarkably good speeds were put up.

Safety and crowd discipline at sand meetings were under close ACU scrutiny. It is worth noting that, from Easter 1925, an RAC/ACU ban on 'Speed Trials' on public roads was in force, pending an inquiry into accidents at the Kop Hill hill-climb meeting in which four spectators were injured. Even when this investigation had been completed the prohibition was never actually lifted, in the sense that the ACU and RAC refused any application from motoring organisations to run competitions on public highways and rights-of-way. So, accessible arenas where high-speed and long-distance motor competitions could be viewed by the public on the mainland of Britain were suddenly at a premium. When *The Motor Cycle* continues with a description of the ten-mile race for 350cc machines, as 'providing the first thrill of the day', there is an underlying caveat for the Pendine meeting:

> Lap 1 saw LV Thomas (Sunbeam) leading, closely followed by TJ Phillips (344 Zenith), CJ Kingston (Sunbeam), GE Rowley (AJS), and George Grinton (New Imperial). Coming round in approximately the same order on lap 2 the riders made for the home

turn in a bunch, and Rowley got hemmed in between LV Thomas and the spectators – who, incidentally, were very troublesome throughout the day. Having to choose between the crowd or his fellow competitor, Rowley chose the latter, and both men crashed in spectacular style, the rest of the field missing them by inches only.

The accident did not stop the race, but made a considerable difference in the order of combat. The Zenith dropped out and the New Imperial of George Grinton found itself in a clear lead, which it held to the end.

10 miles > 350cc
G Grinton, Edinburgh (New Imperial)
V Anstice, Bath (Douglas)
E Mundey, B'ham (New Imperial)
Winner's time: 10 mins 57secs.

10 miles > 275cc
G Grinton, Edinburgh (New Imperial)
M Isaac (New Imperial)
Winner's time: 11 mins 40secs.

10 miles > 660cc
W Wilkinson, Malton (Sunbeam)
A Nicklin, Blaina (Sunbeam)
JW David W'hampton (Sunbeam)
Winner's time: 9 mins 24 secs.

10 miles: unlimited
E Mundey B'ham (596 New Hudson)
W Wilkinson (Sunbeam)
H Langman, Shipley (Scott)
Winner's time: 9 mins 7secs.

one-mile sprint: unlimited
E Mundey (596 New Hudson)
A Nicklin (Sunbeam)
George Dance (Sunbeam)
Winner's time: 45 secs.

30 miles: unlimited
E Mundey (596 New Hudson)
W Wilkinson (Sunbeam)
E Mainwaring, Keighley (Scott)
Winner's time: 28 mins 20 secs.

Sidecars: unlimited
H Langman (Scott)
V Anstice (Douglas)
TJ Phillips (Zenith)
Winner's time: 11mins 26 secs.

CLOSED EVENTS

one-mile sprint > 350cc
CL James, Llanelly (Rex-Acme)
Wm Edwards (AJS)
J Thomas, Neath (AJS)
Winner's time: 46 secs.

10 miles > 350cc
Wm Edwards (AJS)
J Thomas (AJS)
M Isaac (Sunbeam)
Winner's time: 10 mins 48 secs.

10 miles: unlimited
P Rogers, Llanelly (Sunbeam)
M Griffiths (Sunbeam)
C James, Llanelly (Sunbeam)
Winner's time: 9 mins 58secs.

One-mile sprint: unlimited
A Nicklin (Sunbeam)
Frank Griffiths, Glanamman (Sunbeam)
CI James, Llanelly (Sunbeam)
Winner's time: 11 mins 19secs.

one-mile sprint: unlimited
C Sgonina (S. Special)
A Nicklin, Blaina (Sunbeam)
J Thomas (AJS)

NOVICE CLASS

4 miles > 500cc
P Rogers (Sunbeam)
CL Kingston, Newport (Sunbeam)
Frank Griffiths (Sunbeam)

LIGHT CARS

(£12 TAX)
Bassett, Swansea (Rhode)
AP Brown, Mumbles (Alvis)
Albert Henstock, Carmarthen (Rhode)

CHAMPIONSHIP CLASSES

4 miles > 175cc
ETM Stephens (.?.)
Oscar Evans, Brynamman (Excelsior)

10 miles > 275cc
J Edwards (Ariel)
P Rogers (New Imperial)
W Evans, Llanpumsaint (New Imperial)
Winner's time: 13mins 59secs

25 miles > 350cc
M Isaac (Sunbeam)
VR McKenzie, H'west (AJS)
Tudor Williams, St Clears (AJS)
Winner's time: 27mins. 35Secs.

50 miles: unlimited
JE Kettle, Newport (Scott Squirrel)
LF Griffiths, Cardiff (Norton)
C Sgonina (S. Special)
Winner's time: 52 mins 35 secs

LIGHT CARS

5 miles: (£12 tax)
C Sgonina, Penarth (GN)
Louis Pierard, Llandilo (Alvis)
JA Maluis, Cardiff (Morris Cowley)

C Sgonina (GN), 1925. *[Photo courtesy of Mrs Sgonina/AB Demaus]*

Sunbeams had had a remarkable day out, despite the weather. In both amateur and trade categories they had come home in procession, giving AJS more than a run for their money. New Imperial, in the hands of such experts as George Grinton and Ed Mundey showed very well.

New Imperial

In the Lightweight classes New Imperials were always a popular choice. They were still reliant on proprietary JAP and sometimes Blackburne engines – as were Cotton, OK, Rex, Zenith and many others. But New Imps were well put-together and renowned for good steering and braking, which made them the choice of discriminating riders in these categories, including 'semi-professional' local boys – Morris Isaac, Percy Rogers, Ivor Thomas and Eddie Stephens. JAP engine reliability was a vulnerable factor in all makes which raced with them, particularly the smaller capacity units when subjected to high revs and stress-loadings. Under the direction of twenty year-old design engineer, Matt Wright, in 1926, 'New Imps' would soon come out with their own engines which would power them to an impressive five IoM TT victories between the wars: four Lightweight and one Junior win – equalling Velocette's record and coming second only to Norton with a staggering eighteen.

Welsh TT, 1925

If Monday had been a wet day, Tuesday was wetter – the day of the 'Welsh TT'. Yet, despite the rain, the sands were in good condition for racing, except when it came to the business of the start. As *The Motor Cycle* of August, 13th reported

> Immediately the machines were put on the line the wheels simply sank into the wet sand, and many riders stopped their engines at the fall of the flag.

There was nothing for it but to devise a new starting procedure – that of the 'trailing start' – where the bicycles trailed behind a moving automobile, the Starter being perched on 'the step'[72] with his flag. This was 'infinitely more spectacular than the standing start.' It certainly proved so in the 100-mile Welsh TT, as the Starter fell off, 'sustaining slight injuries', poor man.

Jack Thomas, the Neath AJS agent, was an excellent advertisement for his wares in the 350cc race over fifty miles, setting a 'very hot pace' on the ohv sports model. The lap was a five-mile circuit, and at the end of the first lap he was leading by half a mile. After four laps he was a whole five-mile lap ahead, having broken the lap record (4 mins 30 secs), and he'd covered 25 miles in 18 mins 30 secs (81.08 mph). Then, of course, engine trouble – and he packed up.

Leading the 'rat pack' meanwhile, some distance behind, had been the Cotton of SS Evans, followed by P Rogers (Sunbeam), M Isaac (Sunbeam) and V Anstice (Douglas). This situation was defended until the 9th lap, when Evans failed to appear, admitting Rogers into the lead – which he proudly held. Meantime, there had been a side-show for 250s going on, with many retirements. In just under the hour, Rees Thomas came in on his New Imperial, pursued by George Grinton on a similar machine. The finishing order for the 50-mile race was:

---

[72]Running-board?

50 miles > 350cc
P Rogers (Sunbeam)
V Anstice (Douglas)
SS Evans (Cotton)
- Davies (Dot-JAP)

50 miles > 250cc
RE Thomas (New Imperial)
G Grinton (New Imperial)

Percy Rogers (Sunbeam).

Cotton: SS Evans

The appearance of SS Evans of Chepstow on the 350cc Cotton drew attention to a future race-winning association. It was that of an extremely tenacious rider, with an attractive style, upon as sweet-handling a bicycle as it was possible to buy in the early mid-twenties. Until a very young Irishman called Stanley Woods made a brilliant debut appearance on such a machine, with a Blackburne engine, which accidentally caught fire in refuelling in the 1922 Junior IoM TT – even so coming in fifth, and the following year first – no one had much heard of Cotton. But it had one of the best designed and constructed frames in the industry.

Assembled in Gloucester by FW Cotton, the triangulated, unstressed and rigid frame was an excellent basis for a lightweight racing machine. Relying on JAP or specially-prepared, high compression, ohv Blackburne engines, the 250 and 350cc Cotton racers were very competitive, because of their power-to-weight ratio and excellent steering. After 1927, Blackburnes supplied an ohc engine which, being tall, altered the centre of gravity and defiled the road-holding virtues of this elegant marque. Among its adherents on Pendine in those heady days were Luther Davies, Percy Rogers, DJ Jones, Alex Grey of Cardiff, AW Goode of Swansea, CF Edwards of Shrewsbury and CH Jayne – all with varying degrees of accomplishment. None were anywhere near as successful as SS Evans, whose supreme achievement was in claiming the 500cc Trophy in the 1931 100-mile race, second behind JH Carr's Brough. Altogether on his Cottons, he secured eight firsts and five second places on the beach, against stiff competition – usually provided by Ron Parkinson on the AJS.

The scene was set for the main event of the day, the 100-mile 'Welsh TT'. Out of a large field which entered the 'trailing start', 26 completed the first lap, but only 15 or 16 the second – all affected by water on the electrics, or other mishaps – both mechanical and gravitational. The two Douglases of Freddie Dixon and Vic Anstice were first round the 5-mile course on lap one, but then out went Anstice with trouble, allowing George-William Patchett, in his first 'big race' with the Brough Superior, into second place. The duel between Brough and Douglas on this occasion was one of the finest spectacles of brinkmanship ever witnessed at Pendine. Here were two 'hard men' pitched against one another on the fastest machines known. On each corner either Dixon or Patchett would leave the braking just that little bit later, or power the drift that little bit harder, to nose out and up the straight to gain a narrow lead, destined to be lost again at the next turn. For seven laps they drove like this, till something had to give. Would it be the JAP No 2 cylinder? No: a Douglas valve. Patchett could afford momentarily to ease back and 'coast' a little, as his nearest rival was Mostyn Griffiths, on the Triumph 'Riccy' and Alex Grey on a Norton, both trailing by about a mile.

The Brough then began running unevenly, and Patchett dived into the depot where a carburettor problem was diagnosed. Two laps went by before Patchett was out again, replenished and running sweetly. The leaders were now Mostyn Griffiths, (Triumph-Ricardo), Alex Grey (Norton), Langman (Scott), David (Sunbeam) and Mainwaring (Scott). The rest of the field were as distant as memory.

Patchett turned the burner right up on the Brough and overtook back-markers at a terrific pace, soon getting the leaders in his sights, and then in among them, like a fox through the chickens. Lap 13 was an unlucky one for rivals Griffiths and Grey, both of whom ground to a halt. They had been doing so well. Patchett was through into the lead, and going at a furious rate that was reflected in his record winning time of 86 minutes, including a six-minute stop (69.76 mph). Two minutes faster than Needham's tour with the SS80 the previous year. Patchett had driven a blinder.

Mostyn Griffiths, unhappily for a relative beginner and a local boy who had been leading the Welsh TT, failed to re-start the Triumph; unlike Grey, who got his Norton going and drove dazzlingly into second place.

WELSH TT, 1925

100 miles: unlimited
G-W Patchett (Brough Superior)

100 miles > 500cc
A Grey (Norton)
W Mewis (Norton)
AM Harry (New Hudson)
Fastest lap: F Dixon
(Douglas 3 mins 49⅓ secs)

George-William Patchett (McEvoy).

G-W Patchett

This victory in the Welsh TT was George-William Patchett's one and only real success on Pendine, though wherever he was racing he was always seriously in contention. He was a tremendous presence on the racing circuit, the butt of all sorts of good-natured humour. But Patchett was 'the real thing', imbued as he was with the requisite amount of 'Tiger' and technical sensibility. He had first-rate Brooklands and IoM credentials, both as development engineer and driver. Patchett as a motor cycle designer is best remembered for his involvement with CA Birkin in the development of the McEvoy motor cycle and his 1931 Jawa 500 racer.

What is now largely forgotten is his later patent, which he was obliged to develop abroad in Belgium with FN. 'The Patchett gun', known in military circles as the Stirling, was conceived in dramatic circumstances. The blue-print was smuggled out of Czechoslovakia where Janacek, under the noses of the Nazis, were about to go into production with it at the outbreak of World War Two. Some time later, the design was taken on by the War Office. Somewhat unjustly, it was dubbed the 'Stirling' sub-machine gun, after SAS founder, David Stirling. A sophisticated, silenced version, developed primarily for SAS and RM Special Boat Services use, was accorded the 'Patchett' nomenclature and adopted as a NATO weapon.

First Welsh Sidecar TT

The first Welsh Sidecar TT was run off on the Wednesday morning. There were three memorable features of that race. The first was the brilliant performance of the puny little 344cc Zenith of TJ Phillips, against the muscular Harleys, Broughs and Douglases. The other lasting impression was that of George Grinton's Harley-Davidson literally breathing fire, like a dragon, directly onto his legs and all over his unfortunate passenger, as the machine was allowed to start minus its exhaust pipes.

The rider appeared to be surrounded by flames every time he cornered. Spectators awaited his appearance each lap with bated breath, expecting to see him and his outfit burst into flames, but fortunately he escaped any such calamity.[73]

And the third lasting memory was entry in the sidecar event of the man who had won the very first Isle of Man TT sidecar trophy, in 1923. Freddie Dixon, chief engineer of the Douglas concern, was down with his curious 'banking sidecar'[74]. There were eight outfits at the start, and Dixon made a brilliant getaway with the 596cc Douglas, almost taking the lap-scorers by surprise at the end of the first two-mile lap, one minute and fifty-five seconds later. Behind him were George Grinton and the Scott of Langman. These positions were held beyond the half-way mark, when Grinton ran completely out of brakes and continued on for some considerable distance into the landscape before he could reverse direction and catch up with the field – Langman in particular – who occupied his second place. Not for long, however, for the brake-less fire-breathing Grinton had him – and came home a worthy second to the far-out-of-sight Dixon. Langman dropped out with clutch-trouble.

FIRST WELSH SIDECAR TT, 1925

50 miles: sidecars unlimited

FW Dixon (Douglas)	TJ Phillips (344 Zenith)
G Grinton (Harley-Davidson)	I Thomas (Douglas)
CF Edwards (Brough Superior)	Fastest lap: Dixon – 1min 55 secs.

FW Dixon

Freddie Dixon is one of the immortal 'characters' of motor racing. It is said that he, above others, was 'the man who put the Roar into the Roaring Twenties'! Born in Stockton-on-Tees in 1892, he was a self-taught engineer and a complete all-rounder as a driver – making as much of a name for himself behind the wheel of supercharged Rileys in later life as he did on motor cycles as a younger man. During the First World War he became Staff Sergeant in the (R)ASC, after which he started his own business in Middlesborough, selling and repairing motorcycles.

Even before the war Dixon had developed a penchant for big American 'irons', such as Indian and Harley-Davidson – brutal machines to control at high speed over rough roads. His strength was Samsonite, and his riding-style decidedly trans-Atlantic. Dixon demanded foot-boards, a left-hand throttle and a foot clutch. He hated goggles, preferring a fly-screen. In his motor cycle racing career Dixon will always be associated with the Bristol firm of Douglas, to whom he brought considerable engineering skill in innovation, as well as top-flight riding ability. Brough Superior and HRD, at different times, also derived benefit from Fred's engineering and riding genius. He loved Pendine and was enormously popular with the crowds.

---

[73] *The Motor Cycle,* Aug 13th, 1925.
[74] On loan to NMM, Beaulieu, from Bob Thomas, Ramsey, IoM. The passenger controlled the 'tilt' by means of a long lever.

JGP Thomas & Babs, October 1925.

9. Tommy Thomas's Babs

The World Land Speed Record

JG Parry Thomas (1)

THE racing motorist John Godfrey Parry Thomas was at the height of his fame in the summer of 1926. He was world-famous. Under the revised regulations relating to international records he was the holder of more than twenty, including five world records in Class B (5,000 – 8,000cc), with the Leyland-Thomas. He lacked the smooth charm and photogenic good-looks of a Malcolm Campbell or Henry Segrave. In appearance, he looked more like a craggy hill-farmer from Snowdonia[75] except that he was at least a foot too tall! Thomas was heavily-built and strong, with a mouthful of gnarled teeth. On racing occasions he was usually scruffily-dressed, in baggy trousers and familiar Fair Isle pullover, leather helmet or crashed trilby – all liberally oil-smeared. He exhibited an economy with words not uncommon among engineers, which meant he did not exactly court an adoring following. A bachelor, he avowed a liking for children – little girls in particular – that did not entail stigma at that time.[76]

Thomas, like many of his contemporaries, and car-racing drivers of later generations, began on motor cycles. In his early days he owned a series of them before his first car, a Pipe. While still an engineering student in London, at the Central Technical College, South Kensington, he had taken fastest time-of-day at Brockley Hill, in 1905, on a 350cc Kerry.[77]

Nobody ever called him 'John' or 'Parry'. His family knew him as 'Godfrey', and the motor racing fraternity called him 'Mr Thomas', 'Thomas' or 'Tommy'. Posterity seems to have thought up the 'Parry Thomas'. As a racing driver, at Brooklands and on Continental tracks, he was celebrated for his fearlessness. His 'Thomas Swoops' and 'Thomas Dives' were by-words for breathtaking manoeuvres – whereby he would accelerate down off the edge of the 'wall-of-death' banking at Brooklands when others were slowing down. Captioned and head-lined by the press as 'Dare-

---

[75] RE (Rees) Thomas, Gloag, in an HTV interview (May 10th, 1969) remembers Parry Thomas as '*Mwy fel ffarmwr nag unrhiw byd arall*'. (More like a farmer than anything else).

[76] He was a children's hospital visitor – at the Belgrave and Great Ormond St. He endowed a cot at the latter. He would sometimes refuse to autograph - other than for small girls! 'Boys is nasty!'

[77] Manufactured by the East London Rubber Co, using proprietary Kelecom or Abingdon engines.

Devil Tommy', 'Speed-King, Thomas', 'Le Diable Audacieux' or 'The Hermit of Brooklands' – in recognition of his ascetic bachelor life-style – he was in some ways every schoolboy's role-model; but by no means a heart-throb or a ladies' man.

Parry Thomas was one of the most brilliantly inventive development engineers of his generation. He could turn his mind to anything electrical or mechanical, from designing and building electronic transmissions for buses and lorries to innovating vehicle- and aero-engines. He designed a radial aero-engine during WW1 and afterwards a Rolls Royce-beating luxury car, the Leyland Eight. It was packed with new features – years ahead of their time in 1922 – servo brakes, variable-rake steering-column and anti-roll-bars. He designed and built from scratch championship-winning racing cars, of which his Leyland-Thomas and the supercharged, overhead-camshaft, straight-eight 1½ litre 'Flat-iron' Thomas-Specials were the best known. There were those who seriously thought that he was indulging himself – and squandering his considerable genius – on the frivolity of motor racing.

The Higham Special

When, in 1925, the glamorous young Count Zborowski was killed in the Italian Grand Prix at Monza, in the manner of his father before him – at the wheel of a racing car – Thomas went down to the dispersal sale at his friend's Higham estate in Kent and bought for a song his racing car, the American aero-engined 'Higham Special'.[78] The machine had been built by Zborowski's friend and technical adviser, Clive Gallop, on a light Rubery Owen chassis. The bodywork design, by Blythe brothers of Canterbury, which made it look like a grounded Zeppelin, was something of a dog's dinner. This did not matter to Tommy, who was not obsessed with aesthetics. His sights had become set on the Land Speed Record, and this acquisition appeared to him an inspired and affordable method of approach.

Godfrey Thomas, the clergyman's son from Bwlch-y-Cibiau in Montgomeryshire, was not a wealthy man; unlike Malcolm Campbell, a man of independent means, whose LSR car-in-the-making was rumoured to be costing into five figures – an astronomical sum in those days. Since leaving his position as chief engineer at Leyland's, Thomas led a freelance existence. He worked as his own design-engineer and became a bounty-hunter, usually living beyond his means. But he was without responsibility, and had confidence in his ability to win through. Like Campbell though, he had come to the conclusion that the conventional racing car was no longer capable of challenging for the World Land Speed Record, now that a speed well above 150 mph was required. Sights were being set on three-miles-a-minute, and even 200mph.

---

[78] £125.

'Babs'

While Campbell's engineers were building from scratch the 450 hp Napier Lion-engined Blue Bird, Tommy Thomas, in his usual 'up-and-at-'em' manner, rolled up his sleeves in his workshop at the Brooklands circuit and re-worked the Higham Special, whose power potential was also in the region of 420-450 bhp. Among the modifications he put in hand were self-designed pistons, revised carburation, a higher compression ratio, a Leyland front axle, chassis adjustments and body modifications that, unscientifically, offered gestures in the direction of 'streamlining'. So different a car was she by the end of the summer that he decided to re-name her. A mechanic had jokingly chalked 'Baby' on the cylinder block of the behemoth 27, 000cc engine. A frequent visitor to the garage was a little Scots-girl neighbour, Barbara Stuart, who from time-to-time supervised the re-build[79]. She was called 'Babs', for short. (There have been other claimants to the source of inspiration, like Barbara Frazer-Nash, Barbara White and various other explanations)[80]. It is thought that the cost of converting the Higham into Babs was around £850, inclusive of the purchase price.

JG Parry Thomas took the 'new' car down to Pendine for trials on the beach in October, 1925; but not before consulting local coast guard and beach-expert, Wilfred Morgan. He knew that the beach was at its best during a spring tide period. Though they are 'high' tides, spring tides at low tide leave the beach smooth and level and are 'out' for a longer period, allowing the beach more time to dry out and harden. Morgan, however, was not in charge of the weather – which was sulky and disobliging throughout the three days' testing. The flying spray of water-and-sand thwarted any serious attempts at a high-speed run and, on Wednesday, 22nd October, Babs was loaded back on to a lorry and transported home to the garage at Brooklands, to iron out some teething troubles.

For an historic few days at the end of 1925, Babs and Blue Bird stood side-by-side on an exhibition stand at the Royal Horticultural Hall, in London, for the Schoolboys' Exhibition. Every other day Campbell and Thomas took it in turns to answer eager questions from the hordes of 'little horrors' who crowded round the heroes and their monster cars – straight out of the pages of *Hotspur* and *Boy's Own Paper*. This public occasion for Tommy Thomas, an inherently shy man, was something of an ordeal, as he disliked the limelight and anything resembling hero-worship.

The Race to Build the Record-breaker

Over the winter of 1925 and spring of 1926 the motoring press was full of reports and rumours of the 'race' in progress involving preparation of the cars designed for the Land Speed Record. The 10-litre Djelmo, producing 355 bhp, which had been under

---

[79] Pers. letter from S Campbell, St Ives, NSW, Australia, 30-iv-86: re his aunt Mrs B Adams (nee Stuart).
[80] These are too numerous to mention. 'Babs' was as frequent a diminutive term of endearment in 1925 as 'Babe' is today. The nick-name somehow grew from there.

construction for two years, was reported as 'undergoing further trials'. Campbell's new 22.3-litre Napier Blue Bird was taking shape. Its bodywork was in the hands of coachbuilders. Meanwhile Sunbeam, under the direction of Louis Coatalen, took their new 'blown'[81] V-twelve 4-lire car, 'Lady Bird' (after the sponsor's wife) to Southport at the turn of the year. She had a power-to-weight ratio comparable to Babs – weighing-in at only 18 cwts and with about 305 bhp on tap. From the outset the Rootes supercharger proved troublesome. Chassis-flexing over the undulations caused the blower's alloy casing to split – with the result that the rotor blades fouled the housing and began to self-destruct. The casing split six times in all.

Rather than abandon the attempt (timekeepers were standing-by) Major Henry Segrave persuaded Sunbeam's Chief Engineer, Capt Irving, to do an overnight repair job that would hold for three minutes – a single return run. Unfortunately, on the second leg, Segrave hit a gully that caused the car to become air-borne and his foot to kick forward on the throttle while the wheels were off the ground. Engine revs soared. The supercharger blew itself to smithereens. Luckily, this happened after he had passed the 1 kilometre post on a return run, and he found he had set the kilometre record at a new high of 152.33 mph: 1.25 mph above Campbell's record. Success of a kind, but it had proved an expensive exercise, and effectively put an end to the lightweight, quart-in-a-pint-pot approach.

Coatalen's next concept, a Sunbeam designed for 200 mph, was to be a colossal-displacement[82] beast, whose power-output would be around 800 bhp. (Afterwards somewhat unkindly-named 'The Slug'). Babs was at the 'fine-tuning' stage, Parry Thomas working on her beside his 'chief engineer', Ken Taylor, and apprentices, among them John Cobb. She was soon to reward them by becoming the fastest car in the world. *The Motor* for April 27th, 1926, an auspicious day, carried a detailed technical report of Babs's mechanical progress – read, no doubt, with as much care at Povey Cross as at Sunbeam's in Wolverhampton.

A 400 hp Car for Short-distance Records.
Mr JGP Thomas's 12-cylinder Aeroplane-engined Leviathan

During the past week the work of tuning Mr JG Parry Thomas's 400 hp racing car 'Babs' approached completion, and it is anticipated that he will be attacking world's records on this car during the current week; some details of the chassis are therefore opportune. The power unit is a Liberty aero engine of Vee type, the bore and stroke being 127 mm and 177 mm respectively, which result in a cubic capacity of 27,059cc.

The special induction system is of considerable interest, four carburettors being employed. Two induction pipes are placed between the banks of cylinders, feeding the ports through branching connections, the carburettors being fitted to the ends of these pipes. Near the centre of each pipe a baffle is introduced, which cuts down the cross-sectional area.

---

[81]Supercharged: mechanically air-forced induction. (Turbo-charged: re-cycled exhaust-force gases).
[82]Two x 22-litre Sunbeam Matabele aero-engines.

Babs, 1926.

Each of the carburettors fitted at the front is provided with an air intake scoop facing forwards, and additional scoops placed below these are connected with conduits running between the banks of cylinders and terminate in semi-circular pipes which conduct the air to the intake branches of the two rear carburettors.

The radiator slants backwards and is partly cowled, and a header tank containing water is fitted under the fairing at the point where this is swept upwards towards the steering wheel.

The steering box is supported on a large bracket in a high position, so that the steering column is not far from being horizontal, and the drop arm links, etc., are all constructed on massive lines. Semi-elliptical springing is employed fore and aft, the front springs being underslung, and Hartford duplex shock absorbers are fitted. Radius rods are used to locate the I-section rear axle, and the drive to the rear wheels being conveyed through chains and sprockets from a countershaft and differential located behind the gearbox.

Four speeds and a reverse are provided by the centrally controlled gearbox, and the clutch is of multiple-disc type; no flywheel is employed. The engine is fitted with overhead camshafts, which operate two valves per cylinder.

Parry Thomas Achieves WLSR, 170.624 mph

On that same day, April 27th, only hours after the weekly motoring journal was on the news-stands Babs was roaring up the Sands once again. And then down again. Misfiring and issuing black smoke from her exhaust, too. Nevertheless, Col Lindsay

Lloyd was able to confirm that, by an impressive margin of some 16 mph, Tommy Thomas was now the fastest man in the world. Occasion for jubilation, certainly: but not so much to the tall, heavy-jowled, sullen-looking Welshman. That figure could soon be improved upon. Back to the Beach Hotel garage.

After a night of engineering activity, Babs was out on the sand again the following morning, sounding much healthier, though still misfiring occasionally. Farm workers out in the fields and people for miles around could hear Babs's cacophony like distant military gunfire.[83] Good as his word, Thomas raised the record to even greater heights: 171.09 mph for the kilometre and 171.624 for the mile. It was a famous victory: celebrated in *The Times* the following day by a full-page advertisement, taken out by the sponsors, Shell-Mex. Babs, it appears, had done further runs on standard-grade, 'red can' petrol, which enabled the company to boast that, 'though slower speeds are achieved' (than the WLSR), they had smashed Campbell's record 'on the same fuel and oil available to the public'.

At the end of the second run Thomas had, ominously, discovered that one of his specially-strong shock absorbers was about to part company with its mounting. The securing nut was holding by less than half a thread. 'Had it dropped', comments *The Motor,* 'it would have formed a sprag, possibly with very unpleasant results'.

It is worth quoting in full *The Autocar* correspondent's eye-witness account of Pendine's most famous occasion:

> ...The organisation of the entire affair was in the hands of Shell-Mex, Limited, the car being transported in a Scammell six-wheeler to Pendine and back. The measured distance was indicated by a great number of flags, each stretched tightly between two posts planted in the sand, on either side of the course, making an avenue along which the car was to run. Masts supported in old oil drums buried below the surface marked the beginning and end of the measured section.
>
> On Monday the course was marked out and tested with the aid of LG Callingham's well-known and sorely-tried 30-98 hp Vauxhall, 'Elizabeth Tiger', which is a familiar feature at all race meetings, and which spent most of its time doing 70 mph *minus* its torque member. In all, there were assembled ten cars, including the RAC machines and the signal wagon, five lorries, and seven motor cycles, six of which were used by stout-hearted policemen, in spiked helmets, who ran races of their own, and the seventh by a doctor for the occasion. Fifty-three people in all were needed officially for these purposes.
>
> A great number of large wooden platforms, rather like rectangular duck boards, were constructed for use if 'Babs' had to come to rest, in which event the wheels began to sink in the sand immediately, and a gang of men were told off and drilled to keep the car moving until it had all four wheels were on the boards. The wisdom of this was shown when Lt Comm Mackenzie-Grieve's Morris Oxford suddenly commenced to sink with all hands and had to be dug out with much labour, thus entailing a mock court-martial later for its owner.

---

[83]JL Harries, Cadno Farm, pers. comm. c. 1950.

Thomas commenced operations on the Tuesday, when the assembly of notables from the RAC had been duly penned in a roped enclosure, and the usual display of temper from the electrical timing apparatus properly overcome. 'Babs's forced induction pipes over the radiator had been removed and their outlet holes in the bonnet closed up, but even then the engine ran irregularly and emitted clouds of black smoke. There were six complete runs over the course, which, as already announced, broke both records handsomely, the best being 169.238 for the kilometre (272.45kph) and 168.074 mph for the mile, while the highest speed was no less than 172.331 mph. This attempt was made on 60% Shell aviation spirit and 40% benzole. Some other attempts on red can Shell, which had been sealed and provided by the RAC, also broke the old world's records, but not by such a wide margin.

On Wednesday, everyone having ascertained that Mackenzie-Grieve's car was firmly on the duck boards, another run was made, the setting of 'Babs's carburettors having been altered without, however, curing the misfiring. The mean speed of the runs, nevertheless, beat the previous day's figures, and raised the average for the kilometre to the astonishing figure of 171.09 mph (275.229 kph) for the mile to 170.624, a truly wonderful performance, 18 mph faster than the old record. Curiously enough the best one-way run was not as good as on Monday. During all these runs the car had to be kept moving until it was safely on the boards from which it had to start, and while running Thomas had to keep up the air pressure in the petrol tank with the hand pump. Moreover the car 'snaked' considerably.

The attempt on the standing records was not successful for a curious reason. Strips of matting 30ft long were spread and pegged over the timing tapes, so that the car rested on one end of each strip, its front wheels nearly on the strip. The moment the clutch was engaged the Dunlop-tyred wheels raced madly, creating such intense heat that the water came away from them as steam and the smell of burning rubber was intense, the car slewed sideways off the mats, and the time lost at the start frustrated the attempt entirely. Moreover, 'Babs' began to sulk a little and the misfiring became worse. During this day's run the mixture of aviation spirit with benzole was again used. Shell triple oil was in the engine throughout.

Several Brooklands enthusiasts were present, RB Howey and J Cobb from the start, and JEP Howey driving up from Selsey one day, then returning home the same day. Obviously, Thomas can do even better, and a maximum of 200 mph is not so very unlikely at some future date in more favourable circumstances.

Among the components and accessories Thomas was using were Shell oil and spirit, KLG plugs, Dunlop tyres, Hartford shock absorbers, Marles steering, Mosely Float-on-Air cushions, Laystall camshafts, Zenith carburettors, Delco-Remy ignition, Coventry driving chains, Tecalemit greasers, CAV unspillable batteries, Ferodo brake and clutch linings, Auster-Triplex windscreen, Rudge-Whitworth wire wheels, Terry's valve springs, Wellworthy piston rings and Miralite pistons.

Congratulations came pouring in from the motoring world at large. Pendine was, for that moment of glory, the most famous place in the world. Campbell's response was that of a gentleman and a sportsman. He wrote a letter of congratulation, published in *The Motor* and *The Autocar*:

> I should like to add my heartiest congratulations to the many others which Mr Parry Thomas has already received after his recent attack on world's records.
>
> To break old world's records with a margin of over 20 mph is a truly marvellous performance, deserving of the highest praise, and one which will never be forgotten.
>
> Whether these records stand or not matters little, as Mr Thomas will always have the satisfaction of having been the first man in recent years to have beaten the most coveted (of) records by this huge margin.

Prince Djelaleddin also wrote from Paris, congratulating Thomas, but added, carpingly:

> 'However, I think that Djelmo is sufficiently more modern to be able to beat Babs, and, in any case, there will be some good sport during the next few weeks'.

The Prince had not realised that the General Strike, which brought Britain's infrastructure to a halt during the summer of 1926, would prevent the transportation of Djelmo to Pendine. It also saw Godfrey Parry Thomas as a volunteer, driving a London bus, to the amusement of passengers, whose jokes about his not stopping at halts 'so as not to spoil his time', were endless.

Whitsun 1926

The Whitsun 1926 Welsh Championship motor cycle meeting at Pendine was a very enjoyable occasion, with a great turnout. The very fast little Zenith of TJ Phillips, that had done so well in the sidecar TT of 1925, worried LV Thomas on his meticulously-prepared and dominant Sunbeam Sprint for the first six or seven laps of the 25-mile Welsh Championship race for 350s. Phillips, recovered from August Bank Holiday Monday's collision, made the mistake of riding the clutch while cornering and burnt it out, though he managed to ride on to finish down the field. CL Kingston came up into third place with a JAP-HRD, and Case came in third on his AJS.

C Sgonina

The changing times were reflected in the realisation that the valiant Charles Sgonina's name, mounted on his (latterly) twin-cam 'Sgonina Special', was no longer among the entries. This fiercely competitive and intelligent rider, who carried within him an uncommon understanding of machinery, was tempered by the real heroic stuff. He had turned professional for just one season, in 1921:

> About this time I thought I was good enough to race in some of the real events and got fixed up with Triumphs through an advertisement I noticed in one of the Motor Cycle papers. I went to the Island full of hope for the TT races but after my first practice lap didn't feel happy as I had gone around as quickly as I could but found that my time would have to be halved for me to be in the running. I put in as many practice laps as

> possible, my lap times improving with every lap. In fact, I started with great hopes. A thing I learnt during practice was never to let my eyes wander from the road. Seeing some friends waving to me when I was going round the course I took my eyes off the road for a fraction of a second and found myself riding on the pavement. Quite a shock, I can tell you, and I had my leg pulled, as one of the papers called me a 'pavement artist'.
>
> I was third to start in the race and after one and a half hectic laps, went out with a broken valve when in 7th place.
>
> Next, over to France for the French Grand Prix which was to be run at the Le Mans course. We started from Le Havre and rode the machines across France to Le Mans. I don't know how far we travelled but it must have been about 250 miles. The course really suited me and I was very happy about doing something. Unlike the TT you could practise any old time and we had great fun going flat out through a bunch of chickens – but French chickens know how to look after themselves! Another time I can remember going round with Freddie (Edmond) who was one of the team. I was alongside him at about 70mph when we saw a cloud of dust ahead. About half way through it I noticed a steam roller and wondered what happened to Freddie and pulled up. Freddie also pulled up and said 'That was a close one! I heard my clutch lever go click against the back wheel of that steam roller!'
>
> For the race, I started rather gently then went practically flat out, stopping half way to fill up with petrol and oil. I was rather troubled by the calcium chloride they put on the roads to keep down the dust which, if swallowed, gives you a sore throat. I finished third and we were able to gargle in champagne. My mechanic stripped the engine for measurement and as we had a large case of champagne, he was unable to put it together again!

A burst tyre, while lying third in this, the first Belgian Grand Prix, caused Charlie to stop to replace the tube. The cooling of the engine resulted in a poppet valve going down as soon as he re-started.

> The next event was the 500-mile race at Brooklands and, as I had never been on that track before, it was quite an experience and great fun. In the race itself I was well in the running when the big end put me out. Fred Dixon burst a tyre in front of me and was thrown at about 90mph. He rolled over and over, bits of his clothing coming off and I thought 'Poor Freddie won't be riding for a long time', but he was really tough and I noticed him later on back in the race again.[84]

Sgonina, it is said, was himself injured in an accident in 1925, at Margam Park, which shortened a colourful racing career on motor cycles. An inventive engineer, whose family business, making the 'sharp ends' of compressed-air road drills, based in Cardiff, afforded him an independent life-style. This was to end, after the accident, with his marriage and emigration to the USA where, for a number of years, he worked as a technical consultant for the Gillette razor company. Nortons should have head-hunted him in 1922!

---

[84]Quoted from the text of a prepared talk to some unknown audience, by kind permission of AB Demaus.

It is most likely that the metallurgical expertise derived from hard-metal technology in daily use in the Flotsam works, Llanishen, served him well in the pioneering the various overhead valve Specials. There are few recorded instances of Sgonina Specials falling out through burnt or dropped valves. These machines and his mechanical adroitness are now considered to have been so far ahead of their time, as to merit a special place in engineering and motor racing history.[85] *Motor Cycling* was aware of its significance in 1922:

> The Sgonina Special is a novel type of machine, constructed solely by its rider, a Cardiff genius, and was noted to possess remarkable accelerative powers.

The Sgonina Special, still in existence somewhere, deserves to be declared a Pendine and Welsh national treasure.

Curiously, in a single lonely reprise, Charles Sgonina was to turn up in the Pendine entry list, on the Sgonina Special, several years later, in 1933, without registering any success. Had he left America, one wonders, or was he just on holiday? Was this an intended come-back where he discovered he had lost his former touch, or that progress had left him and the Special far behind? He again re-appears in the Welsh motor racing scene after the Second World War, his fascination having graduated to car-racing.[86]

In order to start the 50-mile race, there was a delay while the marshals endeavoured to clear the crowd off the course. The organisers always made the mistake of allowing spectators onto the seaward-side of the course and the centre reservation so that, like chickens confronted with a road, whoever was on one side of the course, preferred to be on the other – which led to continual problems.

When they did get started, the twenty-two machines faced a mile-up and mile-down circuit, and a fast-disappearing Zenith-JAP exhaust, piloted by the tenacious FA Grey. The Zenith led the field convincingly for over fifteen laps, pursued by Kettle's Scott and Mostyn Griffiths's Sunbeam. Then the big Zenith faded – and a battle royal ensued between the Sunbeam and the Scott. Kettle dropped the Scott badly on one corner, and delayed somewhat in straightening out his machine, before he re-mounted and in a brilliant exhibition of skill and determination gave it the full works to overtake the Griffiths Sunbeam before the last lap.

One-mile sprint > 350cc
C (Cliff) James, Llanelly (Rex-Acme)
LV Thomas (Sunbeam)

one-mile sprint (unlimited)
LI Davies (HRD)
A Nicklin (Sunbeam)

---

[85] See *Motor Cycling*: Aug 11, 1955, 'Twenty years Early - A Double Knocker Special of 33 Years Ago' by John Griffith. Also *Motor Sport*: Jan 1976, 'The Sgoninas' by W(illiam) B(oddy).

[86] As late as 1954, the elder-statesman Sgonina was seen pointing a DB 2/4 Aston Martin up-hill at Lydstep, for fastest time in class, and doing battle on Fairwood Aerodrome with Colin Chapman (Lotus) and a youthful Peter Collins, also in an Aston, in the *Daily Telegraph* National Sports Car Race.

AUGUST, 1926

NOVICE CLASS

One-mile sprint > 350cc
W Tucker, Carmarthen (Raleigh)
- Hughes (New Imperial)

WELSH CHAMPIONSHIPS, 1926

25 miles > 350cc
LV Thomas (Sunbeam)
CL Kingston Newport (HRD)
- Case (AJS)

50 miles > unlimited
JE Kettle, Newport (Scott)
M Griffiths (Sunbeam)
- Griffiths (Norton)

LIGHT CARS

> £12 tax
Albert Henstock, Carmarthen (Rhodes Sports)

LV Thomas (Sunbeam 347cc ohv Sprint). [© *LV Thomas collection*]

August, 1926

The August Bank Holiday meeting in 1926 was held in what began as perfect weather conditions. The organisers were the West South Wales ACU, together with the Carmarthen and Neath clubs. A neap tide necessitated a two-hour break for lunch, between the Welsh Centre's events of the morning and the Open Championships of the afternoon. And no one complained. There was good racing in the morning but, as *The Motor Cycle* comments, somewhat disingenuously, 'nothing of a spectacular nature occurred'.[87]

---

[87] Reminiscent of the banner-headline: 'Small earthquake in Peru. Not many killed.'!

There was a Sunbeam/AJS scrap in the 350cc 10-mile race. C Bowles and F Carter went at it hammer-and-tongs, until the AJS succumbed and Bowles led the JAP-engined Zenith of TJ Phillips over the line, by some 80 yards.

Mostyn Griffiths (Sunbeam) gave RE Thomas, Gloag, (Brough Superior), a good run for his money in the unlimited 10-mile event. The Brough was all carefully protected with wire gauze against the flying sand and only managed a thirty-yard lead at the flag, against the Long-stroke Sunbeam which was never separated from the big V-twin by more than a few feet throughout.

A surprise thunder-shower did, however, mar the lunch-break somewhat, and wetted the sand enough to cause some eliminations and provoke 'interesting' cornering in the open championships:

> The 275 race was dull, but the 350 ten-mile event was ample compensation. JH Simpson, the well-known AJS rider, took the lead on the first lap, and had to fight hard to retain it; he was threatened all the time by LV Thomas (Sunbeam) whose lurid, but controlled skids provided a thrill on every lap. FW Dixon (Douglas) picked up very well, for after a slow start he finished third.[88]

The ten-mile race for machines not exceeding 560cc capacity lost a lot of starters. The Douglas of Anstice stopped out on the course and Dixon's similar machine after the turn was firing on only one cylinder. The Scottish Championship contender, Edward Mundey, brought his New Imperial in well ahead of VR McKenzie's Norton. Mckenzie, from Haverfordwest, was a noted rider and an engineer who knew how to cosset machinery. It was evidently a dull race, though, as there were the only two finishers.

There was more excitement in the series of one-mile sprints that followed, so much so that the crowd had to be restrained. A sign went up at the Start/Finish: 'No racing until the course is clear'. This was brought about by some very close racing between the Douglases of Anstice and Dixon, Simpson's AJS and the Scottish ace's New Imperial. Like heavyweights in the ring they slugged it out to finish on even points, neck-and-neck. Spectators were in an uproar. Marshals and police then engaged in crowd-control – and in the process arrested a pick-pocket!

There were nine starters for the 30-mile race. The Zenith rider, Alex Grey, led for the first four laps, to be passed on the fifth by Rees Thomas, Gloag, on the Brough Superior. The Brough had run out of brakes on the first lap, charging the crowd – luckily without incident. It was neck-and-neck thereafter until the Zenith gave out with a split tank. Thomas had made the error of starting with a half-full tank and so was obliged to pull in for fuel, allowing Dixon through with the Douglas, hotly pursued by E Mundey (New Hudson) and Mostyn Griffiths on The Sunbeam. Though Thomas came out again after refuelling, he was never again in contention, and retired with plug trouble. The result is given as:

---

[88] *The Motor Cycle:* Aug 5th, 1926.

30 miles: unlimited
F Dixon (Douglas)
E Mundey (New Hudson)
M Griffiths (Sunbeam)
Winner's time: 24m 19secs (74.0 mph).

There followed a ten-mile side-car race in which three-wheeler Morgan cars were eligible. RT Horton's Morgan led for two miles from Alex Grey, who had somehow cured his Zenith's split fuel tank. A private Douglas battle went on in the rear, between Anstice and Dixon. Dixon's cornering was apparently, once again, 'lurid' – if only judging from the agonised expression on the face of his suffering passenger!

WELSH CENTRE CLASS RESULTS.
(No distances given)
275cc
CF Edwards (New Imperial)
JE Davies (Cotton)

350cc
C Bowles (Sunbeam)
TJ Philips (Zenith)
M Isaac (Sunbeam)

NOVICE

500cc
D Ripps (Norton)
- Watkins (New Hudson)
- Price (Sunbeam)

unlimited >
RE Thomas, Gloag (Brough Superior)
M Griffiths (Sunbeam)

OPEN CHAMPIONSHIP

10 miles > 275cc
(DJ) Jones (Cotton)
(L) Davies (Levis)
CF Edwards (New Imperial)

10 miles > 350cc
JH Simpson (AJS)
LV Thomas (Sunbeam)
FW Dixon (Douglas)
Winner's time: 8m 31.2 secs (70.5 mph).

10 miles > 560cc
E Mundey (New Hudson)
VR McKenzie (Norton)
Winner's time: 8m 19.6 secs (72.1 mph).

10 miles: unlimited
RE Thomas (Brough Superior)
V Anstice (Douglas)
A Nicklin (Sunbeam)
Winner's time: 7mins 59secs (75.2 mph).

SPRINTS

One mile > 350cc
JH Simpson (AJS)
FW Dixon (Douglas)
C Bowles (Sunbeam)

one mile: unlimited
JH Simpson (AJS)
FW Dixon (Douglas)
E Mundey (New Hudson)

30 miles: unlimited
E Mundey (New Hudson)
M Griffiths (Sunbeam)
Winner's time: 24m 19 secs (74 mph).

SIDE-CARS

10 miles: unlimited
A Grey (Zenith)
RT Horton (Morgan)
V Anstice (Douglas)

Simpson had had one of his best days at Pendine, taking home with him some more prize-money – and the prospect of lovely silverware for his mantel-shelf.

RE Thomas, Glogue (Brough Superior). [© RE Thomas collection]

The 1926 August meeting was a three-day event. The 'Roaring Twenties' were at their height. Life was tremendous fun and Pendine was 'it': where the excitement was 'at'. The hats were small, the skirts short, the beads and cigarette-holders were long. Neath and District Motor Club were the organisers of the Welsh TT which was run on Tuesday, August 3rd. *Motor Cycling* maintains in its coverage that

> The Welsh TT now ranks as one of the most important events of the year, and the standard of racing witnessed at Pendine certainly justifies this position.

Attendance Estimates

The Welsh TT at Pendine had grown to a position unquestionably important within the context of the British motor racing calendar. So far as the Welsh sporting and social agenda was concerned there were very few events that attracted more enthusiasts and casual spectators – the National Eisteddfod, religious conventions and major agricultural shows excepted. Estimates vary. Exact figures are difficult to estimate, in the absence of 'turnstile' counts or pedestrian ticket sales. A close analysis from contemporary photographs is often revealing; and it should be possible to interpolate from their evidence attendance numbers at a given moment. But in a three-day event people came and went. Journalists when claiming, as they often did, 'Record Crowds Attend Welsh Speed Championships', are consistently shy about naming numbers – but it is thought (and can be seen) that crowds, varyingly appraised at between 3,000-5,000 daily, invariably turned out to watch *Rasus Pendein*, Pendine Races, in the years between 1905 and 1955.

There are other, anecdotal, estimates for the Welsh TT period that suggest figures of between 9,000 and 30,000. The previously-given lower figure is perhaps as conservative as the higher bracket probably tends towards exaggeration. Comparison with national sand-racing meetings in Scotland and England would, nevertheless, tend to temper this view. From the columns of 'The Blue 'un' and the 'Green 'un', it is seen that 40,000 is given as top crowd-size estimates for Redcar, Southport and St Andrews on different occasions in the twenties and thirties. No such figure is anywhere published as a claim for Pendine, but it has often been said that more turned out to witness a Welsh TT than attended a rugby football International at Swansea or Cardiff in the twenties which, if true, undoubtedly implies very large crowds at Pendine.[89]

---

[89] Attendance numbers are very difficult to estimate, especially as the August meeting was a three-day event, for which people camped out in the dunes. Some estimates of crowds in the region of 30,000 are impossible to corroborate. The largest single turnout in all probability was to see 'S Wood', in 1935, when it is thought there were in the region of 25,000 present. Many believed this to be the Pendine debut of 'the greatest TT rider of all', Stanley Woods, whereas it was, in fact, S 'Ginger' Wood, very much a top-flight rider in his own right. If many were disappointed, it could not have been by the exhibition this rider put up on the day. He won the four top-of-the-bill events. Some, like the *Western Mail* reporter, remained in ignorance! Crowds of 40,000 are reported on Saltburn sands at this time.

In the early days especially, when personal motorised transport ownership – a car or motor cycle – was the exception rather than the rule, it is fascinating to speculate how so many people managed to travel to Pendine. The nearest rail-head was St Clears. From there, the pedestrian method, the horse-and-cart, 'the chara' and the 'safety' bicycle were undoubtedly at the forefront. Then, when they arrived at Pendine, one wonders how race-goers were catered for and accommodated (not to mention the glaring absence of any 'facilities' – except for the sand-dunes!) Many camped out in tents in the dunes for several days, making a holiday of it. What misery it must have been on wet race-days (and they were frequent) without a vestige of shelter; and then to retrace one's steps, soaked to the skin and shivering, back over weary miles after a rained-on meeting.

It is equally hard for us now to appreciate the excitement that motor cycle racing's demonstration of sheer speed and raw energy represented in those days. Far-flung rural Wales in the 1920s was still largely a horse-drawn culture – where the passing of a car or a steam-roller was occasion for curiosity and comment. Motors were bound by a blanket 20-mph speed limit (until 1930), so to see motorbikes in close combat at 'sixty' – much less 'a hundred' must have been gloriously exciting – not to say alarming to some. The trek to Pendine was evidently worth it, for spectators in their thousands were undeterred by weather.

So far as the Welsh TT was concerned, it was easier of access than the Isle of Man TT – though to many, only just. Pendine advertised itself as 'The TT on the mainland' – probably to the annoyance of the Isle of Man authorities. Rail networks in Britain at this time were at their most extensive and efficient, but it was still a long walk from St Clears to the famous beach. Even via Laugharne Burrows it would represent a walk of six or seven miles to the top of the beach; and a further six for a glass of lemonade, a Vimto or a cup of tea at the Avola Tea Rooms or sarsaparilla at Rabaiotti's Welcome Cafe, by any route. Dr Lindsay had remarked in an after dinner speech that the GWR would need to think in terms of a branch line to Pendine. There was certainly a need. Every charabanc that could be mustered was requisitioned to supplement the regular connecting service from St Clears station to Pendine, via Laugharne. The most historic of these was known as 'the Dickie Lake', derived from an old Laugharne livery stables. It was run originally with horse-drawn brakes and, after the 'Fourteen-eighteen War', Tudor Williams of St Clears modernised it with Ford cars and charabancs. There was a rival service also, 'very prompt on time', operated by the Ebsworths of Marros.[90]

Another factor which made the Welsh TT an attraction over the Isle of Man was its compactness. Spectators saw the field go by every two or four minutes, depending on the length of course marked out for the day. And they could stroll around the paddock and see the bikes and their riders at close quarters. The Welsh, having a national predisposition for celebrity-watching, enjoyed rubbing shoulders with, and eavesdropping on, 'celebs'.

---

[90] Langdon, Carmarthen Library Sound Archive, 1977.

'Only last week he was in the paper'.

'Shorter than you'd think!'

They could see the look in the eyes of men who had broken records at Brooklands, gone faster than anyone had dared. Or perhaps come back from the Isle of Man TT where they had ridden to glory *on that actual machine*. You could touch it – admire the shine on the tank and the wear on the tyres. They could hear the sounds of fury and taste the smells of danger. They were heady days for all involved – riders, organisers and spectators. For two generations in the twentieth century, be they motor racing enthusiasts or not, mention of the name 'Pendine' conveyed excitement of a special sort.

Entry to the IoM Senior TT was confined to machines with engine capacity below 500cc, whereas the 'Pendine TT' was a usually a 'big bike' spectacle. Coventry Eagle, Douglas, Harley-Davidson, Indian, Zenith, McEvoy and Brough Superior machines were to be seen being put through their paces. Some of these had engine capacities of 1000cc and over, providing a challenge for full works-tuned, ex-IoM TT road-racers – from the thoroughbred stables of Sunbeam, AJS, Norton, Scott, New Imperial, HRD and others.

Brough Superior dominated the Unlimited category at Pendine for best part of a decade, from 1924 onwards – winning the Welsh TT successively in 1924, 1925, 1926 and 1927, with CM Needham, George Patchett and then Tommy Spann, in the saddle. JH Carr then picked up the Brough baton to win the Welsh Hundred twice in succession before 1933. George Brough placed tremendous importance on publicity. In the absence of IoM TT participation, Welsh TT/Hundred successes at Pendine were the highest equivalent achievement available to him. Flat-out record-breaking successes at Brooklands or Arpajon were all very well. They sent out different messages to the potential customer. Staying ahead of the field for the duration in the cut-and-thrust of a 100-mile TT was beyond dispute, even on the rippled beach. Could this Superiority on sand, perhaps, have persuaded as discriminating a customer as Lawrence of Arabia to buy the first of his seven Broughs! We know that he came down to Pendine to watch his beloved marque performing there in anger.[91]

The fifty-mile race in 1926, which preceded the Welsh TT, was over a two-mile course. The sand was in perfect condition. Within the 350cc category was run simultaneously a 250cc class which only attracted three entries, one of these, CF Edwards, had bad luck on the start-line, oiling-up a plug. It took him a lap and a half to sort it out. The field got away without him, Freddie Dixon taking the lead on the Douglas, hotly pursued by George Rowley (AJS). These two duelled for ten laps, until Rowley, to everyone's surprise, stole past on cornering and held that position until the flag. F Carter, on an AJS, had provided as much of a spectacle as the leaders in trying to keep pace with TJ Phillips who was lying third on a Zenith, challenged on and off by Jack Thomas's AJS. Carter's footwork on the corners was all that kept him from certain fall.

---

[91]See note on JH Carr 1932/3.

In the 250cc event, WB Davies's Cotton pulled in and did not re-start, letting CF Edwards into the remaining placing – second. Carter, third overall, after refuelling, had his carburettor fall off, so that Ed Mundey came up into third place on the New Hudson and Morris Isaac, who had not been going all that well, hit fourth place, with luck.

Welsh TT, 1926

One of the great advantages of Pendine, when the sand was in good condition, or indeed bad, was that the organisers could 'roll out' a completely new circuit at will, like a carpet, by moving the flags up or down the beach. For the hundred-mile TT, they chose a five-mile circuit higher up the sands. There were again classes within the race, and the roar of the 1,000ccs, above the 750s and the 500s at the start-line was quite awesome. The beach itself vibrated, undulated like a trampoline, under the riders' boots. Over twenty starters took the line. But there was serious criticism of the Neath club's race organisation on eight pretty major issues when *The Motor Cycle* was published a few days later:

> The 100-mile Welsh TT was staged immediately after the 50-mile event in the morning in spite of the fact that it had been generally announced for 2.30 pm; this change was responsible for at least one competitor failing to come to the line. Three classes – 1,000, 750cc and 500cc – were run together, which method, although two of the classes were small, made the race very difficult to follow; moreover, there was no lap scoring for the benefit of the spectators. Further, to cause confusion, there were also several competitors not named in the programme, and others with numbers which did not agree with the programme. Then several competitors were down to ride both 500cc and 750cc machines, and there was no way of discovering which race they were in. No 'official' times were taken. The race, including as it did many famous names, was worthy of better organisation.

There was not much doubt as to who was the favourite. Tommy Spann was round and up the shoreline like an arrow with the 110mph works SS100, pursued by Rees Thomas, Gloag, also on a Brough Superior – 'winner of 20 firsts and fastest time of day at Oxwich and Pendine'. In third place, and leading the 500s, was Jimmie Simpson on the AJS. In close-formation behind, lay Joe Craig (Norton), Freddie Dixon (Douglas)[DD 9854], and Tommy Simister (Triumph). William-George Patchett's mount on this outing was the big Zenith, in place of his McEvoy. He was out at the end of the first lap, as was Rees Thomas who, in trying to pass Spann, over-revved the Brough, seizing the front cylinder and causing the con-rod to breach a large hole in the crank-case. Simpson, who was also trying hard, got by Spann who, for the while, was happy to cruise along in his wake. In third and fourth places were the two works Douglases of Dixon and Anstice. The highest placed privateer remaining on lap three was the Cirencester man, WG Freeguard, on a Scott. He entered the corner too fast and came off, as did Alex Grey on his Norton. Both Freeguard and Grey restarted and got away again.

Spann overhauled Simpson on the tenth lap, the halfway mark. His time for the first 50 miles was 37mins 50secs (66.66 mph). The Scott of Alex Thom was in trouble with its gear-linkage. Freddie Dixon, wearing a broad grin, was putting on an exhibition of wild cornering. Anstice had passed Simpson into second place. Simpson retired on lap 15, giving George Dance second place. When Anstice also went out – with a seized clutch – Boobyear was in the act of catching up to take third place, leading a pack of Nortons. The other Norton men were AV Clarke, LF Griffiths and Alex Grey. Jack David was seen coming round with only half a Sunbeam handle-bar. But it was Leslie Griffiths who urged his Norton forward into third place before the flag. His had been a splendidly consistent ride for this young Bridgend man, destined in future for the kind of local celebrity accorded to the truly dedicated amateur.

Joe Craig

Joe Craig, an Ulsterman, on one of the Norton factory's none-too-successful Walter Moore-designed, overhead-valve push-rod engined 500s, was recently back from what he accounted the toughest race he had ever run in – Solitude, over the hills of the Black Forest. A combination of rain, mist and algal moss on the road landed him in hospital. His record avowed that he had won the Senior Manx Grand Prix on a side-valve 16H Norton in 1923, and the 600cc class in the Ulster that same year on a Model 18. He repeated the performance in the Ulster in 1924. This day at Pendine was not his. Perhaps he was not fully recovered. Not really considered a good rider (and reputedly a terrible driver!), Craig was shortly to be appointed competitions manager at Nortons. He was said to be a foul-mouthed martinet in the workplace, and though completely self-taught in engineering theory and practice, Joe was to supervise Norton's Everest climb to fame. This, with others, he achieved by means of the amazing overhead-cam engine after 1928 and, in the early fifties, the McCandless Featherbed frame and the 'Double-knocker' Manx racing engine.[92]

The reason for Dixon's 'sandboy' grin became clear only at the end: he had been canny enough to have entered the 496cc Douglas for the 750cc and the 500cc events. So, he walked off with both awards! This was typical of Dixon, who was 'always up to sommat'.[93] His puckish face told the story of a delightfully impish character.

WELSH TT, 1926

100 miles: unlimited
T Spann (Brough Superior)

100 miles > 750cc
F Dixon (Douglas)
A Thom (Scott)
HG Freeguard (Scott)

---

[92]Few realise that this engine (x4), developed by Norton engineer, Leo Kuzmicki with Francis Beart, was the basis of the successful Formula One Vanwall racing car which was the first British car to win a World Championship British Grand Prix (T Brooks/S Moss, 1957).

[93]FW Dixon's maxim, confronted with something that interested him, was 'Sommat to learn 'ere, lad!'

100 miles > 500cc
F Dixon (Douglas)
LF Griffiths (Norton)
A Grey (Norton)

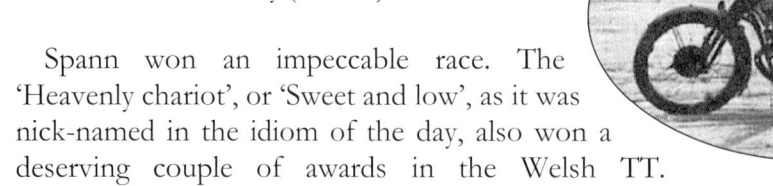

Spann won an impeccable race. The 'Heavenly chariot', or 'Sweet and low', as it was nick-named in the idiom of the day, also won a deserving couple of awards in the Welsh TT. And Dixon was to drive 'the boxer' home to his advantage in the Sidecar TT, the following day.

Wednesday morning saw the staging of The Welsh Sidecar TT event. The sensation of the day was that Parker (Douglas) took a lady passenger out for ballast. 'This was a novelty', asserts *Motor Cycling*, 'and caused quite a sensation – even a glow of pride – amongst members of her own sex, who were there'. The race was won by Dixon, by a clear lap, 'with the ease and skill of a born rider'. His passenger performed impeccably on his famous 'banking' sidecar outfit.[94] CF Edwards's Brough combination came in second. The third-placed Zenith did very well, considering they burst a tyre on the ninth lap and went in for a replacement, which Patchett provided

---
[94]On permanent display in the Montague Motor Museum, Beaulieu.

George Brough, Tommy Spann and Freddie Dixon, 1926. [*Morton's Motor Cycle Media*]

in inimitable fashion, in seconds flat. Boobyer, with the Norton outfit [NY5793], came in second to Philips's Zenith in the 500cc class.

Freddie Dixon had a special liking for sidecar racing. The principle of his banking sidecar was that the 'chair' was passenger controlled. He (or she) could, to a certain extent, counter centrifugal force by altering its centre of gravity by means of two levers connected to the axle. The idea worked well. It is strange that the patent was never further developed. His famous victory in 1923 notwithstanding, Dixon had been out in the Isle of Man for the Sidecar TTs of 1924 and 1925, but had had to content himself merely with fastest lap on both occasions.

The organisers came in for some criticism again. This time for staging this particular event on the Wednesday morning, as it made difficulties for competitors and spectators alike. *Motor Cycling* also suggested that crowd control left quite a lot to be desired, leaving the Neath and District Motor Club and the West South Wales Centre with food for thought.

WELSH SIDECAR TT, 1926

50 miles: unlimited
F Dixon (Douglas)
CF Edwards (Brough Superior)
TJ Phillips (Zenith)
A Boobyer (Norton)

The World Land Speed Record

Malcolm Campbell (3): 174.8 mph

In the dying days of the old year, 1926, Campbell was down at Pendine with his brand-new Napier-Campbell, Blue Bird. If Babs, at 35 cwt, had a tendency to sink into the sand, the new Blue Bird, weighing-in at over 3 tons, needed sheet-steel duckboards to keep her from self-interment. She was as beautiful to look at as poor Babs was ungainly. The Napier was strong-looking and purposeful – with a simple, graceful, 'designed' line.

In battered pork-pie hat and belted leather coat, 'Tommy' Thomas was at Pendine to see the Napier perform. Perhaps he had motored down in the Invicta that he had on trial. But the day was to prove a disappointment. From the moment the twelve cylinders of the tuned aero engine exploded alive at the bottom of the ramp onto the beach, the agonised rasp of unmeshed cogs refusing the selectors grated on everyone's ears. All was far from well within the gearbox. Top gear could not be engaged at all. Campbell and Thomas discussed what should be done and, though Villa[95] and his mechanics worked all night in the garage of the Beach Hotel, by morning it was clear that they had a major engineering problem which could only be solved with equipment back at base. And so, ignominiously, Campbell's shiny new toy had to be loaded back on to its transporter and carried back to Povey Cross – without even having got its feet wet.

Three weeks later Malcolm Campbell was back, and conditions were again unsuited to his purpose. Rivulets and pools of standing water added to the hazards of soft-sand patches. The beach was flailed by blustery squalls. Nevertheless, as the course was ready and marked out, Campbell wanted to 'have a go – to see what she would do'. The answer was – just marginally better than Babs. In one direction only, the new Blue Bird achieved 172.869 mph over the mile. And so the record stayed with Babs. Campbell says he saw 176 mph on his speedometer, but at that pace he would have, more than occasionally, been air-borne and inducing wheel-spin. He did not attempt a return record run, satisfied that the car was in good heart and that, in favourable conditions, he would be looking at three-miles-a-minute. Neap tides precluded any further attempts on the beach for a week or so. The Campbell entourage returned to base for some final adjustments before the assault.

The WLSR 'race' was now very seriously 'on', for Segrave's twin-engined 1,000 hp 'juggernaut' Sunbeam car, 'The Slug', and back-up team were ready – and would soon be on the high seas, bound for Daytona Beach in Florida. Accord had been arrived at between Europe and America on World Landspeed Record ground rules. By America's joining the International Association of Recognised Automobile Clubs, World Land Speed Records would henceforth be acknowledged on both sides of the Atlantic. Daytona beach was more than twice as long as Pendine.

John Godfrey Parry Thomas knew that if Malcolm Campbell was able to beat Babs's 1926 WLSR, it would not be by very much. However alluring she looked, and

---

[95] Leo Villa: vide 'Life with the Speed King' (Marshall, Harris and Baldwin, 1977).

even though she'd cost ten times as much as Babs, Blue Bird with 400 hp and a dry weight of three tons was still out-classed by Babs's power-to-weight ratio of 300 bhp-per-ton[96]. Babs on form could certainly achieve the 180 mph goal; at a stretch, possibly even approach 200. But 200 mph was probably, and realistically, outside Pendine's and Babs's safety parameters. Babs had been accorded a lot of detailed attention over the winter months. A new induction system seemed to cure the misfire problem. A shaft-drive transmission was considered, and then rejected, pro tem: Segrave's 1,000 hp Sunbeam had opted for chain drive. A sloping radiator presented a less wind-resistant profile. The suspension had been modified to give Babs a lower centre of gravity. An aluminium streamline fairing was fabricated to cover the drive chains.

Blue Bird was on the beach on Friday, February 2nd, 1927. Campbell was eager, and 180 mph seemed to be within his grasp. But it was not to be. Gales blew every day and the beach was awash with water and debris carried in by the turbulent waves. Campbell waited many days, growing fat on the generous hospitality of the Ebsworth family, who ran the Beach Hotel. Hams hung from the ceiling of the kitchen, where liberal portions of ham-and-eggs restored the hungry, shivering helpers and calmed the frustrations of men in a hurry. Campbell wrote[97]:

---

[96] Babs's Liberty engine was being prepared at the Hermitage workshop to produce 600 bhp. *The Brooklands Gazette*, April 1925.
[97] *Speed on Wheels* (Sampson Low, 1949).

Day after day I tried for the record. Day after day I had to give up. But on firm stretches of sand *Blue Bird* behaved splendidly, and over one run I actually touched 171.3 mph. We tried again, and this time I came into the mile at fully 170 mph, when the car ran into another of those soft, wet patches of sand. Immediately it skidded sideways and slid off the course, travelling like that for about half a mile, chopping down one of the marker flag posts as it went. Fortunately I kept control, but the mishap ruined the effort.

For the next two weeks the state of the tide would not allow any further attempts. Then the weather became vile. We had to use a plough to cut furrows along the beach to drain the water away and secure something like a dry course when the water was out. At last a day came when the conditions improved. By this time I almost felt desperate as I started off.

The car accelerated marvellously. I soon knew that I was certainly travelling far faster than I had ever gone before. The wind pressure was tremendous, and the noise of the wind drowned all sound from the car itself. The sensation of speed was exhilarating, and during part of that run *Blue Bird* was actually travelling at 184 mph – just over three miles a minute, The speed recorded over the measured distance, however, was 179 mph. I still had the return trip to make to achieve the record.

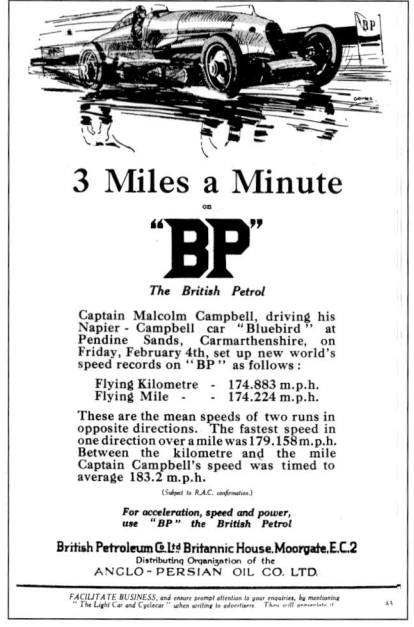

Everything went all right at the start of the return journey, and the car was doing 175 mph, when a sudden bump jerked me upward in the cockpit. My head was caught by the airstream, and my goggles were torn away; there was a furious rush of water and sand, which, of course, stung my eyes so that I was temporarily blinded. I had to take a hand from the wheel to clear them, but managed to keep my foot hard down on the throttle pedal, and by the greatest of good luck the machine remained straight, although a certain amount of speed was lost.

Campbell had averaged 174.2 mph for the mile and 174.8 for the kilometre. Blue Bird was now the fastest car in the world, having beaten Babs by 3.6 mph.

The World Land Speed Record

JG Parry Thomas (2): Poor Tommy, poor Babs

Tommy Parry Thomas was not unduly worried by this. In fact, he had calculated on a far greater margin from Campbell's attempt. The important challenge of a three-miles-a-minute-average still remained; and was there for the taking. Both he and Campbell knew it could only be a temporary glory, for once Segrave got his Sunbeam cracking on Daytona, he would soon make old Babs and new Blue Bird redundant. A lot of money in bonuses and prize money was hanging on this venture into the unknown. It was essential to bag this record. And quickly. Would Babs hold together? He had held some test runs on Brooklands, but was restricted to short bursts of a mile, as the track was under repair. The engine still was not running evenly. More time was needed. But there was no time left. A booking for February 14th at the Beach Hotel had been made, but a ferocious influenza epidemic was raging the land and Tommy caught it so badly he had to cancel Pendine at the last moment. News was that Segrave's passage on the *Berengaria* was booked for March 1st. So, new arrangements were hurriedly phoned through to Pendine for the 1st, 2nd and 3rd of March – when the tide would be right.

Babs was taken down to Pendine on a trailer, towed behind a lorry carrying all the paraphernalia that her master was used to assembling for the big event. Godfrey drove down in an open car, in the hope that the fresh air would blow away the vestiges of the 'flu that he just did not seem to be able to shake off. By the time he arrived at the Beach Hotel, he was frozen cold and shivering – and had very likely either excited a relapse or, worse, had given himself pneumonia. Unusually for him, he was not long before going to bed. In the middle of the night he called down for extra blankets.

The weather was poor the next day. He watched most of it from bed, or from the chair in his sitting-room. White horses cantered in from Carmarthen Bay. The sky loured. The usual entourage were keeping themselves warm and amused in the bar below: Col Lindsay Lloyd, the RAC time-keeper; Commander Mackenzie-Grieve

Babs on slipway, March, 1926.

who was *Chargé d'Affairs*. Reid Railton, Thomas's technical adviser, had arrived down, to observe. A Mr Buckley was present from Dunlop's and Shell's Mr Delacourt was there. Every time the sky brightened Tommy, looking grey and drawn, a big, fawn woolly-scarf round his neck and protecting his chest, walked the beach to assess conditions. But two days were irretrievably lost.

On Thursday, March 3rd, things were better. And Thursday, to a superstitious man, was a good day for breaking records. He would not make an attempt on a Friday. The course was prepared, and set. The 4½ litre Bentley of Major Callingham of Shell-Mex set off up the beach, as arranged, to let the time-keepers know that Thomas was in position and ready to make his first pass. Babs made a reasonably fast first run. Not fast enough to be challenging. When the car came to the turn, he stopped her for adjustments, as she was misfiring again and issuing black smoke through the exhaust. The KLG plugs were changed for new ones, and the screwdriver was applied to the four Zenith carburettors. A couple more runs were tried. The back off-side wheel was not right. The Dunlop men changed it.

Run three was 'up' the beach, east, away from the village. Callingham and Pullen, Thomas's mechanic, were spectating from the timing box at the westward end of the measured mile. Babs thundered past, going 'full-pelt'. As she disappeared in a cloud of sand and spray into the distance, Pullen saw suddenly 'an unusual amount of sand being thrown up. This amount increased'. The engine cut out. Babs was somersaulting. Momentous silence. They sped in the Bentley to the scene. It was three-quarters-of-a-mile away. There Babs had stopped. She was now bent, lop-sided: slewed around, facing the sea. A huge skid. A tyre and wheel-rim missing. Things on the sand. Gulls wheeling. Blood. Fire from the engine, near the petrol tank. Flames flashed up: and an awful tower of black smoke palled upwards, sizzling. Pullen ran,

Tragedy

selflessly, to the burning wreck and saw the most horrible sight. He turned off the petrol and snipped the ignition wires. The fire flashed and roared. With determined effort, he tried to pull his friend's big body from the inferno. It was trapped, the car had twisted. Terrific heat. Pullen was getting badly cooked in his struggle. Others arrived, with extinguishers, and together they succeeded. And laid him, his broken body, on the sand. Poor Tommy. Poor Babs.

The Inquest: the reported circumstances

At the inquest, the coroner, Rowland L Thomas, found that 'The late Mr Parry Thomas died as the result of wounds of (*sic*) the head, the result of a motor accident'.

The inquest was a farce. The cause of death, the sequence of the accident, had clearly not been adequately investigated, or identified. Harold Pullen and LG Callingham made the following statement(s) about the state of the car before the trials – when it was thought to be:

> in as good a condition as a mechanic could leave it... (Pullen)

and

> in such condition that was a fit and proper one by service, construction and attention for the test trials undertaken and was as sound as . . . [? breaks off]. I should like to say that Mr Thomas was fit and well on the morning of the tragedy, and I have never seen him in better spirits. I want to place it on record that the Royal Automobile Club asked me to explain the technical condition leading to the accident. (Callingham)

Reid Railton added his endorsement to the above statements 'as to the general condition of the car'.

The cause of the accident will never now be known: nor in a sense does it matter. No amount of investigation will bring back the man *The Motor*, in Shakesperian tones, acknowledged as

> A great good-hearted fellow and withall a man who knew how to take defeat equally as well as victory, JG Parry Thomas, the best-known and most popular of all British racing drivers.

Theories about the cause of the catastrophe will continue to exercise and provide chatter for 'motorists' for generations to come. Factors that needed investigation at the time, though, for the future safety of others, include:

Wheel balancing was a practically unknown science in 1927. The effect, at 180 mph, of unbalanced and flexible spoke-wire wheels revolving at somewhere in the region of 2,000 rpm would be to create a tremendous amount of vibration and some distortion – sufficient to shed a tyre.[98] Vibration, combined with the flexing of tyres, air-borne at intervals, then grounding with forces above 1½ tons while transmitting 400 – 450 hp, could provoke fatigue, leading to wheel disintegration or the bursting or shedding of a tyre. No one today would think of subjecting wire wheels to these loadings, in extreme conditions.

Babs was observed by Pullen and Callingham to swerve violently first of all, in the sequence of events leading up to Parry Thomas's death. A burst or thrown tyre would cause a violent skid.

Equally, a wheel breaking up and casting a spoke in between the drive-chain and the sprocket (a likely cause of breakage that could have resulted in the transmission chain throwing), would result in a 'snatch' that also could well excite a skid. Protective discs, intended as streamlining, were fitted to both inside and outside rims of Babs's front wheels, but only to the outer rims of the rear wheels. Reid Railton's observation (not mentioned in the inquest) that the perfect-fit groove of a harder metal wheel-spoke was in evidence on the tooth of a sprocket, pointed to a wheel disintegration *before* the chain severed. Whether this was before the commencement of the skid, or after, we will never know.

Dr Alexander Lindsay, the Medical officer in attendance, submitted that sherds of Thomas's skull were deposited on the sand in the vicinity of the commencement of the skid – indicating that the driver's head had struck against something early in the accident.

To have suggested wheel or tyre deficiencies as a possible cause of the tragedy at the inquest would have implicated Rudge-Whitworth or Dunlops, who had just changed that particular wheel and/or tyre on the turn before the fatal run.

---

[98]The wheel distortion often visible in contemporary photographs derives from the bending of light rays within the camera.

ACCIDENT CAUSES

Handling and stability: There are always stability problems attached to driving vehicles at high speed on sand. Some racing drivers, even of the first division, can not tolerate the feeling that a speed-wobble always seems imminent. Thomas himself was to experience high-speed skids on the beach, as did Campbell, Foresti and, later, Bob Berry. When Thomas took delivery of the Higham Special, the first modification was to replace the front axle with one he had brought from Leylands. He also moved the engine back in the chassis, in order to correct a handling problem. In 1926, during a practice run, he experienced a speed wobble that developed into a severe skid, induced by a soft patch. He managed, by sheer driving ability, to control it. The narrow, practically treadless, tyres gave very little in the way of tractional stability. With so much power being laid down, wheel-spin in response to throttle application was almost perpetual; so it was not an option to 'power' out of a wobble or a skid. Added to this was a tendency for the tyres' tread to narrow under centrifugal force to a V-profile, resulting in contact of as little as an inch, critically reducing traction.[99]

In the winter of 1926/7 Parry Thomas again altered the suspension, lowering it – and the car's centre of gravity, indicating that he was still concerned about handling and stability. Babs, on Thursday, March 3rd, 1927, had on board ballast of two-and-a-half hundredweight of lead, contained in two cylinders, one fitted transversely in the back of the car and the other carried in a box in the 'passenger' side. The vehicle had not been properly tested with these makeshift modifications in place, either on Brooklands or on the beach.

It is worth noting a theory put forward by Alvis designer Captain Smith-Clarke a year later when an application for a record attempt on Pendine was refused by the RAC. His observations were in respect of two accidents in Landspeed Record-breaking attempts on sand – one of them, Lockhart's, fatal – that had occurred at a later date than Thomas's, at speeds approaching 200 mph. Foresti's Djelmo came to grief in similar circumstances

> The design and weight of Lockhart's car were such that 200 mph was a critical speed for the suspension, so that the slightest shock would set up wheel tramp – that extraordinary phenomenon which may be described as criss-cross vibration of the axles, causing the wheels to move up and down alternately, leaving the road in severe circumstances. This tramping is usually associated with high-speed wheel shimmy, but may occur independently.
>
> [This] is confirmed by the report of an eye-witness who saw Lockhart's accident at close quarters. This witness said that the car sped towards him as steadily as an arrow, running perfectly and accelerating, with every detail clearly defined. Suddenly it appeared blurred and commenced to behave like an elephant with rolling gait; in his own words 'the car seemed to walk in a fashion horrible to witness instead of rolling along'. When the 'walk' became sufficiently violent, the car rolled over.
>
> This witness stated that an examination of the tracks on the sands showed that the near-side and the off-side wheels had been alternately leaving the track in giant strides

---

[99] Dunlops' advice to Bob Berry, 1959.

of 30 ft or so, making the car completely uncontrollable. It seems that in order to be certain of raising the critical tramping speed above the maximum speed of which a record-breaking car is capable it is essential that the total weight should be very considerable; witness the fact that the cars which were most steady at 200 mph were also the heaviest – Segrave's Sunbeam and Keech's Triplex.[100]

This tendency may be related to, or could be exacerbated by

Gyroscopic imbalance: It is not clear at what speed the Liberty engine was turning over during the heat of the record attempt, or whether Thomas had ever run her flat out. It is a principle of mechanics that the torque-effect of a high-powered, even low-revving, engine is akin to that of a gyroscope, which is to say capable of tilting the unit over in a twisting motion on its mountings, perhaps causing the chassis to bend, but in any event inclining the vehicle to instability. This tendency could fail to show up in testing where revs above a certain critical figure had not been experienced. Such higher-than-experience revs could occur on full-throttle in a wheel-spin event after an undulation, when the load was suddenly released as the vehicle became momentarily air-borne. Campbell makes reference to this gyroscopic phenomenon as being something he was beginning to learn, and to guard against.

Streamlining and aerodynamics: As speeds in excess of 150mph were not common experience in 1926/7 – encountered on a handful of occasions for a matter of seconds only by a few racing drivers and some adventurous aviators – the implications of wind-force on a moving vehicle had not been considered scientifically, beyond 'streamlining' to reduce resistance and increase speed. The 'lift' effect that leads to the 'take-off' of an aircraft at a critical speed was well enough known in avionics, but its counter-application in high-speed car design to aid stability was at that time nowhere in evidence. And it would be quite some while before the science of aerodynamics was required to be applied in motor car and motor cycle design.[101] The weight factor in 1927 was believed to be a sufficiently stabilising element.

Misfiring and black smoke: The 'engineers' in their submission to the inquest maintained that the stricken car 'was a fit and proper one by service, construction and attention for the test trials undertaken and was as sound as ...(?)'. Babs was, in truth, mechanically as unsound as her driver was unwell. The somewhat arcane and vacuous language in which the statement is couched would seem deliberately not to make its meaning clear. The statement is not scientific. The phraseology would not have satisfied a court of law. One surmises that it could not have satisfied the RAC,

---

[100] 'What Killed Lockhart?' *The Motor,* May 22, 1928.
[101] The present author well remembers the tendency for his Porsche 911S (pre-1970) to run out of steering at 130+mph!

the supervising body. The obsequious words served a purpose: to bamboozle a 'country' coroner, amid the confusion and emotion in the aftermath of the occasion – especially when spiced with praise for the selfless heroics of Pullen, co-signatory of the statement.

Reference should have been made to the misfiring of the engine and the black smoke. The misfiring was not insignificant. It could have occasioned jolts and stresses on the transmission – specifically the chains – sufficient eventually to cause them failure.[102] This conspicuous fault was not disclosed. Coventry Chains were sponsors. Malfunctioning ignition could cause misfiring and result in smoke. The plugs were KLG.

Black smoke was an unhealthy sign. Any knowledgeable driver or engineer would hesitate to see driven at speed, much less at high-revs for sustained periods, an engine issuing smoke of any kind. Black smoke, in particular, is usually an indication of poorly-fitting piston rings or valve guides; sometimes over-rich induction or malfunctioning ignition. Oil that leaks through the valve-guides or piston rings burns. If the ignition timing is out and the carburation over-rich, unburnt fuel issues forth and explodes in the exhaust heat. When exhaust smoke occurs, it can be the warning signal for piston-failure, leading to engine-seizure. The pistons were supplied by Miralite and the rings by Wellworthy. JGP T had, it's true, modified the pistons. He was a highly-skilled engineer, not one to make elementary miscalculations. But the engine was not right. Far from it.

Health: There was a medical officer present, in case of mishap, but he was not directed to assess the medical condition of the driver before the event. There is very little doubt that JG Parry Thomas was medically unfit for the undertaking on March 3rd, 1927. The assertion made by Major AG Callingham, the Shell-Mex representative, in his statement to the Coroner's court, that Thomas, on the morning of 3rd of March, 'was fit and well and never in better spirits' cannot be taken seriously. Thomas was not himself on that day. Renowned for a gentle disposition, he was in a foul temper. He snapped at his mechanics and rejected a good-luck mascot from the little daughter of the Beach Hotel with 'I put not my faith in false gods', though he was especially patient with children. Callingham's health assessment of Thomas is unqualified lay comment, and not admissible. There is plenty of evidence to indicate that Thomas was quite seriously unwell. He was suffering a long-term and debilitating bout of a particularly virulent form of influenza that had developed into severe bronchitis. His doctor in Surrey had advised him 'to stay in bed for two more weeks'. Thomas knew, when he loaded up for the journey to Pendine on February 28th, that he was unfit to travel. By the time he reached Oxford he felt so unwell that he was in two minds about turning back or breaking his journey. He told a reporter:

---

[102] Owen Wynn-Owen, consulted on this technicality (15-vii-98) did not seem to think so.

> My doctors did not want me to take the risk, but I felt I must go down to get back that which I had lost. It was only after I had been driving a few miles that I realised how much the illness had undermined my health. I felt I should have to abandon the idea of reaching Pendine, and would have to stop at Oxford. I pushed on however and eventually completed the journey by nightfall.

A post-mortem examination would have revealed whether his illness was even more serious. He may have been concealing pneumonia or pleurisy. In that event, heart failure is an adjunct not uncommon, especially in circumstances of high stress. Tommy had experienced severe coughing fits at the Beach Hotel, such that Mrs Ebsworth had brought him hot milk at 4 am that morning. Had it happened that he had been overcome by a coughing convulsion at the wheel, it is quite feasible for him to have lost momentary control, so that the accident would have been consequential.[103]

Faced with a 'now or never' decision, Thomas, a man of fearless disposition, and feeling characteristically indestructible, had made the wrong decision. What is also obvious is that his state of health warped his judgement, for reasons that follow.

Financial pressures: Godfrey Parry Thomas was almost penniless when he died. Had he, as 'the best-known British racing driver of his generation' and a leading designer-constructor of his own marque, been active in the late twentieth century's racing circus, he would have been a tax-exile multi-millionaire. But as it was, he was under pressure and, though he had broken over a hundred records and won, in five years, a comparatively short racing career, at least 150 gold and silver trophies and had been placed 72 times in motor races – including 35 firsts and 20 second places – it was a hand-to-mouth existence, what would have been called in his native language: *'Dala llygoden a'i bwyta hi'*[104]. Motor racing, if not the sport of kings in 1927, was still a gentleman's sport: and gentlemen did not pay – or get paid. He knew that this was his last chance at the WLSR with Babs and on Pendine.

An inherently nice and decent man, Tommy did not like to let people down – the sponsors, his helpers and the press. From all angles he was 'a driven man'. Segrave would, for sure, pass the 180 mph target at the end of March, and probably even smash the two hundred barrier with The Slug on Daytona. And he, Thomas, would not be in a position to challenge after that, because it would mean a specially-commissioned and sponsored car to go on from there to 250, then 300 mph. It would mean 'cap-in-hand' sponsorship-seeking, competing in a world arena under the spotlight of publicity and dealing with big business. Not what he, at 42 years of age, wanted to do in life – or so it must have seemed to a sick man gazing out at grey skies from his chair in the Beach Hotel.

---

[103] Dr 'Sandy' Lindsay, medical practitioner son of Dr Alexander Lindsay, RAC official Medical Officer on duty at Pendine on 3rd of March, 1927, gives credence to this theory held by his late father.

[104] Like the owl, which he resembled, 'Catching a mouse and eating it'.

John Godfrey Parry Thomas has been badly served by time. Because of his shyness, his lack of glamour and Welsh birth, he has been side-lined in English motor racing history. The achievement of that 17.50 mph increment over Campbell's record was sufficient evidence of his pre-eminent ability. His death, and the manner of it, has become his fame. His life, and its example, should be better known. He deserves remembrance for his genius, his heroism and his humanity.

Two weeks after JG Parry Thomas's funeral, on the 29th March, 1927, Henry Segrave broke the World Land Speed Record on Daytona beach Florida, USA, at a speed of 203.79 mph for the measured mile:[105]

'Sic transit gloria mundi'

Whitsun 1927

McEvoy

At the Whitsun meet, 1927, for which there is no editorial coverage, apart from a *Carmarthen Journal* result report, we note the appearance of an exciting-to-look-at McEvoy. It is thought to have been an example powered by a V-twin, overhead-camshaft British Anzani engine, rather than the push-rod 988 or 998cc JAP[106]. McEvoy was short-lived as a make, owing to the tragic death in TT practice of its mentor and financial backer, Michael Birkin. Among the cognoscenti, the big racing Mac is still considered to possess one of the most purposefully simple and elegant lines in the history of racing motor cycle design. George Patchett believed sufficiently in McEvoys to leave Brough Superior and become their racing manager.

LV Thomas of Swansea was out, making a tremendous impression with the overhead-camshaft (74 x 81mm) 348cc KSS[107] Velocette, a cracking little machine that would evolve into the legendary KTT. 'LV T' was, within a year, to transfer his allegiance briefly back to his old Sunbeam and then on to an overhead-cam Norton.

Camshafts and Velocettes

It will forever be debated as to why the Velocette's record in The Pendine Book of Gold is written up so thin, considering its outstanding qualities as a light, fast, good-handling racing machine – and an exceptionally reliable one. Camshaft Velos were going great guns at a time when rival manufacturers were still experiencing mighty problems with plain overhead valve arrangement. In the early twenties, local boys Harry Church and 'D' Jones had some very solid successes with Velocettes in both 220cc (two-stroke) and 249cc (four-stroke) form. This elusive 'D Jones', to whose name an impressive record of successes on Pendine attaches, had some further first-

---

[105]'Thus pass the glories of the world'.
[106]Personal comment: M Griffiths/E Hughes c. 1957.
[107]'Kamshaft Special Sports' or 'TT' models.

LV Thomas (Norton ohv Model 18). [*MA Clare photo*]

place wins in 1933 in the 350cc class on a camshaft Velocette.[108] After LV T's brief fling in 1927/28, it had to wait until JD Daniels's brief sorties with the Mk V1 KTT in the late 'thirties and DD Snow's successes with the Mk V111 in the late 'forties and early 'fifties before the Velocette was again giving a proper account of itself on the sands.

Camshafts were becoming a main topic in 1927.

The limitations of side-valve and push-rod operated overhead-valve operating systems in racing motorcycle racing engines had long been recognised. Above a certain engine speed push-rods have a tendency to flex and distort under the hammer-action of cams and reciprocating springs. This results in a phenomenon known as 'valve-bounce' or 'float' at what is, *de facto,* maximum revs – where a loss of power occurs. In 1926, this could often mean that power would fall off as soon as 5,500 – 6,000 rpm were seen on the tachometer. When the camshaft is positioned above the piston/cylinder head in order for the cams to operate directly on the valve stems, then there should, in theory, be no such limitation. Certainly it facilitates the adoption of hemispherical heads for better valve configuration and breathing and results in higher engine speeds.

As far as the manufacturers were concerned, existing standard production engines – even those with the less-efficient side-valves – developed, in Rolls Royce's immortal phrase, 'adequate power' for a home-market where there was a 20mph

---

[108] There is also a 'DJ' Jones doing well at that time; it is not certain whether or not they are the same person.

blanket speed limit. Aero-engines and racing cars had long been using overhead cams in order to achieve better gas-flow, increased torque and power – and Grand Touring cars, built for Continental high-speed travel, were fast adopting the ohc arrangement.

It was also seen by the motor cycle manufacturers that racing success was highly persuasive in terms of sales. Following Velocette's lead, many of them reasoned that, in order to stay ahead of the game, they would pretty soon need to devise and adopt their own overhead-camshaft system to increase piston speed. Reliability was the problem. In their overhead camshaft development Sunbeams had not had very much success, nor AJS, nor indeed JA Prestwick – who were looking more at high-camshafts, in order to reduce push-rod inertia. Nortons had even been very slow even in changing over from side-valves to overhead! Blackburne had developed a camshaft engine alongside Velocette. So had Matchless. British Anzani, with aero-engine experience, were making strides with dependability. All overhead valve applications struck snags. Metals broke down when subjected to heat and impact pressure. Partly to do with fuel quality, burnt, bent, or worse, dropped exhaust valves were endemic. An added problem with the overhead camshaft configuration was that enclosure of the heavy gearing – necessary for proper lubrication – interfered with cooling. Motor cars had water-cooled engines. And then, the expense.

Peugeot had been early pioneers of ohc, though their cylinders had a tendency to crack in long-distance races. They had not advanced their technology much further in a decade until, as they saw it, metallurgy caught up. Peugeot's little single ohc engine was noticeably more successful in competition after 1923. It would be 1927 before Norton and AJS came out with their camshaft contenders.

When one thinks of Charles Sgonina and his solitary pioneering work in Llanishen, Cardiff, begun in 1921, admiration grows for his courage and imaginative genius.

Overhead camshaft machines, as represented by the Velocette of LV Thomas, Nick Carter's Matchless, EC Williams's McEvoy-Anzani and LF Griffiths's new CS1 Norton, demonstrated their superiority to the crowd at Pendine.

The story of the day, as reported, was as follows:

WELSH CHAMPIONSHIP

25 miles > 350cc
LV Thomas (Velocette)
Wm Edwards (New Imperial)
N Carter (Matchless)

One-mile sprint > 275cc
Wm Edwards (Dunelt)
ETM Stephens (Ariel)

one-mile sprint > 350cc
N Carter (Matchless)
LV Thomas (Velocette)
TJ Phillips (Zenith)

one-mile sprint: unlimited
AW Nicklin (Sunbeam)
A Grey (Norton)
EC Williams, Morriston (McEvoy-Anzani)

10-mile sprint > 350 (sv)
J Ll Jenkins (Douglas)

10-mile sprint > 350cc
SS Evans, Chepstow (Cotton)
Wm Edwards (New Imperial)
N Carter (Matchless)

10-mile sprint > 500cc
A Grey (Norton)
LF Griffiths (Norton)
EW Thomas (Norton)

10-mile sprint: unlimited
RE Thomas (Brough Superior)
LF Griffiths (Norton)
A Grey (Norton)

WELSH CHAMPIONSHIP, WHITSUN, 1927

50 miles > 500cc
N Carter (Matchless)
AR Boobyer, Pontypridd (Zenith)
LF Griffiths (Norton)

50 miles: unlimited
RE Thomas (Brough Superior)
N Carter (Matchless)
AR Boobyer (Zenith)

William 'Billy' Edwards

Billy Edwards of Towy Garage, at the age of 35, had ridden his last race on Pendine. He was one of the stalwarts, who had been involved from the veteran years with motor cycle sport in West Wales. His had been one of the first agencies in Carmarthen, after Bradbury Jones, when Humber, Verus and Omega had seemed like machines with a promising sporting future. Billy was one of a large family, born to railway ganger at Llety'r Giach, a little cottage on the banks of the Gwili, near Conwil Elfed, in 1892. He began work as a farm-servant. His interest in bicycles and his penchant for repairing them led to his opening a business, a bicycle shop, in Bridge Street, Carmarthen, before the First World War. He was one of the founder members of the Carmarthen Motor Cycle and Light Car Club, which really only came into its own after the war when it took serious cognisance of the potential within their patch, which was the beach at Pendine.

Wm Edwards (Omega).

Billy did not compete in the 1921 TT in Dr Lindsay's team, sponsored by the club, which comprised Norton riders, but he did ride a 'works' AJS at the Island, as a privateer.[109] He had the makings of a good rider. That same guile and determination which he demonstrated as a self-made businessman, exhibited itself when he was in the saddle!

---

[109] Lloyd Edwards (son), pers reminiscence, July, 1999.

August 1927

It was a star-studded August Bank Holiday meeting at Pendine in 1927, and packed with surprises. Tommy Spann, winner of the 1926 Welsh TT, was on the No 1 Brough SS100. Sporting Welsh dragons on the tank, Brough's sports-racing model was now christened the 'Pendine'.[110] Freddie Dixon, after his long association with Douglas, had moved on and thrown his weight in behind the HRD concern, being at the same time secured on retainers with George Brough Ltd and JA Prestwick engines. His friend from Douglas days, Clarry Wood, was back at Pendine with him to pilot the second JAP-engined HRD, the dedicated racing outfit of Howard Rees Davies, the brilliant ex-AJS TT-rider and development engineer. George Patchett was the McEvoy man; and Len Parker represented Douglas from the Kingswood, Bristol, works. Among the local celebrities was Rees E Thomas, Gloag, on his privately-owned Brough Superior; LV Thomas and LF Griffiths were both on privately-entered Nortons; E Gordon Bennett, the Gorseinon ironmonger and ACU committee man, was out on a Scott. George Gregor of Mumbles, heir to the Swansea Gregor Bros sawmill and timber business, and a very fine rider on grass and sand, was making his debut appearance on Pendine on a Rudge-Whitworth, which had four valves per cylinder and a four-speed gearbox. Nick Carter of Blaina was on the 350 'camshaft' Matchless, a rare and fast little machine. Carter was a crack rider. The scene was set for some great racing and a famous occasion.

The Bank Holiday Monday's racing conditions were far from ideal, with squally showers blowing in from the Bristol Channel. Nevertheless, there were some needle contests between supermen and machines from both Trade and Private categories. The West South Wales Centre ACU were the organising body and the morning began with a series of 10-mile events.

There was a splendid duel between a surprise late entry, Jimmie Guthrie's New Hudson, and the young LV Thomas's Velocette, in the 350cc event. The canny Welshman passed the flying Scot on the final straight, winning by a bare two yards. It was a white-knuckled race that had the huge crowd on their toes from the outset.

It was a rare occasion when a Triumph took the lead at Pendine, but in the 560cc class Tommy Simister, who had come third in the Senior IoM TT (65.75 mph), showed Dixon a clean pair of heels on the first lap, only to be out-ridden finally by Dixon who took the race, with team-mate Clarry Wood coming in third on the second of the HRDs.

In the 'big banger' event that followed, G-W Patchett's overhead camshaft McEvoy proved very fast in the opening laps, leading Tommy Spann and RE Thomas's Brough Superiors in no uncertain manner, until the dreaded seizure on lap three – a No 2 piston. Thomas, having hit a wet trough, had a spectacular crash – in which he was only bruised but his handlebars were broken. This left Spann well out in front, with the Triumph of Simister second and CP Wood third on the HRD.

---

[110] The 'Pendine' was first exhibited at the 1926 Olympia show with Welsh Dragon insignia on the tank.

LV Thomas's Velocette proved incredibly fast in the mile sprint, winning by over 50 yards from Dixon on the HRD and 70 yards ahead of Phillips on the Zenith. He must have been on rocket fuel!

It was not Dixon's, or HRD's, day. Pendine was often an unlucky place for him, as well as for Patchett. When Nicklin got past him on the Sunbeam in the 560 event, he had to content himself with, again, just out-classing Simister.

The Unlimited mile-sprint provided an exciting spectacle. Patchett, on the spare McEvoy, was astonished to find himself 30 yards behind the Brough of Dixon at the end of the mile: the Brough doing well over the ton in full-cry second gear. Nicklin was fortunate to come in third on the Sunbeam. He no doubt felt somewhat blown away!

This particular Brough of Dixon's, which had taken the 130 mph flying mile at Arpajon, is well described by Dennis May in *Pastmasters of Speed*:

> For students of this Golden Age of motorcycling, Dixon is associated with one particular Brough Superior, a bicycle of distinctive appearance, low in ground clearance and with a very long gear lever like a crusader's sword. Another feature was the steel-sheeted shroud over the carburation department: the JAP engine, which Fred had built with his own hands and also partly designed, used one carburettor per cylinder, an arrangement he was anxious to conceal from prying eyes. Leaving out the Douglas, which had had a carburettor per cylinder since the early twenties, this BS was, Fred believes, the first to employ the multi-gasworks principle, which subsequently formed the basis of all his better breathing essays on unsupercharged cars.

It must be remembered that, all jests and chicanery aside, 'FD' was a serious creative engineer. Fred was an 'ingénieur' in the first meaning of the word, ingenious and pragmatic – with machinery. The fact that he happened also to be a world-class driver was a lucky case of lightning striking twice. Natural charmer, George Brough was the marketing man: he was 'both showman and salesman'.[111] Fred was the engineer. The combination of Dixon and George was, potentially, a masterly creative association. It was to result in many historic innovations, among them, in years to come, the scarcely-realised four-cylinder Brough 'Golden Dream'.

In the 30-mile Unlimited, chain trouble cost Dixon success when he had the Brough well out in front. Simister seized the moment to put the Triumph in the lead only to be thwarted by engine failure on lap thirteen. Mainwaring took the healthy-sounding Scott up into first position on the leader-board, where it remained. SS Evans (Cotton) came in second and AM Harry (New Hudson) third.

In the sidecar event, the acceleration CF Edwards urged from his Brough was remarkable. No one could hold a light to him. Poor Patchett, trying his utmost, taking the final corner flat out, overturned – causing the whole outfit to fly into the air, catapulting his passenger as if from a mangonel. George-William was pretty much unhurt, but suffered mild concussion and memory loss at the scene, but was declared fighting fit again the following day.

---

[111] National Motor Cycle Museum, Solihull, publicity copy.

The Last Welsh TT, 1927

Tuesday was the day for the 1927 Welsh TT. George Brough was there; Connie, Mrs Brough, too. Expectation was running high. Brough Superiors had already won the Welsh TT three times in succession (Needham, Patchett, Spann); so could they achieve the seemingly impossible and make it four? There were those who were there determined to prevent them.

RE Thomas, Glogue

George Brough could afford to be relaxed. It did not matter to him who won – on a Brough! He had a long-standing relationship with RE Thomas, an important promoter of the marque in south and west Wales. His 'customer care' is demonstrated by the personal letter to Thomas (June 24th, 1926)[112] explaining in detail the settings for the machine the works had prepared for him. He adds words of caution about handling the clutch in particular.

> To: Messrs RE Thomas & Co, Ltd., Glogue.
> Dear Sirs,
> Your machine is leaving here on the midnight train to-night and I have personally been to the station to see that it is put into a straight through coach and it will arrive at Gloag Station tomorrow afternoon.
>
> With regard to the machine itself, she is in perfect condition and able to win anything which I am sure you will do when you get thoroughly used to the handling of her. If you will take careful note of the following remarks it will help you considerably.
>
> I have sent the machine equipped with K.L.G. 230 Sparking Plugs. These should be kept in and used in all your practice sprints, and the pair of 244 Plugs should only be put in immediately before the start of a race because they are apt to oil up very quickly. The Mechanical Oil Pump is set so as not to give too much Oil while practising and running comparatively slowly. For the mile sprint I would advise you to keep the Oil where it is, and providing the Engine is not smoking unduly at the start give her a pump by hand immediately before the fall of the flag. The same remarks apply for the 20 mile Race and do not forget to give her a pump at the end of the first mile. For the 20 Mile Race turn the Mechanical Pump Indicator half way between the on and off position so as to increase the supply of Oil through the Pump and at the end of every mile give an extra pump by hand. The fuel to be used is half Aviation Petrol and half Benzole. The biggest trouble likely to be on the 20 Mile Race like all other Machines, is the Clutch, and I strongly advise you to use this as little as ever possible. Brake well before the turns and go through Gears only using the Clutch the smallest amount possible on the bend itself. If you can manage without using the Clutch so much the better. By this I mean slipping the Clutch in second Gear instead of going into bottom. They are all brand new Plates in the Clutch, as these might take up be sure and check your Clutch lever to see that you have a certain amount of play, that is to be sure that

---

[112]Reproduced courtesy of Denzil Thomas (son), with original spelling and punctuation.

the Clutch Wire is not tight causing the plate to hold apart slightly. In getting off the mark for the mile sprint let her rev right up in second, that is to approximately 70 M.P.H. before changing into top gear.

You will of course take off your Silencers and Rear Mudguard and Carrier for the Racing. When you have got used to the handling of the Machine I do not think that anything in that part of the country will be able to live with you.

Please let me have a line saying how you get on, and wishing you the best of luck,
I am,
Yours sincerely,
Geo Brough.
NB. The machine is capable of a maximum speed of 115 M.P.H.

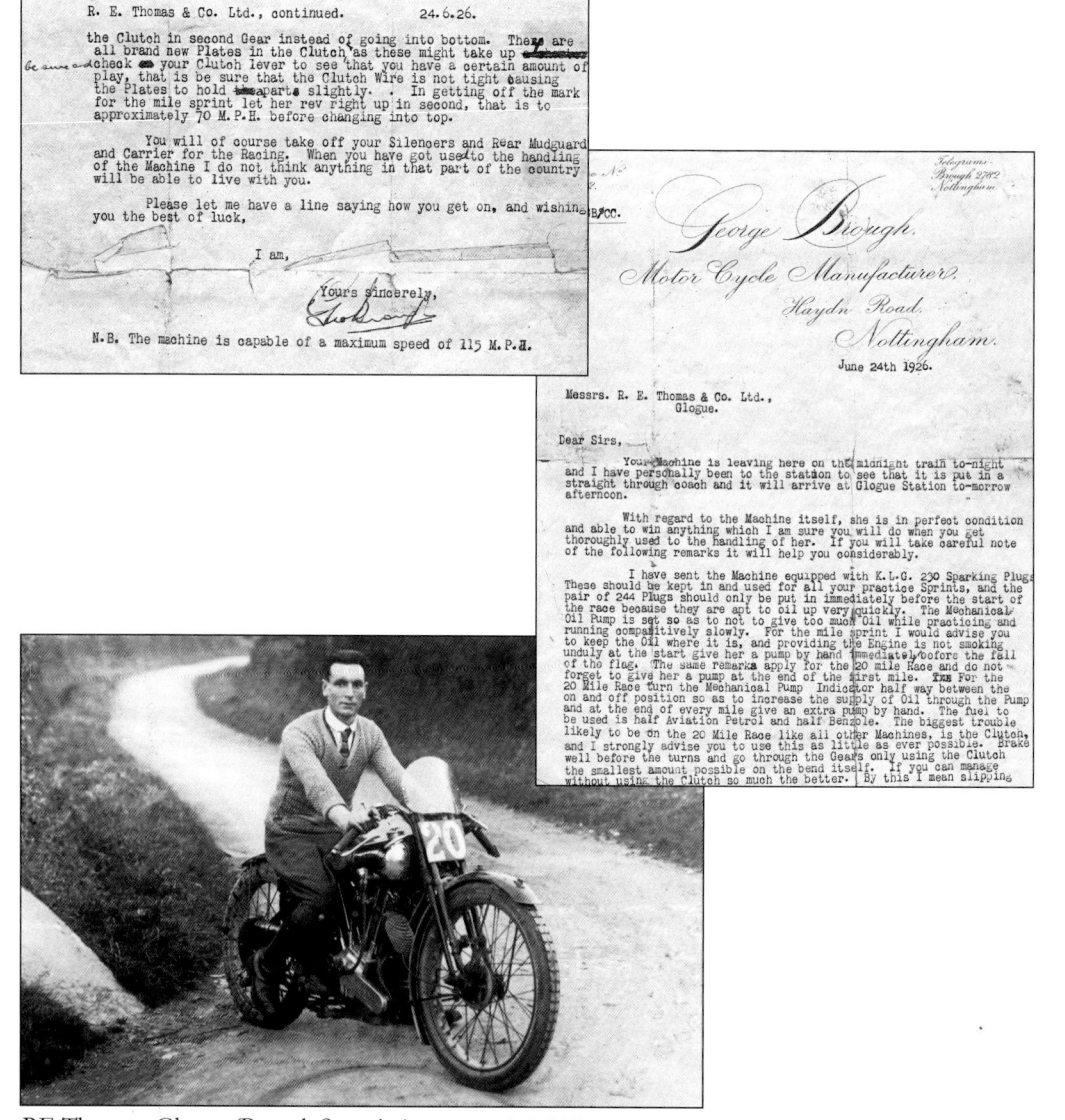

RE Thomas, Glogue (Brough Superior).   [© *RE Thomas collection*]

Jimmie Guthrie

The Motor Cycle (dated August 11th) is in jocular mode over the day's proceedings

> To the utter confusion of the pessimistic prophets the fine weather which prevailed on August Bank Holiday continued on Tuesday and Wednesday for the Welsh 'TT' races at Pendine. The receding tide left that wonderful stretch of sand absolutely flat, and the absence of any of the usual cross wind held promise of some fast speeds being attained.
>
> Rumour and counter rumour flickered about the beach as the size of the crowd grew, and some fabulous stories were related about the speeds attained by Dixon during the early hours of the morning in some practice laps. The fact that to have done any laps in the early morning would have necessitated a periscope being fitted to Dixon's HRD did not deter the rumour merchants!

The fifty-mile Junior (250s and 350s) race was run-off shortly after noon. Two lightweights were entered as against sixteen 'full-bores'. CJP Dodson, newly signed by Marston as works Sunbeam rider was, curiously, credited as a private entrant on the race-card. Jack David had his own Sunbeam. On Cottons were Alex Grey, WB Williams, SS Evans and CF Jayne. The lightweight Cotton-Blackburne of Williams having the new ohc engine, potentially very fast. Eddie Stephens and CF Carter were aboard New Imperials. Freddie Dixon and DG Brockington were on new HRDs: FD's being the official 'works' entry. Nick Carter fielded his ohc Matchless. LV Thomas was on the ohc Velocette, TJ Phillips on a Zenith, CL Pullman on a Rex-Acme and Jack Thomas, Neath, was the sole AJS rider.

J Guthrie

A late entry for Tuesday's proceedings was Jimmie Guthrie, at that time relatively unknown except to talent-spotters. He was, when word got round, a central attraction. The tough but personable young Scot, fresh from his electrifying circuits of the Isle of Man in the Senior TT (second at 66.8 mph) on the works New Hudson, was down with the great Bert Le Vack.[113]

The crowd were in for a treat – privileged to witness Guthrie's 'brilliant and unique method of cornering on sand'. As Le Vack said of him, 'He lays the thing practically on its side, then slams everything open and goes round in a complete slide, filling your face with flying sand.'[114]

Pendine witnessed some of the very best TT and International road-racers in action during the 'Golden Era', and it is difficult to single out who among them was the greatest. In all probability, Jimmie Guthrie would top any pole of road-racing legends seen performing there, even above Alec Bennett, Freddie Dixon, Charlie Dodson, Wal Handley, Jimmie Simpson and Herbert Le Vack. Although he had a

---

[113] H Le Vack (No 51) and J Guthrie's (No 52), names against New Hudson mount numbers, are uniquely hand-stamped - in violet ink - into the programme entry list for Tuesday, August 2nd, 1926 - indicating significant late-entries.

[114] Dennis May: 'Bert Le Vack', *Motor Cycling*, July 10th, 1958.

brief interlude with AJS, in 1930, when he won the Lightweight TT and a Junior in the German GP, Jimmie's remaining career was conducted on works Nortons – as No 2 to Stanley Woods and 'Crasher' White, and then as their No 1 rider, when Woods left Nortons and 'went European'. From 1934 until his tragic death in the German GP in 1937, Guthrie seemed to win every major event going. The list is long and impressive (26 TTs and GPs). He had several bad falls, but his sheer 'guts' and determination to win urged him back into the saddle. It is this quality of bravery combined with driving ability in the highest category, that was to make Jimmie Guthrie, 'the Hawick Express', a legend.

H Le Vack

Le Vack himself is considered by some to be the greatest racing motor cyclist of his generation. He was development engineer with JA Prestwich, and the history of motor cycle sport would have taken a different course in his absence. Undoubtedly, he was also among the best, most courageous, of 'speed-men'. He had earned his spurs at Brooklands and on the Island. When it came to breaking speed-records, Bert had columns in the record books. He was the 'brains' in matters of innovation, in engine and chassis tuning; and in detail preparation he was always the 'hands-on'

H Le Vack (New Hudson).

engineer. In this he was rivalled only by Freddie Dixon, and one thinks of George Dance and HR Davies, but he was somewhat in a different league from any other:

> His precision and exactitude as a fitter were, of course, proverbial, and as a fuel brewer he was on a shelf by himself. A substance called wood naphtha[115] (synonymous with methyl alcohol?) was the basis for Bert's dope formula... Le Vack was never a designer in the sense of translating his ideas on the drawing board, but his word was certainly law (at JAPs, New Hudson and Motosacoche) on the racing and development side.[116]

The new racing New Hudson was largely Le Vack's brain-child; together he and Guthrie were making a serious bid for sports-racing primacy. The Pendine trip was, presumably, a test-bed outing. Jimmie Guthrie, a star in the ascendant, was as determined to show off the TT New Hudson as was Freddie Dixon to demonstrate the potency of the HRD. Their ideals were curiously similar. A most intriguing contest was in prospect. The lap was a short-course mile in either direction. They were both in for an early shock.

Guthrie, another World War One despatch rider and an ex-KOSB hard man, set the pace from the beginning with a sensational getaway in the 10-mile race for 350s, pursued by Dixon who had LV Thomas's Velocette on his tail. On the second lap, 'by dint of superb cornering at impossible speeds, Thomas brought his Velocette into first place on the second lap and held it to the finish'.[117] Guthrie and Dixon continued to do battle, seemingly evenly-matched – Dixon preferring the wide sweep on corners, scattering the crowd, whilst Guthrie made it round in a series of powered skids. But, try as they would, they could not approach the flying Thomas, whose idiosyncratic cornering style, reminiscent of American or Australian dirt-track racing, was captured by the cartoonist Grimes.[118] Thomas was never less than 300 yards ahead of the field throughout. The crowd were agog at the battle for second place between the two IoM TT riders: but after one supreme effort to overhaul Dixon at half-way, Guthrie over-cooked the New Hudson and was out. It was lap 13, and an unlucky one for Alex Grey, too, who went out after having held a very steady and strategic fourth place. SS Evans then brought his Cotton-JAP into third place, as a result of several other retirements down the field. Eddie Stephens was unopposed at the end of the 250 class, and the roar of applause from the crowd for the local heroes, LV Thomas in particular, was tremendous. It had been a quite stunning ride.

The Titans were soon lining up for the superbike event. Dixon was in the Brough Superior camp for this one, fielding a prototype machine, shorter in the chassis and with a higher centre of gravity. He had his eye on George Patchett with the big McEvoy, whose avowed intent was to put a stop to the Broughs. Local Brough hero

---
[115] A product of the silver birch tree. There was a naphtha production industry in the Brechfa area of Carmarthenshire in the early decades of the 20th century.
[116] Dennis May: 'Bert Le Vack', *Motor Cycling*, July 10th, 1958.
[117] *Motor Cycling*.
[118] In *The Motor Cycle* (Aug 11th, 1927).

RE Thomas, Gloag, who, with twenty 'Firsts' to his credit, was after Spann's colours. Someone had to staunch the haemorrhage of trophies over the border! Thomas, alas, had to scratch at the very last moment, to the disappointment of the crowd. T Spann, aboard the other works SS100 was joint favourite.

T Spann

Tommy Spann had begun a distinguished racing career in 1923, when he entered the IoM Junior TT on a Dot. Later, he was to ride works Sunbeams, as well as Raleigh, New Imperial, AJS and Jawa machines. Pendine was one of his favourite and most successful venues. A keen Territorial Army man, he later served with distinction in the Second World War, rising to the rank of Colonel after tours in Africa, the Middle East and Germany. This all-round speed man is best remembered as a Brooklands record breaker and the only man to win the Welsh TT twice in succession.

It was one of the most distinguished fields that Pendine would ever witness. A third of the competitors were 'TT' or Brooklands heroes. George Dance was on a 493cc TT Sunbeam; Clarry Wood was engaged to ride for HRD: W Mewis, the Norton team man, was there; T Simister was with the Triumph works entry; Len Parker's was the solo Douglas contender; H Le Vack and Jimmie Guthrie were on their New Hudsons.

There was no works entry from Bradford. Scott was represented by privateer, Eddie Mainwaring of Keighley, Yorkshire, as well as by local entrants, E Gordon Bennett and DA Jones; EM Thomas was on a privately-entered McEvoy and A Boobyer on the big Zenith-JAP was another Brough challenger. Local combatants were LV Thomas and LF Griffiths on Nortons, Cyril Williams on an HRD and George Gregor and Mostyn Griffiths on Rudge-Whitworth machines. Alex Grey and Nick Carter were placing their faith in the 'camshaft' Matchless potency.

Patchett's McEvoy 'looked the business' as he got away from the dead start to establish a clear lead from Dixon and Spann at the end of the first 2½-mile straight. As early as lap two, the one-litre McEvoy was even beginning to overhaul those back-markers still on lap one. It was some machine; Patchett 'one hell of a rider!' Carter's Matchless, much to its credit, was leading the 500 bunch and the two Scotts of Mainwaring and Gordon Bennett had the leading Brough Superiors in their sights. Then Dixon's experimental mount proved a damp squib, as it groaned to a halt on lap two. The frame had not stood the test: the engine was trailing the ground. By now the 'Big Mac' was setting such a blistering pace that the anxious question on everyone's lips was 'Would it last?'

The answer came on lap four: sadly, no.

> A sensation was created in the third lap; the now familiar black jersey and yellow sleeves of Patchett was replaced in the lead by the wasp jersey of Spann, and E Mainwaring (Scott) had crept up to second place, with AV Carter (Sunbeam) lying a close third and leading the 500cc class. The news gradually leaked through that Patchett had had gearbox trouble and was almost out of the running.

From the fourth lap to the ninth the leaders were in that order, although LF Griffiths (Norton) constituted a continual threat to AV Carter; and CP Wood on a big HRD, gradually crept through the field and lay second to Mainwaring in the 750cc class.

On the tenth lap GW Patchett (McEvoy) came down the straight like a flash, nearly twenty miles behind the leaders and, cornering in a daring fashion, gave the spectators an unexpected thrill by fighting his machine in wonderful skid with the front wheel locked hard over. During the stop he had changed a complete clutch.[119]

Spann's, till then, had been the only 1,000cc machine left running – the Zenith having blown up as well. AV Carter (Sunbeam) was now second and E Mainwaring, on his works-prepared Scott, third. LF Griffiths was progressing smoothly at fourth. And, fifth – to everyone's astonishment was, none other than Fred Dixon – on an HRD! The wily old fox had entered an HRD with a 'nominee' for the 500cc class. He had stopped the nominated rider out on the course and taken command of his entry!

Spann was so well out in front that, even when he came in for fuel, he did not lose his lead. So he continued to circulate at around the 90 mph mark, apparently enjoying himself: the Brough gurgling contentedly. The scrap to watch was the Sunbeam and the Scott, vying for second place. Both makes had undergone detail design changes in recent years. Scotts now had a more conventional saddle-tank appearance, though they were still water-cooled and two-stroke-engined. Sunbeams were still dithering with push rods and side-valvers. E Mainwaring's Scott whirred past the Sunbeam on the half-way mark; a tussle that was to continue to the last.

A similar contest lower down the field was being staged by George Dance on his 'parallel' big Sunbeam, with W Mewis on a privately-entered CS1 Norton. They were lying ninth and tenth, respectively. Clarry Wood had put on his usual smooth performance. Having been up in third place, he had to content himself finally in bringing the HRD home sixth behind the camshaft Nortons of JK Gardner and LF Griffiths. LV Thomas was seventh on a Norton. In the Mainwaring-Carter duel, there was an unfortunate conclusion, as Carter, unwisely, took a signal from a spectator to mean he had one more lap to go, and so, in slowing as if for the corner, was beaten into second place by Mainwaring. Mainwaring thereby won the 750cc class and Carter the 500.

Towards the end, Spann had developed gearbox trouble and, thanks to the tremendous torque and flexibility of the 'KTOR' 998cc JAP engine, was able to take the corners in top, engaging George Brough in 'crescendo conversation' on the lower corner, a very sprightly George sprinting alongside him for fifty yards each time round! Tommy Spann won his second Welsh TT, and Brough's fourth consecutive Welsh TT.

Again Spann and Broughs made for home with the magnificent and coveted Welsh TT Trophy. It was never seen again, as that was an end on the the Welsh TT. It was also, if not the end of the glory days for Pendine Races, then 'the beginning of the end'. There was unpleasantness in store.

---

[119] *The Motor Cycle* August 11th, 1927.

Time and Tide.— PENDINE POSTURES.

Len Parker (Douglas) really gets down to it on corners.

Nick Carter, the Matchless rider, acts as a passenger in the big class.

Tommy Spann(ing) the oversize tank of his victorious Brough Superior.

The classic pose of T. J. Phillips (Norton) suggests a statuesque group for the Welsh T.T. Trophy.

Freddy Dixon (H.R.D.) quite unconcerned about what his back wheel is doing.

N. H. Buckley (Scott) and his passenger in their Turkish bath.

C. F. Edwards. Model by Brough. Paints by Parsons.

Patchett removes the deflated sidecar tyre from Alec Grey's Norton in one-fifth second.

Pessimistic friends bid good-bye to Patchett's passenger, Elvy Thomas.

OPEN EVENTS

10 miles > 275cc
ETM Stephens (New Imperial)
J Edwards (Stephens Special)

10 miles > 350cc
LV Thomas (Velocette)
J Guthrie, Hawick (New Hudson)

10 miles > 500cc
FW Dixon (HRD)
T Simister, Macclesfield (Triumph)
GE Gregor, Mumbles (Rudge)

10 miles: unlimited
T Spann, Didsbury (Brough Superior)
T Simister (Triumph)
CP Wood, Bradford (HRD)

One-mile sprint > 350cc
LV Thomas (Velocette)
FW Dixon (HRD)

one-mile sprint > 560cc
AW Nicklin (Sunbeam)
FW Dixon (HRD)
T Simister (Triumph)

one-mile sprint: unlimited
FW Dixon (Brough Superior)
T Spann (Brough Superior)
AW Nicklin (Sunbeam)

30-mile sprint: unlimited
E Norman, Manchester (Scott)
SS Evans (Cotton-JAP)
AM Harry, B'ham (New Hudson)

CLOSED EVENTS

10 miles > 275cc
ETM Stephens (New Imperial)
CF Edwards (New Imperial)
J Edwards (Stephens Special)

10 miles > 350cc
LV Thomas (Velocette)
C Bowles (Sunbeam)
TJ Phillips (Zenith)

10 miles > 560cc
N Carter (Matchless)
GE Gregor (Rudge)

10 miles: unlimited
A Williams, Killay (Douglas)
EW Thomas, Mumbles (Norton)
C Williams, Morriston (HRD)

WELSH TT, 1927

100 miles: unlimited
T Spann (Brough Superior)

100 miles > 750cc
E Mainwaring (Scott)

100 miles > 500cc
AV Carter (Sunbeam)
JK Gardner (Norton)
LF Griffiths (Norton)
CP Wood (HRD)
LV Thomas (Norton)

George Dance does not feature anywhere in the results. He was 34 years of age, still not too old for the cut-and-thrust, but the black-and-gold marque, to which he remained ever loyal, and which were now an ICI subsidiary, seemingly were. Sunbeams 'smoke-house' were still wrestling with overhead camshafts. As a centre of excellence and design, they had not kept apace. The once 'top people's' machine – beautifully engineered and finished – was now run-of-the-mill. It was George's last race on Pendine. The unchallengable sprint champion, he was soon to retire from racing to devote himself to the more-relaxing-on-the-nerves occupation of market-gardening.

In an amusing little article, written and illustrated by Leslie Grimes, an occasional contributor of cartoons to *The Motor Cycle,* the author/illustrator takes a trip to Pendine to experience the Welsh Sidecar TT, on Wednesday, Aug 3, 1927. His reference to a Ford-tonner-load of red ribbon is now obscure:

Time and Tide: An Appreciation of Pendine Sands and the Men who Race Upon Them.
Occasionally I 'hold things' for one of those fellows who throw things about, in return for which he breathes down my neck when I am sketching and talks compression ratios. So we said we'd do Pendine – he to race a bus or two and me to find passengers for him to use up.

He said I would find the boys a hard-riding crowd, who ride for the love of the sport, there being no bonii to speak of.

And so they were.

A private duel or a close finish is life's blood to them, and their cornering makes your heart two-stroke.

A very knowledgeable lot of spectators there are at Pendine, which is a bit out of the way; but a solid stream of motor cycles started at dawn and emptied itself onto the long stretch of sand.

What a spot for a holiday! Three days of racing, five miles of firm, flat sand, lovely country and living cheap!

Low cost of living
You can arrive there impromptu and pitch a tent among the sand dunes, or put up at a local inn in one of the outlying villages at a very low rate. We ourselves were agreeably surprised to find the charge for bed and beck stuff was only four and six a night.[120]

The staple diet of the Welsh seems to be ham and eggs – the ham very much salted; but the meals seem to be forgotten during the three day's racing. Licensing hours are – well, you soon find out or else you don't! Rain is the only trouble; it is always due for a Bank Holiday, but like the meals is also forgotten. As for the sand – give the old hogbus a real holiday next year. You can ride the machine at the maker's guaranteed speed all day, tide permitting. You can do skid-cornering all out, pick yourself up, and kick the bent bits straight – and blind away again.

It brings out a lot of the good points and faults of the bus. The most noticeable weakness would appear to be the silencer clips, and many a poor rider has had to ride with open exhausts, due to the silencer coming adrift. You find silencers all along the beach!

No objection to Noise.
As the few houses are all at one end of the course no objection is taken, so riders endure the noise in silence. Wire gauze over the carburettor and valve parts is advisable if you have got only one machine, and a bathing cap taped over the magneto is a necessity on damp days.

Of course, there isn't the Brighton touch about Pendine, so you can leave the dress suit out of your bag to make room for a spare piston and a few plugs. Evenings are usually spent putting the motor right, so time does not hang heavy.

Yes, it is the ideal holiday place for the motor cyclist!

---

[120] 22.5 p.

As for the racing it is easy to follow and exciting to watch, and cornering is super-lurid. The way they risk 'bending' the models and their own necks is hair-raising, and may we take to fishing or ludo if it ever ceases to thrill.

And what more thrilling sight than three or four sidecar 'thous' batting up the straight leaving braking to the last fifth of a second in the race for the corner flags! Something like the arrival of a covey of 15-inch shells all together. There is never a dull moment, between racing and, for the motor cycle sportsman, the sporting spirit rages all the time.

The leading man will blow up, and within a few moments will be urging or assisting the runner-up. A man will pull in and the cheering mob, having diagnosed the trouble before he stops, will put things right – quickly and methodically.

Quick filling is a fine art, two petrol cans going at once while someone examines and fills the oil tanks and lubricates the chains. Smart enough to please a track man out for records. All the while machines shriek by locking and unlocking, forks whipping and tyres juddering, riders lying flat out on their tanks, and passengers wiping their helmets in the sand. They have about as much care of their limbs as they have of – say – their language.

Quite refreshing is the way they take a lose, and quite unconcerned as to the ultimate placings or prizes. Every motor cyclist who goes to Pendine keeps a warm spot for these races, and joins the band of regulars. There is a disquieting rumour that certain brass hats are running a Ford tonner down next year, with a load of red ribbon.

Still, here's hoping.

New Hudson

Guthrie and Le Vack had had a disappointing outing on Pendine on the New Hudsons. But Pendine, even on a fine, dry day, was a very different experience from Brooklands or the Isle of Man. A make that was always in the running, New Hudson, a nice-looking and easy-handling marque, had a sports/racing image from which it tended to fall short in the ultimate trials.

Le Vack had taken charge of developing the 1926 racing programme. He probably did not allow enough time to get things in order for the IoM TT, as none of the NHs finished. Emphasis had been laid on brakes: 8-inch-diameter internal-expanding type were fitted to the front (foot-operated front and rear), alloy fins being sweated on to the drums. This was an innovation that would last until the adoption of disc brakes.

Early in 1927, having spent the winter eradicating faults, he took himself off to Brooklands. There he succeeded in being the first man to crack the 100mph lap on a 500cc machine – only just, at 100.01! Shortly afterwards, Guthrie did him proud by coming in second at 68.9mph in the IoM Senior. And another New Hudson came in seventh. With a bored-out 591cc engine, Bert Le Vack then won the 600cc class of the Brooklands 200-mile at 69.9mph. After that, New Hudson were never in serious contention. For one thing, they had no development left in their ohv engines to meet the superior power-output of overhead-cam units being fielded by AJS, Norton, Velocette and Matchless. Eddie Mundey and George Grinton campaigned New

Hudsons faithfully and with success, as did Swansea's George Gregor. AM Harry would be lucky enough to be awarded the Pendine Trophy for the Welsh 100-mile race in 1928, riding a 500. In the circumstances deserved but, without criticism, probably by default.

The Welsh TT side-car event was staged on Wednesday afternoon. There were twelve starters on the 'mile-up, mile-down' circuit. Freddie Dixon had borrowed some welding equipment from Gilbert, Ashwell Garage, and was back in business. There were two Brough Superior outfits on parade, apart from Freddie's; the formidable Brough 'chair-specialist' CF Edwards was on the line, squaring up against the inimitable Patchett and the McEvoy combination. A Boobyer was aboard the 500cc JAP-Zenith outfit; CP Wood – a private entrant – piloted the big HRD with sidecar, L Parker the works Douglas; TJ Phillips, GH Tucker and W Mewis were on the line with Nortons; Gordon Bennett and NH Buckley[121] turned out on Scotts; Alex Grey rode a Matchless, WJ Clifford an AJS and C Nicholson a Rudge. Altogether a record and colourful field.

CF Edwards

CF Edwards of Cirencester the side-car specialist was, not surprisingly, first away, followed by Patchett and Dixon, whose Brough Superior outfit was rumoured to be something of a secret weapon, but was a slower third into the top bend. Up there, Edwards's foot slipped off the brake, causing a 'moment' for his passenger and allowing Patchett through with a lead of 30 yards or so. Dixon was wearing the Pendine jinx again, for on lap three he had mechanical trouble and retired. Then Patchett broke a piston and his race was also run, leaving Edwards in the lead, followed by Len Parker (Douglas) and Clarence Wood (HRD). Wood's gear-lever came adrift at half-way and Buckley and Grey went out. This led to movement up the leader-board of local man, E Gordon Bennett (Scott), into third place, and the Zenith of Boobyer to fourth.

Edwards was next seen driving the Brough one-handed, as his handlebar had broken. It did not seem to have slowed him up any! In he went for fuel, and Parker occupied his place in the lead. But not for long, as Edwards was soon out, 'up and at him' and took him, single-handed, on the very next lap. He held and gradually increased his lead through to the finish. Only three others were left at the flag: Parker, Boobyer and Gordon Bennett. Bennett did well to bring the Scott home, as there was conspicuous clutch malodour around the outfit. Clutch failure was a bugbear of the Scott marque in sidecar racing.[122] It had been a bitter-sweet competition, but the Broughs had chalked up yet another TT win at Pendine. They, at least, were well pleased.

---

[121] Norman Buckley, Water Speed record-holder on Lake Windermere.
[122] Pers. comm. E Gordon Bennett via Dave James, Jan, 1999.

WELSH SIDECAR TT, 1927

50 miles: unlimited
CF Edwards (Brough Superior)
L Parker (Douglas)
A Boobyer (Zenith-JAP)
EG Bennett (Scott)

CF Edwards (Brough Superior).

George Brough

There was clearly a special relationship between Brough and Pendine. George Brough was a man ahead of his time in many ways. He had been brought up to a sound understanding of engineering principles, but what put him ahead in the game was that, better than anyone among his peers, he knew the importance of publicity and public relations. In that, he was a pioneer of modern marketing techniques. George knew there was a limit to the value, in terms of sales, of breaking flying kilometre and mile records at

Brooklands's arid concrete bowl. To the man-in-the street this was noteworthy, but distantly relevant – when he was officially confined to 20mph. What potential customers needed was to see and hear (and smell!) Broughs close-at-hand. The sight and sound of them competing was worth a million words in advertising copy! The way to promote them was at close-quarters, in familiar surroundings, matched against their rivals. Local and national hill-climbs were one such place. The Six Days Trial and other endurance events demonstrated dependability of one sort. The Isle of Man would have exhibited another, except that there were no classes for Brough Superiors in the IoM TT. Southport, St Andrews and Pendine were the only competition arenas with anything like equivalent status. At these sand occasions Broughs were exposed to dedicated public scrutiny for several days; and they could there demonstrate their genuine 'Superiority' before the press and many tens of thousands.

George Brough was the son of pioneer motor cycle and motor car manufacturer, William Edward Brough. The Brough Motor Cycle Company, founded in 1902, was a good deal better than a hundred or so other makers which bought-in components, designed their tank colophon, and went into business. Brough senior was an inventive engineer, capable of designing and building his own engines. He was at the luxury end of the market, and his manufacture and finish were to the very highest standards, so that comparisons with Rolls Royce were made long before the *sobriquet* was attached to his son's creations. It would somehow be more accurate to describe the Brough Superior as 'the Bentley of motor cycles'. Neither Rolls nor Royce were particularly concerned about out-and-out performance – unlike 'WO' and 'GB'.

Sons George and William had served meaningful apprenticeships at the little factory in Vernon Road, Bashford, Derbyshire: William in particular early proving himself a more-than-useful rider of his father's products. George and his brother entered their first motor cycle trial as schoolboys, in 1906, on dad's Broughs. William, on this, his first outing, the ACC End-to-End, won a gold medal. Young George came in three days behind the last man, having pedalled most of the way! But that experience he would put behind him, for in his career as a competition motor cyclist George Brough would win some 250 gold medals and over a hundred cups. He won the Scottish Six Days in 1912 with only one gear. Three years running, 1910-12, he won the London-Edinburgh-and-back Trial. On 'Old Bill', the original SS80, in 1923, he took 51 fastest-times in 52

Tommy Spann and the Broughs, 1927.

[*Morton's Motor Cycle Media*]

The SS100 'Pendine'.

outings. He won the Alpine Cup on the original SS100 and the Austrian 8-day trial, in 1925. And, as late as 1929, in his fortieth year, he would personally take fastest-time on Pendine.

Father Brough did not see eye-to-eye with his younger son in his ambition to build very high-performance luxury machines for a niche market. So, in 1919, George Brough set up on his own. 'I suppose', his father concluded, when George announced his first bike, 'that makes me Brough Inferior!'.

George Brough was an innovator, 'PR man' and a salesman, but his other great strength was as an organiser. Had he gone the whole-hog into show business, he would have been a great success as a film or theatre producer. When he bought or commissioned components from other manufacturers his criteria were very precise, his standards very high. Sturmey-Archer made special 120-ton steel gears for Brough. The engine manufacturers, JA Prestwich of Tottenham, grew to have the greatest respect for him. JAP engines were stamped: 'Special for Brough'. Many elements of JAP, MAG and Bar & Stroud engine design and innovation were at George Brough's instigation. Features we take for granted, such as the saddle tank, the fly-screen or twin headlights, were Brough innovations. The very concept of the superbike was a product of George's resolve and vision, and his determination continually to develop and refine potential, using customer and tester feed-back. This he did with intelligence and restraint.

'GB' was an assiduous correspondent and chatterer with his customers, all of whom relied upon him as a friend. He was in little doubt of his achievement: as he himself comments – 'There never was a masterpiece but that it was copiously copied ... the fact that (the Brough Superior) has been copied more than any other make of motor cycle is in itself significant'. He must have been thinking especially of Coventry Eagle, a blatant, cheaper imitation – and also of McEvoy.

The puzzle is that, with the high cost of all this painstaking attention to detail and a total manufacturing output of only 6,000 units or so, retailing at an average of £150, over the twenty years from 1920 to 1940, what it was that George, who lived in some style, did besides to earn a living! £45,000 p.a., as an average turnover, in the twenties and thirties, though, was a lot healthier than would seem to us to be the case. In fact, George died a wealthy man, leaving a net estate of £101,070-5-0d, at his death on 12th Jan, 1970. He specifically remembers thirty faithful employees in his will, some with shares in George Brough, Ltd, others with £50 legacies.[123]

Gilbert Davies, the Ashwell

An institution that had been growing up in the village of Pendine, in a quiet way, found fuller expression in the opening of the new Ashwell Garage in 1927, under the proprietorship of Mr Gilbert Davies. No study of the story of Pendine racing would be complete without paying tribute to the pivotal role played by 'Gilbert the Ashwell'. This well-loved character, remembered for his calm, unflappable manner, his enduring kindliness, his black funeral suit and wide-brimmed Homberg hat 'all oily',[124] was always available as a solution to all manner of problems, not all of them mechanical!

[123] Grant of Probate, Nottingham Dist. Prob. Register.
[124] Pers. reminiscences: Gordon Perrott, DD Snow, D Parkinson and countless others!

[Ashwell collection photo.]

Ashwell House, from which the business takes its name, still stands on the hill leading out of Pendine. It was in a little shed adjacent that Gilbert learned his trade as apprentice to his uncle. The larger premises with general shop attached which occupies a prime site next to the Spring Well Inn in the village centre, on the foreshore, was first port of call for the majority of riders and record-breakers on arrival at Pendine. Many would have been in touch by telephone before setting out from Middlesborough, Wakefield, Manchester or Weybridge, to know the state of the beach, the weather, the gossip.

The garage was always a hive of activity before and on race days. A great deal of 'borrowing' went on. Nothing was ever denied or too much trouble, even if it took all night. The tools that were lent – the screws, nuts, bolts given, the bits and pieces devised are without number. There was not much talk of coin! Gilbert enjoyed every minute of it. 'Come on now, boys!', he would summon heroes, nuisances and geniuses, at ten o' clock, 'I got a bed to go to. No more working on the bikes till morning!' And all the racers, their tools, spares and paraphernalia would be locked up for the night. (Enthusiasts and nostalgia addicts still come and stare into that corrugated Aladdin's cavern and dream about the treasures it secured, time out of mind). If there was a real problem, and someone – say – needed a gearbox stripped and rebuilt, Gilbert would 'hear the chimes at midnight' – and well beyond! He loved the whole circus, knew everybody, and kept wise counsel.

He died in 1976, aged 65.

Whitsun 1928

The Whitsun Welsh Speed Championships put on by the Carmarthen Motor Cycle and Light Car Club's annual Welsh Championship Speed Trials on the Beach at Pendine were run off on Monday, May 28th, 1928. There was a large turnout of spectators in the perfect weather conditions, though the entry was not so very well subscribed from Wales or from outside: 30 entries in total, was one of the lowest recorded.

The organising committee were: Judges – Messrs WC Davies, Wm Edwards and H Church. Chief Steward was Dr Alexander Lindsay; Chief Marshal, Mr G Sheehan; Clerk of the Course, Mr WA Thomas; Starter, Mr John Jenkins; Time-keeper, Mr W Williams; Competitors' Steward, Lieut EO Wanliss; Hon Gen Sec, MR D Prothero-Jones; Hon Treasurer, Mr GO Thomas; Hon competitors' secretary, Mr A Thomas.

The official results were as follows:

One-mile sprint > 350cc
SS Evans, Coleford (Cotton)
TJ Phillips, Port Talbot (Zenith)
C Williams, Morriston (AJS)

one-mile sprint > 500cc
A Grey (Norton)
LF Griffiths (Norton)
C Bowles, Morriston (Sunbeam)

one mile sprint: unlimited
RE Thomas (Brough Superior)
LF Griffiths (Norton)
A Grey (Matchless)

10 miles > 350 (sv)
J Ll Jenkins (Douglas)

10 miles > 350cc
SS Evans (Cotton)
GE Gregor (New Hudson)
TJ Phillips (Zenith)

10 miles > 500cc
GE Gregor (Rudge)
AM Harry, B'ham (New Hudson)
TJ Phillips, Port Talbot (Zenith)

10 miles: unlimited
LF Griffiths (Norton)
GE Gregor (Rudge)
A Grey (Norton)

WELSH CHAMPIONSHIPS, 1928

50 miles > 350cc
SS Evans (Cotton)
GE Gregor (New Hudson)
C Williams, Morriston (AJS)
Winner's time: 23mins 54 secs.

50 miles > 500cc
AM Harry (New Hudson)
ETM Stephens (Rudge)
RH Baker, Merthyr (Norton)

SIDECARS & THREE-WHEELERS

20 miles: unlimited
HJ Davies, Pontlliw (Brough Superior)

10 miles for light cars
RC Thomas P'pool Rd (Alvis)
H Richards, Cardiff (FIAT)
Dr Lindsay (Morris Oxford)
Winner's time: 13 mins 26 secs.

Entrants who do not feature in the final results were, as a matter of interest and record, PC Watkins, Ystrad (New Hudson); A Phillips, Carmarthen (Scott); AR Boobyer, Pontypridd (Norton); Cripps of Ammanford (Norton); CH Morris, Clydach (Norton); GV Cooper, Pontardawe (Sunbeam); AW Nicklin, Blaina (Sunbeam); Cliff Hughes, Llangennech (AJS); LW Norman, Cirencester (Cotton); J Thomas, Neath (AJS); G Mitcham, Tredegar (New Imperial); RI Davies, Tredegar (.?.); DP Wilkins, Edgbaston (Norton); JE Kettle, Bristol (Scott); DJ Jones, Swansea (Aero-Morgan); HC Lones (*sic*), West Hagley (Morgan).

The World Land Speed Record:

Guilio Foresti & Djelmo

Among the spectators at the Whitsun meet was a fairly long-term guest at the Beach Hotel. He was a charismatic character, familiar to village locals for his efforts at speaking Welsh and his atrocious distortions of the English language. The Italian, Grand Prix racing driver, Guilio Foresti, who drove Bugattis with some success, was 'waiting for parts' to repair his Land Speed Record car. The 10-litre Djelmo was a purpose-built challenger that had broken while undergoing trials.

In early July, it successfully ran at 120, 160 and 174 mph. Parked up in the Beach Hotel garage, the Djelmo became somewhat vague in purpose: she was an anachronism. Malcolm Campbell's return average of 174.88 mph on Pendine, in 1926, with the Napier Blue Bird had probably defined the beach's limits. Henry Segrave's response, a shattering 203.79 mph, with the 1,000 hp Sunbeam, at Daytona in March moved the WLSR onto an entirely different plane. Djelmo was out of the picture.

When Djelmo had originally been commissioned in 1924 it was as a contestant in the three-mile-a-minute land-speed challenge. Designed along the lines of earlier Sunbeam and Bugatti Grand Prix racing cars, many argued that Djelaleddin had been sold a 'pup' as, from 1925 on, when speeds exceeded 150 mph, it was realised that the 'Bugatti-style' concept with its high centre of gravity and short chassis, was too inherently unstable. Through no fault of Foresti's, who was basically hired to drive it, the car was too long making its appearance from the design and development stage for him ever to be in contention. Once 'World' status of the Land Speed Record contest had been more or less ratified, there was a race 'on' between manufacturers and privateers across the northern hemisphere. It was impressive the way Sunbeams progressively enlarged their thinking from the 18.23-litre car of Lee Guinness and Campbell, to Segrave's 4-litre supercharged lightweight and then the heavy, twin-engined, 44-litre Slug – all within the time that the Djelmo camp were tinkering.

The events that comprise the Djelmo story do not make good reading, as there is nothing but a catalogue of misadventure and droll incompetence to impart. Djelmo was running again by the end of August. On the 29th, while practising, Foresti hit a soft patch, skidded, keeled over on two wheels, had a very nasty moment, miraculously recovered and returned to base – shaken.

On the following day, which happened to be Foresti's birthday, fortune was no more inclined to shine on him than the sun. It remained dull and misty all day.

Djelmo. [© *Lindsay collection*]

Djelmo. [© *Lindsay collection*]

The sand was too wet for speeds above 100 mph, so he 'called it a day' after essaying some standing-start drags. On the way back to the Beach Hotel he collided with a private car near the ramp – which caused a fire to break out in Djelmo's engine-room – luckily put out before too much damage was done. The following day the car, straight-off, suffered a major breakdown and Foresti had to send away to France for replacement parts.

These parts were not received until November, by which time Foresti's vocabulary had widened, his accent much improved. On the first day's trials the water pump went and a fault developed in the gearbox, providing Gilbert Davies of nearby Ashwell Garage with a welcome interlude from decoking heads and mending punctures. Re-building the racing gearbox meant working all night, as the official RAC timekeepers were only booked for one more day.

On its first pass up the beach next morning – and under acceleration at between 140 and 150 mph – the car began to lope, then to slew one way, then another, as she passed her stability limit. Foresti fought hard to contain the inevitable skid and sideways tumble: instead, Djelmo hit a marker post head-on. The miscreant car began a somersault; then fell back on her side, with the driver half in, half out of the cockpit. She was still on at well over hundred, issuing fighting-bull roars. Another toss, and Foresti was thrown clear – the car banging on like a tin can blown in the wind.

When Djelmo came to rest all rushed up, expecting a grim repetition of Parry Thomas's fate. Smoke hung heavily in the air. Then, like the ghost of Hamlet's father out of the mist, the irrepressible Foresti appeared, nursing a broken shoulder – a smiling, limping specimen of the walking-wounded. Blood was pouring down his face, his hair all gone. He had to all intents and purposes been scalped.

This somewhat bogus effort brought to an end World Land Speed Record attempts for wheel-driven cars on Pendine – and, for that matter, in Great Britain. Djelmo was scrapped. Foresti, after a sojourn in Carmarthen hospital, returned with his glamorous, opera-singer wife to a fast life in Rome. Perhaps he had some fond memories of Pendine: none, for sure, of Djelmo. He never came back.

Djelmo. [© *Lindsay collection*]

RE Thomas drops the Brough. [*Morton's Motor Cycle Media*]

10. Fall from Grace

The Welsh TT trophy

THAT Pendine's star continued in the ascendant in 1928 was taken for granted. It was suddenly all to change. The beach, recently made world-famous by motoring achievement, was about to see its prestige – as hosting one of the leading events of the British motor-sporting calendar – fall from grace. And it becomes apparent that this opprobrium was partially self-inflicted. A combination of organisational ineptitude and failure to curb the thoughtlessness of a few people among the crowds of spectators spoilt it for everyone.

Loss of the 'Welsh TT' title was a blow to the organisers of the 1928 August Bank Holiday meeting. It meant also that their Welsh TT trophy was redundant. Tommy Spann had 'lifted' it two years in succession, and was obviously looking forward to the opportunity of taking possession of it. George Brough, it seems, at one time proudly displayed it in his Haydn Road offices and at his home, 'Pendine', Mansfield Road, Redhill. But at this point the trophy is lost from sight. In the absence of the Neath and Carmarthen clubs' records – which are said to have been lost – it is only possible to speculate; but it would be good to trace its whereabouts.

Two new major awards had made their appearance by this time. John Bull (tyres) had come forward in 1924 with their Challenge Trophy, awarded to the Carmarthen Motor Cycle for the Welsh TT. It seems not to have been used for this purpose, so much as for the winner of the 'Big' race at Whitsun. JE Kettle won it in 1924 and 1926; RE Thomas, 1927; AM Harry, 1928. Nick Carter won it in 1929 for his performance in the Welsh Hundred on the 350 camshaft Matchless in the 500cc class. JH Carr was awarded 'The John Bull TT cup' for the hundred-mile race on August Bank Holiday, 1931. In 1932, when he repeated his performance, he was given a new Carmarthen Motor Cycle & Light Car Club trophy.

These cups, happily, have survived. The (Fred) Olsson Cup, which we also still have, has its origin in August 1927. On that occasion it was awarded to Gordon Bennett on the Scott. All its subsequent winners appear to have been members of Swansea Motor Club, rewarded for the best performance of a club member at the August meeting on Pendine

It had long been thought in some circles that the 'TT' nomenclature was a touch 'grand' for a sand-meeting. It was an ideal that attached uniquely to the Isle of Man races. There was a perception that the WSW Centre ACU and the organising clubs were, perhaps unwittingly, guilty of 'passing-off' the historic and prestigious Tourist Trophy ideal to their own advantage and to the benefit of the manufacturers who used the words 'Welsh TT' in advertising. George Brough had made much of the Brough Superior winning this award four times on the trot. Douglas and New Hudson clarioned their victories, even their placings, at Pendine in the motor cycling press, as did various oil companies, Lodge and Champion plugs, John Bull, Dunlop and other tyre manufacturers.

The TT

Pendine and the Isle of Man were vastly different propositions. A trophy awarded in the veteran days of motor cycling for the first home after a gruelling, high-speed motor tour of the 37-odd mile, rough, mountain circuit that took in most of the topography of an inhabited island, was deserved in ways that differed from repeated 'speed trial' laps up and down a level, sandy shore. The handle, 'TT', was perceived as being misused – as an indicator of status. There had never been a formal request to use the name; there was no agreement or licence relating to its use. In the bewildering avenues of copyright law the title 'TT' could, if challenged, be defined as commercial or 'intellectual property'. If it had come to litigation, the allegation of unauthorised use for advantage was undeniable and therefore indefensible. So the 1928 August Welsh Open Championship 100-mile race was officially re-named 'The Welsh Hundred' – though, for a decade or more, people still referred to it as 'the Welsh TT'. It was a blow to Pendine's status.

What had become apparent to the ACU and the motor cycle racing fraternity at large was that Pendine Races had acquired something of a bad name. Whether withdrawal of the title was a safeguard against possible reflection upon the prestige of the IoM TT is not certain.

There was growing criticism in the press, which obviously reached the eyes and ears of the ACU, about safety and discipline. It was known that a lot of drinking (behaviour frowned upon by the chapels) went on at race weekends, and this, regrettably, extended to officials and even, in some cases, the riders. This was not unique to Pendine! It was part of the carnival atmosphere of any race-meeting, but the combination of drink and speed was potentially lethal. Considering the vast crowds and the speeds of the machines, Pendine had been very lucky with its accident record. There are tales of riders who set off, unsteadily, up the straight and only turned when they sighted Laugharne! In August 1928, when George Brough won the fastest time-of-day, in the unlimited mile sprint, it was estimated that he was travelling in excess of 110mph at the flag. All that protected the crowds was a single slack strand of wire, hurriedly assembled on the day, after high tide. The dangers were self-evident.

There were any number of spills involving riders on the soft sands, of course. Few received much worse than abrasions. The 'spills and thrills' were an important part of the spectacle. One spectator had received minor injuries in 1927, and the press sensibly urged the organisers to put their house in order. This admonishment was not taken seriously enough. Another person was to be hurt in 1928, as a consequence of inadequate marshalling and insufficient crowd discipline. There was an outcry. This resulted in the laying of blame – and a quarrel between the Neath and Carmarthen clubs.

The three-day programme of past years had imposed a tremendous strain on the organisational capacity of people who were, after all, volunteers, enthusiasts and amateurs. From 1929 onwards, Neath and District were deprived of their specific responsibility for organising the 'big race' in Pendine. Administration of both Whitsun and August Bank Holiday meetings was, from that year on, undertaken by the Carmarthen club alone, under the rules and auspices of the West South Wales Centre. The Swansea club held occasional Easter meetings as a warm-up to the season. These were technically not 'Open' to others than members of the WSW Centre but outsiders anxious to compete only had to pay their subscription to a local club to circumvent this limitation.

Eddie Mainwaring of Keighley, the Scott rider, an old-hand at sand-racing venues throughout the country, had brought down a talented young rider friend for the Bank Holiday motor cycle jamboree at Pendine, in the person of JH 'Jack' Carr. A fellow-member of the Southport Motor Club, a farmer and butcher from Skipton, West Yorkshire, Carr does not appear to have participated in Monday's proceedings. On his Brough Superior he was destined for fame on Pendine.

The debut appearance of RF Parkinson, of Lindthorpe, in the race programme was the commencement of a long association between this very fine rider and Pendine. Ronnie Parkinson's name is synonymous with AJS – one 350 in particular. He also later achieved many successes at Pendine on Douglas motor cycles in association with his friend, Freddy Dixon.

The Bank Holiday Monday weather was fine, the racing of a good standard. *The Carmarthen Journal* affirms that 'thousands' (it does not say how many) attended the meeting, organised by the West South Wales Centre ACU, Neath and the Carmarthen & District Motor Cycle & Light Car Club. The spectators were fairly boisterous, crowding the finishing-line and crossing the track during the racing. Everyone was riveted by Ronnie Parkinson's immaculately tailored, whiter-than-white overalls and his sensational cornering technique on the little AJS.

It concluded as follows:

OPEN EVENTS

One-mile sprint > 275cc
V Anstice (OK Supreme)
LV Thomas (OK Supreme)
JE Davies, Llanwrda (Levis)

one-mile sprint > 350cc
RF Parkinson, Linthorpe (AJS)

GE Rowley, W'hampton (AJS)
LV Thomas (Velocette)

one-mile sprint > 500cc
AW Nicklin, Blaina (Sunbeam)
LV Thomas (Norton)
C Bowles, Morriston (Sunbeam)

one-mile sprint: unlimited
George Brough (Brough Superior)
RE Thomas (Brough Superior)
AW Nicklin (Sunbeam)

10 miles > 275cc
LV Thomas (OK Supreme)
CF Edwards, Cirencester (Cotton)
WD Powell, Brecon (Dunelt)

10 miles > 350cc
RF Parkinson (AJS)
SS Evans (Cotton-JAP)
GE Rowley (AJS)

10 miles > 500cc
GE Gregor, Mumbles (Rudge)
E Mainwaring (Scott)
DH Evans, Merthyr (Rudge)

10 miles: unlimited
E Mainwaring (Scott)
T Spann (Brough Superior)

25 miles > 350cc
SS Evans (Cotton-JAP)

50 miles: unlimited
DP Williams, Edgbaston (Norton)
Alex Grey (Cotton-Blackburne)
RE Thomas (Bough Superior)

CLOSED EVENTS

One-mile sprint > 350cc
AW Nicklin (Sunbeam)
TJ Phillips, Aberavon (Zenith)
N Carter, Brynmawr (Matchless)

one-mile sprint > 500cc
N Carter (Matchless)
AW Nicklin (Sunbeam)
C (Cyril) Bowles, Morriston (Sunbeam)

10 miles > 275cc
LV Thomas (OK Supreme)
WD Powell (Dunelt)
JE Davies (Levis)

10 miles > 350cc
Nick Carter (Matchless)
C Bowles (Sunbeam)
LV Thomas (Velocette)

10 miles > 500cc
C Bowles (Sunbeam)
Nick Carter (Matchless)

10 miles > unlimited
RE Thomas (Brough Superior)
A Williams, Killay (Douglas)
EW Thomas, Mumbles (Norton)
C Williams, Morriston (AJS)

The *Carmarthen Journal* is silent on the organisational chaos and the weather that marred the second day of August Bank Holiday's proceedings. 'RE Thomas, Gloag, had an accident on his Brough Superior involving a spectator, Daniel Jones, Penrheol, Cross Hands' is all it reports. It omits to mention that, in the words of *The Motor Cycle*, 'inadequate preparations for crowd control had been made, with the result that competitors were much hampered by spectators swarming onto the course.'

'Heavy Rain and Poor Organisation Wreck Classic Welsh Sand Race'

was the unpalatable banner headline in *Motor Cycling* 's race report on August 15th, 1928, describing Tuesday's programme. *The Motor Cycle,* under a paragraph headed, 'Lax Marshalling', is critical of the men on the ground:

Conditions for the riders were not made any easier by the rather slack organisation. Spectators drifted about the course in the most casual manner, becoming a danger to themselves and to the competitors, and the marshalling was totally inadequate to deal with the situation. Thus, the result of the 100 mile race is, at the time of writing, a matter of doubt, due to the fact that it was possible for a rider to cut some of the course without being noticed and, although it is probable that every rider who finished completed the full distance, the officials made the disconcerting discovery that the records of the lap scorers at either end of the course did not tally.

Tuesday was a truly awful day from every point of view. Even the most dogged of spectators cut their losses, and made for home. The sensible decision – to postpone the programme till the following day – should have been taken. Conditions for racing motor cycles on the beach could only have been worse if the tide had actually been *in*: the sands in many places were under inches of water. The rain, descending in a horizontal tidal wave, obliged the few remaining spectators to huddle in groups on the leeward-side of any vehicle or feature. Officials and marshals moved about like wet cats after drowned rats. Riders were soaked through to the skin and subjected to considerable pain and discomfort from the cold and the stinging, driving rain. Many wore makeshift face-masks. Often, visibility was so bad that they could not see where they were going. It was an exceptionally dangerous situation. Machines broke down in droves. Clutches slipped, high-tension leads, plugs and magnetos were soused. A phenomenal number of spark-plugs were employed – some being cannibalised from machines belonging to members of the public. One rider used 18 plugs in a single race!

In the 50-mile event, out of five starters in the 250cc class only one was still circulating at quarter distance – so he was 'flagged in to save time'. The 350 class was more of a contest; and the exhibition of 'dirt-track' skid-cornering by RF Parkinson (AJS) was possibly the only piece of merriment that the day provided. LV Thomas, duelling with him, attempted a similar show, but to lesser effect. Parkinson had problems and went out on lap eleven. It had taken Simpson eight laps to get his AJS started, and when he did, he drove like one possessed, blowing everyone away, until he himself blew up. CH Jayne, on a Cotton, came in first, followed by GF Rowley on the works AJS and CL Pullman (Velocette). Many riders had retired from the sheer cold and physical exhaustion. But still the organisers bone-headedly went ahead with the main event, 'The Welsh Hundred.'

For this, the big race, Brough Superiors were lined up in force, the reverberating pulse of their big V-twin engines uttering their trade-mark 'potato-potato'-sound against the wind and the rain. In the van was top man, Tommy Spann, winner of the Welsh TT in 1926 and 1927, sporting his familiar wasp-striped jersey, which he wore over his leathers.

The handsome JH Carr, who was to make a name for himself as a Manx Grand Prix rider, made his debut appearance on Pendine for the Hundred. He had recently enjoyed brilliant successes at Southport and Blackpool riding an SS100 'Pendine' model Brough Superior, with the 8/45 KTOR JAP engine. He was in future destined to emulate Spann's racing record in the Welsh Speed Championships. West Carmarthenshire was a long way from Ilkley Moor but, anxious to see and experience the track where his machine had derived its birth and breeding, they both received something of a baptism! CF Edwards, L Currie and RE Thomas were out on similar mounts: all of them hoping to maintain the succession of fortune that Brough enjoyed at Pendine. George Brough was down from Nottingham to see the fun. He himself had managed fastest time-of-day in the mile sprint.

Driving Rain

Just before the start of the Hundred, the rainpour got even worse. Cancellation was suggested. But no. Conditions rapidly became so atrocious that, of the twenty-five lined up at the start, a dozen stopped on the first lap. Two faltering Broughs held the lead for the first two laps (Spann and Currie), followed by DP Wilkins's Norton and a very plucky George Gregor on his four-valve Rudge, who temporarily took the lead when the waterlogged Broughs slowed. The course soon began to look like the aftermath of a battle, with flags and signs flattened to the ground and inert machines strewn and abandoned over its whole length. The gale reached near-hurricane.

The only indication that there was a sporting event in progress was the occasional passage of a coughing, spluttering machine. Somewhere out there was AM Harry on the New Hudson. EG Bennett, with the Scott, took a turn at the lead for a couple of laps – then went bang. Spann's was the only Brough left in the running. Even he was trailing – behind Mewis's Norton and Clarke on an Ariel. The lap scorers were all at sea as to which order they were in. There was suspicion – and evidence – that certain competitors had 'cut through' half and three-quarters of the way up the course, as records between time-keepers at top and bottom ends were found not to tally.

And there they left it. No result was available at the finish. It was a disgrace. A committee meeting would be called later in the week to assess claims. Eventually, first place was awarded to AM Harry, Birmingham, (New Hudson) who was deemed to have covered the distance.

Owing largely to the weather and poor decision-making, the Neath club had lost control of the situation. Having taken the decision to start the race, there was obdurate inability to abandon when it became impossible to assess progress. Conditions were clearly dangerous to the public and competitors alike. The Neath and Carmarthen clubs had been too inclined to be relaxed about crowd control in previous years. They had received warnings. Reports of these events indicate that they had not taken heed. The sad result was an injured spectator and that their combined negligence was to bring Pendine Races to the verge of disrepute. Things would never be quite the same again. Glamour would fade: the 'glory days' were over.

FIASCO

WELSH HUNDRED, 1928

Result on the day: 'Inconclusive'. After some deliberation the award was ascribed to:

AM Harry (New Hudson)

'Cyclops', writing his Sports Gossip column in *The Motor Cycle*, on August, 22nd, 1928, following general reports and rumours of the fiasco that occurred at the Bank Holiday meet (he is referring more particularly to Tuesday's happenings), says

> The Pendine meeting seems to have been a pretty bad fizzle, judging from what one has overheard about it and the responsible officials of the organising clubs should take seriously to heart the lessons that were so obviously forced upon their notice on the recent unfortunate occasion. The fixture has always been treated as one of first-class importance, but it has lost most of its prestige by this year's happenings, and possible entrants will want a lot of persuasion before they will be prepared to take it seriously in 1929. Really, at this time of day, it seems incredible that in an important open event like the Welsh Hundred things should have been allowed to become so hopelessly mixed up that the winner could not be found without a committee meeting being held days after the event.
>
> It was so deplorable that the crowd should have got so much out of hand when the Carmarthen club was holding its speed trials on the Monday, and indeed the only matter for congratulation was that but a single competitor (*sic*) got knocked down and got away with nothing worse than a fractured leg. That is quite bad enough; a precisely similar accident at Kop[125] was responsible for the cancellation of speed trials that temporarily paralysed the sport in 1925, and what happened at Pendine might quite easily have resulted in the prohibition of all sand racing, a thing that our 'Jix'[126] could bring about without much difficulty, I believe, if he felt so inclined. So, if the Pendine meeting is to be held next year there will have to be some fairly careful thinking between now and then.

Wednesday was a lovely, bright-blue day, with a fresh, westerly wind: a day that would have been perfect for the previous day's business. The 10-mile sidecar event had classes for unlimited machines. The 50-miler was for 500s and 750s. There were ten entries and the laps were a mile up and a mile down the beach.

In the ten-mile event, CF Edwards, of Seven Sisters, predictably, took the lead on the Brough outfit – with Jack Carr, similarly equipped, in pursuit. The popular Clarence P Wood was on the works Douglas, and the 'official' Norton of Mewis held up third until Edwards went out on the last-but-one lap. Gordon Bennett, with the Scott outfit got through and held second position until the last lap. He lost ground owing to the Scott's ailing clutch. Then Carr, who led briefly, retired with mechanical trouble and Clarry Wood took the lead, which he held to the end. The official result was

---

[125] Kop Hill, in the Chilterns, near Princess Risborough, Buckinghamshire, was the premier hill-climb event in the sporting calendar. When, at the Essex club's Easter meeting in March, 1925, two spectacular accidents, one involving a car (Bugatti) and the other a motor cycle (Allchin's Zenith-JAP), occurred, the RAC and ACU jointly refused to license all further speed events on public highways. This ban did not become enshrined in law until the 1930 Road Traffic Act.

[126] Obscure: the Home Secretary's nick-name?

SIDECARS

50 miles > 750cc
CP Wood (Douglas)
EG Bennett (Scott)

50 miles > 500cc
W Mewis (Norton)
AR Boobyer (Zenith)
L Nicholason (Rudge)

10 miles: unlimited
CP Wood (Douglas)
W Mewis (Norton)
AR Boobyer (Zenith)
L Nicholason, Stoke-on-Trent (Norton)

N Carter (ohc Matchless). [*MA Clare photo*]

Whitsun 1929

The Whitsun meeting in 1929 apparently 'attracted large crowds onto the famous sands … in which some of the crack motor cyclists of the country competed'. We have no more than that, which sounds vaguely familiar, from the *Western Mail*. The official results are published as follows:

One-mile sprint > 350cc
RF Parkinson (AJS)
SS Evans (Cotton)
ETM Stephens (New Hudson)

one-mile sprint > 500cc
RF Parkinson (AJS)

N Carter (Matchless)
LV Thomas (Norton)

one-mile sprint: unlimited
GE Gregor (Rudge-Whitworth)
RE Thomas (Brough Superior)
EG Bennett (Scott)

WELSH CHAMPIONSHIP

25 miles > 350cc
RF Parkinson (AJS)
ETM Stephens (New Hudson)
FH Chambers, Mosely (New Hudson)
Winner's time: 23 mins 50 secs.

50 miles > 500cc
N Carter (Matchless)
J John, Llandebie (Norton)
AJ Lennox, Cardiff (Rudge)
Winner's time: 50 mins 16 secs.

50 miles: unlimited
N Carter (Matchless)
EG Bennett (Scott)
Winner's time: 46 mins 16secs.

SIDE-CARS

20 miles: unlimited
N Carter (Matchless)
EG Bennett (Scott)

E Gordon Bennett (Scott). [*MA Clare photo*]

RF Parkinson (AJS).
[*Morton's Motor Cycle Media*]

11. The Man in White & the Skipton Butcher

August 1929

IN 1929, jazz music added a touch of gaiety to the August Bank Holiday Monday proceedings. Al Jolson cried for his Mammy; a shrill singer kept insisting that they wouldn't believe her. The new public address system provided a race commentary and blared out some of the 'Desert Song' hits in between official announcements from the Race Control van. There is every indication from press reports that the organising clubs, found 'guilty as charged' of mismanagement in previous years, had thought long and hard. *Motor Cycling*, in its August 14th coverage, says

> In past years justifiable criticism has been levelled at the organisation of this, the most important Welsh fixture of the season, but this time the officials of the Carmarthen and Neath clubs had really put their backs into the job of making the meeting as safe as possible for both riders and spectators.

A week later, the same journal adds

> As we have already stated, great improvements have already been made in the running of events for this year and a wire rope, attached to huge wooden boxes of sand, was used to keep the crowd of many thousands under control.

The Motor Cycle, deeply critical of slip-shod standards of crowd control and organisational efficiency in past years, comments:

> This year the organisation was much better than it has been in the past, the spectators being well controlled and the course kept clear.

The weather was ideal throughout and the meeting was described by both leading motor cycling journals as 'a success'. 'Elvy' Thomas ran away with the first race, the ten-mile for 500s, on Monday. Opening his lead to half a mile by the fourth lap, on the CS1 Norton, Thomas led his Swansea friend, George Gregor, by half a mile on lap four. Nick Carter's ride was one of amazement, coming in third when he had not been present at the start! On the 350 'cammy' Matchless he flew past the field like a huntsman going through the hounds. It ended much as it began, except for the conspicuous flight towards third place of the man delayed in the paddock:

10 miles > 500cc
LV Thomas (Norton)
GE Gregor (Rudge-Whitworth)
Nick Carter (Matchless)

One-mile sprint > 350cc
SS Evans (Cotton)
RF Parkinson (AJS)

AJS rider, RF Parkinson, would have won the 350cc one-mile sprint from SS Evans (Cotton) had not his engine cut out on him yards from the finishing-line. He came second in silence.

RW Storey (Brough Superior) with George Brough (cap). [*RW Storey collection photo*]

In the 500cc one-mile sprint, George Gregor had his revenge on LV Thomas, showing that the 499cc four-valve Rudge 'Ulster', running on 'jollop' fuel was a very fast sprint machine. JD Potts, of Brooklands fame, who would shortly win the Isle of Man Senior 'Manx Grand Prix' on a Grindlay Peerless, came in third on that same, heavy, but pleasant-to-look-at machine with its nickel-plated frame and tank. Fired by a twin-port 490cc JAP engine with inclined overhead valves, Bill Lacey had, in August 1928, taken a similar machine (one 'Copper Knob'), round Brooklands for an hour at an average speed of over 100mph. Being the first man to do so on a 500cc bike on British soil, he won *The Motor Cycle* silver cup. Incidentally, that Manx victory was short-lived – as Potts was disqualified, for non-declaration. He did not comply within the definition of an 'amateur'.

one-mile sprint > 500cc
George Gregor (Rudge-Whitworth)
LV Thomas (Norton)
JD Potts (Grindlay Peerless)

one-mile sprint: unlimited
RW Storey (Brough Superior)
RF Parkinson (Douglas)
GE Gregor (Rudge-Whitworth)

In the unlimited capacity mile sprint, RW Storey's Brough Superior, and his over-enthusiasm, ended him up among the flags at the end of the finishing straight. Parkinson was some distance behind him on a very fast, borrowed, Douglas, also going like stink, ahead of George Gregor's Rudge-Whitworth. Exciting stuff, very like modern drag racing. They were all well above the 100mph mark at the finish-line. Storey probably closer to 120, as he collected flags.

The 250cc and 350cc events over ten miles were run contiguously, as was usual. Parkinson's 348 AJS was sounding very sweet in the morning air, and he entertained the crowd with an exhibition of sheer speed and cornering virtuosity from start to finish. No one came within sight of him after the first lap, until he lapped them all on his way to a decisive victory. Evans, on a '250' Cotton, led that category and took second place in the '350', ahead of Anstice on an OK Supreme. Theirs had been an engaging tussle to watch.

10 miles > 350cc	**10 miles > 500cc**
RF Parkinson (AJS)	LV Thomas (Norton)
SS Evans (Cotton)	CP Wood (Douglas)
V Anstice (OK Supreme)	GE Gregor (Rudge-Whitworth)
Winner's time: 8m 53secs.	Winner's time: 8m 34secs (79.29 mph).

Ronnie Parkinson was at the peak of his form at this time. It was just when Bob Berry was just beginning his career in sand-racing and, from the paddock, after breaking the Calthorpe's timing-chain, his gives us a first-hand account of watching the mastery of one of the greatest riders

> So we spent practically all that first meeting watching the unrivalled artistry of Ronnie Parkinson as, with his 185-lb 350 AJS, he led the 500s in race after race. How many times I was to see that wonderful little black-and-gold terror vanish into the distance when I was under the impression I was going fast! Older readers will remember the white-overalled figure, his black gum-booted right foot extended forward, broadsiding the little AJS round the flags and gaining yards on bigger machines. Very few 500s could beat him on acceleration, and none at all could catch him on the bends, while in 250 sprints he stood alone; yet always the model looked as though it had just left the agent's showroom.
>
> It speaks volumes for Parkinson's tuning that the AJS was a 1928 push-rod job, and it was winning against all-comers until he retired from racing, still the unbeaten champion of the 350 class, and holder of more fastest times and 'firsts' than anyone else before or since, on any beach. Curiously, although he sometimes rode a 500 AJS, it never seemed to have the terrific performance of its smaller brother.[110]

The two Swansea local heroes, LV Thomas and George Gregor, were at each other's throats again in the ten-mile race for 500s. George streaked away from the start but 'went a little wild on the second lap', allowing LV Thomas's Norton to streak past him. Clarry Wood was on the tail of both of them, and he needed no persuasion to get through into second himself – thereafter to give LV T a hard time. But the privately-entered Douglas just did not have that bit extra power necessary to take the lead.

[100] 'Nine years on Sand', *Motor Cycling* June 28, 1945.

The Brough Superior rider, JH Carr, on his new 'Pendine' had the unlimited race in the bag, and was shutting down, throttling back, ready to go into the paddock, when he noticed consternation written on everyone's faces. They were signalling him on. Had he seen a chequered flag? No he hadn't. There was another lap to go! Lionel Thomas, who had been tailing him, going very fast on the camshaft Norton, had gone on into the lead. The Skipton butcher's dander rose – and with a snarl, a Bentley whine of gears and trailing a spume of sand, he was away again: up the two-and-a-half mile straight in pursuit of the Norton disappearing, like an insect into the haze. If there ever had been, or was anywhere the slightest doubt that the Brough Superior was the king of Pendine, then, that afternoon, Jack Carr was to make sure no one would ever again question it. Nobody who was there will ever forget it. Carr was in all-or-nothing mode. He called on reserves which only the few real master practitioners of the science of the Brough on sand knew about. It looked like sheer anger, but it was a controlled and phenomenally fast standing-start lap. It took LV Thomas by surprise. As he exited the top bend, feeling for third, the outraged Brough roared by him like a bear; and away down the straight he went, unassailable, to complete his mission at the chequered flag.

10 miles: unlimited
JH Carr (Brough Superior)
LV Thomas (Norton)
RF Parkinson (AJS)
Winner's time: 8m 1sec (85.51 mph).

JH Carr (Brough Superior). [*KE John photo*]

That very dedicated and stylish rider, SS Evans, on the Cotton, did battle with RF Parkinson in the 25-mile race for 350s. A close-fought and entertaining contest. Evans only had it his own way when Parky retired with mechanical trouble, while the brilliant little Blackburne-engined Cotton went on like a watch. But in the Unlimited 30-mile event it was Parkinson all the way on the conspicuously faster Douglas. He won, literally by a mile, in the record time of 24 minutes 33 seconds, having lapped the field – and RW Storey's ailing Brough Superior – twice. He was all set to repeat the feat in the 50-mile race, but his mount, the Bristol works machine, was weary. Thomas, Gloag, passed him on the five-year-old Brough, before the Douglas finally resigned. It was a fine race from there on between the Brough Superior and E Mainwaring's Scott. The Brough held the leading edge and CH Jayne came in third on the very neat and tidy Cotton.

WELSH HUNDRED, 1929

25 miles > 350cc
SS Evans (Cotton)

30 miles: unlimited
RF Parkinson (Douglas)
Winner's time: 24 mins 33 secs.

50 miles: unlimited
RE Thomas (Brough Superior)
E Mainwaring (Scott)
CH Jayne (Cotton)
Winner's time: 44mins 35secs (65.09 mph).

GE Gregor

CP Wood (Douglas) pulled out all the stops in the sidecar race. He was way out in front when his engine failed. CF Edwards (Brough Superior) went on to win the event, stuck in one gear, as the clutch packed in early in the race. He did well to stay ahead and go the distance in 19 mins 4secs. It was to be George Gregor's last race at Pendine, before he left to try his hand at rubber planting in Malaya. In twelve outings at Pendine he had scored four firsts, five seconds – and had come third three times. A very creditable performance by a fine, self-assured rider.

E Gordon Bennett & George Gregor (Douglas). [*Clifford H Evans photo*]

After a glorious Bank Holiday Monday, the day of the big race, 'The Welsh 100', woke dismal. Rain poured steadily down on the beach. Every one dreaded the memory of the previous year's washout. The ever-temperamental weather over Carmarthen Bay changed again. By mid-morning, the rain had petered out and a drying wind picked up from the Atlantic. Little plumes of dry sand blew against bare legs and into unprotected eyes. Enough blue sky had appeared by eleven o'clock to make a sailor's trousers and the day looked much more promising for the business of motor cycle racing on sand.

RF Parkinson of Middlesborough, in tight-fitting, shining-white overalls, was ready for it; and it at once looked as if the sleek black AJS belonged in a different category, the way he went off into the distance, away from the small field of eight entries. He soon came round and up behind them, shadowed only by SS Evans, going strongly on another shiny black machine, a Cotton. FH Chambers (New Hudson) was lying a long third. For a while the Cotton came up and really began to issue a challenge, then a dying fall, as the engine began to jolt and splutter from fuel starvation.

Parkinson was now so far out on his own that the crowd turned its attention to a Cotton/OK Supreme tussle that was joined in the 250 class. Edwards and Anstice were relishing the fun, until Edwards's Cotton seemed to lose power, and he faded into the background – and out. Then a shock. At 44 miles Parkinson was missing. The 'AJ' had given up soldiering, thrown down its cap and belt and said, 'Thus far and no further!' So, who *was* there? Out from obscurity, in among the back-markers, appeared FH Chambers again. He had been motoring along nice and steadily on the New Hudson. The only 350-man still going, he was the winner. Anstice came second – and first: in the 250 class. All the others failed to finish.

50 miles > 350cc   **50 miles > 250cc**
FH Chambers (New Hudson)   V Anstice (OK Supreme)

FH Chambers (New Hudson). [*Morton's Motor Cycle Media*]

The beach dried out nicely over the lunch hour, a good omen for the important event of the day. The course was extended to 2½ miles – for the twenty, five-mile laps. Some of the big boys would need to refuel and take on oil, perhaps twice. There was one sticky patch to negotiate at the top-end where the turn had been for the morning's racing. Apart from that, everything was hunky-dory, the crowd and competitors alike 'remembering not past-years'!

There was a line-up of twenty-one riders. Not a very good entry, by Welsh-TT-of-the-past standards – and not quite so many 'top-drawer' stars as had formerly been seen. Had the adverse publicity that adhered to the previous year's organisational débâcle taken immediate effect? CP Wood and RF Parkinson were campaigning Wood-Dixon-prepared 'big' Douglases. JH Carr, RW Storey and RE Thomas were the Brough Superior riders. All machines had received administrations from Ted Lester, Brough's engineer, who was in attendance with the familiar black Chevrolet van, decorated in Brough Superior livery. Storey was on the 'works' entry, Rees Thomas's bike had been delivered back by rail from Haydn Road; Jack Carr had, as usual, driven down from West Yorkshire on the 8/45 SS100 'Pendine', relying on his friends Ron Storey and Ted Lester to 'tweak' it in the *parc fermé* before racing commenced.[127] George Brough was there to offer advice and encouragement.

W Mewis was among the few 'works' riders present, on a Norton. Local riders LF Griffiths and LV Thomas were the 'private' Norton men in with a chance: E Gordon Bennett, Gorseinon, JE Kettle, Newport, and E Mainwaring, Keighly, turned out on Scotts; and there was AV Carter (Sunbeam) and PJ Saunders (Rudge-Whitworth) who would be mentioned in dispatches.

Whatever alchemy had been placed upon the two 750cc Douglases, it worked like magic. From a 'dead', push-start, Clarry Wood was away up the road like a scorched hare, leaving the roar of 'the pack' well behind him – a pack led by his team-mate, Ronnie Parkinson, whose gleaming white racing overalls could be made out a mile away.

Unexpectedly, the Broughs were not having it their own way. Storey and Carr were in close attendance on the flying Douglas of Parkinson by lap three, on the principle that if the 'Bristol boxers' kept up such a hot pace they would sooner or later blow up or shake themselves to pieces. Douglases were notoriously weak in the frame. Dixon was holding out chalked messages for Clarry and Parky, and George Brough was signalling cryptically to the Brough boys.

Carr overtook Parkinson, and Storey followed. Storey slipped by Carr. Then Carr dropped back to third on the fourth lap. As nothing of Wood was visible, Carr reasoned that he had fallen by the wayside and that the lead was his for the taking, in time: so, *festina lente,* make haste slowly. The Brough camp soon apprised him of his

---

[127]'Jack Carr would think nothing of riding from Skipton to Pendine, race 100 miles, and ride the bike home again. He was the most determined of our privateer riders and a great chap.' Ted Lester's reminiscences, quoted in the Brough Superior Club *Newsletter.* Carr often transported his 350 New Imperial, 500 Norton and the Brough in his Jowett van 'when he needed other tools for the job.' (Roland & George Carr, pers. recollections, June 1999.)

delusion, by way of broad physical exhortations from George! Jack Carr once again lay down on the tank, turned up the burner, found and passed Parkinson, then Storey. The Brough could be heard for miles around sounding off into the middle distance in search of the elusive Wood on the wizardly Douglas. But he did not find him, for on the seventh lap, after sustaining a fall on the bottom bend, the 'Pendine' shortly died under him from its exertions and Jack became a spectator. Then Ron Storey started losing power and dropped down the field to sixth place. A carburettor jet was working loose. A quick visit to the depot and he was out again and, it was plain, this newcomer to Pendine had quickly learned the mastery of it – because he worked his way back up the field to second place by lap nine. On an unlucky thirteenth lap, he had a similar mishap to Carr's, falling, dropping the Brough and taking in a shovelful of sand through the air-intake. Unwisely, he drove on, disappearing into the sea mist and was not seen again. The Brough challenge was over. RE Thomas was still circulating; his famous, but now superannuated, machine was nowhere in contention.

So remarkable was CP Wood's progress that he was already lapping the leaders of the pack by three-quarter distance – a five-mile lead! On the leader board were IoM TT works rider Mewis (Norton), riding very well – and by now well ahead of Parkinson; PJ Saunders on the Rudge-Whitworth came next, leading LF Griffiths on the Norton and EG Bennett on Clarence Wood's old favourite, the Scott. It was a real scramble for third place. Mewis stopped to help a fellow Norton rider, JJ Johns, a beginner, who had somehow strayed way off course and crashed heavily into an old wreck on the shore-line. This let Parkinson into second place; but Mewis, after his mercy-mission, reckoned he still had sufficient time in hand to collect the 500cc Trophy. He had, just – one second's time! Winning by a 'hare's breadth', Mewis certainly deserved his place. The injured rider was described the following day as 'going on quite favourably'.

CP Wood, FW Dixon and RF Parkinson (Douglas).
[*Morton's Motor Cycle Media*]

The finishing-order was Wood, Parkinson, Mewis, Saunders, Griffiths, Bennett.

WELSH 'HUNDRED', 1929

100-miles > 750cc
CP Wood (Douglas)
RF Parkinson (Douglas)
EG Bennett (Scott)

100-miles > 500cc
W Mewis (Norton)
PJ Saunders (Rudge Whitworth)
LF Griffiths (Norton)
Winner's time not published.

Wednesday was another fine day for racing on the sands, but the entry for the 50-mile side-car event was down on previous years. There were only seven competitors. Nevertheless, it turned out to be a memorable race – less for speed than for acrobatics. CF Edwards was the only entrant in the heavyweight class, his Brough Superior making such a sensational getaway on the first lap that he found he had broken the standing start course record, with a time of 1 minute 48 seconds. CP Wood was not far behind him with the 600cc Douglas combination, followed by the Grindlay Peerless of JD Potts and DK Mansell's Norton outfit. On the third lap, Edwards had what he thought was plug trouble, but it turned out to be magneto and, for the purposes of the race, it was terminal.

Dutch Salute

This left Wood well in the lead for a while, until his engine began to misfire, allowing Mansell to steal the march on him, but not without nearly losing his passenger on one bend where Wood's deceptively fast cornering tempted him to defy the laws of physics. Wood then elected to go in for a plug change, which gave Mansell a clear lead. When Wood came out again he encountered another difficulty. The wheel of his chair collapsed. Pulling in at the depot to demonstrate this circumstance to the mechanics – passenger on pillion and side-car wheel in the air – he received an unexpected reception from Freddie Dixon, who sent him out again, sharpish, with a flea in his ear. An unnecessary encumbrance a wheel. 'Get out there, Clarry, and show 'em what you're made of!' So, the Douglas did six laps at the 'Dutch salute', with the passenger experiencing the most uncomfortable ride of his career, riding pillion skew-whiff on the rear mudguard at speeds fast enough to win Wood second-in-class and third overall. History does not record Clarry's or his passenger's observations to Dixon at the finish.

SIDECARS

50-miles > 750cc
DK Mansell (Norton)
CP Wood (Douglas)

50-miles > 500cc
A Grey (Matchless)
JD Potts (Grindlay-Peerless)
Winner's time: 52 mins 45 secs

Clarry's 'Dutch Salute'. [*Morton's Motor Cycle Media*]

August 1930: Wall Street crash knock-on

There is no record of a Whitsun meeting in 1930. Other speed activity was planned. The World Landspeed Record for motorcycles stood at 134mph and, in the last week of May, JS Wright, the Brooklands ace, came down to Pendine with the OEC-Temple for a crack at it. But the weather said no. That same machine, with a colourful history, was to return to Pendine in highly modified form some thirty years later, in the possession of Bob Berry, for unfinished business. Business that would remain unfinished.

Of the staging of The Welsh Hundred in 1930, we have very little to go on. In fact, only a 50-mile race appears to have been run. It is likely that the truncation of the meeting may have been a consequence of the tide. A (high) tide occurring in the middle-part of the day on Tuesday, would have posed difficulties for the organisers of a sand-race meeting involving two separate events over distances of thirty, fifty and a hundred miles. The three-day programme of events that comprised the Welsh Speed Championships August fixture had become condensed into a one-day event, for reasons that we can guess.

As the ragtime roar departed the Twenties, it was replaced by a down-beat blues that opened the Thirties – the Depression. The Wall Street collapse reverberated throughout Western economies with dire economic consequences. Money was scarce, manufacturing and sales were in the doldrums. Few could indulge themselves any more in expensive luxuries, as represented by sports and racing motor cycles. The manufacturers all but ceased sending official entries down to Pendine after 1929, so that the attraction and glamour of the proceedings were in this respect significantly diminished.

What is also circumstantially evident, looking back, is bad blood between the Carmarthen and Neath clubs, for they no longer combined forces to run the – no doubt over-ambitious – three-day event. The loss and destruction of the Minutes of both clubs, is a major handicap to the historian in tracing all factors that led to the loss of prestige from 1927/8 onwards. That the West South Wales Section ACU were doing their best with damage-limitation and assurances for the future can be seen from this unambiguous 'Important Notice' prominently placed on the cover of the August meeting Official Programme, on sale at 1/-:

> **The ACU have issued a permit for the Pendine Speed Championships, with the strict proviso that all spectators shall stand well away from the course and shall not, under any circumstances, walk or stand on the Course. ACU officials will be present and will immediately stop the meeting if this order is not obeyed.**

Spectators and organisers clearly held the future of the Pendine meeting in their own hands. There was no lack of conviction on the part of the authorities if it had come to it: they would have aborted the meeting and it is unlikely that the licence to stage another race meeting at Pendine would ever again have been granted. This could have affected sand meetings all over the country, as had occurred at Style Kop. Luckily, crowd discipline on Bank Holiday 1930, was beyond reproach.

An unattributed rider observes, vis-à-vis his new sprung-frame Brough, in *The Carmarthen Journal* -

> 'It gives you the impression of flying; you can't feel a bump.'[128] said one of the Brough Superior riders at Pendine Races on August Bank Holiday Monday. The famous sands indeed could never be in better condition than they were on that day, and hundreds of motoring folk congregated to watch Carmarthen and District Motor Cycle and Light Car Club's Welsh Speed Championships.
>
> The 50-mile race for any power was run simultaneously with the 30-mile race for 500cc machines.
>
> CP Wood of Bradford on a Douglas led for 5 laps till both tyres collapsed. JH Carr of Skipton (Brough Superior) led till the 16th lap, thus winning the 30-mile event. RF Parkinson took the lead on a Douglas when Carr stopped briefly and held the lead to the end when there were only two machines left running.

In almost its last comment on Pendine Races, *The Journal* is still rather quaintly referring to motor cycle enthusiasts as 'motoring folk'.

---

[128] This was probably JH Carr, referring to his newly-acquired machine (Frame 950X).

Stinsford's Chater Lea

The first appearance of a colourful local 'character', always to be associated with Pendine, is noted in the 10-mile race. Tudor Williams, of Stinsford Bakery in St Clears, known naturally enough as 'Tudor Stinsford', was well placed on the Chater-Lea. He also raced a Rex-Acme. Nicholas Phillips remembers how he practised racing on the A40 road between St Clears and Bancyfelin, to the annoyance and chagrin of Sergeant Williams of St Clears. 'I also remember I was given permission to ride astride or rather sit astride his machine and what a thrill that was, sitting practically prone on the machine, the handle-bars being well down towards the front wheel. Unfortunately, Tudor did not have any wins at Pendine – his machine, so they said, was too light and not suitable for sand racing.'[129]

The published results were:

One-mile sprint > 350cc
RF Parkinson, Linthorpe (AJS)
SS Evans (Cotton-JAP)
ETM Stephens (.?.)

10 miles > 500cc
LV Thomas (Sunbeam)
LF Griffiths (Norton)

one-mile sprint > 500cc
LV Thomas (Sunbeam)
CR Sanderson (Rudge)
RF Parkinson (AJS)

one-mile sprint: unlimited
JH Carr (Brough Superior)
RW Storey (Brough Superior)

10 miles > 350cc
FH Chambers (New Hudson)
Tudor Williams, St Clears (Chater-Lea)

10 miles > 500cc
CR Sanderson (Rudge)
LV Thomas (Sunbeam)
LF Griffiths (Norton)

10 miles: unlimited
CP Wood (Douglas)
JH Carr (Brough Superior)

20 miles > 350cc
RF Parkinson (AJS)
FH Chambers (New Hudson)

50 miles: unlimited
RF Parkinson (Douglas)
JH Carr (Bough Superior)

SIDECARS

20 miles: unlimited
JH Carr (Brough Superior)
RF Parkinson (Douglas)

August 1931

Judging by the scarcity of race reports and editorial material in the press generally, it was becoming increasingly evident that Pendine had lost ground as the major national sporting and social event it had aspired to be in former years. The 1931 August Bank Holiday Welsh Hundred meeting at Pendine was again a low-key affair. The reports in the motorcycling press accorded to a sand meeting in Southport, for instance, merit half a page at least of editorial coverage, illustrated by a montage of

---

[129]Nicholas Phillips, Llanwrda. Pers. letter, 1986.

photographs, whereas Pendine receives less than six inches of plain type in single column, recording final placings. Photographs of racing at Pendine in the press from 1930 onwards become exceptionally scarce. *Motor Cycling* confirms that 'there was a very small entry for (both) the 50- and the 100-mile races', in August 1930.

Looking at the list of entrants for the 1931 Open Championship classes, only a few 'old friends', stalwarts from across Offa's Dyke, thought it worthwhile to make the journey. None of them works entrants any more. Jack Carr was down from Skipton, West Yorks, with a new JAP engine – upgraded to 8/50 horse-power – in his Brough, accompanied by Ron Storey, as mechanic and 's/c passenger'. Clarry Wood, whose Manningham Lane, Bradford, motor cycle business had fallen victim to the Slump, came over with a very nice works Douglas. SS Evans, Gloucester, had the Cotton-JAP. James Beck had travelled the furthest, from Edinburgh, with the Diamond-JAP; and CR Sanderson, Durham, had the Rudge-Whitworth.

To those in the know, all cracking machines and riders – well worth the entrance fee to witness. Otherwise it was LF Griffiths, Bridgend, and Reg Good of Swansea on Nortons – Reg's first outing on Pendine; Gordon Bennett, Gorseinon, on a Douglas; AS Truman, Newport, on a Scott; RE Thomas, Glogue, on the Brough; Stanley Davies, 'Stan the Manse' son of Mansel Davies, Llanfyrnach, on a Rudge 500; and the 'Carmarthen boys' Eddie and Iago Stephens, J Evans, J Andrews, RM Rees, J Stoodley – and Tudor Williams from St Clears.

RM Rees was a men's outfitter in Carmarthen, and, for such a mild and gentle soul, a very combative rider, who rode Rudge, OK Supreme, P&M and, later, Triumph Twin machines with some panache. He was for many years a hard-working Secretary and committee-member of the Carmarthen club. Many considered Iago Stephens a far better rider than his brother, Eddie. Iago's career was cut short by an accident when his motor cycle came into collision with a lorry near Newcastle Emlyn. He had not had many years to prove the theory.

> I well remember spectators' comments to the effect that if Eddie was trailing behind in any race he would always bend down from the seat and 'fiddle around' with the engine indicating that he had some kind of engine trouble which he probably hoped would excuse his rather back position in the field.[130]

'They' made much the same comment about Handel and his brother, Luther. The brother was always said to be the better rider, if a trifle wild. Billy Edwards's brother, Jim, was also given a crank of the handle. But, looking at the record (and racing is about winning, not 'style'), it is Eddie, Handel and Billy who carried home the silverware!

The brief *Motor Cycling* race report tells us that

> After a stormy night the weather cleared up, and with the change of the tide the famous sands were left in very good condition. From all parts of South Wales large crowds thronged to the shore, but the club soon had matters well under control.
> The course measured two miles to the lap.

---

[130] Nicholas Phillips. Pers. letter, 1986.

Crowd discipline problems at Pendine were evidently still on the agenda, and the reporter had been briefed!

In the 50/100-mile (combined) race Clarry Wood had trouble on the start line which put him out of contention, much to the crowd's disappointment. Jack Carr got clean away from the pack on the 998cc Brough and was three laps ahead of the field at half-way. He circulated at a steady average of 75 mph on the short course all the way to the flag. An exemplary performance, but altogether an unexciting spectacle.

'El Orence'

An enigmatic character was present in the crowd. A concealed excitement. His celebrated name has since become synonymous with the Brough Superior motor cycle. 352087 Aircraftsman Ross, who had changed his name first to John Hulme Ross in 1922 and then, when discovered by the press, to TE Shaw, had motored over (usually at very high speed: 80 – 100mph wherever possible) from his sparse cottage, Cloud's Hill, near Bovington, Dorset. Mounted on his SS100 Brough 'Pendalpine', he had come to Pendine to observe and support a Brough rider he very much admired, Jack Carr. It was TE Lawrence, Lawrence of Arabia. 'Orence' had read about, and heard from George Brough of Carr's prowess on the 'Pendine'. The two enthusiasts' paths had crossed at the works in Haydn Road, Nottingham, and they became friends. Lawrence, unlike Carr, changed his machines annually, as he clocked up huge road-mileages. Lawrence had seven Broughs in succession, each christened, respectively, George: (I, II, VI, etc).

According to Carr, it was a windy day. The sand was dry and blowing sand devils, like grape-shot, into the riders' faces. For protection, Lawrence 'gave [him] on Pendine Sands a handkerchief to put over [his] face'.[131] It certainly brought him luck on this occasion!

The official results for August, 1931, were as follows:

OPEN CLASSES:

25miles > 350cc
J (James) Beck (Diamond-JAP)
Iago Stephens (Stephens Special)
J Stoodley (AJS)

THE WELSH HUNDRED, 1931

50 miles: unlimited
JH Carr (Brough Superior)
J Beck (Diamond-JAP)
SS Evans (Cotton-JAP)

100 miles: unlimited
JH Carr (Brough Superior)
SS Evans (Cotton-JAP)
CR (Reg) Good, Swansea (Norton)

100 miles > 500cc
SS Evans (Cotton-JAP)
CR Good (Norton)

SIDECARS

20 miles: unlimited
CP Wood (Douglas)

---

[131] *Craven Herald & Pioneer* (Yorkshire) report (undated clipping: c.1956). Also Roland and George Carr (son and brother) pers. comm. Oct 1998.

CLOSED CLASSES	NOVICE CLASS
50 miles > 500cc	**10 miles 350 > 600cc**
J Andrews (Ariel)	CR Good (Norton)
I Stephens (SS)	J Andrews (Ariel)
25 miles >350cc	
I Stephens (SS)	

It was CP Wood's farewell to Wales. In his fortieth year, it was time to hang up his goggles. He worked as technical adviser to Humber of Coventry until the Second World War and, when hostilities ended, he is said to have opened another garage business at Hunmanby, near Scarborough. Over the ten years he raced at Pendine, on Scotts, HRDs and Douglases, he had always 'put up a good show', and was a darling of the crowd for the entertainment he invariably provided. Clarry was a great rider. He paid the price of the sport he loved in the guise of a disfiguring scar to one side of his face, incurred in a fall at the Isle of Man. He bore it with great fortitude and dignity.

George Eyston

Captain George Eyston was on the beach in the spring of 1932 with his MG project record-breaking car, EX 127. It was a disappointment to him and the company that, despite passes up and down the beach at 122 mph, he was not accorded the two-mile-a-minute record for 500-750cc cars. This was entirely due to a technical fault on the RAC's timing equipment. All the officials would admit of is 116.89 mph.

August 1932

The entry list for the 1932 August Bank Holiday Welsh Speed Championships at Pendine was down to 23. It had been even smaller, at 20, in 1931. But times were hard. The Depression was biting. Soup kitchens and riots. It was a crisis time for everyone – not just the organisers of sporting events.

Motor Cycling's columnist 'Carbon' laments the decline in the entries for Pendine in 'Everybody's Business' – the 12th August issue. He points out the high cost of competition and the meagre rewards on offer in the form of prize money and bonuses. 'There was no money in racing in those days', Jack Carr is quoted as saying[132], 'You took what you could get. The Brough company used to come and watch, but never looked at me. Then one day George Brough rang me up and asked me to send the bike for them to do it up.' A few modifications were carried out on the engine and a new and larger tank fitted.

---

[132] *Craven Herald & Pioneer*: c.1956.

OFFICIAL PROGRAMME   **PRICE 1/-**

Carmarthen Motor Cycle and Light Car Club
(Affiliated to West South Wales Centre A.C.U.)

Annual Open
WELSH SPEED CHAMPIONSHIPS

for Motor Cycles, Motor Cycles & Sidecars, & Three-Wheelers, on

PENDINE SANDS
August Bank Holiday, Aug. 1st, 1932

IMPORTANT NOTICE

The A.C.U. have issued a permit for the Pendine Speed Championships, with the strict proviso that all spectators shall stand well away from the Course, and shall not, under any circumstances, walk or stand on the Course. A.C.U. Officials will be present and will immediately stop the meeting if this order is not obeyed.

The Committee of the West South Wales Centre A.C.U. therefore ask the Public in the interest of the sport, and their own safety, to assist them to the utmost in this matter.

Commencing at 10.30 a.m.

J. H. Carr (left), winner of the 50 and 100 miles championships, Pendine Sands, 1931

"The Motor Cycle" Photograph

Contains all the news and pictures of motor cycle sporting events.

EVERY THURSDAY, 3ᴅ

THE MOTOR CYCLE
The Motor Cyclist's Newspaper

JH Carr

It is appropriate that a photograph of JH Carr, who had won both the 50-mile and 100-mile events the previous year, adorns the front cover of the race programme. He is being congratulated by his friend, Brough racing man, Ron Storey: Storey in his familiar Fair Isle pullover. In the league table of Pendine motor cycle racers (in the 'private' or 'amateur' category) Carr is, according to form,[133] the most successful competitor of all, with a 75% success rate. Of the eight events he entered and finished, Jack won 6 – five of them championships – and came second twice. His nearest challenger was to be RJD 'Bob' Burnie of Swansea, with 58.82% success rate – over a much higher number of events entered. Carr's success, he acknowledged, was in no small measure due to the engineering skills of Brough's Ted Lester and Ron Storey, and the close working relationship they developed over the years.

Jack Carr was very discriminating when it came to his choice of mounts for the differing classes and styles of events he entered. He 'always liked to have a good bike' – endeavouring to ride what he considered the nearest Brough equivalents for the classes of event entered. He won the Junior Manx Grand Prix on a 350 New Imperial, in 1932, having come third in the 1931 Senior on a 490 Norton. He rated New Imperials very highly. A JAP-engined HRD would be his mount for the 1934 Senior Manx. Had Broughs made a 350 and a 500, no doubt they would have been his choice! He used the New Imp and the Norton in sand and road-racing events where one-litre engines were ineligible. The racing versions of these thoroughbreds were built with similar devotion to detail and uncompromising dedication to speed as Broughs. All were virtually bespoke products. This could not, alas, be said of production Nortons of the day.[134]

Jack stuck to the heavyweight SS100 model Brough throughout his racing career, changing it in 1928 and 1930, as far as records reveal. He maintained that in racing, once you are fortunate enough to have come upon one of those one-in-many-thousand racing engines, you are reluctant to part with it. But as Broughs/JAPs were subtly changing specification year-by-year, it was necessary to part with an old friend every so often in order to stay ahead of the game. Bob Berry, who was lucky enough to acquire Jack Carr's last 'Pendine' when it was 'pensioned off', maintained it was the most successful racing machine that Haydn Road ever produced. It won, he said, over a hundred 'Firsts', before being adapted to form the basis of Berry's record-breaker in 1948.[135] Frame 950X had a long association with Pendine Sands.

Jack Carr was a rider of exceptional ability, not only on sand, but as a road-racer. His name was invariably among the leaders at Southport Speed Championships where he was certified at speeds between 105 and 110 mph over the measured mile

---

[133]'Form' is calculated for the present purpose by the formula: placings/entries/%. This is admittedly arbitrary, as it enables visiting stars who won every event entered on a single visit to score maximum credits, dislodging, for instance, George Dance from his unquestionable pre-eminence overall and in the 'Trade' category. George Dance and Jack Carr were the 'top men', the 'Kings' of Pendine. (See Appendix II).

[134]See Bert Hopwood: *What Ever Happened to the British Motor Cycle Industry?* (Haynes/Foulis, 1981)

[135]In Berry's hand-written 'autobiographical' draft, via Bob Thredder.

JH Carr (Brough Superior, SS100 'Pendine'). [© *JH Carr collection*]

on the Brough.[136] He rode altogether seven times in the Manx Grand Prix. It was to be 'JH C's' last appearance at Pendine, as the organisers, in their wisdom, outlawed Broughs and their equivalents from competition until the petrol-rationed days that followed the second world war.

We learn from Carr's archive that William 'Bill' Lyons, designer and manufacturer of Swallow Sidecars (later of 'SS' Jaguar fame), was also at that time an enthusiastic visitor to sand-racing venues such as Southport and Pendine, with his sales manager, the celebrated Howard R Davies. Broughs used the Swallow and Hughes side-cars in combination racing.

RJD Burnie

By a quirk of fate, Bob Burnie was making his maiden appearance at Pendine at this meeting, on August 1st, 1932, on a 350cc Norton – always to be his favoured mount. The crowd who turned out on that fine day in August were privileged to see the two finest amateurs on Pendine pitted against each other. At the height of their respective careers Carr and Burnie were sufficiently able to have turned professional. Neither had the need to. As men of means (Burnie, an accountant at Fort Dunlop, was described as 'monied' and Carr was a successful businessman) they could afford to indulge themselves in the best available machines – and raced purely for fun.

Eddie Stephens and his brother Iago, of Carmarthen, had entered an ohv 350cc Calthorpe, a 493cc Model 90 Sunbeam and a 'bitza' Stephens Special. Jack Carr rode his New Imperial for the 350cc event. 'New Imps' were conventional, ohv, push-rod-engined machines of 346cc capacity, with mechanical lubrication via twin Pilgrim pumps. Though not conspicuously fast, they were beautifully engineered and handled outstandingly well. LF Griffiths of Bridgend was out on a 490 Norton, and always a formidable opponent. Clarry Wood had a big 750cc works Douglas, designed for the unlimited category and the sidecar event; and other Douglases were entered by J Stoodley of Carmarthen, AC Dobson of Coventry and N Treseder of Swansea. This was the first appearance of the name Treseder on the Pendine entry list. Norman and his son, (also Norman: 'Nobby'), were to score many successes on the beach over three decades. A crack Southport sand-man, J Blundell, had brought a 490 Norton down to try his luck on Pendine; and other Norton-mounted men were RM Crocker, Jack Davies of Swansea and CH Browning of Newport. Blundell elected to ride a Chater Lea for the 350 events, whereas F Fitt of Swansea and D Jones of Llandebie were on Rudge-Whitworth cycles for the 500cc 'Closed' events. D Jones was to put on a impressive show with the Rudge. There was a single Scott entry – AS Truman of Newport and the sole AJS was ridden by Alfie Griffiths of Carmarthen. CS Andrews of Carmarthen was on an Ariel, as was J Jones of Conwil Elvet. W Daniels of Trimsaran was out on a Dunelt. SS Evans, Coleford, was a late entry on his Brough Superior.

---

[136] ACU Certificates of Speed, dated Oct 4th, 1930 and Sept 10th, 1932, affirm speeds of 108.59 mph and 110.74mph at Southport Foreshore.

The Last Sidecar Race

There was a very small entry for the sidecar event. As a consequence, it was decided to make it the last contest of its kind. It is extraordinary to think that only a few years earlier the Welsh Sidecar TT was mounted as a special feature on the Wednesday morning of the three-day Bank Holiday event. The works teams stayed over for it and it was always well subscribed, drawing excited crowds of thousands for what was considered hilarious entertainment. Sidecar racing looked a lot more dangerous than it actually was, especially on sand. The manufacturers, worried about falling sales, became anxious to deflect doubts relating to passenger security implicit in the image of dare-devil risk-taking.

The official results as published in Tuesday's *Western Mail,* and *The Carmarthen Journal* of the 5th June were:

OPEN CLASSES:

25miles > 350cc
J H Carr (New Imperial)
(Only finisher)

WELSH HUNDRED, 1932

50 miles: unlimited
JH Carr (Brough Superior)
LF Griffiths (Norton)
J Blundell (Norton)

100 miles: unlimited
JH Carr (Brough Superior)
LF Griffiths (Norton)

10 miles: sidecar
CP Wood (Douglas)
SS Evans (Brough Superior)

CLOSED CLASSES

10 miles > 350cc
D Jones, Llandebie (Rudge Whitworth)
A Griffiths, Carmarthen (AJS)

10 miles > 500cc
D Jones (Rudge)
GS Andrews (Ariel)
A Griffiths (AJS)

50 miles: unlimited
D Jones (Rudge)
GS Andrews (Ariel)
(No winners' times given).

End of the 'Glory Days': August 1933

The man in the white suit was back in August, 1933. Ronnie Parkinson was the last of the old faithfuls 'from away'. He was the only 'celebrity' rider who had enrolled. There were no Unlimited classes for the 'big beasties' any more – another nail in the Pendine coffin. The organisers, in their wisdom, had ruled that 600cc was to be the engine size-limit for the 'big' race. This meant no more Brough Superiors, Coventry-Eagles, big Douglases, Grindlay-Peerless, Harley-Davidsons, Indians, McEvoys, Zeniths, or similar big, multi-cylinder exotica – those brutal machines that had thrilled the crowds since 1920; and the 100-mile race was again cut to 50. Pendine's Welsh Open Speed Championships were looking very like old King Lear, stripped of his courtiers, his honoraria, his dignity, year by year. Even press coverage, locally and nationally, was reduced to a brief, dismissive, paragraph.

The character of the event was going through a metamorphosis and it would re-emerge, pitched at a different level of interest and excitement. But it was sad to see the glamour of those glory days fade away, like beauty from a face. To some extent the glory was thrown away; but society and the nature of the sport was changing. Sand-racing events on Southport, St Andrews and elsewhere were experiencing a down-turn, but not to the extent that it affected Pendine in the early thirties.

Car ownership and interest in car-racing was fast overtaking that of the motor cycle. So far as motor cycle competition was concerned, greater emphasis was being placed on international road-racing and Grands Prix on the continent of Europe by manufacturers, oil and tyre companies and component-makers. Their advertising budgets were restricted by the economic down-turn and they chose to focus upon the wider, international achievement. Motor cycle sport, that once had threatened to oust 'the sport of kings', had become a specialist, minority interest.

The days of the great rider-manufacturers, those corner-stones of British enterprise and motor sporting life, had largely drawn to a close. There emerged 'career' development engineers, like Val Page and Edward Turner, whose ability to persuade board-rooms on policy and design was all-important. The amateur rider-tuners, creators of 'go faster' motors and 'specials' would, of course, continue as essential life-blood in motor racing.

The small high-performance motor car was becoming available as a viable alternative to the sporting motor cycle and at a price that was affordable. Roads and road surfaces, in particular, were improving, so that the appeal of the motor car over the motor cycle, among the young in particular, was fast taking hold. Austin, Morgan, Riley, MG, Singer and Wolseley designed and priced their little sporting models at the bachelor motor cyclist as a way of changing his (or her) status. Many did not want change, but nature took its course!

The sport of dirt-track, or speedway, racing had been imported from the USA via Australia in 1927, and became an overnight sensation. This diverted the attention of many riders and several manufacturers from other forms of racing, sand-racing being the obvious. There was real money in speedway, where there was little or none in sand-racing. Douglas, for instance, sold – and a great many for export – 1,300 speedway machines in 1929 alone. A tremendous demand for Rudge dirt-racers had the factory working overtime. They, and the JAP, competed directly with the very light weight Douglas.

'D Jones'

That elusive 'D Jones' (a name commoner in Wales than the ubiquitous John Smith!) disappears from the listings at this meeting. A Swansea club member, possibly from the Llandybïe – Pontarddulais area, he (or together with a name-sake) rode Rudge and Velocette machines from 1923 onwards and scores a very high rating in

Pendine's 'Hall of Fame'. D Jones emerges as the most successful local amateur in Closed events. In six outings he took five straight firsts, and one third place. In the quotient of performance this is top-of-the list, and second only to RJD Burnie and the legendary JH Carr in Open competition. Alas, he is one of those riders whose brilliant performances were of passing interest at the time. He never 'made a name', while history now records him as one of the very best.[137]

McNulty & Sivell

Two new names that were to become stalwarts of future sporting occasions made their way into the Pendine listings: PG Sivell, a Swansea club member, and J McNulty of Carmarthen (formerly Neath). McNulty was revered not only by circumstance of his being an Inland Revenue tax inspector but by dint of authority on his Rudge. Percy Sivell and John McNulty were to serve many faithful years on the WSW Wales Centre committee of the Auto Cycle Union, McNulty in particular being the local delegate to Headquarters and remembered for his punctilious attention to detail and blistering eye when he functioned as ACU scrutineer.

Sgonina

A surprise listing among the entries is that of Charles Sgonina, absent since 1925. Evidently he had returned from the USA – either permanently or on leave, having taken a post with the Gillette razor company. It is remarkable that the Sgonina Special, in storage for ten years, was back on Pendine for a gulp of sea-air. The SS was a hobby engineer's inspired effort at a 'double-knocker' Norton. It had taken that redoubtable firm the intervening time to perfect their 'single-knocker'. The double-knocker Norton was still twenty years away.

Norton 'Camshaft One'

The new 'International' CS1 Norton was lean and mean-looking. LS Cordingley had brought one down and demonstrated its potency to the Pendine crowd. Close-scrutiny in the paddock revealed that the 'cricket bat' timing cover was replaced, and the exhaust came out of the 'right' (both senses!) side. It was a work of art. The former Walter Moore-designed single overhead camshaft configuration, based on the classic 490cc (79 x 100mm) Norton bottom end, had successfully been refined by Joe Craig and Arthur Carroll. Bearings and lubrication had been improved. It was now a powerful and reliable heat-exchanger. This represented the bench-mark for future racing-engine design, destined to become the finest single-cylinder racing engine of all time.

---

[137] At the time of going to press the identity of this rider (or riders) had not been unveiled. Was 'he', as Ken George has suggested (pers. comm. Jan. 1999), a father-and-son succession of riders who earned the unflattering sobriquet of 'Dai Fall-off?' They were good when they stayed on!

AUGUST, 1934

OPEN EVENTS
THE WELSH HUNDRED, 1933

25 miles > 350cc
D Jones, Swansea (Velocette)
ETM Stephens (Calthorpe)
J McNulty (Rudge)

50 miles > 600cc
ETM Stephens (Sunbeam)
RJD Burnie (Norton)
N Treseder (Douglas)

CLOSED EVENTS

10 miles > 350cc
RF Parkinson (AJS)
J McNulty (Rudge)
D Jones (Velocette)

10 miles > 600cc
LS Cordingley (Norton)
E Smith, B' ham (Ariel)
ETM Stephens (Sunbeam)

LIGHT CARS

25 miles: light cars
AM Evans, Pendine (MG Magna)
J Thomas, Neath (Singer)
CR Henwood, Swansea (Singer)

OPEN

10 miles: light cars
AM Evans, Pendine (MG Magna)
J Thomas, (Singer)
CR Henwood, Swansea (Singer)
(Precisely the same order/result as for the 25-mile above)

Jack Thomas, the Neath motor dealer, had run his last race on Pendine in a little Singer sports car, coming characteristically second even in that. Though a motor cycle rider of the first standing in Wales, with several IoM outings to his credit, he was almost always unlucky on Pendine, coming in first only once in twenty outings. He had scored ten runner-up places. This seems to have been the last 'Light Car' event run on the beach in connection with the Welsh Speed Trials.

August 1934

The 1934 Annual Speed Trials at Pendine were run off in near-perfect conditions. Evidence of the worst of the Depression being over is reflected in the upsurge of interest. A local correspondent observes in *The Motor Cycle* that the course is 'considered by many to be Europe's finest speedway'. Judging by 'the number of vehicles and spectators on the beach', he suggests, 'it must have constituted a record crowd'. But he does not hazard an estimate of numbers. The correspondent emphasises that 'Throughout the meeting the organisation was exceedingly good and reflected great credit on the organisers'. He had been carefully briefed. In case no one had considered the matter, he advises that, 'Incidentally, the mile sprints clearly demonstrated the advantages possessed by the supertuned works motors'. There were no works-entries, though some entrants did send their engines to the works for overhaul. Parkinson was one such, but he trusted no one and always re-built and tuned his own engines, even after they had been back to the works!

RF Parkinson

This is illustrated in 'The White Devil of Pendine' – a prominent profile of RF Parkinson which appeared in *Motor Cycling*. Somewhere behind his Middlesborough men's outfitters shop, the part-time racing motorcyclist had a workshop where he prepared his engines for racing. The interviewer, 'Castor', noted it was Very Clean. When he received a brand-new engine from the Wolverhampton works, Parkinson's procedure was as follows:

> I have it right to bits and put it up to my own satisfaction; then, I can blame myself if anything blows up, and probably gain a bit of experience from it too. Ninety-nine times the works racing staff will do the job as well as I can myself . . . but if I weren't to go over it, I should kick myself when something went wrong the hundredth time.

Names on the Pendine race programme entry list come and go. LS Cordingley, from Haslingden, north of Manchester, who appears again with his very fast camshaft Norton, was a considerable rider. His name is seen in the MGP listings and at sand meetings on Blackpool, Southport, Scarborough and Redcar sands, always somewhere in contention. He was Parkinson's main rival on the day. Strangers, E Smith and C Bowers of Birmingham came down with 500 Ariels and were never heard of again. AA Ashbury of Birmingham, who entered on a Velocette, was also a newcomer, as was L Kingston of Swansea, entered on Velocette and Sunbeam machines. A Ballard of Malvern is another casual Pendine entrant on a Norton.

Some old stalwarts and those who were to become long-serving 'Pendiners', present in strength and depth, included Eddie Stephens on a model 30 Sunbeam, Leslie Griffiths, Bob Burnie, Percy Sivell and Reg Good on Nortons. John McNulty is on a Rudge and Eddie's brother Iago Stephens, absent for a while, has entered on a jocularly-named 'Old Un'.

The Light Car Classes included TT Nisbet, Carmarthen and C Bowen, Whitland, in MGs; CR Henwood, Swansea in a Singer, LC Phillips, Narberth, entered a Morris and the only other contestant, a mysterious one that Handel Davies conjured up – something 'On Trial'. The car races over 5, 10 and 20 miles seem all to have been cancelled – presumably, from the paucity of entry, from lack of interest. A **Cancelled** stamp is punched on the 'Car Classes Restricted' page.

From the account published in *Motor Cycling* , it seems to have been a lovely day, against the weather forecast. The day's sport was upset by non-starters and retirements from minor mechanical misfortunes, resulting in a spectacle about as thrilling as a church fête, with Parkinson's artistic cornering the sole memory to carry away:

> By [lunch] time the competitors' paddock was littered with crocked models, and only four competitors came to the line [for the 25-mile race]. Parkinson's AJS was again to the fore, his speed on the straights and beautifully clean cornering being a treat to watch. PG Sivell, on a very standard-looking Norton, and MacNully [*sic*], on a rather slow Rudge, third. A special prize must surely go to AE Davies, who gamely rode a very old, flat-tanked AJS.

OPEN EVENTS

One mile sprint > 350cc
RF Parkinson (348 AJS)
PG Sivell (348 Norton)

one mile sprint > 600cc
E Ballard, Malvern (Norton)
RJD Burnie (490 Norton)
RF Parkinson (348 AJS)

10 miles > 350cc
RF Parkinson (348 AJS)
PG Sivell (348 Norton)

10 miles > 600cc
RJD Burnie (490 Norton)
LS Cordingley (490 Norton)

25 miles > 350cc
RF Parkinson (348 AJS)
PG Sivell (348 Norton)

THE WELSH HUNDRED, 1934

50 miles > 600cc
LS Cordingley (490 Norton)
RJD Burnie (490 Norton)
ETM Stephens (493 Sunbeam)

(No closed events are recorded).

PG Sivell (Norton) & RF Parkinson (AJS). [© *Photo courtesy of Mrs J Sivell*]

RJD Burnie (New Imperial 492cc V-twin), August 1936.

Stanley Wood (left), with ETM Stephens at the Nelson Hotel. CMC&LCC annual dinner and award ceremony, Dec 1935.
[*George Weeks photo*]

12. Stanley Wood on Pendine

August 1935

THE *Western Mail*, Wales's 'National Daily' got it wrong, on August 6th, 1935, when it reported in a column headline that 'STANLEY WOODS WINS FOUR RACES', on a New Imperial, in the 'Welsh Speed Championships at Pendine'. The Cardiff broadsheet expresses no excitement over what would have been the first, and sensational, appearance in Wales of the legendary Stanley Woods, 10 times TT-winner, and the best racing motor cyclist in the world. This sporting coup occupies a six-inch column of race-result reportage, tucked away at the foot of the racing page. Arrival on the patch of a motor racing legend deserved more fulsome coverage.

Except that it was untrue. In August 1935, Woods was in Italy. He had left Husqvarna, to whom he had been signed for an unhappy year to ride the 500 V-twin, and changed stables – to the Italian Moto Guzzi concern. He was attached to them in international road racing competition on the continental circuit. For 'home' events he had agreed to be retained by Velocette. He never raced on sand. Nor for New Imperial.

It was not good enough to get it *nearly* right. A Stanley Wood did win four races at Pendine on works-prepared New Imperials that August Bank Holiday Monday. Many people, like the *Western Mail's* man, did come away believing they had seen the Great Dubliner. The rider they had seen was TT-rider, S 'Ginger' Wood. Ginger was a celebrity in his own right. He put on a demonstration of his prowess before a crowd estimated by *The Carmarthen Journal* at 20,000. It looks very much as if Wood had been enticed to appear as a 'draw', part of a policy to revive Pendine's flagging fortunes by inviting a celebrity rider each year. Stanley, aka 'Ginger', was an imaginative choice.

Ginger Wood

Ginger Wood had been involved with New Imperial at Brooklands in 1934 and 1935. *The Motor Cycle* had offered a prize for the first multi-cylinder 500cc British motor cycle to cover 100 miles in one hour on a British track. On that same 60-degree 500cc V-twin (62.5 x 80 mm) push-rod engined New Imperial, Ginger had covered 100.41 miles at Brooklands within the hour. He was timed at over 122 mph over the half-mile, while circulating the Brooklands track at a 107.8 mph lap average. Lapping Brooklands on an improved version of the 'New Imp 500' later in 1935, Ginger Wood had raised the lap record for a 500 to 115.82 mph. It was a beast of a machine to handle, due to its unwieldy steering and high centre of gravity. He was a very skilled and courageous rider.

It was the unlucky fate of Ginger Wood to have 'marked' his near-namesake in international motor-cycle road-racing. At a time when Nortons was the place to be for any 'top drawer' rider, Nortons already had their quota of best men – Woods, Jimmie Simpson, Jimmie Guthrie and Walter Rusk. Joe Craig, who did not like Ginger, gave him a 'one chance' ride with Nortons at the Dutch GP on one occasion, warning him against dropping the bike. Ginger, who had all the way lain third to Guthrie in the wet, came in third – which was not good enough for Craig. There just was not another stable – the equal of Nortons – to which he could turn, though he rode for George Patchett on Jawas, for FN and Vincent. He made a mistake in turning down a BMW works place.

Bob Burnie was out on a 350 Norton; Leslie Griffiths of Bridgend, a Norton loyalist throughout his long racing career, unusually for him, appeared on an OK Supreme. The pretty little Jones-designed ohc engine performed surprisingly well for him in the 350 class. Lionel Thomas was giving the Sunbeam 'Sprint' an outing, and Percy Sivell of Swansea was winding up his trials-based ES2 Norton. Brothers Iago and Eddie Stephens had Sunbeam and Rudge mounts, respectively. AS Griffiths of Carmarthen had chosen an Ariel and his club-mate RM Rees was on a very fast Rudge. New names were TOE James of Swansea on a BSA and GV Parfitt, Swansea, on a Norton. E Ballard was over from Malvern with a Norton and J Mansfield of Clithero was also Norton-mounted. G Johnson of Ystalyfera was on a Panther – a rarity for Pendine. But with Stanley Wood there and on brilliant form on the works New Imperials, no one else was to get much of a look in.

The official results were

One mile sprint > 350cc
LF Griffiths (OK Supreme)
RJD Burnie (348 Norton)
LS Cordingley (348 Norton)

one mile sprint > 500cc
S Wood (New Imperial)
LF Griffiths (Norton)
E Ballard, Malvern (Norton)

10 miles > 250cc
S Wood (New Imperial)

10 miles > 350cc
RJD Burnie (Norton)
LS Cordingley (Norton)
AS Griffiths, Carmarthen (Excelsior)

10 miles > 500cc
S Wood (New Imperial)
LF Griffiths (Norton)
RJD Burnie (Norton)

25 miles > 350cc
RJD Burnie (Norton)
LV Thomas (Sunbeam)
PG Sivell (Norton)

THE WELSH HUNDRED, 1935

50 miles > 500cc
S Wood (New Imperial)
LF Griffiths (Norton)

50 miles > 350cc
RJD Burnie (Norton)
PG Sivell (Norton)

'Flying Spray'.

George Eyston (2)

Mr Wilfred Morgan had been contacted by Capt George Eyston who paid a flying visit to Pendine in December, 1935. Mr Morgan, 'whose advice on the beach [condition] had always been much sought after by all the speed aces who have visited Pendine',[138] was a coastguard and the recognised local fount of knowledge on predicting the vagaries of water tables and tides. February's spring tides, he predicted, would be the optimum period to contemplate a record attempt.

Eyston's interest was centred on a heavy-oil engine, designed by Harry Ricardo. His car 'Flying Spray' – so called when fitted with the 17-litre V-12 (un-named, 'secret') engine, on trial for the RAF – was dubbed 'Speed of the Wind' when accommodating the 21-litre Rolls Royce 'Kestrel' petrol engine, with which he had secured records at Utah.[139] In diesel trim it also exhibited some external modifications: namely, a massive duralmin tubular oil-cooler on the scuttle and a curious three-tier 'clear-vision' windscreen, designed specifically to overcome problems of flying spray on Pendine. It worked on the principle of air-stream deflection. The driver was actually looking out through a space between the three

---

[138] *The Motor* Dec 10, 1935.
[139] Dylan Thomas in his masterpiece, *Under Milk Wood,* makes oblique reference to this through one of his characters, the obdurate farmer, Utah Watkins, who lives at the fictional Salt Lake Farm. Salt House Farm was, in fact, in the poet's line of sight as he looked out of his 'writing shed' at the Boat House, above the Taf estuary, towards Laugharne Burrows and the 'top' end of Pendine beach where Land Speed Record machines had once roared.

screens, placed so that they diverted draught, sand and 'flying spray' to one side. The cockpit was fitted with a special, protective 'hard-top'.

During the third week of February, 1936, GET Eyston made some trial passes up and down the beach in 'Flying Spray', finding that sand drag was holding him back from his 140 mph target, to beat American Dave Evans's 137 mph for a diesel car over the 'flying' mile and kilometre. He would need to lower the rear axle ratio before seriously attempting the record. Though he had intended to return to Pendine for the bid, he decided subsequently to cut his losses and make for the Bonneville Flats near Salt Lake City, USA.

August 1936

1936: A strong south-west wind, but perfect conditions prevailed on Monday, August 3rd. According to *The Welshman*

> An almost incessant stream of motor vehicles of every class and description poured in during the morning from all parts of the country.

Motor vehicles were permitted on to the beach, parked facing the course in double and treble column between the dunes and the 'down' straight. Some enthusiasts and competitors pitched tents in the dunes and camped for two or three days. A small residential caravan or two were seen above the high tide-line, some with motor bikes in bits. Striped awnings, sun-umbrellas, canvas wind-breaks, afforded shelter. Mobile refreshment vendors came. Some had carts; others with vans or lorries offered milky tea with sand and gritty sandwiches. You could buy 'pop' – ginger beer, sarsaparilla, and dandelion-and-burdock – and ice cream. From the smell of onions you could get home-made faggots, peas, sausages – and chips. There were boxes of oranges, plums and William pears on the lorries. These were sold in brown paper bags.

Most women brought their own food, if they were country Welsh – not trusting 'bought' meals. You boiled the kettle over an oil-stove or a fire of dry driftwood on which salty bacon and eggs could be fried. The handiest was cold hard boileds, with lettuce, tomatoes, meat or cheese. Tea from the flask, or Camp coffee.

There were bookies shouting odds. You could have your photo 'pulled' by the man who threw a black cloth over his head; or have your fortune told in a little tent where there was a long queue of women and the odd, silly, fellow. There was a tattooist; and a strong man with chains around his body. Sometimes, if the weather was fine enough, a couple of planes flew in from Swansea. You could have a flip round the bay in a bi-plane that trailed a banner advertising Craven 'A' or Shell petrol. The cost was 5/-.

It was a day by the sea. For some. Children built sandcastles and played games in the dunes where sweethearts lay and people came to 'look' and pee. Dogs barked. Motors revved and banged. Mothers buttered the bread and cut ham. Sisters squinted at the Fair-isled young fellows with pipes, in baggy slacks. The men evaluated the new cars and the latest-model bikes and knew about the engines and some of the riders. Grandmas fussed, while grandfathers remembered Sgonina and drank brown ale from a flagon; then slept under a knotted handkerchief, their trousers rolled up at the calf.

The noise of the start was quite terrific – like a roll of thunder. The ground shuddered – and the smell of methyl fuel and Castrol 'Racing' oil hung on in the air, intoxicating and unforgettable. It was hard to see, unless you were small enough to squeeze through to the front, under the wire. The dunes were too far. Just after the start of a race – when the bikes had gone 'up' – there was this hush. Like in the lull between the races, the sea boomed and sighed at a distance. You could hear the sea, and the gulls cry, 'Pendine!'.

Something of a celebrity appearance was that of 'M Davies, Llanfyrnach' who was entered on a 498cc Sunbeam. This was Mansel Davies, now in his mid-fifties, who had won the first 'official' motor cycle race on the beach thirty years earlier on his brother's Humber motor bicycle, bravely having a nostalgic 'go'! The Davieses Llanfyrnach ran a transport and garage business, and had become agents for Sunbeam motor cycles in the early twenties. An unusual motor cycle in any event was the little SOS entered by J Treseder. A machine with a water-cooled engine, the brain

RJD Burnie (Norton). [*Clifford H Evans photo*]

child of Len Vale-Onslow of Worcester, it unfortunately gave an inauspicious account of itself. Being the only entry in the 350cc Closed class the trophy was guaranteed. But, on the very first lap, it broke down. Included in the entry-list we find one or two 'star' names: Norton man, LS Cordingley of Haslingden, who had scored successes in the 1934 Welsh Speed Championships against RF Parkinson's AJS; both men entered again, this time on the new 'Inter' Nortons. JB 'Joey' Moss of Manchester, an Excelsior Manxman adherent on this occasion, was another one to watch; and, importantly for Wales, 1936 saw the debut of a man destined for great things in his racing career, JD (Jack) Daniels of Swansea, who was entered on Norton machines, learning his way – but making no particular impression on this occasion.

OPEN EVENTS
One mile sprint > 350cc
RJD Burnie (348 Norton)
ETM Stephens (Rudge)
LS Cordingley (348 Norton)

One mile sprint > 600cc
LF Griffiths (Norton)
AS Griffiths, Carmarthen (Ariel)
ETM Stephens (Rudge)

10 miles > 350cc
RJD Burnie (348 Norton)
LS Cordingley (348 Norton)
J McNulty (Rudge)

10 miles > 600cc
LF Griffiths (Norton)
ETM Stephens (Rudge)
EG Bennett (Ariel)

THE WELSH HUNDRED, 1936
25 miles >350cc
RJD Burnie (348 Norton)
PG Sivell (348 Norton)

50 miles > 600cc
RJD Burnie (490 Norton)
LS Cordingley (490 Norton)
(Only two finishers)

Nortons were beginning to sweep the board in competition, in a way which must have been disheartening for other manufacturers. Bob Burnie had had a magnificent day out, his reputation for contumely somewhat justified!

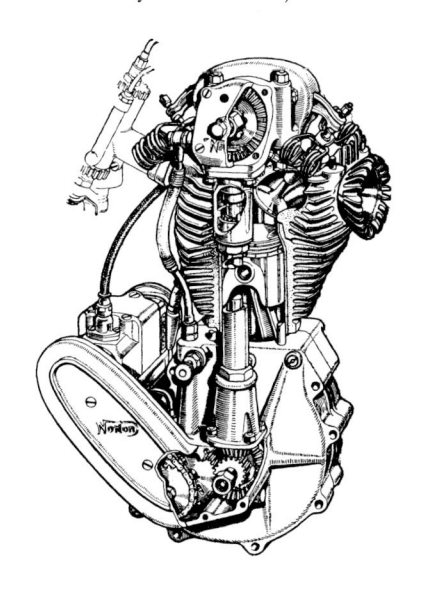

13. The First Welsh Grand Prix

August 1937

SOMEONE had a brilliant idea for 1937. 'The Welsh TT' as a title for the August Bank Holiday Hundred-mile race on Pendine sands, having been dropped ten years earlier, things – from a prestige point of view – had faced downhill ever since. A new title for the big race was being suggested – as 'The Welsh Hundred' did not exactly have them rolling in the aisles. Neither was it actually descriptive of (as-often-as-not) a 50-mile race. Now, the title 'The Welsh Grand Prix' definitely had a certain ring about it, and nobody could say them nay, nor lay claim to exclusivity.[140] The term 'Grand Prix' ('Big Prize') was in general use throughout the sporting world.

And so the first Welsh Grand Prix was run off at Pendine on Monday, August 2nd, 1937. The categories 'Senior' and 'Junior' were adopted to designate the 600cc x 50-mile category, and 350cc x 25-miles, respectively. There was still no Unlimited category on this occasion; but that mistake would be rectified in the future.

The £25 'big prize', with John Bull[141] Cup and replica, did not attract any 'stars' or very many 'foreigners' in 1937. There were no old friends of Pendine such as Wood, Anstice, Cordingley or Parkinson. Corporate accountant, DR Griffith, '*Cymro ar wasgar*' (exiled Welshman), was home from London. He fielded a classy New Hudson. EA Beckham, a Londoner, was on an exciting TT-Replica Vincent-HRD Comet – the first to be seen on Pendine.[142] The rising Swansea ace, JD Daniels, was seen on a Mk V1 KTT Velocette and a 348 Norton.

The local stars were out in force: ETM Stephens, LF Griffiths, LV Thomas and N Treseder – all on 490 Nortons. RJD Burnie, in addition to his usual favoured 348 Norton, had brought down from Birmingham an intriguing works, V-twin, (492cc) New Imperial. The rumour was that Bob Burnie, through connections with Nortons, may have been evaluating it. (He need not have bothered, for New Imperial were to fail in 1937). Gordon Bennett, always original, was at the start-line on an Ariel, as was CS Andrews of Carmarthen.

LF Griffiths was the envy of all on the day. Its Bracebridge Street packing-crate straw still in evidence, his brand-new Norton 'International' had been rolled out. It had

---

[140](Or '*Gwobr Fawr Cymru*'?: not quite as beguiling as 'The Welsh Grand Prix', somehow!)
[141]The tyre company.
[142]A sprung-frame 500cc JAP-engined version, as there were no classes above 600cc. The 1000cc twin had just been announced.

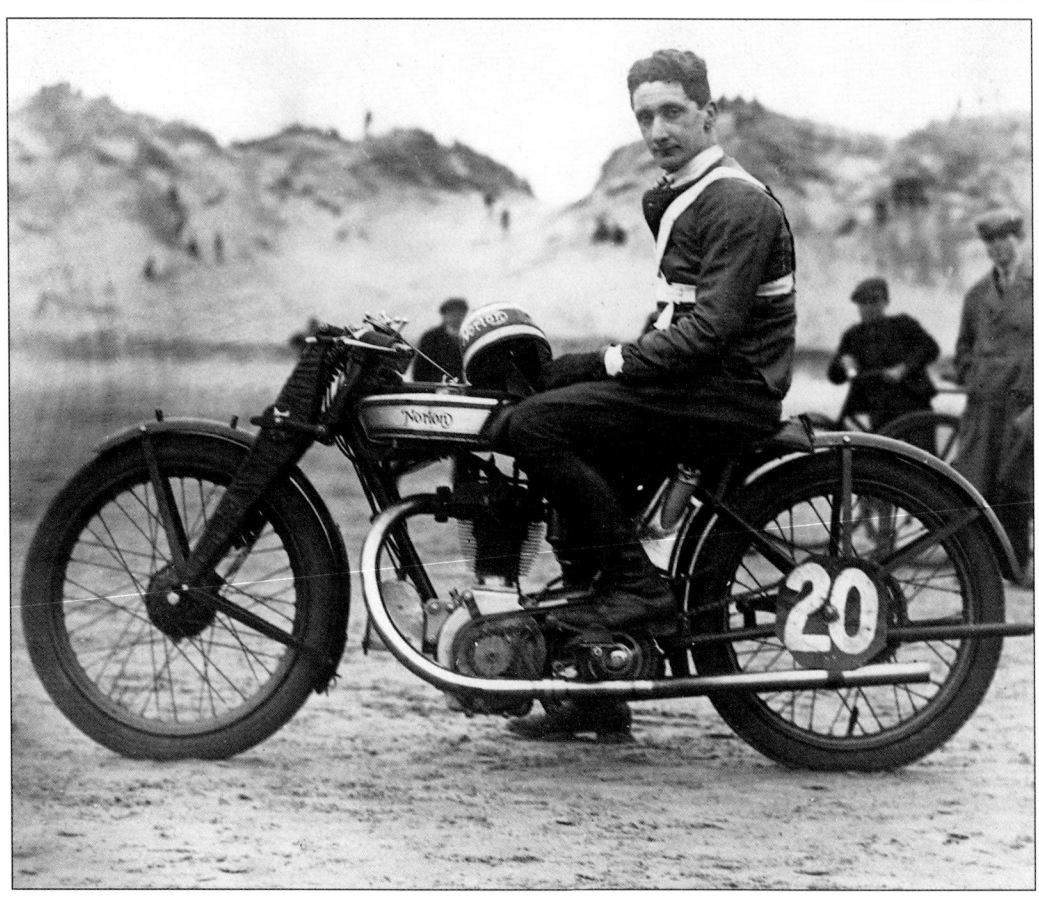

LF Griffiths: above, Aug 1927 (Norton Model 18); below, Aug 1950 (Manx Norton). [*LA Lusardi photo*]

innovative 'garden gate' rear suspension: plungers resembling big hinges supporting its frame, without damping.[143] Nortons had been very slow in developing fully-sprung suspension, on the principle that 'what was good enough for the Isle of Man was good enough' – for all occasions. The new Norton frame would in time more than prove its worth, but in 1937 the ohc engine's reliability was still suspect in long-distance events. Nevertheless, Leslie swept the board with his 'new toy', the Nortons on this occasion emphatically living up to Harold Daniel's coinage: 'Unapproachable'.

One-mile sprint > 350cc
RJD Burnie (Norton)
JSA Humphries (OK Supreme)
G Thomas, Swansea (Norton)

one-mile sprint > 600cc
LF Griffiths (Norton)
ETM Stephens (Norton)
JSA Humphries (OK Supreme)

10 miles > 600cc
LF Griffiths (Norton)

ETM Stephens (Norton)
LV Thomas (Norton)

4 miles > 350cc
JD Daniels (Velocette)
DW Protheroe, Llanelly (Velocette)
RC Lewis, Carmarthen (Triumph)

25 miles > 350cc
RJD Burnie (Norton)
JD Daniels (Norton)
LV Thomas (Sunbeam)

A field of some fifteen riders and their motor cycles lined up for the rolling start of the first Welsh Grand Prix. Burnie was tipped – on the New Imperial.

THE FIRST WELSH GRAND PRIX, 1937

50 miles > 600cc
LF Griffiths (490 Norton)
ETM Stephens (490 Norton)
JD Daniels (348 Norton)
N Treseder (490 Norton)
CS Andrews (Ariel)
EA Beckham (Vincent-HRD)
Winner's Average Speed: 76mph.

LF Griffiths

An elusive, introvert and sometimes truculent character, Leslie Frederick Griffiths, motor cycle dealer and specialist motor engineer of Bridgend, was a distinctive stylist on a racing motorcycle. His familiar orange and brown, wasp-striped helmet, reminiscent of Tommy Spann's shirt, and No 11 plate (after his business and home address – No 11, Ewenny Road) symbolised at Pendine the local defence against

---

[143] Leslie Griffiths's riding-style was very easy to distinguish from a distance, especially in profile, as he always adopted a very upright stance. DD Snow, in conversation (Aug 1998), described him as 'a very upright gentleman'. Perfect!

works entrants and marauding outsiders. His first placing in this, the first Welsh Grand Prix, was well-deserved and possibly long overdue, though he generally scored best in sprint events.[144] Sand-racing was his speciality; Pendine, in his long career in motor cycle racing, his favourite venue.[145] He began racing in 1921, and made his first appearance on Pendine in 1922, riding a Sunbeam in the first 100-mile Welsh TT. Leslie won the last Pendine race in 1955.

Les Griffiths's was the life of the sporting bachelor for most of his racing days. Athletic, a first-class rugby player – who is said to have trialled for Wales – and fond of dog-and-gun pursuits, he was a curious mixture of shyness and the gregarious. A friend described him as 'a half-pint man on the edge of the crowd'. Les kept to himself. Always the owner of a 'smart' car, whether a Wolesley Hornet or an ex-Hawthorn 140-engined XK-120 Jaguar, he cut something of a dash around the watering holes of Bridgend and the Vale[146]. Rarely did he ride motor cycles on the road: 'Far too dangerous!' He married a long-standing lady-friend quite late in life.

His racing stance, easily distinguishable, being of the 'up' variety, could be detected from a distance. Using his body as an 'air-brake' on the approach to corners, in a pronounced sit-up-and-beg attitude, while changing down smoothly, he was always light on brakes. Elbows out, he employed his own, wide, racing line that was clean and unfussed, reminiscent of that other great sand-racing artist, CP 'Clarry' Wood[147]. Film footage exists[148] of LF G racing against that doyen of sand-racers, Fred Rist, at Pendine, in 1951. The contrast could not be more pronounced – Fred, foot stuck out, showering sand on the corners like a snow-plough, Leslie riding immaculately round the rim, like a disdainful maiden aunt, devoid of histrionics, but equally quick. Not such a spectacle for the crowd, perhaps, but getting there in the end. And fast!

Bob Burnie's venture on the V-twin 499 New Imperial was a tribute to his driving skill. Evidently impressed by Ginger Wood's amazing performance the previous year, he may not have realised the extent to which Ginger's strength and bravery had disguised the porcine handling qualities of the 'Vee Imp'. Nevertheless, he put up a sensational show in the Grand Prix, gallantly contesting with JD Daniels and ETM Stephens – both on 500 Nortons – for third and second place, until trouble struck on lap 24. The squabble had kept the crowd on its toes. 'The Imp was conspicuously faster on the straight bits, but handling and reliability were bugbears. It needed a lot

---

[144]His off-the-mark sprint technique involved a straight-pipe extension to his exhaust, secured by weak pin - which soon broke under pressure - and jettisoned itself! (Haydn Rees, 1998).

[145]LF G is known to have competed in the Porthcawl opening (post-war) sand meeting in 1921,where he gained 3 firsts. He was at the Ewenny Hill-climb meeting in 1923,where he won the Ewenny Cup for fastest time-of-day and firsts in the 500, 750 & and Unlimited classes. He came second three times at Abergarw (Hill-climb) in 1924. On a Rex-Acme Blackburne he came first in the half-mile sprint for 350cc machines, also in 1924. He won the Handel Davies cup at Oxwich, July, 1926 and the 10- and 20-mile races at Port Talbot, 1926. His name is regularly among the entries for Pembrey, Port Talbot and 'Swansea Sands' (Oxwich?) throughout the twenties. (From 'Record of Successes Notice' in the former Ewenny St office, ghoulishly headed: 'They never wear out, they are passed on to the next-of-kin').

[146]Pers. reminiscences: Messrs A Allen, B Hurley, H Rees, G Perrott and P Smith, 1998.

[147]*Vide* Denis Parkinson: *Foreword*, above.

[148]*Vintage Motorcycling* Vol 1. Freelance TV Prods, Baglan, W. Glam. SA12 8DG.

STANDARD CLASSES

more development'[149]. Treseder over-reached himself on lap 18. He took a bend too fast and went wide, hit a patch of wet sand and went 'a-over-t', but was only winded, not hurt. He bravely resumed. This was the Pendine spirit!

ETM Stephens (New Imperial). [*LA Lusardi photo*]

30 miles > 350cc
RJD Burnie (348 Norton)
JD Daniels (348 Norton)
LV Thomas (348 Norton)

OPEN EVENTS

10 miles > 600cc
LF Griffiths (Norton)
P Williams (Rudge)
ETM Stephens (Norton)

STANDARD MACHINES

10 miles > 350cc
JD Daniels (Velocette)
DW Protheroe (Velocette)
RC Lewis (Triumph)

10 miles > 600cc
JD Daniels (Velocette)
DW Protheroe (Velocette)
RC Lewis (Triumph)
(Precisely as above)

FOUNDER'S CUP

25 miles > 350cc
RJD Burnie Norton)
JD Daniels (Norton)
LV Thomas (Sunbeam)

10-mile sprint > 600cc
LF Griffiths (499 Norton)
ETM Stephens (490 Norton)
LV Thomas (490 Norton)

Eddie Stephens, Carmarthen, came off in the Junior and was unable to continue. JD Daniels rode the last lap holding his carburettor in place with one hand.

---
[149]Pers. comm. RM Rees, Nov 1998.

Whitsun 1938

At both Whitsun and August Bank Holiday 'Welsh Speed Races' in 1938, a new idea was tried out. As a pure safety consideration, there was a certain logic in separating racing machines from standard models in direct competition. Even with the engine-capacity limitation imposed in recent years, full-race-trim 500 Nortons were capable of speeds and acceleration not far short of the superbikes of a recently by-gone era. They were hitting 100 – 110mph on the straights, Brough-fashion; and to have one of these come up behind a 250 Dunelt, or a small commuter Matchless, in a race involving mixed classes, was vexatious. A race among standard machines served the useful purpose of bringing on beginners, a theatre where they could learn the lines and project themselves towards a performance. To make it interesting, some of the older generation, great riders from the past, like Handel Davies, joined in occasionally.

There was also some value – from a consumer stand-point – in seeing how one catalogue machine fared in terms of performance and stamina against another. In theory, the spectacle and perspective were improved and clarified by separation into distinct categories. The difficulty, often debated at ACU centre and at club level was, of course, in defining a 'standard' – as opposed to a 'racing' machine. A great number of 'road-legal' motor cycles were ridden to Pendine, raced, and ridden home again! Races for 'bog standard' bikes, especially the lightweights, could be tedious to watch, unless imported or local 'needle' arose – as could occur with the Treseder boys.

From the foxing, the water marks and pocket-damage on a copy of a programme for the June 6th meeting, Whit Monday, it was something more than a damp day. According to *The Western Mail*:

> Heavy rain, accompanied by a strong south-westerly wind, marred the second part of the Welsh open speed races on Pendine Sands under the auspices of the Carmarthen Motor Cycle and Light Car Club. In spite of the weather, however, a good size crowd witnessed some close finishes.

The entry was an especially good one from the south Wales clubs. The Carmarthen clubmen, out in force, numbered: garage-proprietor ETM Stephens (New Imperial, Triumph, Norton), taxman, J McNulty (Rudge), men's outfitter, RM Rees (OK Supreme), agricultural contractor, WH Tucker (Excelsior), garage proprietor, RC Lewis (Norton), engineers CS Andrews and B Edwards (Ariels). Swansea fielded RJD Burnie (Norton), LV Thomas (Sunbeam), G Thomas (Velocette), W Williams (600cc Scott) and DJ Snell on a 596cc Douglas – (though this machine is listed as 494cc). Handel Davies had come with a battered-looking 250 Matchless which, nevertheless, was in good enough fettle to win him the sprint. RC Hazel had come down from Coventry with his 349 Rudge, FC Trott of Birmingham had a 349 Norton and LF Griffiths, Bridgend, had entered the 490 Norton.

The official results:

STANDARD CLASSES

One-mile sprint > 250cc
H (Handel) Davies (Matchless)
RM Rees, Carmarthen (OK Supreme)

one mile sprint > 350cc
ETM Stephens (Triumph)
FC Trott, Birmingham (349 Norton)
WH Tucker (Excelsior)

one mile sprint > 600cc
B Edwards (Ariel)
ETM Stephens (Triumph)
P Williams, Swansea (Rudge)

4 miles > 250cc
G Thomas (Velocette)
RM Rees (OK Supreme)
H Davies (Matchless)

4 miles > 350cc
ETM Stephens (350 Triumph)
FC Trott (349 Norton)

4 miles > 600cc
ETM Stephens (Triumph)
B Edwards, Carmarthen (Ariel)
P Williams (Rudge)

10 miles > 250cc
H Davies (Matchless)
G Thomas (Velocette)

10 miles > 350cc
ETM Stephens (Triumph)
RM Rees, Carmarthen (OK Supreme)

10 miles > 600cc
ETM Stephens (Triumph)
CS Andrews (Ariel)
P Williams (Rudge)

RACING CLASSES

One-mile sprint > 350cc
RJD Burnie (Norton)
G Thomas, Swansea (Norton)
RC Hazel, Coventry (Rudge)

one mile sprint > 600cc
LF Griffiths (490 Norton)
ETM Stephens (499 Norton)

5 miles > 350cc
RJD Burnie (349 Norton)
ETM Stephens (348 New Imperial)
RC Hazell, Coventry (Rudge)

5 miles > 600cc
LF Griffiths (490 Norton)
ETM Stephens (499 Norton)
DJ Snell (596cc Douglas)

10 miles > 600cc
LF Griffiths (490 Norton)
ETM Stephens (499 Norton)

30 miles > 350cc
RJD Burnie (349 Norton)
ETM Stephens (348 New Imperial)

30 miles > 600cc
LF Griffiths (490 Norton)
RJD Burnie (349 Norton)
ETM Stephens (499 Norton)

Tommy McEwan (Norton), August, 1938. [*LA Lusardi* photo]

T McEwan (Norton), 1937.

14. The Fife Flier

August 1938

THE August Bank Holiday Monday Welsh Speed Championships meeting at Pendine in 1938 included separate classes for standard and racing machines. The main events were the Welsh Junior and Senior Grands Prix, to take place in the afternoon. The organisers were the Carmarthen Motor Cycle and Light Car Club. There was an improved number of entries (48 listed), a number of 'star' riders and, by the unblemished crispness of the surviving annotated race programme, in this instance a fine and dry day. To begin with!

The celebrity riders attracted to the event, offering a £20 prize and a John Bull Cup replica, were Norton ace Tommy McEwan, the Scottish national champion, who virtually swept the board in the open classes, and the up-and-coming Jack Brett, Leeds, also on a Norton. Another Manx Grand Prix rider, Wilf Billington of Manchester (Rudge), made his first appearance. Both he and Brett were somewhat overshadowed on this outing.

Local heroes, celebrities in their own right, LF Griffiths, LV Thomas, RJD Burnie and ETM Stephens were all on Nortons. Bob Burnie, unusually for him, had entered a much-used looking 350 Sunbeam for the sprint event in the morning. The likelihood is that he borrowed LV Thomas's little secret weapon. It gave Tommy McEwan a fright!

Londoners had come down – D Turpin from Wembley, with a 499 Sunbeam; from Putney, WH Griffiths with a 497 Ariel; and EA Beckenham of Fulham again, with the 498 Vincent-HRD.

Formerly based in London, company accountant DR Griffith transferred to Richard Thomas & Baldwin's offices in South Wales. He became a Swansea club member with his intriguingly named 'VMC' which, he said, 'comprised of parts from Various Makes Combined'.[150] His other club-mates were George 'the music shop' Snell (Douglas), Pat Williams (Rudge) and ACU Centre Secretary, E Gordon Bennett (497 Ariel). Notable absentees were Handel Davies and Swansea Comet Club member, JD 'Danny' Daniels.

These two redoubtable members were residing under a temporary cloud, issued forth by the local ACU disciplinary committee in connection with their participation in an 'unauthorised' Grass-Track event in Swansea to raise money for a local school.

---

[150] Pers. conv. 1986.

They were each penalised with a month's suspension from competition within the Centre's area. Men of their experience (Handel as handicapper) should have known better than to involve themselves in a competition which was uninsured by the ACU's public liability policy.[151]

Miss M Lewis – a first for Pendine – was entered on a 500 Norton. RG Davies turned out on a lightweight Excelsior, and DC Gershon on a 498 Excelsior-JAP. The latter all represented Llanelly. And there was a sole Neath rider, G Harry, on a standard lightweight Matchless. Milford Haven man, M McNally, was on a lightweight standard Rudge.

The Carmarthen boys were RC Lewis (Norton), CS Andrews (Ariel), and DL Jenkins (Douglas). Bryn Edwards ('Ocky Tipi') had turned up as well on his favourite Ariel. Handel Davies, that stalwart of Pendine, was on the 250 Excelsior Manxman [OCY 450].

The official results:

**CLOSED
STANDARD MACHINES**

One mile sprint > 250cc
RG Davies, Llanelly (249 Excelsior)
M McNally, Milford (245 Rudge)

one mile sprint > 350
ETM Stephens (350 Triumph)
G Morgan, Carmarthen (Excelsior)

one mile sprint > 600cc
Miss M Lewis, Llanelly (Norton)
B Edwards (Ariel)

10 miles > 250cc
RG Davies, Llanelly (249 Excelsior)
G Harry, Neath (250 Matchless)

10 miles > 350cc
ETM Stephens (350 Triumph)
J Treseder (248 OK Supreme)

10 miles > 600cc
ETM Stephens (Norton)
EG Bennett (498 Ariel)

RACING CLASSES

One mile sprint > 350cc
T McEwan, Fifeshire (348 Norton)
RJD Burnie (347 Sunbeam)

one mile sprint > 600cc
T McEwan (490 Norton)
HW Billington (499 Rudge)

10-miles > 350cc
T McEwan (348 Norton)
RJD Burnie (349 Norton)
ETM Stephens (350 Norton)

10 miles > 600cc
T McEwan (348 Norton)
WH Griffiths, Putney (497 Ariel)
RC Lewis, Carmarthen (498 Norton)

JUNIOR WELSH GRAND PRIX, 1938

30 miles > 350cc
RJD Burnie (349 Norton)
ETM Stephens (348 New Imperial)

SENIOR WELSH GRAND PRIX

30 miles > 600cc
LF Griffiths (490 Norton)
RJD Burnie (349 Norton)
ETM Stephens (499 Norton)

---

[151] ACU West South Wales Centre Minutes: July 3rd, 1938.

T McEwan

McEwan is curiously absent from the Grand Prix championship events, whether from mechanical problems or 'indisposition' is not recorded. On form, he was one of those outstanding riders – fast, safe and unbeatable. Always tipped for 'works' rides, Tommy McEwan was dogged by ill-luck. Year after year, Tommy started among the favourites in the TT but invariably fell short of the high honours of which he was capable. In the Manx he often finished on the podium: 4th in the Senior both in 1935 and 1937, and second in the Junior in 1938. His worst fate was to run out of fuel when lying second on the last lap in the 1946 Junior TT. In the 1951 Senior TT, McEwan was fourth, behind Duke, Doran and McCandless. This was his best performance. He was the first private entrant home. Lack of professionalism in attention to detail deprived him of a career in the first rank. Those who knew him make comparison with Guthrie and McIntyre. It is said McEwan was guilty sometimes of enjoying the fruits of victory without having accomplished his goal. He was a mining engineer by profession.

LA Lusardi

In tweed cap and glasses, a photographer appeared on the beach to watch this meeting. He was an amateur with the camera, a cafe-owner by trade, and a man 'with eyes'. That he had an eye, too, for a good motorcycle was evident from the new, high-camshaft, 998cc Vincent-HRD Rapide he had ridden over from Nantymoel.[152] In his pannier he often carried Retina, Roleiflex or Leica cameras, together with many rolls of 'High-speed – ISS' film. He was to become a familiar figure on the bottom corner at Pendine and at other motor-sporting events in South Wales – Aberdare Park, Eppynt, the International Six Days. He liked to photograph motor cycles in action. You'd even see him, some years, at the bottom of Bray Hill or at Kate's Cottage in the first week in June. 'Mr Lusardi' was a gifted action photographer.

Following the débâcle of 1928 when proceedings ended in a shambles, the motor cycling press reduced editorial coverage of Pendine to a minimum; pictorial record even less. Only once throughout the thirties,[153] do photographs of racing at Pendine appear in either of the two leading motorcycling weeklies.

Luigi Arcadio Lusardi was born in the little village of Casaleto in Parma, in 1910. He was an artist born into a family of cafe proprietors. He first came to Wales as a teenager when his mother, Amabile, a widow, decided to follow family and friends and open a cafe in the Rhondda valley. Being academically bright,[154] Luigi returned to

---

[152] A personal friend of Phil(s) Vincent and Irving, of Vincent-HRD fame, LA Lusardi is reputed to have patented the 'B' series Vincent's ingenious prop stands. (J Lusardi: Dec. 1998)

[153] *The Motor Cycle,* Aug 13, 1931. JH Carr in action (KE John). *Motor Cycling,* Aug 12, 1931. RM Parkinson - cornering.

[154] His fluency in the other Latin languages - Spanish, Portuguese and French - was complete. (J Lusardi pers. comm. Dec. 1998).

LA Lusardi and his HRD 'Rapide'. [© *LA Lusardi collection*]

Italy to go to university where he read art and art-history. There he found himself liable for National Service, and when called up he took a commission. Horuzzi & Co, Nantymoel, had meanwhile become famous for its ice-cream and cappuccino – and the warmth of its welcome.

When Mussolini's pact with Hitler meant that Britain was at war with Italy, all Italian males 'of a certain age' were interned. Among them LA Lusardi of Nantymoel who, by some strange quirk of fate, found himself in the Palace Internment Camp, Douglas, Isle of Man, a motor cycle enthusiast's haven! Among the inmates were restaurateur Charles Forte and the painter Sorgiani. The time was not wasted.

When he returned after the war Lusardi married Olga, a Welsh girl. One evening a week he attended photography night-classes in Port Talbot with his friend Reg Lewis of Bridgend. His spare time was taken up with perfecting techniques with the camera and in the dark-room. The basement of the Ogwy Street premises, Nantymoel, gradually transformed into a photographic studio and dark-room. He became, by default, semi-professional. Babies were photographed: 'every bambino in the valley';[155] weddings, coal mines, steam-locomotives, steam-rollers, men, women, dogs farmers, sun-sets and motor cycles. Hundreds of motor cycles.

In a charming monograph, *Hurry Slowly,* unique of its kind,[156] which LA Lusardi bound and illustrated as a little keepsake of his technique in making motor cycle racing studies, he has left us a 'snap-shot' of his manifesto as an action photographer:

---

[155] Pers. reminiscence, John Lusardi, Dec 1998.
[156] Reproduced by kind permission of Wayne Bowen, this is an edited version of a longer essay, probably the text of a talk to a photographic group.

In South Wales we have one of the best sands in the country suitable for racing, at Pendine. Indeed, many well-known riders claim it to be the best. At Pendine the straight is a mile long and, with motor cycles, speeds of well over a hundred miles-an-hour are attained. I believe the record is about 128mph. My favourite spot is at one of the corners where speed is comparatively low and where the skill of the rider really stands out and is easily noted. Here one has to be ready at all times as this is usually the spot for thrills and spills. Fortunately the sands are nice and soft so the rider usually picks everything up and off again in a hurry to make up for lost time.

My opinion is that any type of camera can take reasonable pictures at these events. I have even seen some passable results with a box camera. Of course, the simpler, cheaper cameras have their limitations and are best used when speeds are low and the object [is] coming towards the camera, [and] say, when rounding a corner. With any type of camera, it must follow the moving object in such a smooth way that it is continuously viewed in the finder and the shutter released exactly when the object is on a predetermined spot at which distance the lens is focused. But the movement of following the moving object with the camera must not be stopped the moment the

ETM Stephens (Norton), 1939. [© *ETM Stephens collection*]

ETM Stephens and Jim Bosisto (Nortons), Whitsun, 1939. [*LA Lusardi photos*]

shutter is released, but continued. My position for this 'panning', as it is called, is feet apart and the movement done with the body alone, and not by moving the camera or feet. In this way I have taken photographs of motor cycles passing in front of me at speeds of about 100 mph or even more. These are taken at 1/500th sec. The film I use is the fastest [HP3 or SuperXX – I SS in pre-war days] and I usually have plenty and use plenty because, as can be expected, the chances of failure are many. I use a fast film because one never knows the mood of the weather, and sometimes I find myself not in the open but near trees or some place where quite a lot of light is cut off.

One has to be careful at sand races for here one is in the open – and even the exposure meter seems to go wrong, often resulting in an over-exposure. I usually develop 35mm film in MCM 100 and others in Johnson's Fine Grain, and prefer to have a grainy negative to an under-exposed one.

A good view-finder is almost a 'must' and I believe that the best is the 'open frame' type and not the optical, for one can keep both eyes open and see what is going on. With a Roleiflex I usually use the direct view-finder (the one in which the pupil of the eye reflects in a small mirror). Many do not like this type, but I get good results with it. I would like to boast that I get good results with a folding camera without a direct view-finder, simply by fixing a match-stick on the side of the camera with adhesive tape and holding the camera up so that it 'follows' the match. Not an ideal finder, but it works!

This reminds me that at a sand meeting before the war an old gent had a box camera about the same age as himself – one of those contraptions on which a button is pressed and an exposed plate falls, leaving an un-exposed one in position. He had the camera on a tripod and was busy exposing as the riders were passing at speed. I did not see the results!

Press photographers at these events in South Wales all seem to use plate cameras. The results are very good. I asked why not use a 35mm camera and save a lot of weight, time, trouble, etc. The answer was that the newspapers did not have much faith in such size film. I did see a professional photographer (not a press-man) using a Leica, stopped down to F11 or F16 and exposing at 1/1000 sec. He said he was doing so to get a good depth of focus and making up for lack of speed by developing in Meritol-Caustic. I saw some of his results, and they were very good.

I think that the Leica or Contax should be ideal cameras for this type of work as they have a high shutter speed, a choice of view-finders and the film can be wound on very quickly. In action, one should at the same time set the shutter, so that if anything exciting happens it is possible to take a series of photographs of the same incident. The interchangeability of lenses with these cameras is also a great advantage as close-ups can be taken and, if confined to one place, a wide-angle lens should give good results.

LA Lusardi died in 1985. The immediacy and realism of his work, post-war, persuaded editors to focus once again on the motor racing scene in distant Wales. Club secretaries, who were early recipients of his carefully-finished pictures, variously preserved and lost them.[157] Lusardi's photographs are identifiable by his familiar stamp on the verso. They represent for the motor cycle historian the work of a dedicated craftsman, and a chronicler of our times.

Heavy thunder showers taunted the crowd all afternoon. High into what had been a perfect morning blue sky, hazy and mountainous storm clouds had gathered in towering nimbuses; and in the afternoon lightning flashed out at sea and the artillery of the heavens rumbled and recoiled. An omen, perhaps, for turbulent times that lay just around the corner for Britain, Europe and the world.

---

[157] He religiously and promptly supplied Event-secretaries with proof-prints of his work after every event he attended: cf. *Hurry Slowly*.

Whitsun 1939

Mona Lewis, Llanelly, on her International Norton, made local headlines for her showing at the Pendine Races meeting of 1939 when she beat the men on Whit Monday. She won the mile sprint – a feat she had performed in 1938, which had passed unremarked. She is reported as being the first woman to win outright an event on a sand-track in Great Britain.

J Bosisto

There was a new local name on the entry list, on Whitsun Bank Holiday, Monday, May 29th. It was that of Cornishman, Jim Bosisto, son of Carmarthen's Capitol cinema proprietor. Jim brought with him the airs of a socialite, the credentials of a racing driver, a Manx Norton and a whiff of glamour. Nick-named 'Buzzy', he was a down-to-earth power station engineer at Portishead, Bristol, by trade, but he represented himself as a man who moved mysteriously on the verges of the 'fast set'. His conversation was of the Glory Days at Brooklands, short-chassis four-and-a-halfs and the 'Bentley boys'. He is remembered with affection as one of those rare characters, around whom a mythology grows. And not a bad rider either.

Otherwise, to mix a metaphor, the cast-list was very much 'the mixture as before'. RJD Burnie, ETM Stephens, LF Griffiths on Nortons; Billington down from Chester on the Rudge Replica. RM Rees, the Carmarthen outfitter, too, was out on his 348cc Rudge, which was to discharge him into the atmosphere with aplomb when a brake seized! George Snell had the 596cc Douglas.

Excelsior Manxman

Handel Davies had become very much an Excelsior Manxman fan, and had a lot of fun and local success on this mechanically sound, if somewhat overweight, concept. Handel considered the Excelsior Manxman 'designed for Pendine'. A rugged and fast little bike, the Excelsior marque's early development began, like a hundred others, as 'assembly' jobs, using JAP, Blackburne or Villiers engines. Then, in the early thirties, this, one of the oldest of manufacturers, came out with their own, highly

Handel Davies (Excelsior) and daughter Valerie.

complex, four-valve, overhead camshaft engine, the 'Mechanical Marvel', designed by HJ Hatch. Syd Gleave, on its first outing, won the IoM Lightweight TT on it. But the Mechanical Marvel was considered too sophisticated to go into volume production, and so a simplified version of the Manxman was evolved with first the four-valve head, then two. Its development continued in the hands of Alan Bruce and works riders HG Tyrell-Smith and S 'Ginger' Wood helped make its reputation in 250 and 350 form. It was still winning club races in the fifties.

It was not a good day for LV Thomas and the Sunbeam Sprint. She seized, breaking a crank pin. Lionel's cousin, Hugh Moffatt, Head of Engineering Technology at University College, Swansea, was later to effect a repair, using armour plate steel, to a tolerance of 1.5 thou mm.[158]

There was a high tide in the morning, so proceedings were late in starting. The results were:

STANDARD MACHINES

One-mile sprint > 250cc
RG Davies, Llanelly (249 Excelsior)

4 miles > 600cc
Miss M Lewis, Llanelly (490 Norton)
B Edwards (Ariel)
WH Gardner, Swansea (Rudge)

4 miles > 350cc
RC Lewis, Carmarthen (Norton)
MG Taylor, Mitcheldean (348 Velocette)
H Davies (348 Excelsior)

10 miles > 350cc
P Sivell (348 BSA)

10 miles > 600cc
TR Rees, Swansea (497 Ariel)
RM Rees (498 Triumph Twin)
B Edwards (497 Ariel)

RACING CLASSES

One-mile sprint > 350cc
ETM Stephens (349 Norton)
HW Billington (Rudge)
JF Bosisto (349 Norton)

one-mile sprint > 600cc
RC Lewis, Carmarthen (498 Norton)
HW Billington (Rudge)
LF Griffiths (490 Norton)

6 miles > 350cc
JF Bosisto (349 Norton)
LV Thomas (Sunbeam)
ETM Stephens (350 Norton)

10 miles > 600cc
RC Lewis, Carmarthen (490 Norton)
JF Bosisto (349 Norton)
ETM Stephens (349 Norton)

30 miles > 350cc
RJD Burnie (349 Norton)
ETM Stephens (348 New Imperial)

30 miles > 600cc
LF Griffiths (490 Norton)
RC Lewis (349 Norton)
ETM Stephens (349 Norton)

LF Griffiths won the 30-mile event. But the man-of-the-day was RC Lewis, Carmarthen, who won four races on his 'Inter' Nortons – two in each class. A very creditable day out.

---

[158] HM - pers. comm.

RC Lewis

Cyril Lewis of Johnston, Kilgetty, was a flamboyant character, remembered in later years for his taste in ostentatious American cars, typical of which was a 4,562cc Cadillac he once hill-climbed at Lydstep, in 1954. Cyril was a pugnacious competitor, possessed of plenty of 'tiger' and a jaunty cornering style – scarf flying in the wind. He kicked sand in the faces of those two hardened war-horses of the Swansea club, Bob Burnie and Lionel Thomas, not to mention Leslie Griffiths of Bridgend. The pity was that the war intervened, as RC Lewis looked, on that day, to have a future in the saddle.

RC Lewis (Norton), Whitsun, 1939.　　　　　　　　　　　　　　　　　　[*LA Lusardi photos*]

August 1939

The weather that greeted the 1939 August Bank Holiday meeting, including the Welsh Grand Prix, was memorable and glorious. The standard events were run off in the morning, for which machines had to be fitted with 'silencers etc'. L Harries on an Excelsior Manxman did very well to win both 250cc races. TR Rees, the Lampeter cycle dealer, 'gave a very good performance on a very standard Red Hunter Ariel, winning the 600cc ten-mile race, and gaining second place in the sprint event'.

HC Lamacraft & JB Moss

HC Lamacraft, a Londoner from East Finchley and a photographer by profession, was a veteran in the saddle. He had ridden his first Manx Grand Prix in 1932, where he crashed – but had a list of successes to his name at the Crystal Palace and

Brooklands. Lamacraft and fellow Norton entrant Joe Moss of Manchester were minor celebrities in the worlds of sand-racing and short-circuit road-racing – as was Manchester's Wilf Billington. These were the men to watch and for the local boys to beat. *The Motor Cycle*, for a change, sent a reporter along to witness these 'Closely Contested Sprint and Championship Events'.

> In the racing classes, both ten-mile races were closely contested. H Billington (348 Rudge) got away well in the 350cc event, but lost his lead to E Stephens (348 Norton). A duel for third position was waged between two Norton riders, G Williams and J F Bosisto.
> LF Griffiths again showed his form in the 600cc event and duelled for many laps with JB Moss. Moss gained the advantage towards the end of the race.
> The high-spots of the meeting were undoubtedly the Junior (350cc) and Senior (600cc) Welsh Grands Prix, the former over 30 miles and the latter over 50 miles.
> E Stephens (348 Norton) held the lead in the Junior event for the first few laps, although hotly chased by H Billington whose 348cc Rudge had remarkable acceleration out of the corners. HC Lamacraft was fourth. When Stephens fell back, Billington and Lamacraft fought it out, to finish in that order.
> JB Moss and LF Griffiths, both on 490cc Nortons, made the running in the early stages of the Senior event. There was great excitement when, after leading for several laps, Moss took a spectacular toss, and lost nearly a lap. He recovered well, however, and regained his position two laps from the finish.

An incident involving Handel Davies's elder daughter, Molly, was not reported in the press, and the facts are not altogether clear, but she sustained an accident on the beach, whether in taking a bike (presumably her father's Manxman) up the beach for 'a spin', or during competition is not now known. Her name does not appear on the entry list.[159]

STANDARD CLASS

One-mile sprint > 250cc
L Harris (Excelsior Manxman)
RM Rees (OK Supreme)
JG Davies, Cheltenham (Rudge)

6 miles > 250cc
L Harris (Excelsior)
H Davies (Excelsior)
JG Davies, Cheltenham (Rudge)

one-mile sprint > 350cc
MG Taylor, Micheldean (Velocette)
RC Lewis (Norton)
HA Lawrence, Micheldean (Norton)

10 miles > 350cc
MG Taylor (Velocette)
PG Sivell (BSA)
H Davies (Excelsior Manxman)

one-mile sprint > 600cc
ETM Stephens (490 Norton)
TR Rees, Swansea (497 Ariel)
H Gasgoigne, Chingford (Triumph)

10 miles > 600cc
TR Rees (497 Ariel)
ETM Stephens (490 Norton)
EG Bennett, Swansea (Ariel)

---

[159] Molly Davies, who ran one of her father's motor cycle shops in Swansea, volunteered for the ATS as a DR. She died of meningitis in 1940.

OPEN EVENTS

One-mile sprint > 350cc
JF Bosisto (Norton)
ETM Stephens (Norton)
HC Lamacraft, London (Velocette)

one-mile sprint > 600cc
LF Griffiths (490 Norton)
JB Moss (490 Norton)
RC Lewis (Norton)

10 miles > 350cc
ETM Stephens (Norton)
HW Billington (Rudge)
JF Bosisto (Norton)

10 miles > 600cc
JB Moss (490 Norton)
LF Griffiths (490 Norton)
RC Lewis (Norton)

RACING CLASSES
JUNIOR WELSH GRAND PRIX, 1939

30 miles > 350cc
HW Billington (348 Rudge)
HC Lamacraft (348 Velocette)
JF Bosisto (348 Norton)

SENIOR WELSH GRAND PRIX

50 miles > 500cc
JB Moss (490 Norton)
LF Griffiths (490 Norton)
JA Bates (490 Norton)
(Fastest lap: 78.26 mph)

It was the last Welsh Grand Prix for some years to come.

RM Rees (Rudge), 1939. [*LA Lusardi photo*]

15. Post-war enthusiasm

Easter 1946

SIX years had gone by. The only music of finely-tuned machinery and raw power that had been heard on Pendine in the meantime was the recurring drone of Rolls Royce Merlin engines[160] – on their constant training missions to and from Pembrey airfield, directly across the water, and in defence of the western approaches.

Considering austerity restrictions and petrol rationing, there was a tremendous turn-out for the Swansea Motor Cycle Club's meeting on Pendine on Easter Monday, April 22nd, 1946. This was a gauge of the enthusiasm for Pendine that lay pent-up – for petrol was all but unobtainable. The event was run under the general competition rules of the ACU. It was the first motor cycle race meeting on sand in the British Isles since 1939. The programme was divided into classes for standard, road-going, machines in the morning and dedicated racing-irons after lunch. Forty-five entries are listed – bikes all carefully laid up throughout the war. Among the entrants a reassuring number of old friends; not least, the nostalgic reprise of a half-forgotten sound: the jabber and grunt of a Brough Superior, with its V-twin 998cc JAP engine.

LF Griffiths, having spent the war at Bridgend's REME depot, a civilian in charge of mechanical engineering,[161] brought out the carefully-preserved 490 International Norton that had stood him in such good stead before Munich. His Norton-mounted sparring-partner from before the war, JB Moss of Manchester, had joined the RAF, engaged in more sinister combat, to become one of 'the few' who did not return. LV Thomas, another pre-war rival on the Norton, was in 'mufti', as club steward. Wilf Billington, a Pendine devotee, was down from Chester on a 490 Norton – the speedy Rudge TT Replica having itself succumbed, a victim of the war. Another Pendine enthusiast-in-the-making, a Southport club member who had also travelled from Manchester, was Bob Berry, the Brough man.[162] He had been fortunate to acquire the

---

[160] Hurricanes and Spitfires, Henleys and Beaufighters, Westland Whirlwinds, Blenheims and Halifaxes. Pembrey was a training depot for night-fighters, light bombers and gunnery regiments. The Polish squadrons were trained there.

[161] A familiar figure in this setting, immaculately accoutred in a white coat, he was known as 'the Doctor' (though his appearance was more that of a Consultant), as he never liked to get his hands dirty!

[162] It is surprising to find that Bob Berry, self-styled 'Britain's Fastest Motor Cyclist', ran his business from a very small, run-down premises, a 'Coronation Street', back-street shack, at 1a Ackers Street, Manchester 13 - now demolished. Many have commented on the irony of 'Ackers', as it was what Berry, a first-rate engineer with true single-mindedness, mainly lacked.

First race, 1946 L>R: [4] HW Billington (Norton); [45] RJD Burnie (Norton); [17] B Berry (Brough Superior); [6] N Treseder (Norton). *[LA Lusardi photo]*

great Jack Carr's last 'two-of-everything' 8/50 'Pendine'. Berry had raced it with some success before the war at venues in the north. After the 1948 season he would modify and develop it for an attempt on the World Land Speed Record.

CM Williams was listed as riding a 498cc Norton. RJD, now 'Major', Burnie was there with his 348cc International Norton to the fore. Burnie was said to have been related by marriage to Gilbert Smith 'or someone at Nortons', and that his engines were always favoured with the latest factory racing modifications, some of them 'experimental'. Burnie's somewhat elevated manner and affluent air did not endear him to many of the racing fraternity in those austere times. What none could deny was that he was a cracking good rider, who rode to win.

Bon viveur, 'Captain' George Snell, the Swansea music shop owner, who was always a laugh and the 'life and soul', was turned out on the modified 596cc Douglas that had once belonged to George Gregor. Mounted on the old 'Inter', which he used in between as a trials machine was Reg Good of Neath. Reg was groundsman and caretaker in Clydach. He also brought along a 250 Excelsior Manxman, which had become a great favourite on the beach for its eager turn of speed and superb steering. Percy Sivell, recovered from his pre-war accident (he had taken avoiding action and hit several machines in the paddock), was BSA mounted. TH Poley of Swansea was on a 250 Triumph; N and J Treseder, the Swansea oil suppliers, had brought along a van-load: 250 Triumphs, a 350 Norton and a 498cc Coventry Eagle. The Treseders always had an interesting variety of bikes. Ariel enthusiasts 'Big Eric' Williams and Ben Davies were on 497 and 498cc machines, respectively. Local AJS belief was represented by Jack Phillips – and a newcomer, T Hunkin of Neath, who was on a borrowed flat-tank 350 GR7. This lad was to provide the surprise of the day.

KE John

An account of the latter entry, and a very successful debut one it turned out to be, is vividly documented in a surviving manuscript, which was at one time intended for publication, and has happily been preserved for posterity. A story with such uncommon human interest is rare among motor cycling memorabilia, especially one that reads like a real-life fairy-tale. It was written[163] by Kenneth Edmund John, himself a Pendine rider in the thirties and forties, and a meticulous preparer of his own machines. Ken, after wartime service in the RAF, on demob, found himself and his family virtually homeless. Imbued with the indomitable spirit when confronted with a challenge he wrote

> A chance meeting with some local Neath Motor Club men led to an enquiry about my almost-forgotten competition AJS, that I had last ridden around 1936. 'Could a very promising young member of the club be given the loan of it'? was the somewhat abrupt, but challenging, request. I was quite taken aback to think that anyone still remembered the old 'AJ'. She was a 1926, ohv, 349cc GR7 and – the fact was – that she was stored, for the most part in packing-cases, at my elderly parents' house where, some time before the war, I had dismantled her. I cannot deny being flattered – and somewhat persuaded by their insistence that the young lad in question, one Trehearne Hunkin, had promise – the makings of a first-class competitor. It was left for me to think it over. They gave me a phone number and an address. A farm, near to a town some distance away.
>
> I must admit to being intrigued to know just who this young hopeful might be, being still myself a dedicated motor cycle racing enthusiast; though there had been nothing to stimulate interest during the long years of the war. My wife, on hearing of the encounter and proposition, was unimpressed. There were, as far as she was concerned, more pressing considerations and domestic priorities in those dark and austere times. We, like so many thousands of returning servicemen's families, had a housing problem. We also had a young family. But I was fascinated.
>
> A visit to my parents' house revealed a calamity. A war-time campaign to secure 'metal for victory', especially aluminiums, had resulted in a mix-up. My precious motor cycle spares – set aside in boxes – had, though clearly marked with chalk, inadvertently been given away for the war effort. That settled it; and was, to my mind, the effective end of any restoration plan. The only option was to visit the lad and apprise him of the situation, so that he could find an alternative.
>
> The trouble was that when I presented myself, unannounced, at the farm in Cimla, near Neath, I was met with such kindness and enthusiasm by the young man's relatives, motor club members among them, that I was made to feel as if I had in some way fallen short. (Trehearne was away – so I did not have the opportunity of meeting him). I left, hearing myself making promises to 'look more closely into the matter' and 'to see if anything could be salvaged from the situation'.
>
> Here I was, perched on the horns of a dilemma, wanting very much to help, but really and truly, in a position more in need of help myself, as our domestic situation was

---

[163] KE John asserted (June, 1991) that it should be edited.

tenuous indeed: we were virtually homeless, not quite squatters, but effectively under notice to quit – with our future home, an ex-army billet, lying in flat-form in a farmer's field. I must have been mad even to contemplate the bike re-build idea. But the weather improved, and during the early days of 1946, we somehow began to get our future home assembled, while living-out in a rented bungalow in Caswell, near Swansea. It was remote and bucolic – and there was a handy veranda that provided me with a rudimentary workplace. The boxes, turned out, contained discarded-part items – those one sets aside 'in case' – but amounted to more vital bits than I had estimated, or feared lost. Actually, the old AJ was a proposition, however marginal. I was reminded of the lines in the Kipling poem about making a heap of all one's winnings; then losing all, and starting again 'at your beginnings'!

I was gently pursed and encouraged by reassuring voices on the phone. One day, I was paid an unexpected visit by young Hunkin, the putative rider (known for short as 'TH' – his full name required a lot of breath). His driving up to the bungalow in a farm-lorry over terrain which had never been traversed by wheeled vehicle before, was spectacular – and so unconcerned was he, that I was impressed. I even found I had committed myself to a time-table, when the presumptuous 'hunk' coolly announced that he had entered the unresolved machine for six events on Pendine Sands on Easter Bank Holiday Monday, just a few weeks away. 'Six events'! This was placing confidence in a machine and tuner, both not only rusty, but in theory and practice obsolete. Yet there was something about the lad. He was quietly-spoken, strong, a product of the land. And he looked the part. I liked him.

He was not inexperienced either. He had behind him an impressively wide range of competition at club level, and his grasp of the mechanical side also combined to inspire sufficient confidence in me to persuade me to give the project my best shot. He was so young! Temperament was what counted in the cut-and-thrust. How, I wondered, would he cope with the going on sand? He was proposing to collect the bike in a week-or-so's time to put in some practice.

Some missing parts would have to be made-up. My 'bench' consisted of a vice clamped onto the wooden rails of the veranda. I had to fabricate a chain-guard and

'General view', 1947. [*H Adams photo*]

various other crucial items. The old flat-tank was painstakingly cleaned, re-painted and adorned with the AJS colophon. She began to take shape. But there were decisions to be arrived at, technical and lonely ones. Luckily, I still retained a quantity of castor-based lubricant from former times; but fuel was the problem. All that was available was basic, 'pool' petrol, and low grade it was. Around this fundamental element, decisions had to be made concerning ignition, carburettor settings and plugs. What was the likely fuel consumption over the various distances? What gearing would we need? Tyre pressures? It was all largely a matter of memory and experience. Fortunately, somewhere, I had not only mental but written notes which logged the crucial settings. And, yes, they came to hand and gradually to mind!

The rider, young Trehearne Hunkin, had advised me of the number allocated to him. I shall never forget it: No 18. When I finally found myself with tin-snips, file, emery cloth and paint, ensuring that this item looked as professional as I could manage, and taking an almost childish pleasure in it, I knew the job was done. He would, as had been promised, now 'have his chance'.

By this time, of course, the whole family had become involved. Imagine my surprise (and pleasure) when I heard my wife greet the young tyro with familiarity. 'Hope it goes, TH!', she teased, when he duly arrived in the truck to collect his mount. 'He's talked, eaten and slept nothing but AJS these last weeks.'

'*Will* she start?', he nervously asked.

'Nothing surer,' I promised, making a few adjustments and securing lock-wire on vital components.

We were in the field adjacent to the house. The fuel tap was turned on. 'Put her in second. Pull back against the compression. Push forward hard. Clutch out' . . . Bang! Within a length she came alive. The roar of her open exhaust echoed through the surrounding woodland. I gave her the once 'round the field, Hunkin looking on, impressed. She was a very light little bicycle. Somewhere near the 175lb-mark, I seem to remember. That was the secret of her speed and handling. He then bestrode her and, with an easy competence, tested for himself steering, brakes and throttle response. He was even able to cope with the hand gear-change, which must have been a 'first' for him. The boy was a natural. He seemed pleased and satisfied, so we loaded up machine, fuel, oil, tools and spares – such as they were – and arranged to meet at the beach on the morning of Bank Holiday Monday.

The day shone as bright as one always remembers such days. The trusty little 250 AJS side-car combination transported wife, brood, dog, ex-army tent, utensils and supplies to a cosy nook in the sand dunes, among the holiday crowds. The sea shimmered on the ebb-tide and there was bustling excitement in the paddock where the racing engines were barking and banging. That good smell of Castrol 'R' again. The clear air, and salt of the sea. Some familiar faces from pre-war days. A few missing; and some new young, disconcertingly young, faces in racing leathers and overalls.

'TH' was already in position for the first short sprint.

'Running OK,' was all he said to me. The first event was a miler. No point in distracting him with small-talk. And there was not much more I could do. Knowing the vagaries of motor sport, I felt at the same time elated and subdued. I could have done so much better for him had I had my full complement of spares. But, the die was cast. He was on his own now in a cruel world. Some of the riders were old hands, who took no prisoners. Bob Burnie was down from Birmingham, with his 'Inter' Norton: a crack rider with style and winning determination. Leslie Griffiths, Bridgend – Norton again, a wily and brilliant rider who had won a shelf-full of trophies, including the Welsh Hundred. Wilf Billington from Manchester who, before the war used to race a very fast Rudge, was on a Norton, up against strong contenders like Bob Berry the record-breaker with the Brough – and the Treseders, always in the running. Oh! Dear! What chance did we stand? Still, it would be a good experience for the boy. Everyone has to start somewhere.

The deafening roar of 'standard class' tuned engines brought me back with a jolt from my reverie. With a boom like thunder the 'field' was off and away. I was afraid to look, in case No 18 was left on the line. A frequent fate of first-timers, especially on sand. I could not pick him out in the melee of the pack. Where the devil was he? What? No! Can't be! No 18 – out in front! In the lead and gaining. He took the flag. It was incredible, almost like a dream.

I went off in search of them. Bike and rider. TH had parked the bike nonchalantly against the wheel of the farm lorry.

'No trouble at all,' he said. 'Runs like oiled silk!'

My hands were shaking as I checked oil and fuel. Added a quart.

'Hell of a vibration on the front forks like,' he added, 'from the tide ridges.' Then, after some reflection, 'Otherwise OK.'

I was shy of looking around too much in case my gaze met that of Reg Good or Jack Phillips, whose machines came rolling in noisily, megaphones shouting their protests. They had all been taken by surprise. Still, it was a one-off, beginner's luck, perhaps. But a brilliant 'Blooding' for the lad on his first Pendine.

The second race, a ten mile-race for racing machines with unlimited engine capacity, was won, fairly predictably, by Wilf Billington on his immaculately-turned-out 490 Inter Norton, from the 996cc Brough Superior of Manchester motor engineer, Bob Berry. It was lucky for them that LF Griffiths was having some trouble with a tyre in the paddock which had prevented him from racing. Those were very fast machines. A tremendous thrill to watch and hear this thoroughbred machinery in action again.

We were on for the next event, a mile sprint for racing machines of 350cc capacity. Almost a repeat field, but with people like Burnie and Billington on the line. This would prove whether the old sweats were caught unawares or whether 'the boy' and my old bike were truly a wonder formula. And that's what emerged. He did it again, almost; coming a convincing second to a very commanding performance by Burnie. People were now taking notice. That was a racing-class event! I just could not believe it. Here was a nineteen-year-old beginner on a bike older than himself, showing these past-masters and the works-men a clean pair of heels!

When Trehearne Hunkin won the 10-mile event for racing machines next, from Billington, they were the only two left running. Burnie, Reg Good, Treseder, and Cyril Williams all on Nortons, had dropped out for one fault or another, leaving Ben Davies, trailing for a while on his Ariel. Then it was a straight fight between the expert on a virtual 'works' machine and the novice on an antique 'banger'. It was an incredible feat. He beat him! The crowd were ecstatic.

'She runs like a dynamo,' our hero said to me when he pulled up. I struggled to find any settings that needed alteration or adjustments that could be made. But it was better to leave well alone. The little GR7 was ticking away like a well-oiled machine should. There were three more events to go, and there was nothing much for me to do, except top up the tanks at intervals, assisted by the Hunkin family who looked mighty pleased with the way things were going, though as a group they were a curiously silent lot, compared to my noisy ones. In the midst of the excitement I was summoned home for tea. I needed it! In the meantime, TH took the ten-mile standard event and, for good measure, came 3rd in the 25-mile Standard Class and second in the 4-mile Standard Class. Not a bad afternoon's work.

TH then announced he had managed to enter the little bicycle for the Grass Track Speedway event in Carmarthen Park, that same evening. This was without prior consultation. Realistically, to compete in a totally different style of event, the bike would need a lot of attention, including a change of gear ratios, different tyres and many detailed adjustments. I was not best pleased, but I agreed, not wanting to be a spoil-sport. He was to take the machine home with him afterwards and return it to me in due course. It had been a long day for our little family. We were all fairly worn-out.

But that evening the spell was broken. She did not oblige him any more. She misfired and over-heated. Though in the weeks that followed, we worked on her for many hours – engine running on the bench – and called in expert advice, the magic spell was broken. At the end of the season the GR7 was returned to her box like the magic toys in the children's story to await another midnight.

Trehearne Hunkin (AJS) and KE John, 1946. [*KE John photo*]

The day's official results were as follows:

STANDARD CLASSES

One-mile sprint > 250cc
TH Poley, Swansea (249 Triumph)
WJ Rees, Swansea (248 Velocette)
CR Good, Swansea (248 Excelsior)

one-mile sprint > 350cc
T Hunkin, Neath (348 AJS)
CR Good (248 Excelsior)
J Phillips, Swansea (250 Rudge)

one-mile sprint >
CM Williams (498 Norton)
BJ Davies, Swansea (490 Ariel)
N Treseder (498 Coventry Eagle)

4 miles > 250cc
TH Poley (249 Triumph)
J Treseder (249 Triumph)
CR Good (Excelsior)

4 miles > 350cc
J Treseder (Triumph)
T Hunkin (AJS)
CR Good (Norton)

4 miles >
CM Williams (Norton)
B Davies (Ariel)
N Treseder (?)

10 miles > 350cc
T Hunkin (AJS)
J Treseder (Triumph)
Winner's time: 8 mins 49.2 secs (62 mph).

25 miles > 250cc
J Treseder (Triumph)
TH Poley (Triumph)
CR Good (Excelsior)

25 miles > 350cc
J Treseder (Triumph)
T H Poley (Triumph)
T Hunkin (AJS)

25 miles >
CM Williams (Norton)
B Davies (Velocette)
N Treseder (Triumph)

RACING CLASSES

One-mile sprint >
HW Billington, Chester (Norton)
B Berry, Chorlton-on-Medlock (Brough Superior)

one-mile sprint > 350cc
RJD Burnie (Norton)
T Hunkin (AJS)
N Treseder (Triumph)

10 miles > 350cc
T Hunkin (AJS)

10 miles >
HW Billington (Norton)

25 miles > 350cc
N Treseder (350 Norton)
J Treseder (Triumph)
CR Good (Norton)

25 miles >
LF Griffiths (Norton)
N Treseder (Norton)
HW Billington (Norton)

The Coventry Eagle entered by Norman Treseder was a rare animal. An old and highly regarded manufacturer, not much known for direct participation themselves in competition, C-E produced very sporting models, particularly the 'Flying' series with 250, 350 and 500cc Matchless engines, of which this was one.

Whit Monday, June 10th, 1946. One-mile sprint for standard class 350cc machines. L>R: [20] D Tynon, Manchester (Norton); [5] DJ Pugh, Cwmtwrch (Velocette); [8] N Treseder, Swansea (Triumph); [11] JBB Edwards, Carmarthen (Ariel); [16] Handel Davies, Swansea (Excelsior). Standing (rear [5]) TW Pugh; TE Hughes between [8] & [10]; extreme right (school cap) the author!
[*Courtesy of Mrs Norma Evans*]

Whitsun 1946

The Welsh Open Speed Trials were held on Pendine on Whit Monday, June 10th, 1946. There was a 10 am start, to suit the tide.

LF Griffiths was on a 490 Manx Norton, as were Wilf Billington and D Tynon of Manchester, on similar machines. CM Williams and CH Morris of Swansea were listed as riding a 498cc Nortons; RJD Burnie was there with the 348cc Norton. Mounted on 'Inters' and 'Manxes' were Reg Good, Neath, and N Treseder, jnr, of Swansea. DJ Pugh and EA Davies of Newport were on 348cc Velocettes. AJS was represented by DH Thomas, Carmarthen, and T Hunkin of Neath.

Notice of a novel attraction was inserted in the programme that gladdened many hearts, remembering days when the Brough was king of Pendine:

> **In between the Standard and Racing Classes Mr BOB BERRY will make an unofficial attempt at the FLYING HALF-MILE RECORD on his 990cc Brough Superior. It is quite an unofficial attempt and is in the nature of a try-out for his machine, which will be streamlined when the official attempt is made at some future date.**

Bob Berry (Brough Superior), 1946. [*Clifford H Evans photo*]

Handel Davies

David Handel Davies must have been especially pleased by the Brough's presence. At the first Welsh Championship meeting after the Great War he had been the proud owner of one of the very first racing-specification 90-bore Brough Superiors to leave Haydn Road, Nottingham. His was probably the first Brough Superior in Wales, and well-known to motor cycling enthusiasts all over south and west Wales who would recognise its distinctive engine-note without seeing it.[164] In the twenties and early thirties Handel's name was synonymous with the Brough Superior and high-performance motor cycles. His Oxford Street, Swansea, shop was a mecca for enthusiasts – as was the famous Brooklands Garage in Garnant. The 248cc Excelsior Manxman that he had entered in the first Welsh Championship meeting after another world war was not quite in the same league, but a little thoroughbred being put through its paces in the expert hands of the 53-year-old veteran rider was a joy to watch.[165]

---

[164] Ernest Hughes. Pers. comm., 1996.

[165] Handel Davies's racing career was blighted by an accident while competing in a hill-climb on the Aberdare Mountain. There are memories of him being carried off the hill on a farm gate. His badly-injured ankle never really recovered and, in later life, he always walked with a pronounced limp.

STANDARD CLASS

One mile sprint > 350cc
DJ Pugh (Velocette 348)
D Tynon (Norton 349)
DH Thomas (AJS 350)
H Davies (Excelsior 248)

one mile sprint > 600cc
JBB Edwards (Ariel 500)
CM Williams (Norton 490)

RACING

30 miles > 600cc
CR Good (348 Norton)

August, 1946

The entry for the afternoon meeting of August Bank Holiday, 1946, was very much a re-run of the Whitsun gathering. Billington, Burnie, Handel Davies, Bryn Edwards, Reg Good, LF Griffiths, T Hunkin, CH Morris, TH Poley and N Treseder. Eddie Stephens was out on 348cc and 490cc Nortons, in addition to the curiosity of the meeting – a beautiful 1,000cc Vincent-HRD [DBX 970] – like Handel's Brough all those years ago, one of the very first off the production line. What a splendid sight it must have been to see it do battle with the Bob Berry Brough Superior in the 50-mile Welsh Grand Prix, later that afternoon. JC Snell-Adcock brought a very fast 498cc Excelsior down from Cheltenham; and DR Griffith was on the whimsically-named 'VMC'.

DR Griffith, 'VMC'

The 'VMC' was constructed of 'Various Makes Combined' – nothing new in the annals of motor cycle competition, especially on sand. Norton gearboxes, Rudge front wheels, Triumph forks were quite the norm as modifications. Pendine saw some very interesting 'Specials' – the Sgonina Specials being pre-eminent among them. There was the Stephens Special, the Old'un, the Veriot-Precision and the IWS. Some very respectable 'makes' of the past were hybrids, assembled entirely from proprietary bits and pieces. Douglas Griffith can be viewed as a serious amateur mechanical engineer and a more than competent rider. His early racing exploits were on a New Hudson, which he used to ride down from London. Given the resources, he might have attained greater distinction. Douglas Griffith, whose name is invariably spelt wrongly in programmes and reports, did what he did for the right reason – fun. His account of the VMC is

> My motor cycle: built in 1946, the engine was a 499cc, Dirt-track JAP (75 brake-horse-power, using pure methyl alcohol); note the large ex-Norton front wheel-brake, which was of prime importance for sandracing: and the four-speed close-ratio Burman gear-box – all interesting museum pieces now!

In 1946 it was a competitive formula but, predictably, the JAP engine, running on dope, proved unreliable in long-distance events. DR Griffith's record on Pendine is disappointing on paper. He was indefatigable and undeterred, however – racing from before the war till the very end of racing at Pendine. He may not have won high honours, but deserves some special recognition for keeping the faith, his courtliness and sportsmanship.

The official results were as follows:

JUNIOR WELSH GRAND PRIX, 1946	SENIOR WELSH GRAND PRIX
30 miles > 350cc	50 miles > 1,000cc
CR Good (348 Norton)	LF Griffiths (490 Norton)

The Daily Mail's correspondent records an unexpected thrill for the crowds that thronged Pendine for the first Welsh motor cycle championships after he war.

> LF Griffiths, Bridgend (Norton), the winner, and Eddie Stephens, Carmarthen, (Norton), who was second, were beginning their thirteenth lap in the first Welsh Grand Prix race of 50 miles when an aeroplane swooped down to a height of 50ft and flew along the course above the heads of the two riders before disappearing into the blue.[166]

Whitsun 1947

The Whitsun meeting, 1947, was held on May 26th. One or two old favourites were out again – Swansea's LV Thomas amused everyone by wheeling out his 22-year-old 347cc Sunbeam Sprint which proved still very competitive. Not to be out-done, DJ Snell had brought over from Swansea the potent 596cc Douglas of similar vintage. The 'bitza bike' VMC was on the beach, tended by DR Griffith, now of Pontypool. JD Daniels was entered on a 490cc Norton. Bob Berry was down from Manchester with Brough and Manx Norton. He, like many another from over Offa's Dyke, was in a love-affair with Pendine which would never let go.

The *Western Mail* were, on this rare occasion, in attendance but evidently inattentive to motor cycling activity on Pendine in the previous year:

> Thrills galore were provided [for] the several thousand spectators who journeyed to the famous stretch of sands at Pendine – the Mecca of British motor racing on Whit-Monday, when, after a lapse of about eight years, the Carmarthen Motor Cycle and Light Car Club revived their annual open Welsh speed races for motor cycles, which proved so popular years ago.
>
> Some of the finest racing motor cyclists in Wales gave a splendid display of riding, equal to anything seen on the sands where many world speed records have been broken. The ideal summer weather attracted an ideal Whitsun crowd equal to the

---

[166] It is tempting to suggest that this prankster may have been the redoubtable Battle of Britain Hurricane pilot, Hardy McHardy, of Taliaris, Llandeilo. Hardy had spent an uncomfortable four years in Stalagluft 3, with Bader, Stanford Tuck and others. This was just the sort of exuberant gesture that secured Hardy a place in local folklore. (See *The Carmarthen Journal* Jan. 9th 1991: 'Life & Times of a Modest Hero', by the present author). Fighter Command, still active at RAF Pembrey, a couple of miles distant across the bay, had no shortage of comedians, either!

attendance of August Bank Holiday races. Large numbers were spread along the natural grandstand provided by the sand dunes, whereas the course was lined for a great distance with motor cars and spectators.

Splendid speeds were set up, especially in the 30-mile race which was really a magnificent one to watch, and was won at a speed of 72 miles an hour by ETM Stephens, Carmarthen. Stephens put up a remarkable show, revealing to the full his experience as an amateur Tourist Trophy rider. He swept the board in the classes for machines up to 600cc and also won two races for machines up to 350cc, thus winning five of the seven events of the day. For the first few laps of the premier event of the day he was also averaging over 80mph.

For the first 20 miles or so of the 30-mile race a thrilling duel was witnessed between ETM Stephens and LF Griffiths, Bridgend. Griffiths is an experienced driver of long standing and never failed to provide the crowd with a treat with his clever cornering at

Douglas Griffith (VMC). [RTB photo]

the finishing post end. He had the advantage over Stephens on the bends, but the Carmarthen man was usually the first coming down the straight, having a faster machine.

Almost on the completion of 11 two-mile laps, Griffiths, to the regret of everyone, was forced to retire, due to a seized engine. Up to this stage no notice had been taken of JD Daniels, of Swansea, who at some distance had been tailing Stephens and Griffiths. Following Griffiths's retirement Stephens naturally took things easier and thus gave Daniels the opportunity 'to come out of the blue' and take the lead without the knowledge of his rival, who, evidently thought he was a lap ahead of the other riders. Daniels, it should be noted, had fallen off his machine through taking the lower bend rather sharp, but remounted.

At the 26-mile stage Daniels, now in the lead, again fell off twice in succession but pluckily remounted and set on his way again and regained the lead, passing Stephens as the latter was taking the bend. Thinking he was now on his last lap, whereas it was his last but one, Daniels flashed past the post at a terrific speed only to hear the bell indicating the last lap. He had evidently not heard the bell, for after going about 200 yards or so he turned behind the crowd to go to the 'camp'. After being gesticulated to by the crowd he once more got back on the course but by now Stephens had a substantial lead. When the riders passed the post however, Daniels was a close second, only the distance of a motor cycle between them.

Daniels was by no means the first to make that misjudgement in the heat of the moment.

Jack Daniels (Norton). [© *JD Daniels collection*]

Bob Burnie won outright the Founder's Cup in the 25 mile race and 'Danny' Daniels had a good day, coming second and third in the 25- and 50-mile races. Les Griffiths set a lap record for the course with a 77.8 mph last lap and a 73.49 race average. He was always after the 80 mph race average.

The results were:

One-mile sprint > 350cc
ETM Stephens (Rudge)
LV Thomas (Sunbeam)
RJD Burnie (348 Norton)

one-mile sprint > 600cc
ETM Stephens (490 Norton)
LF Griffiths (490 Norton)
RJD Burnie (348 Norton)

5 miles > 350cc
RJD Burnie (348 Norton)
LV Thomas (Sunbeam)
KE John, Swansea (AJS)

5 miles > 600cc
ETM Stephens (490 Norton)
RJD Burnie (348 Norton)
LV Thomas (490 Norton)

4 miles > 350cc
J Treseder (Stevens)
D Gates, Swansea (348 Rudge)
C Andrews (250 Ariel)

4 miles > 600cc
JA Beckham, London (Scott)

10 miles > 600cc
ETM Stephens (Norton)
LV Thomas (Norton)
RJD Burnie (348 Norton)

30 miles > 350cc
RJD Burnie (Norton)
J Treseder (Stevens)
J McNulty (Rudge)

30 miles > 600cc
ETM Stephens (Norton)
JD Daniels (Norton)
LV Thomas (Norton)

Rudge

Rudges were out in force and still giving an impressive account of themselves in all classes from 250cc upwards. Proud owners had nurtured them through the war years, longer – sports-racing machines that were, in the main, of 1935/8 vintage. After an impressive seven years, Rudge had pulled out of racing in 1933 – participating by proxy in supplying the Graham Walker/Ernie Nott/Tyrell-Smith syndicate with selected machines and engineering service. When John Vernon Pugh, the motivator behind sports Rudges, died in 1936 there was no one 'in-house' to perpetuate this once formidable force in motor cycle racing.

The 1933 TT Replica and 1928/38 Ulsters, with linked braking systems and adjustable steering dampers, are among the great racing motor cycles of the Vintage era. They found homes and were raced all over the world, where their inventive and robust construction was admired as the best of British manufacturing. TT Reps and Ulsters were not all supplied with radial-valved engines, but production versions of these four-valved bronze-headed machines, where they occur, are very highly-prized.

Rudge introduced a feature on their 1931 TT machines that was to become the *sine qua non* of all racing motor cycles – the megaphone exhaust.

The Treseders had a penchant for interesting bikes. The rare[167] Stevens out on Pendine for this meeting, produced by the Stevens brothers of AJS, following the demise of their main business in 1932 and its sale to Matchless, was a sporting and sweet-handling machine. Stevens development engineer and works rider Tommy Deadman had chalked up some notable competition successes with it, particularly in trials guise.

Riders at Pendine, August 1947:
L>R: ETM Stephens/ Noel Knight/ Bob Berry (Norton No10)/ Norman Treseder/ BJ 'Ben' Davies/ Neville 'Nobby' Treseder/ 'Big Eric' A Williams/ Gwyn Walters/ LF Griffiths (Norton No11)/ Emrys Walters/ Carmody? (non-rider)/ Wilf Billington/ John Penry?/ Denis Parkinson/ Fred Rist/ RJD Burnie/ Reg Good/ John Williams. [MA Clare photo]

---

[167] About 1,000 left the factory.

16. Mr Manx Grand Prix

Conditions for the Welsh Grand Prix in August 1947, were inauspicious. It rained on the morning of the 4th, with louring cloud and a strong wind till after mid day. The start was delayed, as the sands were waterlogged: water table up and vehicles bogged down. There was a very good entry. The celebrity rider was Denis Parkinson of Wakefield who had just won the Junior Clubman's TT in record-breaking style on a Norton.

Denis Parkinson

Parkinson was a highly successful amateur road-racer and a well-schooled sand-racing ace, whose career began in 1929, on a Rex-Acme, at the age of 14. His father, Bill Parkinson, had opened a motor cycle retail business in Wakefield in 1920. It grew into a large and successful business for which racing activity was part of the PR and advertising effort. An amateur racer himself, Bill saw potential and dedication in his son from an early age and methodically taught him the art and science of racing a motor cycle. Denis's record, which eventually included an unprecedented number of Firsts in all classes of competition at Clubman's and Manx level at the Isle of Man, was 8 Scottish championships at St Andrews, 6 Yorkshire championships at Saltburn/Redcar and several others at Southport. He would win two championships at Pendine. His machines were, in the early days, prepared by his father and then, latterly, by the wizardly Francis Beart. On retirement from racing Denis became a journalist and was well-known for his race commentaries on radio and television.

HW Billington

Wilf Billington, another regular Manx Grand Prix challenger, and a sand-racing celebrity of some renown, had driven from Chester, armed with Manx Nortons. Billington had matured as a rider and was to give an incredibly good account of himself in the face of Denis Parkinson and a very battle-scarred local opposition. Bob Berry had come down from Manchester with a Brough Superior and a Norton on the trailer. RJD Burnie, Reg Good, LF Griffiths and Eddie Stephens, represented the Welsh defence, all also Norton-mounted. Altogether it looked like a Norton benefit! Burnie's and Griffiths's engines were invariably factory-tuned.

Start of a race, 1947: L>R: [11] LF Griffiths (Norton); [4] HW Billington (Norton); [6] N Treseder (Norton); [16] N Treseder (Coventry Eagle); [7] J Treseder (Triumph). [*LA Lusardi photo*]

The bottom corner, 1947, L>R: [40] D Parkinson (Norton); [22] FM Rist (BSA); [6] ETM Stephens (Vincent-HRD) [4] HW Billington (Norton). [*LA Lusardi photo*]

The Nortons all, however, had to meet a formidable BSA challenge in the person of FM Rist, the BSA works-man and gifted trials-rider, on Armoury Road B32 350cc 'Gold Star' and A10 650cc, 'Golden Flash' models. Fred was making his first appearance on Pendine. It was a famous occasion.

There were some surprises in store for this distinguished company, with their shining works-prepared Nortons and BSAs. In the 350cc sprint, LV Thomas, on his George Dance-era ohv Sunbeam, streaked home ahead of the whole field led by the canny and quick Reg Good. Hot on his heels: Parkinson, Billington, Burnie and LF Griffiths. The little old Sunbeam, like a hare before the hound-pack made it home safely – by many convincing yards. Elvy 'umbled 'em! Francis Beart was seen scratching his head!

As if that were not salutary lesson enough, LV T then proceeded to trounce Berry and Billington while mounted on the antique (1927) 596cc Douglas, borrowed from George Snell. This was a hybrid machine, ultra-light, despite its dope-filled long-distance tank. The Douglas was fitted with a Norton clutch and gearbox and, according to its owner, 'good for a hundred and twenty miles an hour'.[168] Third time was not lucky for Welshman Thomas, however. This 'Big Dug' was not famous for its staying power. Although he managed to lead Parkinson, Billington and Good in the 10-mile race for two miles, he developed mechanical trouble and thereafter faded from contention. This allowed for a duel between Parkinson and Billington that was well worth the entry fee. Reg Good was a close third to Parkinson's second, when Billington called upon some undeclared reserves and pulled away for a clear lead to the finish. Consolation awaited Parkinson in the unlimited race where the order was reversed.

The Junior Welsh Grand Prix was run off under much better conditions, with the beach rapidly drying off in the wind. Fred Rist, at this meeting, was learning; and had to content himself with watching the cornering techniques of Parkinson and Billington – while doing battle with a very tenacious Reg Good. On the second bend Parkinson overdid it and came off – a rarity for Denis – allowing Good and Rist through, positions which they held to the end, despite Parkinson's best efforts to reassert himself.

The sun came out for the Senior, showing what a fickle place Pendine can be, weatherwise. It proved to be one of the most exciting races ever seen on the beach. Alongside the Brough Superior and the Vincent-HRD at the start, bayed a pack of Nortons. Pendine's sea air was heady with Castrol 'R' and bootleg high-octane fuel.

That very fine Neath club rider, also a Manx Grand Prix contestant, Cliff Edwards, was making his Pendine debut on a 499cc Norton. The 490s of Billington and Parkinson took the lead, leaving Rist (650 BSA) to fight off the heavier machinery, wielded by Bob Berry (Brough) and Eddie Stephens (Vincent). Billington, in a splendid exhibition of machine control, held the lead from Parkinson for eleven laps. LF Griffiths lay fourth at half-way, and Rist fifth until Billington's gearbox went and

---

[168]George Snell, Pers. comm., 1984.

[40] D Parkinson (Norton) leads, 1947 (*Wayne Bowen collection*). [*LA Lusardi photo*]

Closest finish. [40] D Parkinson (Norton) and [11] LF Griffiths (Norton), Welsh Grand Prix, August 1947 (*Wayne Bowen collection*). [*LA Lusardi photo*]

he retired. Reg Good, last year's winner, upped to fourth. Parkinson was now where he always liked to be – well out in front. The famous old Brough was giving a very good account of itself – holding third, then second place until, sadly, it stopped on the last lap, allowing LF Griffiths through. Griffiths, ever the wily tactician, with a huge surge of reserve power and speed, had calculated to take the leader by surprise on the last lap. His calculation fell marginally short, as Parkinson – a hard-road dog himself – powered ahead to the line and made it – by a wheel! The closest finish in the big race ever seen on Pendine.

It was Rob Burnie's Swan-song. After a seemingly barren day for this stylish and sometimes indomitable rider, one of Pendine's very best, the fragrant Bob Burnie disappeared into history; to re-appear some years later in South Africa, where he started a new life, it is said, with a new identity. His name was, however, perpetuated in the Burnie Trophy, awarded for the year's best performance by a Swansea Club rider.

STANDARD CLASSES

One-mile sprint > 250cc
H Davies (Excelsior)
EJ Phillips (BSA)

one-mile sprint > 350cc
TW Pugh (Velocette)
N Treseder Jnr (BSA)
BJ Davies (Velocette)

one-mile sprint > 600cc
CH Morris (Norton)
TW Pugh (Velocette)
CJ Walters (Norton)

10 miles > 250cc
H Davies (Excelsior)

10 miles > 350cc
N Treseder Jnr (BSA)
ET Williams (OK Supreme)

10 miles > 1,000cc
N Treseder jnr (BSA)
CL Banister (HRD)
GJ Walters (Norton)

RACING CLASSES: OPEN

One-mile sprint > 350cc
LV Thomas (Sunbeam)
CR Good (Norton)
D Parkinson (Norton)

one-mile sprint > 600cc
LV Thomas (494 Douglas)
HW Billington (Norton)
B Berry (490 Norton)

10 miles > 350cc
HW Billington (Norton)
D Parkinson (Norton)
CR Good (Norton)

10 miles: unlimited
HW Billington (Norton)
D Parkinson (Norton)
C (Cliff) R Edwards, Aberkenfig (Norton)

JUNIOR WELSH GRAND PRIX, 1947

30 miles > 350cc
HW Billington (Norton)
CR Good (348 Norton)
FM Rist (348 BSA)

SENIOR WELSH GRAND PRIX

50 miles > 1,000cc
D Parkinson (490 Norton)
LF Griffiths (490 Norton)
FM Rist (348 BSA)

Reg Good

A bizarre incident marred the end of what had been a most exciting race. The crowd rushed on to the course to congratulate the winners of the Senior, before the back-markers were all home. Reg Good, doing somewhere near the hundred mark, some distance behind on a Norton, suddenly came upon the scene out of the mirage and, unable to stop, took avoiding action with tremendous selflessness. He hit several parked bikes in the paddock, sustaining serious injury to himself, but miraculously not hurting any member of the public. He deserved a medal for it.

Whitsun 1948

The 1948 Whitsun speed trials of the Carmarthen motor Cycle and Light Car Club meeting on 17th May, was a family affair again, held under ideal conditions for racing. We have no editorial coverage in either specialist weeklies – the 'Green 'un' or the 'Blue 'un'. The *Western Mail* and *Carmarthen Journal* print minimal reports hidden among the sports results.

STANDARD CLASSES

CLOSED

one-mile sprint > 350cc
TW Pugh (Velocette)
AB Drew (BSA)
DH Webster (BSA)

one-mile sprint > 600cc
ETM Stephens (Matchless)
CJ Walters (Triumph)
TW Pugh (Velocette)

10 miles > 1,000cc
ETM Stephens (-?-)
CM Williams (Norton)
AB Drew (BSA)

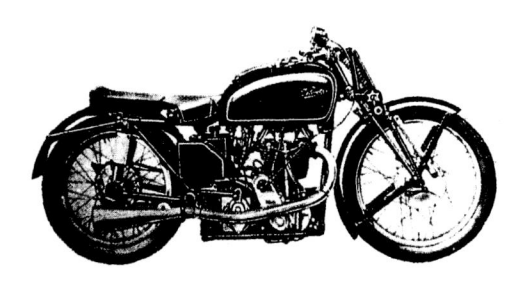

RACING CLASSES

OPEN

One-mile sprint > 350cc
HW Billington (Norton)
AB Drew (BSA)

one-mile sprint > 600cc
D Parkinson (Norton)
LV Thomas (Douglas)
CR Edwards (Norton)

6 miles > 350cc
D Parkinson (Norton)
HW Billington (Norton)
AR Drew (BSA)

30 miles > 600cc
ETM Stephens (?)
CR Edwards (Norton)
D Parkinson (Norton)

10 miles > 1,000cc
CR Edwards (Norton)
HW Billington (Norton)
D Parkinson (Norton)

17. 'Pendine Hundred' Again

August, 1948

After 1948 the Welsh Grand Prix was no longer staged on Pendine, as the West South Wales Centre ACU had managed to negotiate use of a tarmac access-road circuit on a Ministry of Defence gunnery range at Eppynt,[169] near Llywel, between Trecastle and Sennybridge, in Breconshire. The GP was transferred there and Pendine's big race over a hundred miles was re-christened 'The Pendine Hundred': though again, as it turned out, it was usually only over fifty miles – it just felt like a hundred!

Reg Dearden

Reg Dearden's was one of the best-known names in the behind-the-scenes of motor cycle racing in the forties and fifties. It was something of a coup to find him at Pendine with his entourage. From his famous retail premises in Manchester he gave many a young hopeful a first break on one of his immaculately prepared Velocettes or Nortons, among them Les Graham, Gary Hocking and Fergus Anderson. In 1958 Reg was to enter 17 machines in the IoM, and win 16 replicas! Geoff Duke, John Hartle, Dave Chadwick, Ralph Rensen and Terry Shepherd were among others who rode Dearden Nortons to fame if not fortune. Reg was no mean rider himself, and whenever he could, liked to 'have a bit of a go'. He rode in the MGP several times, and Pendine was one of his favourite playgrounds. Rex Young believes Reg was a good deal better on sand than on tarmac.[170] It was a safer place to fall!

JD Daniels

Pendine Sands showed what they thought of this further demotion. On August 2nd, 1948, it rained and it rained. According to *The Motor Cycle*:

> The Pendine Hundred was held on a disappointingly wet day and so was reduced to fifty miles, and what would have been a record crowd trickled away wet and discomforted.[171]

---

[169]The alternate spelling 'Epynt' is considered 'more Welsh', but the likelihood is that the name is of Latin/Goidelic (Irish) origin, containing the meaning 'horses' (Latin *equus*, Goidelic *epos*) and possibly 'wind' (Welsh, 'gwynt'): 'Horses of the Wind'.

[170]Pers. letter Nov, 1998.

[171]Emrys Walters remembers that the sand was so rutted with tyre-marks it resembled a ploughed field. 'If you got into one of those ruts, it was like being caught in a tramline.' (Dec, 1998).

JD Daniels (Norton). [© *JD Daniels collection*]

[12] Reg Dearden (Norton) leads [2] Wilf Billington (Norton), 1948. [*LA Lusardi photo*]

JACK DANIELS

They had travelled to see, among others, a new Welsh star in the ascendant, JD 'Danny' Daniels of Swansea, fresh from winning the Senior Clubman's TT, on a 998cc Vincent-HRD, supplied by Eddie Stephens, Carmarthen, sponsored by Handel Davies and donations from ACU-affiliated clubs all over south Wales. Daniels had 'all the makings', but his showing in the 1948 Pendine Hundred was scarcely remarkable. Perhaps he was a road-racer rather than a sand man. His versatility in all manner of competition, grass-track as well as scramble, nevertheless, was considerable.

Jack Daniels was tragically killed in a road accident on North Road, near Fairwood Common, Swansea, later that year, on November 1st, 1948, riding a MK VII KTT Velocette. 'It was a silly accident for which he was entirely responsible, as he was practising to take a series of bends on the public road that resembled a well-known stretch on the Isle of Man course'.[172] This was a place where Joe Craig and Reg Dearden allegedly looked for talent during practice sessions in the Clubman's and the Manx. According to Denis Parkinson,[173] they went there and listened to exhausts. 'Those lads brave enough not to shut off were considered men who could ride a motor cycle. In my day there were only three or four riders who could take a 500 flat-out through Barregarrow and down to the Thirteenth Milestone – it was so blind you needed a lot of courage. These were the talent'.

On a Sunday morning Daniels, travelling at high speed, hit a roadside bank and was catapulted into the air where he hit a branch of a tree. He died instantly. He was the nearest Wales had come till then to producing a world-class road-racing motor cyclist. His style and *élan* were such that 'you could spot him a mile off'. He exhibited that ease and fluency discernible only in top class riders.

CLOSED

One-mile sprint > 350cc
TW Pugh (Velocette)
JD Daniels, Swansea (Triumph)
W (Wilmot) Evans, Coventry (Matchless)

one-mile sprint > 600cc
TW Pugh (Velocette)
WA Gates, Swansea (497 Ariel)
TH (Henry) Adams, Tenby (499 Rudge)

STANDARD MACHINES

10 miles > 350cc
W Evans (Matchless)
N Treseder (Triumph)
JD Daniels (Triumph)

OPEN

10 miles > 1,000cc
P Cousins, N Lancs (Vincent-HRD 998)
WA Gates (Ariel)
TW Pugh (Velocette)

RACING CLASSES

One-mile sprint > 350cc
H Fletcher, Leeds (OK Supreme-JAP)
D Parkinson (Norton)
PG Barnard, Pontypool (Velocette)

one-mile sprint > 600cc
D Parkinson (Norton)
LF Griffiths (Norton)

6 miles > 350cc
D Parkinson (Norton)
PG Barnard, Pontypool (Velocette)

---

[172]Harold Bragg (business partner and Pendine rider): pers. recollection, June 1998.
[173]'Mr MGP', Patrick Click: *The Classic Motor Cycle*, Nov. 1985.

THE PENDINE HUNDRED, 1948

50 miles > 250cc
J Treseder (Triumph)
TW Pugh (248 Excelsior)

50 miles > 350cc
N Treseder Jnr (BSA)

N Treseder (BSA)
J Treseder (Triumph)

50 miles > 1,000cc
R Dearden (Norton)
N Treseder Jnr (BSA)
N Treseder (BSA)

ETM Stephens

Eddie Stephens lost control and came off the new demonstration Vincent-HRD, Black Lightning, (also dubbed 'Gunga Din'), at high speed in the Unlimited event. He was, for once, wearing racing leathers under his signature overalls. On that critical occasion, Eddie reckoned they saved both life and limb. He persuaded anyone he saw not wearing leathers after that to consider his experience.[174] It was a very close shave indeed, persuading the man who, above all, is most closely associated with Pendine Races, for his tireless enthusiasm and organisational efforts, to hang up his helmet and goggles, in favour of something safer, such as rally-driving! And yet more organisation – at Eppynt and Lydstep.

---

[174]Witnesses maintain that ETM S spun like a top for 50 yards, miraculously missing, as he wove in and out of them, the steel spikes that held the wire crowd barrier - cf. Emrys Walters, Hugh Moffatt & Lloyd Tucker.

ETM Stephens (Norton), 1939. *[LA Lusardi photo]*

18. The Motor Cycle World Land Speed Record

Bob Berry (1)

THERE was motor cycle speed activity on the beach in April 1949 – with something of a difference. The unmistakable double-echo of a highly-tuned V-twin JAP engine thrilled up the beach and then down again, as Bob Berry and his little team from Manchester tested a Brough Superior for a crack at the World Land Speed Record for motor cycles. The bicycle he was riding was familiar enough on the sands, to those with long memories. It was JH Carr's 'Pendine' which Berry had bought (but never paid for!) when Jack gave up racing in 1936. As Skipton men, Carr and Berry were acquainted: and Berry knew well the machine that had the reputation of being the most successful racing Brough ever to come out of Haydn Road. He had himself been racing it at sand venues up and down the country since acquiring it in 1936, winning many 'Firsts' and FTDs. But none, it must be said, at Pendine.

During the war, Berry's Manchester garage and his tyre businesses had both succumbed to Luftwaffe bombs, and he was determined to avenge his 'ruination' on the 'perfidious Hun' by reclaiming for Britain the record previously held by Englishman Eric Fernihough on a Brough at Gyon, Hungary, in April 1937 (169.78 mph). That same year E Henne broke Fernihough's record, raising the World Land Speed Record for a motorcycle to 173.67 mph.

The 'Flying kilometre' for motor cycles had been a preoccupation since the early days of motoring, progressively raised from CR Cook's record of 75.92 mph on the 16th June, 1909, by such heroes as CR Collier (Matchless), Jake de Rosier and Herbert Le Vack (Indians) to CF Temple's 108.48 mph on a 996cc camshaft British Anzani, at Brooklands on the 6th November, 1923. That was the last 'World Flying Kilometre' record for motor cycles retained on British soil.

It annoyed Berry that this record had been held since 1937 on German soil on a German machine, the 'Kompressor', a 493cc blown BMW. Henne had averaged this impressive best of two opposite runs on the autobahn at Frankfurt-am-Main. It was a tremendous speed for its time and a hard act to follow. Berry was against the idea of mechanically forced induction and was intent on upholding the honour of British engineering on a normally-aspirated machine, albeit one of twice the engine capacity.

Prayers for Bob Berry. [H *Adams photo*]

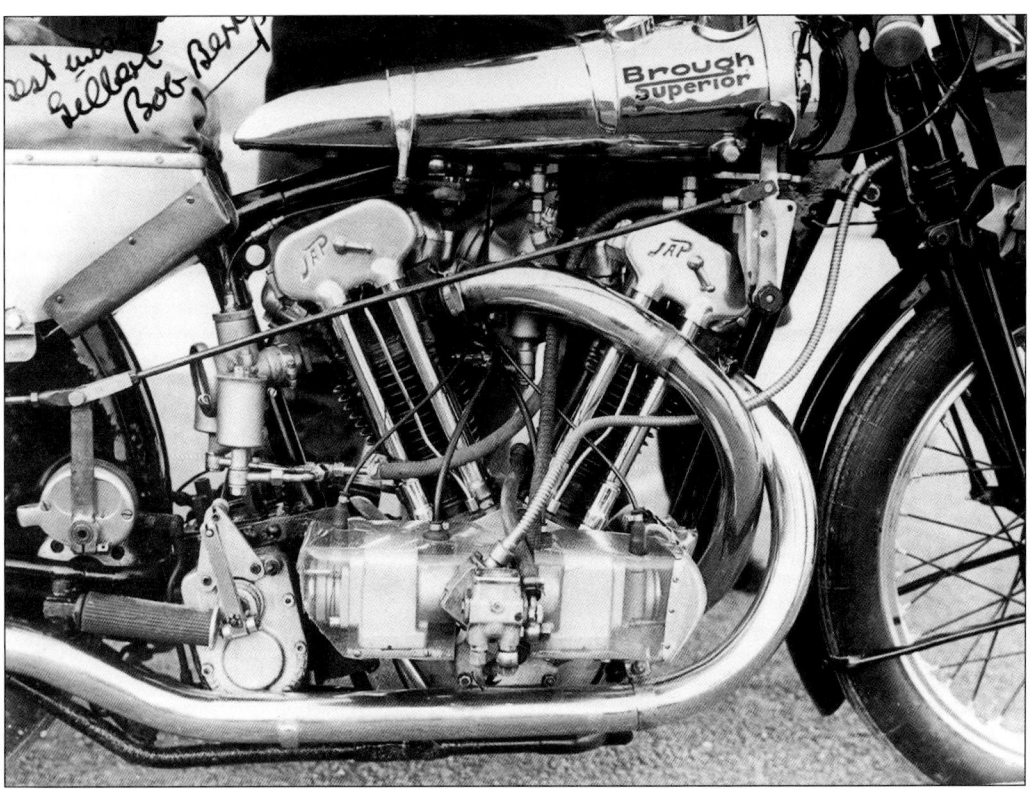

The JAP 'JTOR iron 8/80' (90bhp) engine.

Dearden's Lightning

He would need to persuade more than 95bhp out of the aged JAP engine to be ahead of the BMW on power.

The Motor Cycle, in 1949, was offering a trophy and an award of £500 to the first British rider of a British machine who could bring the record back to this country. At the age of 41 Bob Berry had decided to give up racing and determined to dedicate his efforts in future to bringing the Land Speed Record for motor cycles back to Britain.

With a new 8/75 engine in the old Jack Carr bike, Berry had clocked 126 mph at Southport – on ACU timing. But this was not nearly fast enough; a good Manx Norton in road-race trim could match that. Speeds were rising rapidly as the ohc engine and spring-frame suspensions grew to maturity. Nortons had announced the 'double-knocker' engine, AJS had a secret-weapon 'triple-knocker'. Whether Berry's choice of a virtually obsolete, cast-iron, push-rod and naturally-aspirated engine was the right choice of power-plant for 1949, much less 1961, will remain a matter for debate. A high-camshaft Vincent-HRD twin was a more up-to-date alternative. The Black Lightning engine would produce 100bhp with carburettors, but Reg Dearden was working along the lines of a supercharged version with the Vincent people, and would himself test it at Pendine.[175]

Be that as it may, and as a dedicated Brough man, Berry's answer was another, two-of-everything, SM Greening design, a Prestwich of Tottenham 8/80 engine,[176] the performance curve of which was such that it was faster in second (of three gears) than the 8/75 had been in top. At Brighton Speed trials the 8/80 reached 128 mph in second gear, crossing the finishing line at 140 mph in third – when it was still nowhere near 'flat-out'. Impressive for an obsolete design!

Engine-power, though, was not the nub of the matter, though it was generally conceded that 100 bhp was the minimum requirement to push a machine and rider past 180 mph. *The Motor Cycle* identified the related problems:[177]

> Chief among them are achieving the requisite brake horse-power, and ensuring directional stability at speeds on the exciting side of three-miles-a-minute – faster than man has ever travelled before on two wheels. Unstreamlined machines capable of providing something like 100 bhp even after extensive testing are rare, and enormous development work would be necessary before adequate power and reliability could be obtained from any one of them. To take an existing machine capable of providing enough power and attempt to modify it for full streamlining, which, one imagines, would demand a prone position, would give rise to a host of questions, the answers to which are largely unknown.

At Jabbeke, in 1949, Berry was to capture the Belgian national speed record of 155.9 mph on the Brough in bad weather conditions and twilight gloom, without the fairing. Stability was a severe problem but things, he felt, were moving.

---

[175] Dearden rode the Vincent on the beach in April 1951. He broke the crankpin, just as Stevenage had warned!
[176] Its four float-chambers reminded Freddie Dixon of 'a row of pint-pots on a pub shelf'.
[177] *The Motor Cycle,* 17 February, 1955.

When he came down to Pendine from Chorlton-on-Medlock that spring, Bob Berry decided not to test his machine in streamlined guise. Instead, he had devised a fairing arrangement which enabled him to lie in a prone position, on a 3ft-long Dunlopillo pad, to minimise wind-drag. He reckoned on between 84 and 86 horsepower against the brake at 6,000rpm on the bench with the JAP 8/80.

> On each side of the rear wheel are duralmin T-section horizontal girders, at the rear of which is a cross-bar with footrests; there is also a pivoted gear-change pedal on the offside. The gear-change technique is interesting. A hand-change lever is fitted near the front of the tank. It is coupled to a relay lever near the rear of the tank, the foot-change being connected to the same lever. From the relay lever a rod changes the motion to the positive-stop gear-change mechanism which controls the Sturmey-Archer three-speed box.
>
> First gear is engaged by hand, the machine starts and accelerates, and the change from first to second is also made by hand. At something approaching 90 mph, the change to top gear is made and this is done with the foot. If necessary, foot pressure can be maintained on the pedal to prevent jumping out. Downward changes, as the machine decelerates after its measured distance has been completed will be made by hand.
>
> For the record attempt, special dural rims and shallow-ribbed racing tyres have been supplied by Dunlop, the size being 3.50 x 21 inch.[178]

There is no denying Berry's inventiveness and competence as an engineer. The standard of the work and finish with which his machines were imbued was top class – and in deep contrast to some of the scraggy oil-spouters that were disgraceful to be seen at Brooklands and elsewhere. He was very conscious of being the last in a long and great tradition of Brough Superior riders, 'the Rolls Royce of motorcycles', and did not want to let them, George Brough or Britain down.[179] Above all, he was an unashamed patriot!

Despite all endeavours, the weather took a hand – as it so often did at Pendine when record bids were afoot – and the time-keepers booked for Saturday and Sunday, April 2nd and 3rd, did not even get to lick their pencils. In a way it was as well, because there were lubrication problems. With the very high compression ratios (13 to 1), the rear cylinder was tending to seize. It would be August before Berry could return to bid for the *Motor Cycle* prize.

Whitsun 1949

At the 1949 Whitsun meeting, June 2nd, Reg Good was back on the beach not only with the 348 Norton but with, of all things, a 495cc Moto Guzzi which, more than likely, derived from Leslie Griffiths Motors Ltd, Bridgend, who were the Guzzi agents in South Wales. For those who enjoy 'Not a Lot of People Know That' sort of

---
[178] *The Motor Cycle,* 31st March, 1949.
[179] *Vide* ms 1st draft 'autobiography': Bob Thredder.

information – this is the only foreign, 'Continental', machine ever recorded in the entry for Pendine in fifty years of racing! Except, that is, for a sole NSU in 1919. There may have been Werners on the ACU-tour, in 1909. It is uncertain.

Reg Good, now recovered from his accident in August 1947, when he sustained a broken leg, was bravely back in the saddle securing a placing in the 6-mile event for 350s. There is no indication of Reg having actually raced the Moto Guzzi. It does not appear in the official results and we have no editorial coverage to rely on. It seems that entrants to Pendine Races had been unconsciously practising a 'Little Englander' ('beyond Wales')[180] policy for forty years! There had, of course, been other 'foreign' entries in the twenties – Indians and Harley-Davidsons – but they were English-speaking, 'USA-foreign'! Pendine escaped the Japanese invasion altogether, without effort.

But not the 'Gold Star invasion'. Fred Rist was down from Middlesborough with a vanload of Goldies. Fred had become the man to beat – apart from local giant-killers LV Thomas, LF Griffiths and the quite formidable Treseders – if you could sort out which was which! Reg Dearden was in the entry list, presenting Rist with a challenge.

G Heinze & M Martinelli

Bryn Edwards, Llanstephan, known as 'Ocky Tipi'[181], a local personality, son of a London-to-Paddington 'Castle Class' engine driver, turned up with a brand-new 998cc Vincent-HRD – and not just for show! He was, as they say, there to 'show them the way round'. M Martinelli, Carmarthen, was a newcomer. His mount was a brand-new alloy-head 7R AJS.[182] Martinelli and Gerhard Heinze were, seemingly, ex-prisoners-of-war who had settled in the Carmarthen area. Martinelli is said to have 'married money' and a business in Carmarthen: an explanation of how he could always afford the best and latest racing bike! Martinelli was a good and promising rider, acquitting himself well on tarmac on subsequent outings with the Eddie Stephens stable. Heinze worked for Eddie as a mechanic for a number of years, post 1947, before setting up in the motor business for himself. He was sponsored as a rider by Eddie Stephens Motors, Dearden-fashion. Heinze, a sure-footed and aggressive rider, had a crack at the Manx Grand Prix, on a 490 Norton in 1950, and was entered on a Triumph and a Vincent 500 'Series C' Comet at Eppynt, in 1950 and 51.[183] People, locally, remember him as a somewhat truculent personality.

---

[180]Pembrokeshire, to which Pendine once belonged, was known as 'Little England beyond Wales'. Ref: Edward Laws's little masterpiece of that name.
[181]After the exotic house-name his war-time radio-operator brother imposed.
[182]H Adams: pers. comm., 1998.
[183]Pers. reminiscence, Emrys Walters, 1998.

E Walters & E Rees

Two other local MGP riders were out on the sands in sparring mood – Emrys Walters and Elwyn Rees. Emrys was an Eddie Stephens mechanic, riding a 'firm's bike'. He, too, was a serious contender at Eppynt on his AJS 500. Elwyn, still flying his Gloucester club colours, had worked in aircraft construction throughout the war. He was soon to move back down to Wales to establish the well-known Lampeter agency.

It was a programme packed with interest and local talent.

LV Thomas was to confound everyone again on the 25-year-old push-rod Sunbeam Sprint which beat them all in the 350cc racing-class sprint – and still had the stamina to come second in the 6-mile race.

RACING CLASS

10 miles > 1,000cc
LF Griffiths (Norton)
FM Rist (BSA)
E (Emrys) Walters, Carmarthen (Norton)

30 miles > 350cc
FM Rist (BSA)
LF Griffiths (Norton)
CR Edwards, (Norton)

STANDARD CLASS

One-mile sprint > 350cc
M Martinelli, Carmarthen (AJS)

one-mile sprint > 1,000cc
JBB Edwards (Vincent-HRD)
H Penson, Tenby (BSA)
G Heinze, Carmarthen (Norton)

6 miles > 350cc
M Martinelli (AJS)
TH Adams, Tenby (AJS)
T Johnson, Manchester (BSA)

10 miles > 1,000cc
DM Thomas, Carmarthen (HRD)
E Rees, Staveston (499 Ariel)
H Penson, Tenby (500 BSA)

Gerhard Heinze, Noel Knight and Vince Lloyd. [© Knight collection]

August 1949

August Bank Holiday, 1949, and the beach was still resentful. It rained heavily all day. Reg Dearden was down from Manchester with a vanload of Manx Nortons. Hugh Moffat took his first bow on the start-line, on a very nice – and fast – Rudge Ulster of 1938 vintage, sophisticated by a four-valve-per-cylinder hemispherical bronze head. Hugh was to prove he had taken note of the firm's advertising slogan: 'Don't trudge it, Rudge it!' A skilled engineer, he had helped his cousin, LV Thomas, to rebuild the 350 Sunbeam Sprint after a rocker broke on Oxwich. She was still going like stink!

LV Thomas

This was to be 'Elvy' Thomas's last outing on Pendine, after a colourful career as amateur motor cycle racing driver. In a long association with Pendine he had engaged in hostilities with giants such as Freddie Dixon, Clarry Wood, Jimmie Guthrie, RF and Denis Parkinson – and more than once seen them off! He had begun racing in 1925, on the now-famous little 1924 Sunbeam Sprint that he kept in his possession for the rest of his life.

There are many claims relating to 'George Dance' Sunbeams. Lionel's Sunbeam, which is still intact, has more than the usual claim to Dance affinity. George Dance, as competitions manager at the Marston, supervised its manufacture and preparation. He competed against it and LV Thomas on Pendine and elsewhere in sprint and long-distance events. George would occasionally give Lionel monosyllabic benefit of his wisdom, and a works bike (eg. DA 9995) for him to try, and demonstrate. Lionel always practised from his mentor the 'George Dance getaway': throttle half-to-three-quarters open, second gear. His maxim was: 'At the drop of the flag walk it with all might with both legs onto solid ground, letting the clutch take the punishment. Then flat – to as near a hundred as you dare!'[184]

LV Thomas is said also to have raced a 498cc pushrod Sports Sunbeam. August 1930, is the single instance of him having successfully raced a 500 Sunbeam on Pendine. Interestingly, there was such a machine in his possession (boxed!) at the time of his death. He also raced to good effect an early camshaft 350 Velocette in the late 'twenties, but in the thirties he became a dedicated Norton man.

Lionel Victor Thomas was a red-head. Coming from a comfortably-off, middle-class background – his people were in shipping – he was also a successful businessman in his own right. He was an electrical contractor and, later, he developed a tyre and battery suppliers. Lionel was a sociable character with a ready sense of humour – and said to be great company. 'He was a modest chap of great ability and was never afraid to ask anyone for ideas and thrash them out over a beer – until only what survived his critical argument remained'.[185]

---
[184] Hugh Moffatt, pers. comm.
[185] Dudley C Gershon *Motor Sport,* May 1977.

LV Thomas (Velocette, Norton & trophies). [© *LV Thomas collection*]

LV Thomas (Sunbeam Sprint), George Snell (crouched, left). [*MA Clare photo*]

LVT Special

In later years, when he had finished racing, Lionel designed and built a racing car, 'The LVT Special'. In an early incarnation, when it employed a Brooklands Riley Nine engine in a sports-racing body, it was found to be hopelessly under powered. He later worked on a Lea-Francis power-plant which was discarded as too stressed to be reliable. The story is told of how, after Lionel had rebuilt the engine, he installed it and started it up. The oil-pressure was so tremendous it sprayed the laurels along the Rectory drive![186]

RACING CLASS

30 miles > 350cc
R Dearden (Norton)
LV Thomas (Sunbeam)
T Johnson (Norton)

one-mile sprint > 1,000cc
R Dearden (Norton)
E Walters (Norton)
TW Pugh (Velocette)

6 miles > 350cc
FM Rist (348 BSA)
R Dearden (Norton)
TW Pugh (348 Velocette)

10 miles > 1,000cc
FM Rist (500 BSA)
E Walters (Norton)
DM Thomas (Vincent-HRD)

STANDARD CLASS

One-mile sprint > 350cc
N Treseder, Snr (Triumph)
N Treseder Jnr (Velocette)

one-mile sprint > 1,000cc
J Johnson, Manchester (Vincent-HRD)
G J Walters (498 Rudge)
G Heinze, Carmarthen (Norton)

10 miles > 350cc
N Treseder Snr (348 Triumph)
N Treseder Jnr (348 BSA)
AH Moffat (Rudge)

10 miles > 1,000cc
J Johnson, Manchester (Vincent-HRD)
N Treseder, Snr (Triumph)
G Heinze (Norton)

THE PENDINE HUNDRED, 1949

50 miles > 350cc
WR Williams (Matchless)
N Treseder, snr (249 Triumph)
N Treseder, jnr (249 Triumph)

---

[186] The LVT Special is also said to have had an Alta cross-flow engine, but this is not substantiated. The car, in its final metamorphosis, reg no [LVT 1], emerged as a most handsome, drop-head, grand touring car - a Healey Westland, or an Abbot-bodied Healey Tourer look-alike. It was powered by a high-cam, 'big four' 2.4 litre, 104 bhp Riley engine.

The World Land Speed Record:

Bob Berry (2)

Bob Berry was back in the second week of August 1949, for another crack at the motor cycle Land Speed Record.

> A keen wind blew in off the sea, and Berry was content to cruise his machine back. He expressed himself pleased with the day's work... On Thursday evening, [he] made another unofficial run in each direction along the beach. In spite of a strong off-shore wind and unfavourable sand conditions, the test was very successful. The Manchester man said later that the rev counter of his machine had a speed well in excess of the record.
>
> On the following evening, disaster nearly overtook Berry when he was flashing over the beach at approximately 120 mph in second gear. A patch of soft sand situated a little off the course he would be using for the record attempt caused his front wheel to wobble perilously. The performance of the machine, however, pleased him, and he decided to make an attack on the world's record of 174 mph early on Sunday morning.
>
> Early on Saturday, Berry made several short runs over the beach for a magneto test. He said afterwards that he had reached 7,000 revs in bottom gear.
>
> Keen disappointment was expressed on Sunday morning when a thick coastal mist blanketed the beach, and the attempt was held up until the evening between high and low water. However, the state of the beach was too rippled for an attack in the evening, and Berry decided to wait another few tides before making his speed dash.

But conditions did not permit another attempt. That ended Berry's ambition to bring the motor cycle 'Flying kilometre' record back onto British soil. Events were to take a turn.

Bob Berry - prone.

19. Fabulous Fred

THE Carmarthen MC & LC Club's Spring meeting of 1950 was on 29th May, Whit Monday. There were 40 entries. Eddie Stephens,[187] retired from active racing, assumed the role of a Welsh Reg Dearden, promoting up-and-coming riders, among them Emrys Walters, Gerhard Heinze and D Watkin Jones. These fielded on that day an anthology of potent machinery – two International Nortons, a Vincent 500 and a 7R AJS. M Martinelli of Carmarthen was mounted on a 7R also, as were Emrys's brother, Gwyn, and SW Adams of Saundersfoot. JD Roberts of Saundersfoot was on a 500 AJS. The Pughs of Cwmtwrch were on Velocettes, as was E Waters of Swansea and Des Snow of Merthyr. They were all 350s, presumably a mixture of Mk V1 and Mk V111 KTTs.

DD Snow

Des Snow of Merthyr was destined to become a great favourite with the crowds at Pendine, on his Mk V111 KTT Velocette. A consistently 'tidy' and fast rider, Des was also a versatile performer on grass and tarmac, to be seen at Eppynt or Aberdare Park in the early fifties, locked in battle with the likes of Bob McIntyre, Dickie Dale, Bob Foster and even Les Graham. Des's racing career began in company with his father, a local garage proprietor ('Snow's of Merthyr'), on a rare Indian machine. He later graduated to Coventry Eagle and Triumph before his love affair with Velocettes (first, a Mk V), whose lightness and 'hand-made' quality appealed to this very able and discriminating engineer. Easily capable of high honours in road-racing, he was never able to realise his ambition to 'have a go' at the Manx Grand Prix.

Miss Joan Slack, of Bowden near Wolverhampton, was down with a 350 Velo also, as well as her customary 125 BSA Bantam. DR Griffith, whose name is always wrongly spelt in race programmes and who, on the beach, seemed to inhabit a little private world – with scarcely a word to other competitors – had his potent 499cc JAP-engined VMC in line for an outing. The appropriately-named RS Paddock of Chester, was another with a self-build 'Special' entry, a 347 RSP. Henry Adams, a Saundersfoot club man, was out with his 499 Rudge. Apart from Leslie Griffiths's 490 there were only two other Nortons – that of AW James of Saundersfoot and Reg

---

[187]Eddie was affectionately known as 'Bomp'. His reflex action on handling any motor cycle was to test its compression, until the engine uttered his nick-name!

FM Rist (BSA). [LA Lusardi photo]

DD Snow (Velocette) and family, 1952.

Good's. In the Lightweight category a Tandon, fired by a 125 Villiers two-stroke, was a 'first' for Pendine. The entrant, R Edwards of Neath, was a candidate for some special award or other as the Tandon, conceived as a 'Flat-pack' for the Indian market, was considered the 'Trabant' of motor cycles! It was rivalled by a whole flock of 125 Bantams, ridden by: D Cole, H Vickery, J Thomas and J Billington, all Neath club members. H Williams of Llanelly was the sole Bantam contestant from that club. JW Waters, EJ Freason, K Wilson, G Thomas and EB Mason, all Saundersfoot men, had an assortment of BSA 500s – singles and twins. RJ Ware, Newport, had a 350 Gold Star, as did Nobby Treseder. Norman Treseder, his father, had the sole Triumph entry, a 350 Tiger 80.

Fred Rist's was an early entry, with three machines of 249, 350 and 500cc capacity.

FM Rist

Many riders have been in line for the title 'king of Pendine', but in recent memory none wears the crown more securely than Fredrick Maurice Rist. He was perhaps, correctly, 'the last king of Pendine', as no mortal wears a crown for ever. He stands in a long and distinguished succession that begins with George Dance, Morris Isaac and Freddie Dixon, Clarry Wood and Jimmie Simpson, Tommy Spann and Jack Carr, then RF Parkinson, LF Griffiths, LV Thomas and RJD Burnie, Wilf Billington and Rex Young – not forgetting the ubiquitous D Jones. There were those that were king for a day, like CM Needham, George Patchett, Alec Bennett, Ginger Wood and Tommy McEwan – but Fred, on Pendine with the BSAs, in his day, was magisterial. He wrote,[188] saying

> Pendine, which I recall vividly, and especially the way that you local enthusiasts were always eager to help in one way or another when I used (usually) to come down on my own with a couple of bikes in the van – that the company always loaned me inspite of the event not being one of the officially trade-supported events.
>
> I still, in particular, (will) always be indebted to the proprietor of the little garage, near the little slipway at Pendine, who always met me with a smile and allowed me the use of his workshop and his facilities without ever making any charge as far as I can ever remember. Great Guy.
>
> I also enjoyed staying at a little cottage on the hillside a (few) hundred yards away up on the left on the Saundersfoot road. The lady was always very kind and put up with a fair amount of sand falling out of my leathers (and underclothes, sometimes), as well as the odour of Castrol 'R' and Methanol fuel, which would never smell as good to the good lady as it always did to us!
>
> Of course, Eddie Stephens and his wife were very close and greatly valued friends, ever since I first met them at the 1938 Six Days' Trials at Llandrindod Wells, where Eddie was also taking part in that event on a works Triumph for the 'umpteenth' time, when I was having my first attempt at gold!
>
> Eddie's Carmarthen club and friends, apart from putting on the Pendine races, used also to run a scramble each evening after the sand racing on a farm at Llan 'Lliw', I think[189] which was near the Ministry of Agriculture 'AI' centre.
>
> I used to enjoy the scramble very much, but first the valve cams, tyres and sprockets had to be changed from what I had been using at Pendine a few hours previously.
>
> And at the end of the day, it was always wonderful to be invited 'home' to Eddie's, and enjoy such hospitality and conversation after the events. No wonder Carmarthenshire and Pendine in particular have a special place in my heart for those old days.

(No published result is available for the Whitsun, 1950, meeting at the time of going to press. No doubt, FM R had things pretty much his own way, as far as LF G would let him!).

Fred Rist's reference is a another tribute to Mr Gilbert Davies, Ashwell Garage, Pendine, whose generosity of spirit is remembered by everyone who raced on the beach. The story is told of someone who left a (once) very nice little Sunbeam at the garage, meaning to call back for it. Which he did, fifteen years later. And there it was still safe and sound. Mr Davies excused himself for a moment to the 'office'. Then presented a bill for storage – not far short of £1,500. 'A shilling a day for fifteen years. Good value.' Gilbert's sense of humour!

---

[188] Fred Rist. Pers. letter, 13 March, 1986.
[189] Llanllwch.

August 1950

There was a vast entry of 90 (some of them multiples) for the Pendine Hundred meeting on August 7th, 1950 – though its distance was curtailed to 70 miles – very likely because of the tide. Pre-eminent among the 'hot-shots' were Wilf Billington and Reg Dearden, on 348cc and 499 cc Nortons. They were there, armed, to meet the BSA challenge. The ambience can be seen to have shifted towards the Clubman class of racing. The BSA Gold Star was so good, fast, cheap and successful that it tended to kill all enterprise, the very essence of Pendine. You could buy a Gold Star and, with aggression and a little talent, be formidable, if not competitive. In the same way as it put a stop to the IoM Clubman's and took the 'class' out of the Manx Grand Prix, the Goldie was in danger for a while of turning Pendine into a one marque procession. Many of the entries for the day's racing are in duplicates and triplicates, either dealers airing their wares or thinly-disguised works entrants.

Fred Rist has his name down for BSAs of 250, 350 and 500cc capacity. KTT Velocettes and the 'Boy-Racer' AJS 7Rs were similarly available 'over the counter' ready to race, highly competitive and not that expensive at prices starting below £150. HL Williams of Worcester is over with a vanload of standard and racing Nortons and BSAs – and, of course, Eddie Stephens, as usual, 'entering garages of bikes'. Joan Slack, a very competent rider, schooled by her Royal Military Police despatch-rider father, with three entries (Velocettes and a BSA) had her first real experience of Pendine, being thrown, without harm, in the 70-mile race. Motor and electrical engineer Fitzroy Allen and garage man Wilmot Evans, Triumph works trials riders, take the stage – as does HL Stephens.

Wilmot, (popularly known as 'Mot') a Glanaman man, managing director of Ace Garages, Coventry, was a veteran rider who rode in his first IoM TT in 1926. He finished in the 1949 Junior TT on an AJS, in 61st position – the only time he ever completed a TT. He distinguished himself in trials riding under the Triumph banner as well as in international road-racing *grandes épreuves*. Recently his successes had included successive wins at Eppynt in the Lightweight in 1949 and 1950, on a machine of his own design derived from AJS and Triumph parts. He had earlier visited Pendine in 1948, on a Matchless, and been placed. He was a close friend and rival of Fred Rist.

Rex Young and his pal Douglas Connett were down on a recce from Nortons. They must have been impressed by the turn-out. Not since the great Hubert Hassall's efforts in the first Welsh TT, in 1922, and Joe Craig's tentative appearance in 1926, had Bracebridge Street shown a direct interest in the Pendine races. Leslie Griffiths and Bob Burnie kept a kind of 'watching brief' for Nortons. It is not difficult to understand why sand-racing successes were considered marginal to major manufacturers involved in big league road and circuit racing. The publicity derived was disproportionate to the effort and outlay. Nortons – and this was their hey-day – had a limited competitions budget. Sand-racing was expensive – as it was notoriously destructive of machines.

In the field of 90 entries there are 27 BSAs. All but two appear to be 'Gold Stars'. There are 21 Nortons, 7 Triumphs, 5 AJSes and 4 Velocettes and, amongst others –

Ambassador (3), Excelsior (3), James (3) and Matchless (2). A special mention is deserved for a Python-engined Dunelt, brought all the way from Rochdale by GW Hall. Five machines are in the 600 – 1,000cc category (three 1,000cc Vincent-HRDs, two Triumph 650s) as the Hundred was open again to such exotica, after years of pointless prohibition.

The Manchester painter, Leo Starr, dressed gaudy in bold checks and cap-to-match, stood out among the drab, coupon-dressed spectators and competitors in the paddock. He was entered on a 350 Matchless. An odd combination: artist and racing motor cyclist!

STANDARD MACHINES

2 laps > 125cc
Joan Slack (BSA)

One-mile sprint > 350cc
N Treseder (Triumph)

one-mile sprint > 1,000cc
DM Thomas (HRD)

2 miles > 350cc
N Treseder (Triumph)

10 miles > 1,000cc
A Pickerill, Saundersfoot (499 BSA)

4 laps > 125cc
J Slack (BSA)

RACING

One-mile sprint > 350cc
R Dearden (Norton)

one-mile sprint > 1,000cc
DM Thomas (HRD)

PENDINE HUNDRED, 1950

70 miles: unlimited
FM Rist (499 BSA)

HW Billington had an 'off' day. It was to be his last outing on Pendine. There were younger Lochinvars waiting to steal his shining spurs.

HW Billington (Norton), Aug 1950. [*LA Lusardi photo*]

Whitsun 1951

The 1951 Whitsun meeting on Pendine, organised by the Carmarthen club, was on 14th of May. There was a good entry of some 47 men, women and machines. Joan Slack and her 123cc BSA Bantam and 248cc Velocette comprised the women. AK Young and HJ Hulsman, Neath, were on similar 125 BSA machines. The big BSA challenger was Fred Rist, with a very business-like 645cc special 'Golden Flash', in addition to a 500. Hulsman also fielded an Ambassador, a sweet-sounding Villiers twin-two-stroke-powered bike that just seemed to lack the promised 'get-up-and-go' in its voice. This may have persuaded him at a later date to design, assemble and market the HJH trials and scramble machine, a light-handling little scrapper that made a reputation for itself.

There were 14 BSAs altogether in the paddock. Ivor Eveleigh, Cardiff, MD Davies, Llanelly, J Phillips, Swansea, D Cole, Neath, and N Treseder, Swansea were on 350s; JW Waters, Tenby, D Atkins, Morriston, Llwyd James, Maenclochog, A Pickerskill, Narberth, V Lloyd, Carmarthen, and VB Davies, Morriston, among others, were out on 500s. There were seven Triumphs: D Bolton, Stockport, ST Davies and Dan Thomas, Stevenage, and N Treseder were on 350s; the three 500s were entered by AL Barrow, Stockport, G Heinze, Carmarthen, and H Edwards, Neath. Dan Thomas and his friend, JT Griffiths of Stevenage, also fielded a couple of 998 HRDs; and DW Davies, Llanybyther was on a big Vincent. The Velocette threat came from DD Snow, Merthyr, E Pimlott, Chorlton-cum-Hardy and C Morgan, Llanelly. AJSes were scarce – only JW Waters, Tenby, and JH Barnard of Pontnewydd, on 350s; JDH Roberts of Tenby had a 500 on parade. There was one Royal Enfield (EG Knight, Carmarthen), an Ariel (V Lloyd, Carmarthen), and D Bolton of Stockport had also entered a 350 Matchless. John Mills of Neath was out on his little 248cc Rudge Rapid. The odd-ball was DR Griffith's familiar 499cc VMC.

Rex Young led the Norton challenge on a 499 single-knocker that he had cobbled together from a trials frame, designed for sand-racing. Nortons, for once, were comparatively thin on the ground. Les Griffiths was out, as usual, on his 499cc, Manx/Inter, fitted with Roadholder forks. The other Norton riders were CA Richards, Swansea, P Owen, Johnstone, Pembs, DC Evans, Merthyr, and A Thomas, Pencader.

There are no official results to hand. According to an inscribed race programme, it turned out as follows:

STANDARD CLASSES
Two laps > 125cc
HJ Hulsman, Neath (BSA)
J Slack (BSA)
AK Young, Neath (BSA)

one mile >
DW Davies (Vincent 1,000cc)

4 laps >125cc
HJ Hulsman (BSA)

J Slack ((BSA)
AK Young (BSA)

RACING CLASSES
30 miles > 600cc
FM Rist (BSA)
LF Griffiths (Norton)
DD Snow (Velocette)

10 miles > 1,000cc
FM Rist (BSA 646cc)

J Sutherland (BSA), 1951.

August 1951

August Bank Holiday, 1951 fell on August 6th, a fine summer day. 'Seldom, if ever, have conditions been so perfect at Pendine's famous sands', comments *Motor Cycling*, and *The Motor cycle*, in poetic vein, says that a 'blaze of summer sunshine greeted thousands of holidaymakers, who witnessed some thrilling racing'.

Fred Rist had entered, amongst other machines prepared at the Smallheath, Birmingham works, a 140mph dope-burning version of the 650cc A10 twin 'Golden Flash', geared-down for the sands. ST Sefton was along with him, with BSAs of racing specification. IoM Clubman's rider, J Sutherland, arrived to try his luck with his 350 ZB Gold Star. Rex Young had a 348 and a 490 Norton, devised in the competitions shop, Bracebridge Street. Reg Dearden had been bitten by the Pendine bug. He was ready to go with an immaculately-prepared, pair of Manxes. Joan Slack had the Bantam and a 250 Velocette; and, a first for Pendine in the miniature range, a couple of ultra-lightweight Dots with, respectively, the 123cc and 197cc, 45-degree Villiers engines. They were entered by B Bardsley of Woodford. Dot had recently won the team prize at the Isle of Man. Considering that the 'Devoid-of-trouble' marque, founded in 1903, was one of the oldest motorcycle manufacturers, and one that had been actively involved in racing for the best part of 40 years, it is amazing that this was only the second occasion for Dots to be entered on Pendine, the last occasion being 1928. In a field of 51 there were 21 BSAs, 10 Nortons, 4 AJSes, 4 Triumphs, 2 Velocettes, 2 HRDs, a Royal Enfield, a Rudge, a James, an Ambassador – and various 'Specials' including, of course, the VMC.

As usual, Fred Rist shone by capturing most of the events in the racing classes. His 'cornering was superb'. *Motor Cycling* continues:

> Rist and Young were sliding their machines through the corners in spectacular fashion and drawing steadily away from third man, LF Griffiths. By half-way they had lapped all but Griffiths, and lapped him before the end. Good clean racing and well organised by Carmarthen Motor Cycle Club. It was the largest crowd ever seen on the beach.

Fred Rist's BSAs

FM Rist campaigned three machines on Pendine: a 650, a 500 and a 350. They were not quite the state-of-the-art weaponry that most people imagined – though the 650 was a truly exciting product of the Armoury Road small arms foundry, and an effective mobile test-bed. It was a special: one of two. Its 'twin' was awarded to Gene Theissen who clocked an average of 143.5mph on her on Bonneville's hard, smooth Salt Flats. On tap was 60bhp – 10% more than a Manx Norton.

The engine was a good old push-rod, iron A10, with a 13.5 to 1 compression ratio for alcohol consumption, whose rate on Pendine was 8 mpg! Dope was administered through two Amal TT carburettors, of one-inch choke diameter, 1.5 thou. main jets and separately mounted – remote – float chambers. 'On sand you use twice the jet-size', Fred affirmed. The normal bifurcated inlet manifold was cut off close to the cylinder head, to provide a flange for the carburettors. The engine was, of course, highly polished – so that, as Fred said, 'There are no corners anywhere'.

The Golden Flash had a an A7-type frame, with light-alloy wheel-rims. The tyres were studded Dunlops; brakes were 7-inch front (eventually 8-inch) and the 13-inch megaphone exhausts were $3\frac{7}{8}$-inch diameter, from a lead of $40\frac{1}{2}$-inch exhausts. But it was a flying machine – capable of 145mph, but geared to deliver about 120mph at 6,000rpm on the beach: the lower gearing necessary to counter sand-drag.

The 500 was basically a B34 engine, in a pre-war Empire Star frame. It was slower by 20 mph, and more economical by 2 mpg. The 'Iron Gold Star' had a similar Amal carburettor with a $1\frac{5}{32}$-inch choke. The gear-box was an ex-WD M20, with close ratios, bottom being 4.16, as compared to the 650's 7.36. The 350 was identical in specification, except for jet-sizes.

These bikes were not, then, as people have speculated, prototype, alloy-engined DBD 34s, but good old 'Iron-Stars', brilliant machines – considering they only had push-rod engines. The A10 was only really out-classed when the Double-knocker, Featherbed Nortons and then the Vincent Black Lightnings were unleashed.

FM Rist [4] (BSA 650cc twin, A10: the 140mph 'Golden Flash'), Whitsun 1952. [*LA Lusardi photo*]
(*Courtesy of Wayne Bowen*)

FM Rist [5] (BSA 350 cc B32, 'Iron Star'), 1950. [*LA Lusardi photo*]

STANDARD CLASSES

Two laps > 125cc
HJ Hulsman, Neath (BSA)
J Slack (BSA)
B Bardsley, Woodford (Dot)

One-mile sprint > 350cc
ST Sefton, B'ham (BSA)
N Treseder (BSA)
MD Davies, Llanelli (BSA)

one-mile sprint > 1,000cc
DM Thomas, Stevenage (Vincent-HRD)
ST Sefton (BSA)
E Rees, Carmarthen (Norton)

4 laps >125cc
HJ Hulsman (BSA)
J Slack ((BSA)
B Bardsley (Dot)

10 miles > 350cc
ST Sefton, B'ham (350 BSA)
DD Snow, Merthyr (348 Velocette)
N Treseder (346 Triumph)

10 miles > 1,000cc
ST Sefton (BSA)
DM Thomas (Vincent-HRD)
DW Davies, Llanybyther (HRD)

RACING CLASSES

One-mile sprint > 350cc
RB Young (Norton)
R Dearden (Norton)
FM Rist (BSA)

one-mile sprint > 1,000cc
FM Rist (650 BSA)
DW Davies (HRD)
DR Griffith (VMC)

6 miles > 350cc
RB Young (Norton)
FM Rist (BSA)
R Dearden (Norton)

THE PENDINE HUNDRED, 1951

50 miles > 1,000cc
FM Rist (650 BSA)
RB Young (499Norton)
LF Griffiths ((499 Norton)

50 miles > 250cc
J Slack (248 Velocette)

50 miles > 350cc
R Dearden (349 Norton)

50 miles > 500cc
RB Young (499 Norton)
DR Griffith (VMC)

The 'Hundred' was cut to fifty miles and the two final races of the day were cancelled: the 'Ten-mile' for standard machines not exceeding 1000cc and the 'Six-mile' for racing machines not exceeding 350cc. On such a perfect day, it can only be assumed that someone miscalculated the time of the tide! Unless there was some other cause, now forgotten. Rex Young, who had been racing with his arm in plaster – a broken wrist – knew that he would have to do some serious thinking and persuading when he got back to work in Birmingham, if he was to spike Fred Rist's pilearm.

Rex Young [44] and Doug Connett, August, 1950.   [© RB Young collection]

RB Young [9], (Norton 'Featherbed' 541cc), August, 19502.
[© RB Young collection]

20. Rex is King

August 1952

A MEETING took place at Easter, on the 14th of April, 1952, but no records of it are to hand. LA Lusardi has left a splendid photographic record of that Easter Monday meeting, where it can be seen that it was a wet, blustery day. Fred Rist, Rex Young, Cliff Edwards and DR Griffith were out having a great time, but no press representatives ventured down to the 'Brooklands of the West' to watch the racing on that day.

Whether there was a Whitsun meeting in 1952 is uncertain.

A record post-war crowd attended the 1952 August Bank Holiday meeting on the 4th; according to *Motor Cycling* 'the best crowd ever'. (This seems always to be the case, though no-one at the time ever ventures to put a figure on it!). The relaxation of petrol rationing may have had something to do with the upsurge of interest, though motor cycle racing, owing to the great celebrity of Geoff Duke and the intensifying contest between Nortons and foreign multi-cylinder machines, was enjoying an upsurge generally and great popular vogue.

It was a cool, but fine day, a perfect motor-cycle-racing day. The beach was dry. A similar entry to August Bank Holiday, 1951: Rist and Sefton, over from Birmingham, with Channel Islands champion, NF George of Jersey, leading the Beezer attack, on Goldies. LF Griffiths, Dearden, Young and Connett, armed with Nortons, ready for the BSA onslaught. For a change, there were more Nortons in contention this year – eleven Inters/Manxes as against nine Beezers. Young and Dearden had persuaded Nortons to devise 'secret weapon' 541cc 'big bore' engines for them in Featherbed frames to meet the Rist 'Golden Flash' challenge. And it worked! Rist, for once, was 'sent bootless home'.

Doug Connett from Middlesborough, a good trials man – new to sand-racing, accompanied Rex Young. Well-known in trials, Young's Norton colleague rode the 'spare' machine for the day. There were seven KTT Velocettes, DD Snow leading the Hall Green challenge on his self-prepared Mk V111. Reg Good was out on his 348 Norton. Bob Berry had 'come out of retirement' and was seen driving a Triumph Thunderbird; and AB Drew of Manchester had entered an OK Supreme.

The event for standard production machines was pretty uneventful, but Young and Dearden out on the hot Featherbeds gave Rist a terrible fright in the Racing classes. He had to content himself with second place at best. There was a lovely Velocette duel between DD Snow and the brilliant young LW 'Len' Nicholas of

Carmarthen, and the outcome was only decided by Des's Renolds chain. A similar fate befell NF George while leading the field on the borrowed Vincent-HRD of DM Thomas of Stevenage. George's cornering on the 'big banger' was an excellent spectacle. As a newcomer to Pendine, though with a tremendous track-record in Channel Island racing, he was showing enormous form, as was Doug Connett on the 490 Norton. It was one of the finest days racing ever seen on the beach. The day belonged to Rex Young, whose performance put some of the older spectators in mind of the great George Dance, who was always only in the business of coming in first.

These are the official results:

STANDARD CLASSES

Two laps > 200cc
D Johnson, Cheshire (Dot)
E Rees, Carmarthen (New Imperial)
E Sefton, B'ham (Earles-JAP)

one-mile sprint > 350cc
LW Nichols, Carmarthen (Velocette)
R Cowles, Monkswood (BSA)
ST Sefton, (Earles-JAP)

one-mile sprint > 1,000cc
DM Thomas, Stevenage (Vincent-HRD)
NF George, Jersey (BSA)
ST Sefton (Earles-JAP)

4 laps > 200cc
D Johnson (Dot)
E Rees (New Imperial)
AJ Griffiths (BSA)

4 laps > 250cc
D Bolton, Stockport (Velocette)

10 miles > 350cc
LW Nicholas (348 Velocette)
G Heinze (350 BSA)
R Cowles (BSA)

10 miles > 1,000cc
DM Thomas (Vincent-HRD)
NF George (BSA)
ST Sefton (Earles-JAP)

RACING CLASSES

One-mile sprint > 350cc
RB Young (348 Norton)
R Dearden (348 Norton)
FM Rist (BSA)

one-mile sprint > 1,000cc
RB Young (541 Norton)
FM Rist (650 BSA)
R Dearden (541 Norton)

6 miles > 350cc
RB Young (348 Norton)
DD Snow (Velocette)
FM Rist (BSA)

10 miles > 1,000cc
RB Young (541 Norton)
D Connett (490 Norton)
FM Rist (650 BSA)

THE PENDINE HUNDRED, 1952

50 miles > 1,000cc
RB Young (541 Norton)
D Connett (499 Norton)
DD Snow (Velocette)

RB Young

Rex Young's performance on the day was out of the top drawer. He rode an absolute blinder and won everything he entered. Only George Dance, Alec Bennett, Ginger Wood and Tommy McEwan could boast similar unblemished success on Pendine Sands. Rex was king for the day!

The machines Rex rode for the occasion were of his own conception. He writes

> As I was working at Bracebridge Street, I was able to obtain a spare scramble bike frame into which I cobbled a single ohc motor. The bike was made specially for sand racing & I used it at Redcar and Durage Bay. It was soon apparent however that something faster was required. So I made a second bike, a Manx Featherbed, but the big difference was the double ohc motor which was bored out to 541cc and the compression ratio raised to run on Methanol. I can still remember the engine being run on the dynamometer at Norton & the boys testing it said it was giving 50/60 bhp, which they said was comparable with the petrol works bikes. The output doesn't seem much these days but things have moved on.
>
> The Featherbed sandracer was much quicker than the earlier bike & I believe still holds the Flying kilo at Redcar of 118 mph jointly with George Brown's 1,000cc Vincent.

Rex Young [21] (Norton), Whitsun 1952. Aged 13, in riding mac, gesticulating, 4th from the left, the author caught again! (*Courtesy of Wayne Bowen*). [*LA Lusardi photo*]

Whitsun, 1953 L>R: [17] DR Griffith (VMC); [34] Llwyd James (BSA); [7] Reg Dearden (541cc Norton); Jack Morris (programme) Len Nicholas (BD jacket) J McNulty (Sou'wester). [*RTB photo*]

The Motor Cycle World Land Speed Record:

Bob Berry (3)

Bob Berry, in record-breaker mode, was back on the beach in May 1953, his ambitions still running high. He was talking, not just of breaking the new record that had been set up in December by another German, W Herz, on an NSU at 180.17 mph, but of cracking the 200 and 300 mph barrier! But not on Pendine. 150 mph, he reckoned, was about Pendine's limit for a motor cycle. He had burned a great deal of 'midnight oil' to produce a potent, 'all-enveloped' record breaker. Its greatest design improvement was the adaptation of the frame to a 'prone' riding position. This configuration, now world-famous, was not altogether innovative. George Tucker, in 1929, had modified an AJW Super Four, with a blown 985cc British Anzani engine, into the 'First of the Kneelers' for Brooklands.[190] More recently, American Vincent rider, Roland 'Rowley' Free, had adopted a kneeler chassis for record runs on Bonneville. Free calculated on a speed increase of between 17 and 20 mph above 140 mph. The Brough's fish-tailed, bullet-shaped Electron alloy shell was aerodynamically unscientific, as Bob Berry was to discover.

---

[190]See *Classic Motor Cycle,* July, 1984.

Hairpin valve springs replaced the coil-springs of the proprietary JAP head. This, according to Berry, made a tremendous difference.[191] Compression ratios were up to 14.5 to 1 on the front, and 14.2 to 1 on the rear cylinder – the front being the cooler-running. The power-output of the 8/80 JAP-twin was thereby up-rated to 90 bhp at 6,700 rpm. Stan Greening, JA Prestwich's designer, even ran it on the dynamometer at 7,400rpm and the con-rods held! The standard light-alloy racing cylinder heads had been replaced by cast-iron ones to facilitate quicker warming-up. Induction to the twin carburettors was via air-intake scoops and ram tubes. It was estimated that the scoops contributed an extra 10 bhp at speeds above 160 mph. The Renolds chains, which took a tremendous bashing, were drip-lubricated.

A special heavy-duty clutch was built to counter slip on take-off and at high speed, and on Dunlop's advice, Berry swapped the duralumin wheels for steel, with rolled-thread spokes. 70psi pressures were recommended for the special mix sand-grip speed-record tyres. Dunlop had provided 8-ply silk cord walled tyres of 3.50 x12 ins, with only ⅛ inches of smooth tread as a precaution against tread throw. Berry was full of praise for Dunlops' unstinting help throughout his career as an aspiring record-breaker.

---

[191]From BB's hand-written ms. notes for what might be a first-draft autobiography, via B Thredder.

Bob Berry (Brough Superior) 'Kneeler'.

The idea was to test-run his new machine in July, again without the light-alloy streamlined shell and, given that 160 mph came up without problems (in second gear!), he intended to go back and run it on the road at Jabbecke, near Ostende, or on the autobahn, near Munich, to be officially timed with the streamlining in place. By his calculation, verified by wind-tunnel trials, the streamlining would give him an extra 40 mph. The 'sand-drag' factor had variously been assessed at reducing speed by between 10 and 15%. He was said to be looking at a speed of 240+ mph. With benefit of hindsight and without advanced aerodynamics Berry, had he got there, would undoubtedly have joined a roll-call of 'the late' record-breakers!

During a practice session he foolishly took the machine for 'a spin' up the course, wearing only beach clothes. At 167 mph, very likely due to the fairing, he got into trouble, a half-mile wobble ensued: he lost it – and came off. He was lucky to come out of it alive. Carmarthen hospital treated his fractured collar-bone, smashed teeth and broken toes. His spirit was not broken.

Bob Berry, licking his wounds, disappeared from view for a good few years. He was back, still doggedly canvassing sponsorship, in 1959. The Land Speed Record for motor cycles had progressed somewhat, but was in a muddle at 211 or 214 mph. NSU and Triumph were in legal contention. He had abandoned the kneeler, the fish-tailed 'bullet' based on the remnants of the fabulous old Jack Carr-derived Brough racer, in favour of a 1920s chassis, made famous at Brooklands by Joe Wright around 1930, and that had been involved in the record-attempt scandal on a road near Cork, in Eire.[192] JAPs supplied him with a new engine with cylinder heads and barrels of light alloy, sparked by twin racing magnetos and fed by twin Amal carburettors. Its OEC-Temple-Reynolds Duplex front suspension was damped by the addition of Girling shock absorbers. An extended rear sub-frame had been welded on to carry outrigger footrests and controls, the engine being mounted behind the driver. The linkage to the 4-speed Burman (racing Norton) gearbox had a similar hand/foot change to the earlier version. The whole was enveloped in a specially designed and wind-tunnel-tested bright crimson fibreglass shell, christened variously 'Moby Dick' and 'The Projectile' by the press, but which he referred to as 'The Streamliner'. Fifteen feet long, it was developed with the help of James Livesey, lecturer in aerodynamics at Manchester University, and fabricated from resins supplied by British Resin Products, at HP Pressurecast Ltd, Manchester, a plastics firm which supplied de Havillands. The overall height of the shell was no more than 36 inches, allowing 4 inches ground-clearance.

Berry spent five weeks at Pendine in the summer of 1959, when the combination of beach and weather conditions only met his criteria three times. He was running seriously short of money, being obliged to change his hotel room for modest digs. It was a 'do-or-die' situation. Among the sponsorships he had managed to secure for his proposed sortie to Utah were Amal carburettors, Mobil oil, Dunlop, ICI paints,

---

[192]Wright achieved a World Record of 150.74 mph on the Carrigrohane Straight in 1930. The machine alleged to have been used, when exhibited at Olympia, was revealed **not** to have been the OEC-Temple but the spare machine, a Zenith. The OEC had broken down!

Ferodo linings and Lucas ignition. A patient development engineer, Berry was, nevertheless, able to identify minor changes to the fairing that would strengthen the screen and assist access.

He was back again in the autumn of 1960 when the motor was said to be producing a very-near-to-bursting-point 105 bhp at 6,800 rpm, a power-to-weight ratio of 370bhp per ton.[193] Running on a mixture of pump fuel and ethol/methyl, he saw the equivalent of 200 mph on the rev counter in third gear for a few seconds (186mph on the air speed indicator), and eased off – only to have the cockpit fill with gas. Given the all-enveloped red-hot exhausts, he was riding a two-wheeled bomb! He must have had a fright.

Despite concentrated fund-raising – begging-bowls at Silverstone and the Isle of Man, dances and whist-drives at Pendine – and still more development, he never got his machine to the Salt Lake, Utah; never realised his ambition to be the fastest man on two wheels, for simple lack of cash. His personal account of his final test run at Pendine which appeared in *The Motor Cycle* in edited form, is as follows:

> Let me try and explain the Pendine set-up and its faults and virtues. When in perfect condition the beach is quite probably as good as Bonneville Salt Flats but of course much shorter, the longest stretch I have ever been able to use being five miles. Now for the snags.
>
> The beach can roughly be divided into 2 sections, the first stretch three miles long being usually almost, or quite, perfect, but the farthest two miles, beyond where the sandhills end and the coastline curves inland, are suitable for 150 mph plus perhaps, once in a fortnight. The beach can be perfect at dawn and after a midday tide can be hopeless. It can be in perfect condition for two or three tides but unusable because of cross winds which prevail.
>
> The beach runs from east to west. At dawn the rising sun completely blinds a rider travelling towards the east. At sunset it is perhaps worse in the opposite direction. And usually at dawn and dusk it is windless. Sir Malcolm Campbell spent three months waiting for favourable conditions on one of his record attempts. Amy Johnson and Jim Mollison waited six weeks in (Seafarer) before taking off on their epic trip to America from the famous beach.
>
> In 1959 I waited five weeks and the fastest speed I could attain was 154 mph in second gear, due to soft beaches and three rows of steel posts which run diagonally across my track. These posts spaced 100 yards apart are used for artillery ranges by the Government establishment which uses the beach for weapons testing. Due to having to drive through the posts at an acute angle, the maximum clearance between them and the beach is 10 feet. The posts are almost invisible when approached in a car at 70 mph.
>
> In a streamliner at 150 mph and above, it is impossible to see them at all. When one takes into account that the projectile cannot be steered at over 90 mph thus preventing any possibility of steering round them the posts constitute a bit of a hazard. I returned to Pendine this year to see if I could top 180 mph and thus reach a speed higher than has ever been attained before on land in Britain, and at the same time to see if the bike

---

[193]Formula One GP racing cars of the time had a p/w ratio of between 400 and 425bhp per ton.

stayed straight at this speed. I needed this assurance before going to Bonneville as I have always been against travelling to America with an untried project and should hate to come unstuck in front of 160 million Americans, quite a lot of whom purchase British motorcycles.

This visit to Pendine differed in several ways from previous trials there. First, I had never been so late in the year as most of my previous trials and official attempts at the old record had taken place in July and August at dawn and dusk, that is around 6 am and 8 pm. This time I planned to run in the late mornings, wind and beach permitting.

Until 1959 I had, when not on officially timed runs, been forced to rely on rev counter reading for speeds reached, but of course could not rely on the absolute accuracy of these due to a certain amount of wheel spin on the sand. We realised that at higher speeds than 150 mph, due to the increased wind resistance, wheel slip would be even greater and I wanted accurate speeds for data purposes and drag calculations, it was realised that some other method of speed recording would have to be used. Officially measured distances and timing could not be used due to the fact that any speeds in the region of 180 – 190 mph would be of the duration of only five seconds during which time I would have travelled over a quarter of a mile. Due to the extremely good streamlining of the machine, when the throttle is closed, the speed hardly drops, it just keeps going on at a hell of a bat. There is no front brake and if the rear brake is used at over 100mph it would only lock the wheel and perhaps start a slide. The problem would not arise at Bonneville due to the length of the record strips (12 miles), but at Pendine the slightest delay in shutting off could easily end up with the bike smashing into the cliffs at one end of the beach or running into the estuary at the other end. Quite sticky! Hence the vital need for a dead accurate instrument registering the speed irrespective of wheel spin and also of whichever gear the machine was using, second or third, (it is impossible to get into top gear at Pendine). The answer was an air speed indicator and pilot head from an aeroplane. One was supplied by an enthusiast from Nottingham and was tested and calibrated at Manchester University. The pilot head was fitted to the nose of the machine, projecting 2-6" in front of it where it would be in still air and the 4" dial placed in the nose of the perspex canopy where it could be easily seen whilst travelling at any speed. The pilot head looks like a 20mm cannon on a Spitfire wing and caused many a head to be scratched!

But in operation it is the complete answer to my problems. It is extremely sensitive to the slightest change in speed. When the bike is being towed on the trailer behind my car the air speed needle is registering the speed on the road of the car and trailer.

After waiting fifteen weeks for good weather reports from South Wales, I decided in October to take a chance and go down to Pendine and wait for a favourable opportunity to get in at least two fast runs.

Most amazingly I left Manchester in blazing sunshine on the first day of what proved to be an 'Indian summer' and upon arrival at Pendine found we could not use the beach until the Saturday following due to the Ministry of supply holding night exercises on it.

We were on the beach at 8 am on the Saturday morning in bright sunshine but with a strong breeze blowing offshore at right angles to my course.

We drove along the beach in the car on a 'survey trip' to lay off a suitable course. The sands were in better condition than I had ever seen them and a course was selected

Bob Berry OEC-Temple 'Streamliner', 1960.

on the tide line left by the last tide. The entire length of sand usable was 4.6 miles and necessitated having to travel through three lines of the hated steel posts. We returned to the Pendine end of the beach and unloaded the quarter ton bike from the trailer. Everything was prepared for an instant start and the party sat down to watch the windsock on the beach which was hanging at an angle of 45 degrees. Until that windsock was almost vertical, I dared not ride the bike. Side area of the machine is 150 square feet, she would curve off course and finish up in the sea.

As the sun became hotter, the wind dropped noticeably and at 11.15 we decided that at 11.30 I would get cracking if the wind dropped a little more. At 11.30 I climbed into the cockpit and put on my crash helmet and glare goggles and in that minute, most dramatically the windsock dropped against its pole. Petrol taps were turned on, the bike was pulled back onto compression and then pushed forward. I dropped the clutch and the engine fired at once. I drove the bike across the beach for 200 yards down to the tideline and curved onto the course, gradually opening up and sighting the distant mountains as a course marker. Slowly opening up, the air speed needle swung round to 100 in bottom gear, a quick change into second and still accelerating slowly up to 150mph as I strained to see those steel posts. There they were, and thank heaven I was not heading for them. I flashed through them and opened up until 165 mph showed on the air speed indicator. The exhaust noise was terrific, even inside the cockpit. A quick glance at the instrument panel and as I looked ahead I could see a tiny black dot in the distance. The Land Rover which we were using as a course end marker. I closed the throttle but the Rover rapidly grew in size. Down to 70mph and on with the brake. Down to 10mph. The 'catch crew' ran forward but on an impulse I steered the bike down towards the sea and then turned in an 80 foot circle and turned back towards Pendine 4½ miles away and quite invisible in the distance. I lined the bike up on the 500-foot cliff at the end of the beach and opened the throttle. On this run I was determined, posts or no posts, to really have a go as there would be no time for further runs as the tide was coming in fast and would cover the track I was using. I particularly wanted to exceed 175 mph, as this was the fastest speed ever recorded on land in the British Isles and would tell me all I wanted to know about the stability of the bike.

Up to 80 mph the bike was rolling a little but as she went 'off the handlebars' and on to the streamlining at 100 mph she became rock steady. Change into second gear at 115 and still accelerating at lightning speed. Fully committed now on its course and unable to change direction, we hurtled towards Pendine, 165 on the air speed indicator and into third. 170 -175 and the bike rock steady, 180 and the wind was shrieking round the cockpit, the exhaust not so loud now, a beautifully smooth noise from the engine room at my back. A large tree branch right in my track, I know I cannot avoid it, instinctively I brace myself, a distinct thump and we are over it. The ASI reaches 186 mph and the rev counter shows 200 mph. I wonder why the difference? Wheelspin, of course. I count up to five slowly, that's a quarter of a mile. The distant cliff is flying at me and I cut the throttle back and at once I think I have left it too late. The beach is shrinking unbelievably quickly, 150 -140 -130. The cliff is huge now. I can see the village. Down to 80 and into bottom gear and gently on with the brake, the cockpit is filled with a choking smell of alcohol, ether and nitro benzine. It makes me cough and gasp for air.

The nitro affects my vision and the ether makes me dizzy. Slowly the streamliner loses its speed and with only 300 yards to spare, I stop alongside my two 'catchers' and switch off the big engine. The cockpit reeks of dope and hot oil. I climb out and glance at my watch: 11.35. Just five minutes since I left. A round trip of nine miles. I look at the incoming tide, it is too close to chance another run. But I am more than satisfied. As we stand round the bike, I look towards the windsock. It suddenly billows out and rises to 45 degrees and the wind blows sand devils along the beach. For five minutes there had been just a perfect flat calm!

Strange to think that after five years of building this beautiful monster, her total 'working' life may, in all, be perhaps half an hour!

Idolised by some, reviled by others, Bob Berry's name is indelibly entered in Pendine's ledger of achievement for his motor bicycling efforts on the beach. His self-acclaimed distinction as 'Britain's Fastest Motorcyclist' may hold if his account of the final pass on the OEC-Temple-JAP Streamliner/Projectile is to be believed. It would also have made him the man to achieve the highest one-way speed on mainland Britain at that time. Campbell says he saw 184 mph on the Napier speedometer, at Pendine, as against Berry's claimed 186 on the air speed indicator. We will never know.[194]

---

[194] Bob Berry retired from Manchester to a small cottage in Tegryn, near Llanfyrnach, Pembrokeshire, where he lived, in reduced circumstances, with his friend, Peggy Carodus. He died in 1970, at the age of 62.

Whitsun 1953

Coronation year, 1953, has left us no record (so far!) of an Easter meeting, nor, sadly, one at August Bank Holiday, apart from a set of amateurish photographs, carefully inscribed by Douglas Phillips, a *Western Mail* reporter at that time and better known as a poet. Several correspondents have pronounced that the August meeting was cancelled, on account of an outbreak of foot-and-mouth disease in cattle in Wales.[195] A programme of entries for a Whitsun National Welsh Speed Championship meeting is in existence for the 25th of May. We have no published results. It is possible that Phillips's photographs may actually relate to the Whitsun meeting, though he was not a man to make mistakes.

The star entrants – Dearden, Rist and LF Griffiths do correspond with the Phillips snap-shot. Many familiar names, it has to be said, had in recent years, quietly slipped by the wayside. Dearden again had entered the 541cc Featherbed; DM Thomas is there with the 998 Vincent-HRD; and, lo and behold! – a 996cc Brough Superior, entered by D Pickering of the British Motor Cycle Racing Club. The VMC is on parade, a real old war-horse by now. In a field of 36 there are 13 BSAs, 5 Nortons, 4 Triumphs, two Velocettes a Royal Enfield and a Francis Barnett. One whole page of the 5-page programme is dedicated to warnings of dire consequences of crowd indiscipline:

> '**This course is on WD controlled property and it is absolutely necessary for all spectators to do as they are bidden**'.

. . . otherwise, presumably, they would be put on a charge and shot at dawn!

The writing had been on the wall for a very long time: Pendine was unsafe. All that was protecting crowds of many thousands of people, children, dogs, drunks and the odd half-wit, was a single strand of wire – from machines, sometimes only feet away, hurtling along in bunches, at 100+ mph. It had been an amazing run of luck. In forty years of competition only two spectators had been hurt; only one rider killed[196] and that was during an 'unofficial' practice. The escape, otherwise, was not far short of miraculous.

Whitsun 1954

We have a brief account of the Whitsun meeting at Pendine in 1954. Fred Rist of Neath – he had taken over a dealership in the town – won four out of the eleven events of the day's programme.

---

[195] Gordon Perrott (Pers. comm, 1998) turned up with his friend, Cliff Edwards (Norton), to find the meeting abandoned.

[196] From information supplied by Lloyd Tucker (1998): a Thunderbird rider died in 1952 or 53.

STANDARD CLASS

Two-laps > 500cc
AR Hayes (Norton)
DTL Williams (BSA)

One-mile sprint > 350cc
L (Len) Nicholas, Carmarthen (Velocette)
G Thomas, Saundersfoot (BSA)
J (John) L Mills, Neath (Rudge)

one-mile sprint > 1,000cc
A Phillips, Caerphilly (BSA)
AJ Phillips, Carmarthen (Matchless)
L Nicholas (Velocette)

6 miles > 350cc
FM Rist (BSA)
DD Snow, Merthyr (Velocette)
G Thomas (BSA)

10 miles > 1,000cc
FM Rist (BSA)
DR Griffith (VMC)
LF Griffiths (Norton)

4 laps > 200cc
AR Hayes (Norton)
DTL Williams (BSA)

RACING CLASSES

One-mile sprint > 350cc
L Nicholas (Velocette)
G Thomas (BSA)
JL Mills (Rudge)

one-mile sprint > 1,000cc
A Phillips (BSA)
G Thomas (BSA)
R Greco, Swansea (Triumph)

six miles > 350cc
FM Rist (BSA)
DD Snow (Velocette)
AA Rees, Caerphilly (Norton)

30 miles > 600cc
LF Griffiths (Norton)
DR Griffith (VMC)
DD Snow (Velocette)

10 miles > 1,000cc
FM Rist (BSA)
LF Griffiths (Norton)
DR Griffith (VMC)

August 1954

Of an entry of 35, in August 1954, 17 were Carmarthen club members. Fred Rist was there with 350 and 650 BSAs. Other BSAs were entered by RJ Wild, JD Price, Llwyd James, VG Thomas, A Phillips, and T George. Velocettes were out in force: Des Snow, brought the Mk V111 down from Merthyr, AW Ford had travelled from St Helens with a similar machine, and Carmarthen club member JDH Roberts appeared on a 250, while Bill Doughty and Len Nicholas were mounted on 350s. DR Griffith had wheeled out the old VMC, and Ivor Eveleigh of Cardiff was on another special of his own devising, the IES. There were three Vincent-HRDs, at the time undoubtedly the fastest production machine in the world. Interestingly, Bruce Main Smith, the Norton aficionado and motor-cycle book publisher, was down at Pendine on a big Vincent, as were T Cragg of Westmoreland and DM Thomas of Carmarthen. Cragg's machine was a Vincent Rapide-engined projectile, brought up to Black Lightning specification, housed neatly in a Featherbed Norton frame. It proved uncatchable, even by Fred Rist's tuned 650 BSA – itself a 'wild' machine. Of the five Triumphs entered, the late Jack Daniels's business partner, Harold Bragg, was entered on a 500 GP, as was Arthur

Harris, a national serviceman, who had come over for the day. Well-known as a local scrambler, Arthur was riding the ex-David Whitworth 500GP works Triumph, loaned by Pankhursts of Weymouth's Parkstone branch. Syd Davies was on a 250 Triumph Tiger and Wyn Morgan bestrode a 650 Thunderbird. Veteran Handel Davies was on a Dot 197, as was Gerhard Heinze who had, by this time, left Eddie Stephens Motors and set up his own motor business; and John Mills of Neath, 'the schoolmaster', was on his 250 Rudge Rapid. A Thomason, of the Carmarthen club was, curiously, and as it turned out, justifiably, placing his faith in, of all things, a Calthorpe.

CR Edwards

Only a few years younger than Handel Davies, Leslie Griffiths was, as usual, entered with his 'No 11', a 499cc Norton, but from the total absence of any placings for this very consistently competitive rider, one is bound to conclude that he scratched. There were only two other Nortons entered for the meeting, that of AA Rees, of Caerphilly and Cliff Edwards of Aberkenfig. Cliff Edwards was an able engineer who, after wartime service, where he worked with Leslie Griffiths at the Bridgend REME workshops, he became involved in development of the Kieft racing car with, among others, Gordon Whitehead and Francis Beart. A bachelor and a weight-lifter, Cliff made quite a name for himself in road-racing, locally, at Aberdare Park and the Eppynt mountain circuit. He rode in the Dunrod 'Hundred' and secured a very creditable third place in the Senior Manx Grand Prix.

The remarkable, total absence of AJSes in the entry-list for that day was, no doubt, pure chance – and probably unique.

[10] CR Edwards (Norton) (*Wayne Bowen collection*). [*LA Lusardi photo*]

The unofficial results (from a programme inscription) read as follows:

STANDARD CLASSES

Two laps > 200cc
G Heinze (Dot 197)
H Davies (Dot 197)

one mile sprint > 350 cc
L Nicholas (Velocette)
JD Price, Brecon (BSA 350)
JL Mills, Neath (Rudge 250cc)

one mile sprint > 1,000cc
B Main-Smith (Vincent-HRD)
A Phillips, Caerphilly (BSA 498cc)
L Nicholas, Carmarthen (Velocette 350)

10 miles > 350cc
L Nicholas (Velocette)
JL Mills, Neath (Rudge 250cc)
JD Price, Brecon (BSA 350)

10 miles > 1,000cc
T Cragg, Westmoreland (Vincent-Norton)
B Main-Smith (Vincent-HRD)
A Phillips (BSA)
L Nicholas (Velocette)
L James (BSA 500)

RACING CLASSES

One mile > 350cc
L Nicholas (Velocette)
FM Rist (BSA)
A Thomason (Calthorpe)

one mile > 1,000cc
T Cragg (Vincent-Norton)
FM Rist (BSA)
B Main-Smith (Vincent-HRD)

10 miles > 350cc
FM Rist (BSA)
DD Snow, Merthyr (Velocette)
AA Rees, Caerphilly (Norton)

50 miles > 1,000cc
T Cragg, Westmoreland (Vincent-Norton)
CR Edwards, Ogmore Vale (Norton)
A Harris, Carmarthen (Triumph 500)

50 miles > 250cc
JL Mills (Rudge)

50 miles > 350cc
DD Snow (Velocette)

50 miles > 650cc
CR Edwards (Norton)

10 miles > 1,000cc
T Cragg (Vincent-Norton)
FM Rist (BSA 650)
CR Edwards (Norton)

Tom Cragg

Bruce Main-Smith, who was living in Fishguard at the time, where his people owned an hotel, remembers racing the Vincents on that day:

> Fred Rist was very hard to catch on that 650, running on dope. She was good for 140 up those long straights, but he could handle the bike through corners, getting round at 70mph or so. So he was on top. Tom (Cragg) and I would creep round at 15mph: then, with the Vincents, all you had to do was open up and hang on. We worked hard putting gauze and other protection on (induction systems). Tom's at first was asphyxiated, whereas mine resulted in rocket-propulsion for a while . . . I managed to wrap a brake cable round a sprocket and that was my day done.
>
> Tom Cragg was a water engineer, working on some project transferring water from North Wales to Manchester. A good rider – and that machine was a real hum-dinger! I never heard of him as a racer after that.[197]

---

[197] Bruce Main-Smith, pers. comm. June, 1999.

In that situation, Cragg must have been hitting phenomenal terminal speeds to have consistently beaten Fred Rist. It is a shame that times and speeds were not recorded at the 1954 Welsh National Speed Championships. Tom Cragg's record of straight 'Firsts' on the day, when set against the record, tends to distort the achievement of other great riders of the past. That he was a competent enough rider is self-evident. He must also have been fearless!

The Vincent-Norton concept was an invicible formula, with its Lightning-spec engine's superb power-curve – all the way up to 70bhp – its excellent brakes, despite the extra weight, and the flawless road-holding of the McCandless Featherbed frame. It was a Brough Superior, fifteen years on:

> Accelerating whilst upright produced too much urge for traction in bottom gear. A change into second – and a good one at that, certain every time – brought a marked increase in speed almost as savage. In third one was tramping even at 3,500 rpm. When one opened up a little, not much happened (comparatively speaking) – 'picking up' like a good 'three-fifty'; then, at 3,800, like a good 'five-hundred'. Up to 4,000 – whoops, *hold tight* ! The power's come in and she's away. Keep the motor in the 4 – 6,000rpm band and there's all the urge one can use.
>
> The ability to go imposes the need for stopping quickly and surely. The Norton anchors work well. Cragg says that in spite of their being the old-type of single leading-shoe stopper, they work under race conditions and keep on stopping with no fade to speak of, remembering the extra work with which they must cope. Suspension and cornering are of a high order.[198]

In its way, this would prove a nail in Pendine's coffin. Speeds were now a thin edge off Campbell's 1926 World Land Speed Record – 150mph, and crowd safety was no better than in 1905. It was Fred Rist's last appearance on Pendine. He would have been justifiably sickened by the V-N's manifest superiority. But Fred, ever philosophical, would have concluded that 'Every dog has his day!'

Len Nicholas, a tall, gangling lad – and a very promising rider – also had an outstanding day out on the KTT Velocette. He had an inventive brain for mechanical matters. This led to his being killed in a tragic domestic accident while working on his house in Ferryside.[199] In the 50-miler, on the last corner before the finish on the last lap, Arthur Harris dropped a valve,

> wrecking the engine, such was the poor grade of material available then. However, freewheeling as far as possible, the final few hundred yards had to be pushed for a finish. Completely knackered but worth it. The poor sods in the IoM who ran out of fuel at Governor's Bridge and pushed to the finish will always remain heroes because you are not mentally or physically tuned for that kind of trauma during a race. Any reward following becomes that much sweeter.[200]

---

[198] Bruce Main-Smith, 'A Norton-Vincent Special', *Motor Cycling*, Jan 3, 1957.
[199] E Walters, pers. comm. Jan, 1999.
[200] Pers. letter, A Harris, 18 v 99.

Above: LF Griffiths (Norton) c 1970. Below, in action 1950. [*LA Lusardi photo*]

21. A Glory that has passed

August 1955

THE official entry for The National Welsh Championships on Pendine Sands on August 1st, 1955 was a respectable 40, including some Vintage machinery: a 350cc Calthorpe, a couple of Rudges, a 1928 Sunbeam Model 80 and a 500 JAP. There were seven BSAs and seven Nortons, six Velocettes, three 500 Triumphs, two 7R AJSes, a G45 and a 350 Matchless. There is a 998cc Vincent entered, but no evidence of it having performed. Of the old, familiar, names entered, Leslie (LF) Griffiths, Bridgend, with 20 Pendine firsts already to his name, was there with his faithful Norton to add yet another three. No Fred Rist or LV Thomas, no visiting stars, except for Merthyr's own Des Snow, on the 350 Velocette. DM Thomas, of Buntingford sported a 490 Manx and the Vincent. DR Griffith had a good day out with the VMC. Among the officials were Handel Davies and Dr Lindsay, Pendine veterans from first to last. Eddie Stephens, with more Pendine honours to his name than anybody (29 firsts and 25 second-places), was Clerk-of-the-Course. The (unofficial)[201] results were as follows:

STANDARD

One mile > 350cc
WC Adams, Brynmawr (BSA)
G James, Newcastle Emlyn (BSA)
PH Humphries, Liverpool (BSA)

one mile > 1,000cc
TT Evans, Cheltenham (BSA)
WH Yates, Liverpool (Triumph)
DW James, Saundersfoot (Matchless)

10 miles > 350cc
WC Adams, Ebbw Vale (BSA)
RH Southworth, Caerphilly (BSA)
G James (BSA)

10 miles > 1,000cc
TT Evans (BSA)
WH Yates (Triumph)
H (Harry) Williams, Llanelli (Norton)
P H Humphries (BSA)

RACING

One mile > 350cc
DD Snow, Merthyr (Velocette)
E Walters, Carmarthen (AJS)
PB Nicholson, Cardigan (Matchless)

one mile > 1,000cc
LF Griffiths, Bridgend (499 Norton)
DR Griffith, Swansea (VMC)
EP Evans, Chepstow (Sunbeam)

---

[201] The author is indebted to John Griffiths for a carefully annotated Race Programme.

10 miles > 350cc
DD Snow (Velocette)
E Walters (AJS)
PH Humphries (BSA)
S Wilson, Liverpool (Velocette)

50 miles > 1,000cc
LF Griffiths (Norton)

TT Evans (BSA)
DD Snow (Velocette)

10 miles > 1,000cc
LF Griffiths (Norton)
S Wilson (Velocette)
WH Yates (Triumph)
TT Evans (BSA)

The course was a mile up and a mile down. Les Griffiths's lap times were consistently around 1 minute 30 secs: an average speed of 79.99 mph. He missed the 80 by a whisker! What was it that Malcolm Campbell had fixed on when christening his Sunbeam racing car for speed-trials? The Blue Bird: pursuit of the unattainable. Les, always chasing his own imaginary Blue Bird, had run his and Pendine's last race. It was fitting that he should have led the way to the final flag.

It is sad to have to end this account of such heroic days on a low note. Either the Carmarthen club's Press Department (there wasn't one, of course) was not functioning, or the press itself found little to interest them or their readers any more in what had become a marginalised competition; it is hard to know. We have no published account of the last day of motor cycle racing at Pendine.

Recriminations

There is a Welsh proverb, a variant on 'He who pays the piper calls the tune', it is: '*Diwedd y gân yw y geiniog*' (The end of the song is the penny). Old men who remember, those who were there, lament the passing of Pendine Races. What ended the song, they will tell you, was the penny. Money, or lack of it, finally killed Pendine. Had there been a serious accident or a fatality, it's true, racing might easily have ended sooner, for the racing was very dangerous – and crowd protection and control, of necessity, was minimal.

Putting on a major sporting event with sparse funding and volunteer assistance poses real difficulties. There could be no 'turnstile' revenue from pedestrians as there exists in common law a right for the public to have free access to the shore. Cars and other vehicles were in a different legal category, as they required temporary easement over Stepney Estate riparian property in descending the ramp, for which they were liable to a fee. Even this is a legal 'grey area'. The ramp itself was not Council property. It had been erected in 1909 by public subscription – initially to facilitate that first motor rally, the Motor Union Tour. In fairness, the Estate never laid a claim on the charge, and when on race days cars were admitted onto the beach the (then) Parish Council awarded itself 50% of the proceeds.

Post-war, cars and their occupants were charged 5/- (25p), motor cycles 1/-. Programmes were 2/-, (1/- before the war).

Given those charges, revenue accruing from a notional attendance at a meeting of

5,000 people – conveyed in 1,000 cars and on 1,500 motor cycles, is estimated at £375, plus (say) £150 – £200 from programme sales and franchise licences. Against this, count the cost of public liability insurance, printing posters and programmes and other overheads, including hire of labour for fencing, policing, ambulance stand-by and a public address system. It can be seen that by the time cash prizes and cups were awarded, finances were very tight on receipts to the club of around £250 – £300.(In the absence of the clubs' minutes and balance sheets, guesswork is involved).

The reality was that the event had become too costly to mount. In order to attract 'star' riders with worthwhile cash prizes and by paying 'starting money', some form of commercial sponsorship or local authority grant would have been necessary. Administration of an event as ambitious as the three-day Welsh TT, required the benefit of semi-permanent staff. That dream was beyond the reality of those days. Questions are still being asked concerning the old Parish Council who, over the years, took the lion's share of the revenue from racing and appeared to give proportionately little in return. Looking at Pendine in 1955, with a world-class natural attribute and a history in motor sport of comparable standing, no visible benefit to its infrastructure from the 'Glory Days' had accrued. Very little remained of that vision for its future spelt out by Dr Lindsay when he spoke of the need for the GWR to consider a branch line.

The Museum of Speed

The building of the Museum of Speed at Pendine in 1996, undertaken by the former Carmarthen District Council at a cost of not less than £400,000, much of which was EEC grant-aided, was a very positive beginning. In the short-term, the building provides Babs with 'a home' for a few months each year, and early efforts at interpreting the heroic story of the beach have taken place. But the old story of lack of funding is all-too evident. Pendine, by virtue of the museum's existence, is now in possession of an additional asset which deserves thoughtful exploitation. It is to be hoped that in the future the full potential of this imaginative concept will be recognised, and that it will accordingly be properly funded.

If it is to survive and fulfil its purpose there needs to be a coherent policy for the Museum, a vision for its future.

A basic collection of the machines that made history on the beach needs urgently to be gathered, before they disappear. From time-to-time they, and others like them, should be taken out and demonstrated, as occurs with specimens in the National Motor Cycle Museum and the Sammy Miller Collection. Static exhibits in transport collections have limited intrinsic interest, and the continuance of several such museums is held in question. Activity days, apart from enlisting the many willing enthusiasts' clubs to participate, provide an educational dividend. This is one way to bring future generations into contact with the heroic events that took place on Pendine's great natural arena.

From such initiatives opportunities to take in the wider spectrum spring. Well-conceived audio-visual presentation ('virtual reality') is the modern way of providing children in particular with information that they can draw from. The whole story of man's quest for speed could be told in this way, in the context of Pendine. The village was, after all, the focus of world attention in this matter at one time. Whereas the Museum of Speed would appear to be the obvious and immediate repository for a collection of local exhibits and a focal point for an archive of material relating to motor sport activity in Carmarthenshire, the long-term holds a more significant and colourful prospect. Motors and the quest for speed reflect a vital part of our cultural heritage in the twentieth and the new century. Even in a purely 'Wales' context the opportunity to celebrate the many different aspects of Welsh motor sport, from motor rallying, to the International Six Days and airfield circuit racing, should not be lost to us.

Cavalcade

On that last day of the racing in 1955, acknowledgement of what was passing was required. No one had the presence of mind or the vision to gather the material and write the story from first-hand sources. In forty years it has become fragmented.

Celebration in a cavalcade of memory and the imagination is available. Walk the beach.

From the mists of the past a lean Sunbeam Sprint speeds along the shore, followed by a TT Scott, an AJS 'Big-port', a lightweight New Imperial, a 494cc Douglas, a Brough Superior SS100 'Pendine', an Excelsior Manxman, a KTT Velocette, and a Gold Star BSA: not forgetting, of course, two Nortons – one a side-valve, the other with at least one camshaft! Their fly-past is led by the Sgonina Special and tailed by the JAP-VMC. Bob Berry's futuristic contraption sidles up for remembrance, its old Jack Carr Brough engine burbling: while Blue Bird and Babs, in the distance, roar and bang along the sands. Djelmo has broken down again!

The tangy aroma of Castrol 'R' and methanol blows on the salt-sea spindrift.

As *Rasus Pendein* slipped away into history on August 1st, 1955, it is pleasing to note that Dr Alexander Lindsay was there with Handel Davies: Pendine fixtures and stalwarts from the very beginning. They had seen it through. Also present and high in the roll-call of Pendine middle-era heroes and die-hards were ETM Stephens, LF Griffiths and DR Griffith. Between them, Alex, Handel, Eddie, Leslie and Douglas had won every class of event at one time or another. They had worked hard, enjoyed immensely, met a galaxy of stars and a variety of talents on the beach and jousted with them, the meek and the mighty. Great days. And here it was, a vast epic, at an end

'Like an arrow-shower,
Sent out of sight, somewhere becoming rain'.

Postscript

At the time of going to press, the local Section of the Vintage Motor Cycle Club are in discussion about staging racing on the beach at Pendine at some time in the future. Provided they can reach satisfactory accommodation with the local Community Council, with the Military authorities, and meet ACU requirements on organisational arrangements – including safeguards to the public – we can look forward to a heady whiff of nostalgia, if sufficient numbers of enthusiasts are prepared to expose their precious and venerable machinery to the hazards of salinity.

A note of caution, 'a word to the wise', not intended as discouragement, is offered from experience of a previous attempt at reprise. Ken George, BEM, Llanmilo, for many years regional Centre representative on the ACU General Council, writes:

> One Friday, late in 1970, on my way to London to attend one of our meetings in the company of Fitzroy Allen, the BSA works rider and International Six Days Trial Gold Medallist, we started reminiscing, as is the wont of old motor cycle racing enthusiasts, about 'The Great Old Days' of racing in west Wales. Why had they quietly faded away? 'What happened?', we questioned. Was it cost or lack of enthusiasm that had caused us to lose our local motor sporting fixtures? We were both equally convinced it could not have been for lack of enthusiasm.
>
> We resolved, there and then, to bring the matter before the next meeting of the Motor Cycle Club of Wales, and suggest resurrecting either the Cambrian Trial or Pendine. The decision of the meeting went in favour of Pendine. Fitzroy found himself 'volunteered' as Chairman of a small committee, consisting of Triumph works-rider, Wilmot Evans, Jack Phillips of Swansea, DD Snow, Merthyr, Eric Williams, Llanelli, and myself as Secretary.
>
> When we commenced negotiations with the Pendine Parish Council (as it then was), we were somewhat bemused when they began to run away with the idea that they did not need us, and could perfectly-well put on such an event themselves. When disabused of this assumption (ACU Standing and General Competition rules applied), they countered by awarding themselves the total slipway take, with a nominal £100 to the club 'to run the meeting'. When we pointed out that, relying on volunteer labour, borrowed equipment and all-round good-will, the minimum budget required to stage such a meeting would not be less than £500. Eventually, they agreed to a 50/50 share of the slipway 'gate'. Even so, we lost £100!

The meeting, staged on Saturday, 24th July, 1971, attracted, according to *The Carmarthen Journal*,[202] a good turn-out of spectators, the beach being 'black with cars

---

[202] 30 July, 1971.

'Trannoeth y ffair': ('After the fair') St Clears cross, c.1930.

[*Stanley Phillips photo*]

and people'. But 'not like the old days'. 'Roneoed', stapled, programmes were priced in the new currency – 5p. 'Most sincere thanks' were expressed to the chairman and councillors of the Pendine Parish Council, 'for without their generosity and help . . .' etc. (there would have been no irony in the concluding paragraph of the Acknowledgements!)

On the day, some of the great names of the past were in attendance. Fred Rist was invited. Denis Parkinson, in his role as ITV sports commentator, was apparently on the beach and is said to have written-up the meeting in the press. A very significant Pendine old-timer, 90-year-old Mansel Davies, Llanfyrnach, with whom it had all started, way back, on that Thursday in 1905, was present.

The Stewards were HE Jones, A Bates and Fitzroy Allen. The Judges were 'Mot' Evans and I James. 'Big' Eric Williams acted as Starter, assisted by D Mathews. Jack Phillips was Chief Scrutineer, aided by I Lane and Des Snow. The Paddock Marshall was R Morgan and the Lap Scorer, Mrs Mathews. Jeff Lewis was Chief Marshal and R Dunbar the Clerk-of-the-Course. Ken George was Secretary of the Meeting, for whom the lasting impression was a fine day and a financial nightmare.

Local riders in the entry-list were thin on the ground. J Hill of Pendine, wrongly credited in the programme, was on a 350 AJS. G Bowen, Narberth, was a late entry on a 440 BSA. D Phillips, Boncath, was on a BSA 500.

Motorcycle patrolman and Manx Grand Prix competitor, JB Caffrey, on an A7 BSA 500 twin in full road-race tune was a much-fancied local contender in solo classes. His Ted Young Triumph kneeler, fitted with slicks, proved a handful on corners in the sidecar events. His passenger was MH Davies, Haverfordwest. D Phillips of Boncath had also entered a 500 BSA Gold Star. From Cwmbran came five-times Welsh Scramble Championship winner D Jeremiah on the works 249 CZ trials machine. P Peterson, also on a CZ, was along with him.

In the sidecar event, MG Strong, Boncath, was out on a Tri-Norton and JL Davies of Carmarthen was on a BSA 650 twin; J & G Phillips of Whitland were similarly mounted. The Hogan-JAP of Gareth Llewellyn was a dedicated sand-racing special in a well-supported event for 'combinations'. Several Triumphs, a Helga and Norton-specials from the Wirral, Yarm-on-Tees, Ormskirk, Rainsford, West Houghton St Helens, South Godstone and Oxted formed the opposition.

There were Bultacos from Derby and St Helens. PE Slack was on the Derby entry, accompanied, one guesses, by Joan Slack – a well-known Pendine entrant in former years. There was a Yamaha and a Honda, two 'Pacsis' – a 250 and a 650, four Moto-cross Husqvarnas (annoyingly listed as 'Huskies'), TriBSAs Tridots, Triams and an Elstar. Mounted on 'proper' motor cycles were BJ Wells of Oxted on a BSA 499 Gold Star, B Griffiths of Blackwood, on a 200 Triumph Tiger Cub, B Ross, Erith in Kent, on a 499 Rudge, JS Linstanley of Ellesmere Port on a 500 Velocette and KR Stephenson on what must have been a very intriguingly-devised special, a 'KSS 700' Velocette twin.

The circuit was 880 yards up and half-a-mile down. 'Not at all like times of yore. More a short-circuit speedway or dirt-track on the sands,' Ken George muses. All events were run over five laps. The speeds achieved, as recorded in *The Carmarthen Journal*, were '90mph top, and 60mph lap-average.' The *Journal* pays tribute to the work of the Motor Cycle Club of Wales and hopes that 'with Parish Council consent regular racing will come back in the future'. N Lerrigo, the northern hill-climb ace, had the best of days, winning three events on his mysteriously-named 'Pacsis' machines.

The outcome was:

Five miles > 350cc
N Lerrigo, Co Durham (Pacsis 250)
PH Robinson, Liverpool (Yamaha 250)
PE Slack, Derby (Bultaco 250)

SIDE CARS

5 miles >1300cc
Tebbs bros, Yarm-on-Tees (Domi-No 750)
G Ratcliffe (Triumph 650)
N Roscoe, Wirral (TriBSA 650)

5 miles > 351 > 500cc
J Nicholson, Liverpool ((3A Special)
R Lee, Griffithstown (Husqvarna 460)
H McDonagh, Manchester (Tridot 499)

SIDE CARS

5 miles 1300cc
Tebbs bros (Domi-No 750)
J Phillips, Whitland (Triumph 650)
L Peacock, South Godstone (Triumph 500)

5 miles 350cc >
N Lerrigo (Pacsis 650)
KR Stephenson, Huddersfield (KSS 700)
H McDonagh (Tryam 678)

5 miles solo (allcomers)
L Peacock (BSA 479)
P Peterson, Cwmbran (CZ 360)
N Lerrigo (Pacsis)

SIDE CARS

5 miles >
G Ratcliffe (Triumph 650)
Tebbs bros (Domi-No 650)
JB Caffrey, Haverfordwest
  (Triumph Kneeler)

5 miles solo >
N Lerrigo (Pacsis 650)
J Nicholson (3A Special)
KR Stephenson (KSS 700)

5 miles solo >
J Nicholson (3A Special)
G Bowen, Narberth (BSA 464)
D Roberts, Newport (CZ 360)

There was discontent among competitors who had travelled long distances that no 'starting money' or travel expenses were forth-coming. One gathers it was not the happiest of days. And the Motor Cycle Club of Wales never considered a repeat performance.

Afterword

Introductions and prefaces that authors write are an abomination. Nobody should read them. Nobody, I suspect does, very much. And rightly. It is painful to have to clamber over excuses before you can begin. Prefaces are nothing less than a shameless attempt to pre-empt, to canvass, your critical view. Do painters draw your attention before viewing? Or composers bend your ear with matter-of-fact? They do not. They get straight to it. So should authors of books. They dictate their own intake and exhalation of breath on a chosen subject. They should not be permitted to smother you at the start.

I have chosen to 'tug-boat' you at the finish, like this, and hail you with a whisper, not a megaphone, first with thanks. If you've got this far my living has not been in vain. Thank you for your company. The time I spent was for you and with you. I enjoyed myself.

And, you can relax. I offer no excuses. When I started out on 'Pendine' I knew it could never be perfect or the complete story. Custodians entrusted with the Minutes of the Carmarthen and Neath clubs, those records carefully noted and preserved over the years, failed in their duty. Pathetically, they lost them: the precious record of the Glory Days. They lost the Welsh TT trophy as well.

But for them, it would have been a much better book. These irresponsible men broke the faith with their colleagues, dedicated enthusiasts who organised the Pendine meetings. They denied to future generations the collective memory of tens of thousands who went there as followers. They threw away the grail.

If there is a Round Table of legendary riders they sit there, aghast. Let there be a lesson in it for all keepers of records of human endeavour: the past belongs to the future – not to you to dispose.

Had someone undertaken the task of recording the history of Pendine twenty or more years ago, when there were a great many more first-hand witnesses to examine, the story would, for that, have been a lot more fulsome. Would that I could have been able to do my work sooner.

To find the required amount of 'space' to loll in archives and elbow oily benches is not easy or cheap. What you find is that you pitch up against a barrier piled with life's wearier considerations. And the writing – harder work than digging a trench – requires a significant interlude of spiritual peace, energy and sustained concentration. These were not available to me until a serious illness intervened and I was spared by God, rescued by a fine surgeon and the staff of two hospitals. Then, there, I learned the wisdom of choice. Perhaps you'd say, discovered 'my priorities'.

At last, as you see, I kept the faith. As far as I possibly could. This book has been a long time in the making and the many who have urged me on, those who lent me material – photographs, memories and programmes – and gave me their time, share in this achievement with me.

Others (there are always the others – it's no good pretending to forget – 'begrudgers', as Brendan Behan memorably called them), not many, have not been so gracious. To you, I say 'God Bless you too'.

There's no merit in recrimination, unless it helps us view the future in a positive way. The gift we have received in the Museum of Speed is compensation for what has been lost. The reward in it is inestimable in the opportunity it affords the future. Nothing will restore the passing, never to return, of the golden era. Whatever remains, in the form of memory, record or artefact of the heroic past of Pendine Races, now has a safe and permanent home. There the story I have made a start on telling will be secure for future generations to marvel.

Those surely were Glory Days!

Cliff Edwards (Norton) & friends. [*LA Lusardi photo*]

Acknowledgements

For help along the way with the piecing together of the Pendine story, the author would like to acknowledge the help, guidance and courtesy of Henry Adams, AM Allen, Fitzroy Allen, Titch Allen, Ken Attwell, Doug Baker, Mrs Valerie Bastian, Ted Beckham, Chris Bennett, Bill Boddy, John Borrough, Wayne Bowen, Harold Bragg, Mike Budd, Wendy Bullen, Peter Butler, JB Caffery, S Campbell, Roland and Marion Carr, Robert Cordon Champ, Jim and John Codd, Jim Colburn, John Davies, Annice Collett, Stephen Collier, Ernie Crust, Ben Davies, Bob Davies, Jack Davies, Mrs Jane Davies, John Davies, Mr Kaye Mansel Davies, Raymond Davies, Stan Davies, Yorweth Davies, AB Demaus, Bruce Dowell, Sir Clive Edwards, Bt, JBB Edwards, Lloyd Edwards, Elwyn Evans, IWS Evans, Neville Evans, Mrs Norma Evans, Ivor Eveleigh, Bruce Eynon, Martyn Flower, Ken George, PP Gibbin, Phil Heath, Dave James, Mrs Janice Jenkins, Mrs Jane Jervis, Mrs Joy Jones, Phil Jones, Ray Jones, Dr Trevor Jones, Reg Good, Bryn Gooding, Peter Gray, Mrs IE Gregor, Bill Grey, Douglas and Mrs DR Griffith, Alfie Griffiths, Frank Griffiths, John Griffiths, GM Hayes, Mike Hornby, Brian Hurley, Euros Jones, Peter John, Vic King, Noel Knight, Dr Stefan Knittel, Mike Leatherdale, Cyril Lewis, Dr Sandy Lindsay, Michael Lowndes, John Lusardi, Bruce Main-Smith, Mrs Jean Mather, Andrew Macaulay, Mrs Ruth Thomas McNeilly, Ray Megget, Dillwyn Miles, John Mills, Hugh Moffat, Peter Moon, Ted Ogden, Mrs Josie Owen, Owen Wyn Owen, Bill Page, Denis Parkinson, Len Parry, Sidney Pearse, Flt Com John Peel, Gordon Perrott, DH Phillips, Douglas Phillips, Jack Phillips, Nicholas Phillips, John Powell, DW Protheroe, DJ Pugh, Glyn Pugsley, Dai Purslove, Miles Raven, Haydn Rees, RM Rees, Roddy Rees, Dr Alun Richards, Fred Rist and Fred Rist (jnr), John Rist, Colin Roberts, Ivan Rhodes, Commander LW Roberts, Peter Roydhouse, DB Sanday, Linda Shean, V Short, Noel Simmons, Mrs Jean Sivell, Percy Sivell, Gordon Small, Peter Smith, George Snell, DD Snow, Bill Spick, Mike Stanton, Roger Stephens, George Stevens, Ian Sutherland, Bob Thomas, Denzil Thomas, Johnny Thomas, TSE Thomas, Bob Thredder, Neville 'Nobby', Ida and Karen Treseder, Lloyd Tucker, Emrys Walters, Glenys Watts, Dick Weekes, Gordon Williams, Tudor Williams, Brian Willis, Liz Veasey, Mrs M Van Eagan, Norman Vanhouse, Mike Worthington-Williams and Rex Young.

For personally contributing photographs and other graphic material used in illustration, thanks are due to Henry Adams, Mrs Valerie Bastian, David Bingham, Wayne Bowen, Roland and Marion Carr, Robert Cordon Champ, Ernie Crust, Mrs

Jane Davies, Kaye Mansel Davies, Raymond Davies, AB Demaus, Lloyd Edwards, Ivor Eveleigh, Mrs Norma Evans, PP Gibbin, Dave James, Mrs Janice Jenkins, Ray Jones, Dr Trevor Jones, Reg Good, Peter Grey, Mrs IE Gregor, Douglas and Mrs DR Griffith, John Griffiths, GM Hayes, Brian Hurley, Peter John, Noel Knight, Mike Leatherdale, Cyril Lewis, Dr Sandy Lindsay, John Lusardi, Andrew Macaulay, Ray Megget, Hugh Moffat, Bill Page, Denis Parkinson, Gordon Perrott, Douglas Phillips, Haydn Rees, Fred Rist (jnr), Barry Robinson, Percy Sivell, Peter Smith, George Snell, DD Snow, Roger Stephens, Peter Staughton, Ian Sutherland, Bob Thomas, Denzil Thomas, Johnny Thomas, Mrs Ruth Thomas McNeilly, Bob Thredder, Karen Treseder, Lloyd Tucker, Glenys Watts, Dick Weekes and Rex Young.

Acknowledgement is made to the keepers of Institutional and National collections as follows: Carmarthen Museum; The National Motor Museum, Beaulieu; Morton's Motorcycle Media for access to some remaining images from the files of *The Motor Cycle* and *Motor Cycling*, and for quotations from their columns and to *Motor Sport*. Thanks to the editors of *The Carmarthen Journal, The Western Telegraph* and *The Western Mail* for reference material from their archives. Thanks to Messrs Faber & Faber for the last line of Philip Larkin's 'The Whitsun Weddings' which ends the text. Special thanks to Wayne Bowen for the LA Lusardi collection, to Roland Carr for the JH Carr collection, to Mrs Jane Davies for the LV Thomas collection, to Mrs Janice Jenkins for the JD Daniels collection, Roger Stephens for the ETM Stephens collection and to Peter John for the KE John collection. Thanks also to John Lusardi.

APPENDIX 1

Photograph of the first meeting of the Pembrokeshire Automobile Club at Williamston, Houghton, nr Burton, seat of Sir Owen Scourfield, in 1910.

(Copy in Pembrokeshire County Record Office, Castle Hill, Haverfordwest.

L > R

[CJ 627] Vauxhall 'A' type, chassis/engine nos: A-09-101.

[DE 2] Humber 10/12hp. 4-seater, with dark green side-entrance. Weight 15 cwts. Sir Hugh James Prothero Thomas, Haverfordwest, driving. Percy Hart (chauffeur) in white cap.

[LB 8292] Belsize.

[DE 188] Adams 4-seater, Green, picked out in black, 15cwt. Registered to Gwladys & Mabel Griffiths, Bunker's Hill, Milford Haven.

[R 4863] Riley 2-cyl.

[DE 247] Sunbeam 12/14. Major Stokes and chauffeur, Parry(?) Registered to Col Lloyd Philipps, DSO, Dale Castle, Milford Haven.

[DE 199] Rover 12. John Dean Bland in front in bowler hat; John A Bland standing on running board; Gordon A Bland sitting inside car; chauffeur is Ernest Holt in peaked cap.

[DE ?] (?)

[DE 179] Humber 10/12. Tonneau body, 16 cwt. First reg, Dec 1908. Hugh Mortimer Thomas, Goodwick.

[DE 154] Rover 8hp. Two-seater, 12 cwts. First reg. 18-v-08. John Berridge Gaskell, 115, Charles St, Milford Haven: Hon Sec Pembroke Automobile Club.

(Motor Cycles difficult to identify).

APPENDIX 2

1922 Motorcycles

ABC
Abingdon
Ackland
Acme
Acrolite
AEL
Ajax
AJS
Akkens
Alecto
Allon (Alldays & Onions)
Ariel
Armis
Atlas

Banshee
BAT
Beardmore Precision
Beaumont
Blackburne
Bown
Bradbury
British Radial
British Standard
Brough
Brough Superior
BSA
Burney

Calthorpe
Campion
Carfield
CC
Cedos
Chater Lea
Cleveland
Clement-Garrard
Clyno
CMM
Commery
Consul
Connaught
Corona-Junior
Cotton
Coulson B

Coventry Eagle
Coventry Mascot
Coventry Victor

Dalton
Dayton
Defy-All
Diamond
Dot
Douglas
Dreadnought
Dunelt
Duzmo

Economic
Edmund
Endurance
Excelsior
Elfson
Endurance

Federal/Federation
FB (Fowler & Bingham)
Francis Barnett

Gamage
Gough
Green
GRI
Grigg
Grindlay-Peerless
GSD

Hagg-Tandem
Harley-Davidson*
Harper
Hawker
Hazelwood
HB
HEC
Henderson*
Henley
Hobart
Holroyd

Hoskison
H&R
Humber

Indian*
Invicta
Ivy
Ixion

James
JES
JNU
Juckes

Kempton
Kenilworth
Kingsbury
Kingsway

Lea-Francis
Levis
Lincoln-Elk
LMC

Marloe
Mars
Martin
Martinshaw
Martinsyde
Massey-Arran
Matador
Matchless
McKechnie
McKenzie
Metro-Tyler
Mohawk
Monopole
Montgomery
Morris-Warne
Morton-Adam
Mountaineer
MPH

APPENDIX

Ner-a-car
New Comet
New Courier
New Era
New Gerrard
New Henley
New Hudson
New Imperial
New Knight
Newmount
New Paragon
New Ryder
New Scale
Newton
Nickson
Norbreck
Norton
NUT

OEC
OK(Supreme)
Olympic
Omega
Orbit
Osmond
Overseas

Pax
Peters
P&M (Panther)
Powell
P&P
Priory
Pullin-Groom
PV

Quadrant

Radco
Raleigh
Ray
Raynal
Rebro
Regent
Remus
Revere
Rex-Acme
Reynolds Special
R&H
Rockson
Rover
Royal Enfield
Royal-Ruby
Royal Scot
Rudge
RW Scout

Saltley
Sarco-Reliance
Scott
Seal
Sharratt
Sheffield-Henderson
Silver Prince
Sirrah
Slaney
Southey
Spark
Sparkbrook
Spartan
Stanger

Sun
Sunbeam
Supremoco

Triple-H
Triplette
Triumph
Trump

Vasco
Velocette
Venus
Verus
Victoria
Vincent (HRD)
Vindec
Viper
Vulcan

Waverly
Weaver
Weatherell
Wee McGregor
Wigan-Barlow
Witall
Wizard
Wolf
Wooler

XL

Zenith

*USA

APPENDIX 3

KINGS OF PENDINE: THE TOP FIFTY AMATEURS   CH
[AND ONE QUEEN!]

Rank	Rider	Machine	1sts	2nds	3rds	Events	Points	Av.	Pts
1	JE Kettle	Scott	3	0	0	3	42	14	12
1	AV Carter	Sunbeam/Norton	2	0	0	2	28	14	8
2	JH Carr	Brough/New Imp	6	2	0	8	92	11.5	20
3	T Cragg	Vincent-Norton	4	0	0	4	44	11	4
4	D Jones*	Velocette/Rudge	5	0	1	6	61	10.16	8
5	M Davies	Humber/Sunbeam	3	0	0	3	30	10	0
5	JB Moss	Norton	2	1	0	3	30	10	4
5	M Martinelli	AJS	2	0	0	2	20	10	0
5	JBB Edwards	Vincent-HRD	2	0	0	2	20	10	0
5	HJ Hulsman	BSA	4	0	0	4	40	10	0
6	RE Thomas	Brough/New Imp	8	2	1	11	107	9.72	12
7	RF Parkinson	AJS	14	4	2	20	190	9.5	20
8	SS Evans	Cotton	7	4	1	12	113	9.41	16
8	N Carter	Matchless	7	2	3	12	113	9.41	16
9	HW Billington	Rudge/Norton	6	4	0	10	92	9.2	8
9	RJD Burnie	Norton	20	9	5	34	313	9.2	44
10	J Slack	BSA/Velocette	2	2	0	4	36	9	4
11	TT Evans	BSA	2	1	0	3	26	8.66	0
12	DM Thomas	Vincent-HRD	6	1	1	8	69	8.62	0
13	T McEwan	Norton	3	2	0	5	42	8.4	0
14	M Isaac	Sunbeam/New Imp	17	5	6	28	234	8.35	16
15	FH Chambers	New Hudson	2	1	1	4	33	8.25	4
16	R Dearden	Norton	5	3	2	10	82	8.2	8
17	Wm Edwards	Verus/Omega/AJS	8	8	2	17	138	8.11	4
18	LF Griffiths	Norton	23	20	7	50	403	8.06	32
19	AM Harry	New Hudson	2	1	2	5	40	8	8
20	J Treseder	OK/Triumph/Stevens	5	5	1	11	87	7.9	4
21	N Treseder (Jnr)	Triumph/Velocette	4	4	1	9	71	7.88	4
22	E Mainwaring	Scott	2	2	1	5	39	7.8	4
23	D Parkinson	Norton	5	3	3	11	85	7.72	8
24	CR Edwards	Norton	1	1	1	3	23	7.66	4
24	JL Mills	Rudge	1	1	1	3	23	7.66	4
24	L Nicholas	Velocette	4	0	2	6	46	7.66	0
25	I Thomas	Scott	2	0	2	4	30	7.5	4
25	T Hunkin	AJS	3	2	1	6	45	7.5	0
26	G Grinton	Harley-Dav/New Imp	2	4	0	6	44	7.33	0
27	CF Edwards	Brough/Cotton/N Imp	3	3	2	8	58	7.25	4
28	ETM Stephens	Diam/Norton/N Imp	26	25	12	63	458	7.26	12
29	Ll Davies	ABC/Cotton	4	2	3	9	65	7.22	4
30	A Grey	Match/Norton/Zenith	5	1	5	11	79	7.18	8
31	C Sgonina	Verus/AJS/Nort/SS	10	8	5	23	163	7.08	0
32	LV Thomas	Velo/Norton/'Beam	13	15	9	37	259	7	12
33	FP Bush	Harley-Davidson	3	4	3	10	67	6.7	4
34	CM Needham	Brough-Superior	1	0	2	3	20	6.6	4
35	H Church	Velocette	2	0	2	4	26	6.5	0
36	AW Nicklin	Sunbeam	5	2	5	12	77	6.41	0
37	TW Pugh	Velocette	4	2	4	10	64	6.4	0
38	DD Snow	Velocette	2	4	3	9	57	6.33	4

APPENDIX   319

Rank	Rider	Machine	1sts	2nds	3rds	Events	Points	Av.	Pts
38	J Edwards	Ariel	1	1	1	3	19	6.33	0
39	JD Daniels	Norton/Velocette	2	5	2	9	56	6.22	0
40	N Treseder (Snr)	Doug/C. Eag/Norton	5	5	7	17	105	6.17	4
41	CR Good	Norton	3	4	6	13	80	6.15	8
42	P Sivell	BSA/Norton	1	6	1	8	49	6.12	0
43	H Davies	Brough/Excelsior	4	3	5	12	73	6.08	0
44	G Gregor	New Hudson/Rudge	4	5	5	14	85	6.07	0
45	A Lindsay	Norton	3	6	2	12	72	6	0
45	RM Rees	OK Sup/Rudge/Trium	0	5	0	5	30	6	0
45	D Connett	Norton	0	2	0	2	12	6	0
45	NF George	Norton	0	2	0	2	12	6	0
46	J Bosisto	Norton	2	1	3	6	35	5.83	0
47	M Griffiths	Triumph/'Beam/Nort	1	2	2	5	28	5.6	0
48	VR McKenzie	Triumph/AJS/Norton	0	6	1	7	39	5.57	0
49	RC Lewis	Norton	3	2	6	11	60	5.45	0
50	E Walters	Norton/AJS	0	4	1	5	27	5.4	0
51	J Thomas	AJS	1	9	5	15	79	5.26	0
52	E Rees	Ariel	0	3	1	4	21	5.25	0
53	LS Cordingley	Norton	2	4	6	12	62	5.16	0
54	DR Griffith	New Hudson/VMC	0	4	2	6	30	5	0
54	B Berry	Norton	0	2	1	3	15	5	0
54	A Griffiths	AJS	0	2	1	3	15	5	0
54	G Heinze	BSA/Norton/DOT	1	1	3	5	25	5	0
55	EG Bennett	Scott/Ariel	0	4	3	7	33	4.71	0
56	HC Lamacraft	Velocette	0	1	1	2	9	4.5	0

KINGS OF PENDINE: WORKS RIDERS

Rank	Rider	Machine	1sts	2nds	3rds	Events	Points	Av.	Pts
1	A Bennett	Douglas	1	0	0	1	14	14	4
2	S Wood	New Imperial	4	0	0	4	44	11	4
3	RB Young	Norton	8	1	0	9	94	10.44	8
4	G Dance	Sunbeam	15	0	0	15	150	10	0
4	T Spann	Brough Superior	3	2	0	5	50	10	8
5	H Langman	Scott	3	1	1	5	47	9.4	8
6	JH Simpson	AJS	4	1	1	6	53	8.83	4
7	CP Wood	Scott/HRD/Douglas	11	7	2	20	174	8.7	16
8	V Anstice	Douglas	4	4	0	8	68	8.5	4
9	FW Dixon	Doug/Brough/HRD	7	4	1	12	101	8.41	4
10	WL Handley	REX-ACME	2	0	0	2	16	8	4
10	RW Storey	Brough Superior	1	1	0	2	16	8	0
11	FM Rist	BSA	6	2	4	12	92	7.66	8
12	HR Davies	AJS	2	1	1	4	29	7.25	0
13	H Hassall	Norton	0	1	0	1	6	6	0
13	J Guthrie	New Hudson	0	2	0	2	12	6	0
14	L Parker	Douglas	0	2	1	3	15	5	0

POINTS AWARDED ON THE BASIS:
First 10; Second 6; Third 3; Bonus 4—for first place in a Championship event—or 20 miles and over.
NB: Not definitive. Based on available data (incomplete). To be regarded as an exercise, indicating form.

* N Treseder = father/son, difficult to distinguish in listings; D Jones = possibly two different riders.

INDEX

ABC 23, 40, **42**, 44
Aberavon 3, 17, 103
Ace, G 26, 32
Ace Garages 279
Ackers Street 239
ACU ix, 26, 35, 36, 41, 79, 84, 108, 111, 127, 146, 153, 173, 177, 178, 197, 208, 224, 227, 228, 239, 261, 263, 267, 269, 307
Adams
  SW 275
  TH 263
  WC 303
AJS 24, 25, 27, 35, **37**, 38, 44, 47, 61, 65, 67, 68, 71, 72, 75, 85, 87, 90, 103, 111, 128, 133, 134, 153, 158, 179, 181, 192, 218, 241, 247, 270, 299, 306
AJW m/c 290
Aldridge, EAD 96
Alldays 15, 45
Allen
  E 6
  Fitzroy, 279, 307
Alpine Cup 169
Alvis 104, 110, 145
Amal 283, 292
Amman Valley Dist M/c Club 17, 30
Anderson
  AA 85, 86
  F 261
Anstice, Vic 58, 65, 69, 74, 80, 83, 88, 109, 111, 113, 128, 134, 135, 189, 192
Antiquities of Laugharne 98
Anzani, British 149, 151, 290
Argyll 11
Ariel x, 44, 45, 78, 102, 182, 201, 205, 206, 214, 219, 224, 227, 228, 240, 244, 270, 281
Arnold's Hill 2, 5, 16
Arpajon 133, 154
Ashbury, AA 210
Ashwell Garage 166, 170, 171, 174, 278

Atkins, D 281
Atmos 35
Austin 43, 105
avionics 42, 94
Avro 63, 64

Babs 117, **119**, 120, 122, 123, 124, 138, 139, 140, 141, 142, 144, 145, 146, 148
Baker
  FE 85
  RH 172
Ballard, A 210, 214
Barclay, J/T 104-5
Bardsley, B 282, 285
Barker, WF 77-8, 89-90
Barnard
  JH 281
  PG 263
Barnes 18
Barregarrow 263
Barrow, AL 281
Bashford 168
Basset 110
Beach Hotel ix, 1, 2, 100, 122, 138, 141, 147, 148, 172, 174
Beart, Francis ix, x, xi, 135, 255, 257, 299
Beaufighter 239
Beaulieu 115, 314
Beck, JL 199, 200, 219, 221
Beckham, EA 219, 221, 253
Beeston-Humber, 12
Belgian Nat Speed Record 267
Belsize 12, 315
Bennett
  Alec **73**, 76-8
  E Gordon **153**, 160, 166, 183-5, 194-5, 228
Bentley 45, 142, 168, 190, 234
Berengaria 141
Berry, Bob 145, 239, 240, 244, 249, 255, 257, **265**, 267, 268, 274, 287, 290, 291, 292, 296, 306
'Big-port', AJS 25, 37
Billington, HW 227, 234, 237,

238, 240, 244, 249, 254, **255**, 256, 262, 277, 280
J 277
Birkin, CA 114, 149
Black Mountain 16, 17
Blackburne 28, 37, 38, 45, 48, 54, 69, 77, 85, 86, 111, 112, 157, 190
Blackpill 31, 63
Blaina 78, 153, 172, 179
Blue Bird 96, **100**, 106, 119, 120
Blundell, J 205
Blythe Bros 118
BMW 43, 214, 267
Board, I 58
Bolton, P 281, 288
Bonneville, USA 216, 283, 290, 293, 294
Boobyear, A 135
bookies 35, 38, 88, 216
Boshier-Jones, F 35, 39, 40
Bosisto, J 232, **234**, 235, 237
Bowden 275
Bowen, C 210
Bowers, C 210
Bowles, C 16, 128, 129, 130, 180
Bracebridge Street 51, 282, 289
Bradbury Jones & Co 32
Bradshaw 42, 50, 85, 86, 103
Brechfa 17, 159
Brett, J 227
Bridge Street Garage 21, 45, 54
Bridgend 61, 88, 103, 135, 222, 244, 268, 299
Brighton Speed Trials 267
Brock-Blackburne 37, 38
Brockbank, HF 37
Brockington, DG 157
Brooklands 4, 24, 27, 35, 47, 50, 80, 81, 88, 90, **94**, 96, 98, 114, 117, 119, 123, 125, 133, 145, 158, 160, 165, 188, 196, 213, 287
Brooklands Gazette 139
Brough
  George **167**-9
  William E 168

Brough Superior
  '90-bore' 22, 30, 32, 49-50, 57-8, 62
  SS80 88-89
  SS100 'Pendine' 103, 113, 130, 134, 155-6, 160-3, 169, 188-90, 200, 203, 239-40, 265-8
Brown
  AP 104
  George 289
Browning 205
BSA 21, 45, 88, 103, 235, 237, 240, 257, 275, 277, 278, 279, 281, **283**, 285, 298, 300, 303, 306
Buckley, NH 142, 166
Bugatti 107, 172, 173, 183
Bullock, A 56, 58
Burman gearbox 249, 292
Burnie, RJD 17, 51, **205**, 208, 221, 222, 225, 227, 240, 244, 253, 259, 278, 279
Bush
  FP 22-3, 40, 49, **63**-4
  HH 22, 40, 77
Bwlch-y-Cibau, Mont 118

Cadillac 236
Caffrey, JB 309, 310
Callingham, Major LG 122, 142, 143, 144, 147
Calthorpe 19, 45, 299, 303
cameras 229
Campbell, Malcolm 58, 95, **96**, 98, 100, 101, 104, 105, 106, 117, 138, 140, 146, 304
'Carbon' 201
Cardiff 21, 45, 47, 88, 125, 298
Carmarthen hospital 175, 292
Carmarthen Motor Cycle & Light Car Club 13, 42, **70-1**,100, 171, 179
Carodus, Peggy 296
Carr, JH 179, 190, 200-1, **203**, 205
Carroll, A 208
Carter
  AV 88-91, 193
  N 151, 180,184

Castrol 136, 217, 243, 257, 278, 306
causeway 7
Cefn Sidan 3
Chadwick 261
Chapman Challenge Cup 18, 107, 126
Chater-Lea 45, 85, 86, **198**
Chitty-Chitty-Bang-Bang 94, 96, 107
Christie, P 15
Chrysler 105
Church, H 23, 31, 36, 39
Clarke
  AV 135, 182
  J 18
Clement-Talbot 12
Clifford, J 84, 86, 166
Clithero, Lancs 214
Coatalen, L 107, 120
Cobb, J 120, 123, 281
Cocks, A 32
Colby, JV 13, 15
Cole, D 171
Collier Bros 50, 265
Connett, D 279, 287, 288
Conwil Evans, J 23, 52, 62
Cook 265
Cooper, GV 172
Cordery, Miss 105
Cordingley, L 208, 209, 210, 211, 214, 218
coroner 143, 147
Cotton 45, 48, 86, 102, 111, **112**, 134, 154, 157, 172, 180, 190, 192, 200
Coulson B 26, 31, 32
Cousins, P 263
Coventry Eagle 45, 169, 206, 240, 246
Coygan quarry 101
Cragg, T 298, **300**
Craig, Joe 134, **135**, 214, 263, 279
Crawley 18
Cripps 172
crowd 35, 66, 108, 126, 128, 131, 137, 153, 159, 177, 178, 179, 180, 187, 193, 197, 199, 206, 213, 260, 301

Crwbin 19, 21
'Cyclops' 183
Czechoslovakia 114

Daimler 11, 12, 15, 16
Dance, G 24, 35, 36, 38, 51, **52**, 56, 61, 66, 68, 69, 74, 77, 78, 80, 83, 88, 102, 135, 159, 160, 257, 271, 289
Daniel, Harold 221
Daniels
  JD 'Jack' 105, 205, 218-19, 222-3, 227-8, 250-3, 261, **263**, 298
  W 205
Danish Automobile Club 96
Darracq 6, 11
David, JW 85, 86, 88, 109
Davies,
  AE 210, 247
  BJ 'Ben' 240, 246
  D 103
  DW 281, 285
Davies, Gilbert **170**-1, 174, 278
Davies, Handel 22, 25, 30-32, 45, 49-50, 56-7, 103, 210, 224, 227-8, 234, 237, **248**, 306
Davies, Howard R 24-5, **27**, 34-6
  JE 179-80
  JG 237
  Ll (Luther) 40,42, 54,
  MD 281, 285
Davies, Molly 237
  RG 228
  S 299
  ST 281
  VB 281
  WD 17
Daytona 94, 98, 138, 148, 173
De Dion 11
de Havilland 107
de la Hay, T 65
de Rosier, J 265
Deadman, T 254
Dearden, Reg **261**, 263, 267, 269, 271, 273, 275, 279, 282, 287, 297
Delacourt 142

Delage 105
Delco-Remy 123
Diamond 54, 58, 81, 200
'Dickie Lake', the 132
Discol 81
Dixon, FW 51, 54, 65, 113, **115**, 125, 128, 133, 134, 153, 154, 157, 160, 166, 179, 193, 195, 278
Djelaleddin, Prince 107, 124, 173
Djelmo 107, 119, 124, 145, 172, 173, 174
Dodd, CH 10
Dodson, CJP 157
Dot 112, 160, 282, 283, 295, 299, 300
Doughty, W 298
Douglas 17, 32, 35, 37, 43, 50, **65**, 69, 74, 75, 77, 88, 90, 111, 113, 114, 115, 128, 134, 135, 166, 183, 190, 191, 194, 195, 199, 205, 207, 224, 250, 257, 306
Duke, Geoff 229, 261, 287
Dulais bridge 5
Dunelt 151, 180, 205, 224, 280
Dunlop 99, 123, 142, 144, 145, 205, 268, 283, 291
'Dunlop's Dividend' 17
Dunrod 62, 299
Dusenberg 94
'Dutch Salute' 195

Edmond 125
Edmund 23, 26, 44, 77
Edwards
    B 224-5, 235
    CF 84, 115, 134, 136-7, **166**-7, 183
    CR 260, **299**
    J 78
    JBB 247, 249, 269-70
    MR 84
    R 277
    Wm 21, 23, 45, 48-9, **152**
Enfield 12, 28, 45
Eppynt 79, 229, 261, 264, 269, 270, 275, 279, 299
Esholt Park x

Evans
    AM 209
    D 6
    DC 281
    DH 180
    EP 303
    J 4, 199
    SS **112-13,** 159, 188, 206
    TT 303
Evans, Wilmot 279
Eveleigh, I 281, 298
Ewenny 61, 221, 222
Excelsior x, 45, 224, 228, 280
Excelsior 'Manxman' 218, 228, 234, 236, 240, 248
Eyston, George **201**, 213-14

Fabian Society 44
Fairwood Common 263
Fanoe Islands 96
'Fast Motors Ltd' 88
Fernihough, E 265
Ferodo 65, 123
FIAT 58, 96, 105, 106, 172
Fitt, F 205
'Flapper', The 96
Fletcher, H 263
Flower, Lionel 102
'Flying Flea', The 42
'Flying Spray', The 215
Ford car 45, 58, 104, 132, 164
Foresti, G **107**, 145, 172
fossils 101, 102
Fowler, Rem 25
Francis Barnett 45, 297
Frazer-Nash 119
Freason, EJ 277
Free, Rollie 290
Freeguard, WJ 134

Gallop, C 118
Gardiner, AR 70
Gardner
    AE 58
    JK 161
    WH 235
Garnant 30, 45, 54, 248
Gates, D 253, 263

General Strike 124
geology 101
George
    E 15
    K 307
    NF 287-8
    T 298
Gershon, DC 103, 271
GN 58, 110
'Golden Dream' 154
Golden Grove 17
Good, CR 199, 210, 240, 244, 257, 259, 268
Goode, WA 102, 112
Graham, Les 261, 275
Great House 2
Greco, R 298
Green, E/R 5, 6, 13, 15, 32
Greening, SM 267, 291
Greenish, WH 13
Greenwood, A 88, 89
Gregor, G 153, 160, 182, 187, 189, **191**
Grey, A 88, 89, 113, 128, 134, 159, 304
Griffith, DR ix, 227, **249**, 250, 275, 287, 298, 303
Griffith, Dr A 6
Griffiths
    AS 206, 212, 214
    JT 79, 87, 281
Griffiths, LF 135, **219-22**, 237, 239, 250, 257-8, 302, 306
Griffiths, Mostyn **47**, 67, 86-7, 113, 126-8
Grimes, L 159, 164
Grindlay Peerless **188**, 189, 195
Grindlay-Peerless 45, 195, 206
Grinton, G 56, 61, 62, 80, 81, 85, 88, 108, 109, 110, 114
Guinness, KL 95, 96, 98, 106, 173
Guthrie, J 153, **157**, 159, 165, 214
Gwilliam, AJ 6, 15
GWR 63, 132
Gyon 265
gyroscopic action 101, 146

Halford 47
Hall Green 287
Hancock, DL 85
Handley, WL 80, 81, 85, 86, **88**, 91, 157
Hands 19
Harley-Davidson 20, 25, 40, 44, **49**, 50, 56, 61, 114, 206
Harries, JL 122
Harris
  A 300
  B 69
  H 58
  L 237
Harry, AM 154, 166, 177, 182
Hartle, J 261
Hassal, H 56, 61, **62**
Haverfordwest 2, 5, 13, 16, 32, 309, 310
Hazel, RE 224
Heinze, G **269**, 275, 299
Henderson 50
Henne, E 265
Henstock, A 52, 103, 110, 127
Henwood, CR 209, 210
Hermitage, The 139
'Higham Speial' 106, 107, 118, 119, 145
Hill, H 6
Hills-Johnes 44
Hinde, B 10
Hocking, G 261
Holding, B 85
Hopkins, T 24, 26
Horsell, S 23
Horton, RT 129, 130
Howell, Capt Hind 7, 10
Howey, RB/JEP 123
HRD 27, 124, 133, 153, 154, 157, 159, 160, 161, 166, 201, 203
Hughes
  C 77, 82-3
  TE 102-3
Hughes-Morgan 10, 11, 12, 17
Hulsman, HJ 281, 285
Humber 1, 6, 13, 18, 152
Humphries
  JSA 221
  PH 303

Hunkin, T 240, 241, 242, 244, 246, 247
Hurry Slowly 230
Husqvarna 213, 309
hyena den 101

Ilkley Moor 182
Indian 6, 18, 20, 24, 26, 40, 49, 50, **54**, 115, 265, 275
inquest 143
Invicta 105, 138
Irving, Capt P 229
Isaac, Morris 24, 26, 32, 38, **41**, 48, 54, 61, 67, 68, 70, 73, 76, 81, 85, 87
Isle of Man 23, 27, 40, 42, 47, 73, **132-33**, 169, **177-78**, 229, 263
Ivy 62
Ixion 44

Jacobs, ER 74, 75, 85, 86
Jaguar 205, 222
James
  AW 275
  C(L) 109
  DW 303
  G 303
  Ll 290, 298
  TOE 214
Janacek 114
Jarvis 100
Jawa 114
Jayne, CF 113, 157, 181, 190
Jeffrys, R 10
Jenkins, DL 228
Jeremiah, D 309
'Jix' 183
John, KE **241**-5, 253
John Bull trophy 177, 178, 219, 227
Johnson
  Amy 293
  G 214
  J 273
  T 270
Johnston 236, 281

Jones
  D 67, 278, **207**-8
  DA 160
  S 26
Jones-Lloyd, HA 6, 12, 13
Joynson-Hicks, W 10

Kerry 117
Kestrel engine 215
Kettle, JE 79, 88, 90, 91, 126, 177, 193
Kilgetty 236
King Smith, A 25
Kingston 108, 124
Kingswood, Bristol 153
Kipling, R 44
KLG 98, 123, 142, 147
Knight, EG, 270, 281
Kop hill 28, 108, 183

'Lady Bird' 120
Lagonda 45
Lamacraft, HC **236**, 237
Langdon 132
Lange, V 13
Langman, H 40, 80, 82, 83, 84, 89, 109, 113, 115
Laugharne 7, 13, 101, 132, 215
Lawrence, TE 133, **200**, 237
Laws, Edward 101
League International des Associations Touristes 7
Lee, R 310
Lerrigo, N 310
Lester, Ted 193, 203
Le Vack, H 158-9
Levis 129, 180
Lewis
  Albert 70-1
  B 88
  Miss M 234
  RC 235/6
Leyland 118, 119, 145
Leyland-Thomas 96, 117, 118
Liberty engine 107, 120, 146
Life with the Speed King 138
Lindsay, Dr Alexander 23, 25, 30, **50-51**, 59, 63, 70

INDEX

Linstanley JS 309
Lion engine 108
Little England Beyond Wales 101, 269
Llandebie 185, 205
Llandilo 5, 47, 88, 103, 110
Llanelly 87, 102, 103, 109, 126, 228, 234, 277
Llanfyrnach 1, 32, 217, 309
Llangadog 16
Llanishen 21, 126, 151
Llanstephan 1, 13, 269
Llewelyn, DJ 17
Lloyd, Col L 98, 122, 141
Lockhart, G 145, 146
Lodge 99, 178
Lones, HC 172
Lucas 293
'lurid' 56, 90, 129
Lusardi, LA **229**, 230, 233
LVT Special 273
Lyons, William 205

MacDonald, Tom 3
Mackenzie-Grieve, Comm. 122, 123
Maeterlinck, M 96
MAG 169
Main-Smith, B 300
Mainwaring, E 109, 113, 154, 160, 161, 179, 190
Mallins, JA 105
Manchester 88, 210, 218, 227, 237, 244, 247, 250, 255, 261, 265, 280, 287
Manchester University 292, 294
Mansell, DK 195
Mansfield, J 214
Marriott, F 94
Marros 101, 132
Marston Sunbeam 24, 73, 85, 157
Martin, N 105
Martinelli, M **269**, 270
Martinsyde 33
Mason, EB 277
Massey-Arran 35, 36, 62
Matabele engine 120
Matador 85, 86-**7**
Mayner, EA 105

Mays, R 104
McEvoy 114, 133, 134, **149**, 151, 153, 159, 160, 161, 166, 169
McEwan, T 227, 228, **229**, 289
McKenzie, VR 33, 78, 110
McNally, M 228
McNulty, J **208**, 210, 224, 253, 290
Mercedes 11, 105, 106
Mewis, W 113, 161, 166, 182, 183, 184, 193, 194, 195
MG 201, 207, 209
Middlesborough 115, 192, 210, 287
Miller, L 305
Mills, J 281, 299, 300
Milton, T 94
Milwaukee 24, 49
Miralite 123, 147
Mitchell, ER 26
'Moby Dick' 292
Moffat, AH 235, 271, 273
Mollison, J 293
Moore, Walter 135
Morgan
  C 281
  FN 58
  HFS 18
  JA 17
  Wilfred 119, 215
  W 299
Morgan car 129, 130, 172, 207
Morris car 105, 110, 122, 172, 210
Morris, CH 247
Moss, JB 218, 236, **237**, 239
Moto Guzzi 213, 268, 269
Motor Cycle Museum 52, 154, 305
Motor Museum, Nat: see Beaulieu
Motosacoche 159
Mundey, E 109, 110, 128, 134, 165
Museum of Speed, Pendine 305
Nantycaws 2
Napier 108, 119, 120, 136, 138, 139, 172
Neath Motor Cycle Club 17, 26, 40, 49, 61, 63, 71, 127, 131, 137, 179, 182, 197, 241, 297

Needham, CM 83, 88, 90, 113, 133
Nelson Hotel 35, 62, 103, 212
New Hudson 45, 103, 128, 134, 153, 154, 157, 159, 160, **165**, 178, 182, 183, 192, 219, 249
New Imperial 32, 39, 42, 67, **111**, 212, 213, 219, 222
Newsome 18
Nicholas, LW 287, 288, 298, 300, 301
Nicholson
  C 166
  PB 303
Norton
  BRS 21, 22 25, 28-30
  BS 50/1
  CS1 **208**
  Featherbed, ix, 135, 286, 287, 289, 297, 298, 301
  'Garden gate' 221
  Manx/International 220>
  Model 18 150/1
  ohv experimental 65
Norton
  Garage/'Motors', Blackpill 31, 63
Norton, Tom 41
NSU 11, 290, 292

'Ocky-Tipi': see Edwards, B
O'Donnell 8, 15
O'Donovan 65
OEC 85, 86, 292, 296
OK Supreme x, 189, 192, 214, **259**
Oldfield, B 94
Olympia 25, 44, 153, 292
Omega 24, 32, 45, 47
Ormond Beach 94, 98
Ostende 292
Owen, GF 6
Oxford 147
Oxwich 3, 134, 222, 271

P&M: see Panther
Paddock, RS 275
Pantall, D 15
Panther, (P&M) 19, 199, 214

Parfitt, GV 214
Parker
    I 58, 69, 85
    J 74
    L **82**-3, 88-90, 136, 166
Parkinson
    D ix-xi, **254**-9, 263
    RF 179, 181, 186-195, 206. **210**-11
Pastmasters of Speed 56, 73, 154
Patchett, GW 89, 90, 113, **114**, 134, 136, 153, 155, 159, 160, 161, 166, 278
Peacock, I 310
Pembrey 2, 222, 239, 250
Pembrokeshire Automobile Club 13, 31, 315
Penson, H 270
Peterson, P 309, 310
petrol 21, **51**, **81**, 122, 239, 243
Peugeot 25, 43, 151
Phillips
    A 172, 298
    AJ 298
Phillips, Douglas (end-papers), 297
    Dr 4
    Francis 15
    FD 33
    Sir I 32
    Jack 240, 244, 246
    LC 210
    Nicholas 198
Phillips, TJ 108, 114 5, 124, 128, 163
Pickerill, A 280
Pierard, L 110
Pimlott, E 281
Pipe car 117
Pitman 26
Platt, W 101
Poley, TH 240, 246, 249
Pollard, W Cox 11, 18
Pomilio bomber 107
Pontardawe 172
Pontarddulais 207
Popular Geology 101
Portishead 234
Potts, J 188, 189, 195

Povey Cross 120, 138
Powell, WD 180
Precision 18, 32, 41, 44, 62, 75, 85, 86
Prestwich, JA 158, 169, 291
Price, JD 26, 300
'Projectile, The' 292, 296
Protheroe, DW 221, 223
Prothero-Jones, D 171
Pugh, DJ/TH 247, 249, 253, 259, 263, 273, 275
Pullen, K 142, 143, 144, 147
Pullin, C 65
Pullman, CL 157, 181

Quadrant 11

RAC 95, 99, 100, 106, 108, 122, 123, 141, 145, 146, 174, 201
RAF 63, 239, 241, 250
Railton, R 142, 144
Raleigh 45, 103, 127, 160
Ratcliffe, G 310
Redcar 131, 210, 255, 289
Rees
    AA 298-9
    E 270
    RM 199, 234, 238
    WJ 246
Referee, The 98
REME 239
Renault 15
Renfrey, FJ 1, 2
Renolds 288, 291
Rensen, R 261
Rex 6, 17
Rex-Acme x, 54, 81, 85, 91, 102, 103, 157, 198, 255
Rex Speed King 15
RFC 63, 96
Ricardo, Sir Harry 47, 81
'Riccy' Triumph **47**, 81, 113

Richards
    CA 281
    H 172
Riley 115, 207, 273
Ripps, D 129
Rist, FM ix, 222, 257, 269, **277**, 278, 282, 283, 287, 297

Roberts
    JD 275
    JDH 281
    JN 62
Rogers, P 32, 67, 85, 87, 111, 112
Rolls Royce 33, 100, 118, 150, 168, 215, 239
Rook, RB 18
Rootes 120
Roscoe, N 310
Rover 6, 15, 32, 33
Rowley, G 108, 133, 179, 181
Royal Enfield 45, 46, 81, 85, 283, 297
Royal Horticultural Hall 119
RSPCA 10
Rubery Owen 118
Rudge 18, 26, 67, 99, 102, 144, 153, 182, 188, 193, 194, 206, 207, **253-4**
Rusk, Walter 214

Salmson 105
Salt House 215
Salt Lake 215, 216, 293
Sanderson 198
SAS 114
Saunders, PJ 194
Saundersfoot 7, 98, 275, 277, 280
Sawyer, LE 18
Schimmel-Andrews 7, 267, 288, 310
Scott 44, 51, 56, 61, 62, **66**, 68, 69, 82, 84, 89, 90, 154, 160, 166, 183
Sefton ST 282-4, 287-8
Segrave, H 108, 120, 148-9,
Selby-Clare 27
Sgonina, C 26, **28-30**, 47-9, 55, 57, 59, 110, **124-6**, 208
'Special' 28-31
Sheehan 171
Sheffield-Henderson 48, 56
Shell-Mex 122, 142
shells
    arty. 41, 165
    sea 101-2

INDEX

Shepherd, T 261
Sherman tank 107
Siddeley car 6
sidecar, banking 115, 136
    TT 114, 136, 166-7
Simister, T 134, 160
Simpson, JH 67-8, **71**-2, 74-5, 86-7, 90-1, 181
Singer car 17, 209
Sirrah 28
Sivell, PJ **208**, 210, 211, 214, 240
Skegness 96
Slack, Miss J/PE 281, 309
'Slug', The 120, 138, 148, 173
Smith, Gilbert 209, 240
Smith-Clarke, Capt 145
Snell, G 224, 234, 240
Snell-Adcock 249
Snow, DD 150, **275**, 281, 298, 303
SOS 217
Southport x, 3, 120, 131, 168, 179, 181, 198, 203, 205, 207, 210, 255, 267
Southworth, RH 303
Spann, T 133, 135, 153, **160**, 163, 177, 181, 182, 221
'Speed of the Wind', The 215
Sprague 98
St Andrews 3, 168, 207, 255
St Clears 1, 4, 9, 132, 198
Stanley Steamer 94
'Stan the Manse': see Davies, S
Stephens, ETM ix, 46, **79**, 81, 102, 157, 205, 210, 222, 225, 250, 263, 264, 269, 275, 278, 303
Stephens, Iago 199, 205
Stephens Special 163, 200
Stephenson, KR 309
Stepney, Lady 304
Stevens m/c 37, 50
Stevens-Precision 18
'Stinsford', Tudor 198
Stirling, smg 114
Stoodley, J 199, 205
Storey, RW 189, 190, 193, 194, 199
Strong, MG 309

Sturmey-Archer 169, 268
Sunbeam ix, 24, 40, 42, 54, 56, 59, 61, 64, 65, 69, 73, 74, 83, 86, 88, 103, 108, 110, 151, 157, 160, 163, 205, 227, 235, 257, 270, 271, 303, 306
supercharger 108, 115, 118, 120, 154, 173

Talbot 6, 13, 17
Talog 16
Taylor, MG 235, 237
Tebbs, P 310
Tegryn, Pembs 296
Temple, CF 196, 265, 292, 296
Tenby 7, 26, 98, 99, 104, 270, 281
Terry's springs 123
Thomas
    B 42
    DH 247
    DM 270, 288, 298, 303
Thomas, Dylan 215
    EM 160
    EW 180
    G 74, 221, 224-5, 277
    H 13
    Major HJP 13
Thomas, Ivor 35-6, **40**, 62 89-90
Thomas, Jack, 12, **40**, 277
Thomas, JG Parry **116**-124, 140-149
Thomas, LV 102-4, 128, 149, 153, 159, 181, 189, 250, 257, 271-**273**
    RC 128, 172
Thomas, RE, 'Gloag' 30, 130, 153, **155-6**, 160, 176-7, 180, 194
    TG 48
    VG 298
Thomason, A 299
Toms, RE 23
Treseder
    J 217, 240, 256
    N Jnr 254
    N Snr 240, 254
Trott, FC 224
Tucker, GH/WH 103, 166

Turpin, D 227
Tynon, D 247

Ulster 56, 84, 91, 135
Under Milk Wood 215
Utah 215

valves 37, 46, 47, 51, 65, 150, 151
Vanwall 135
Velocette 23, 36, 45, 69, 81, 86, 102, 111, **149**, 150, 151, 153, 159, 165, 213, 219, 259, 263, 275, 287, 298, 303
Veriot-Precision 41
Vernon Road 168
Vickery, H 277
Villa, L 92, 138
Villiers 24, 81, 108, 277, 281, 282
Vincent, P 27
Vincent-HRD 27, 219, 227, 229, 249, 263, 264, 267, 269
'VMC' 227, **249**
Vulcan 12

Wakefield ix, x, 171, 255
Walker, G 28, 253
Wanliss, Lieut EO 171
Ward, JC 84
Ware, RJ 277
Waters, JW 275, 277, 281
Watkins, PC 129
Weatherell 56, 58
Webster, DH 260
Weigel 11, 12
Wells, BJ 309
Wellstead, HR 105
Welsh Automobile Club 7, 9, 12
Welsh Grand Prix 219, 221, 236, 249, 255, 258, 261
Welsh Hundred 133, 177, 178, 181, 196, 198, 219, 244
Welsh TT 40, 61, 71, 73, 75, 78, 85, 88, 111, 113, 131, 132, 136, 155, 166
Welsh TT trophy 62, **177**, 311
Werts, GL 85, 86
Weybridge 4

Whitehead, G 299
Wild, RJ 298
Wilkins, DP 172, 182
Wilkinson 109
Williams
   C 163, 180
   CM 240, 246
   DTL 298
   EC 151
   ET 259
   H 277
   HL 279
   TJ 12, 16
   W 224
   WB 157
   WR 273
Wilson, K/S 277, 304
Wolverhampton 120, 275
Wood
   CP 56, 60-2, **66-7**, 161-3, 193-6
   CV 105
   S 'Ginger' **213**
Woods, S 112, 158, 213, 214

Wright, J 196
Wright-Precision 18
Wyn-Owen, Owen 147

Yates, WH 303, 304
Young, RB 261, 278, 279, 281, 282, 285, 287, 288, **289**

Zborowski, Count LV 94, 96, 106, 107, 118
Zenith 18, 88, 114, 124, 128, 130, 134, 154, 160, 161, 166

TO FUND HIS RACING CAREER, IN 1927, THE WILY L F GRIFFITHS SET ABOUT SELLING & REPAIRING MOTORCYCLES, FOR THE PUBLIC AND FELLOW 'SPEED-MEN', AT A GARAGE HE BUILT IN BRIDGEND.

OVER 70 YEARS ON, THE NAME AND PREMISES MAY HAVE CHANGED BUT

THE SPIRIT LIVES ON

AT

THUNDER ROAD
— M O T O R C Y C L E S —

INCORPORATING LESLIE GRIFFITHS MOTORS
ESTABLISHED 1927

HONDA   **HONDA**

Thunder Road Motorcycles Ltd
Tremains Road, Bridgend, South Wales, CF31 1TZ.
Tel 01656 661131 Fax 01656 661132 www.ThunderRoad.co.uk
Open Mon to Sat 9am-6pm Sun 11am-4pm

STILL SERVICING SPEED-MEN

AMGUEDDFA CYFLYMDER, PENTYWYN
MUSEUM OF SPEED, PENDINE

Dysgwch am hanes traeth byd-enwog Pentywyn, mewn adeilad newydd trawiadol sy'n bwrw'i drem dros y traeth. Yn yr haf, dewch i weld 'Babs', y car enwog sydd wedi'i adnewyddu, ynghyd â cherbydau cyflym eraill.

Explore the history of Pendine's 'Sands of Speed' in a dramatic new building, overlooking the beach. See the beautifully restored car 'Babs' in the summer and other record breaking and fast vehicles at other times.

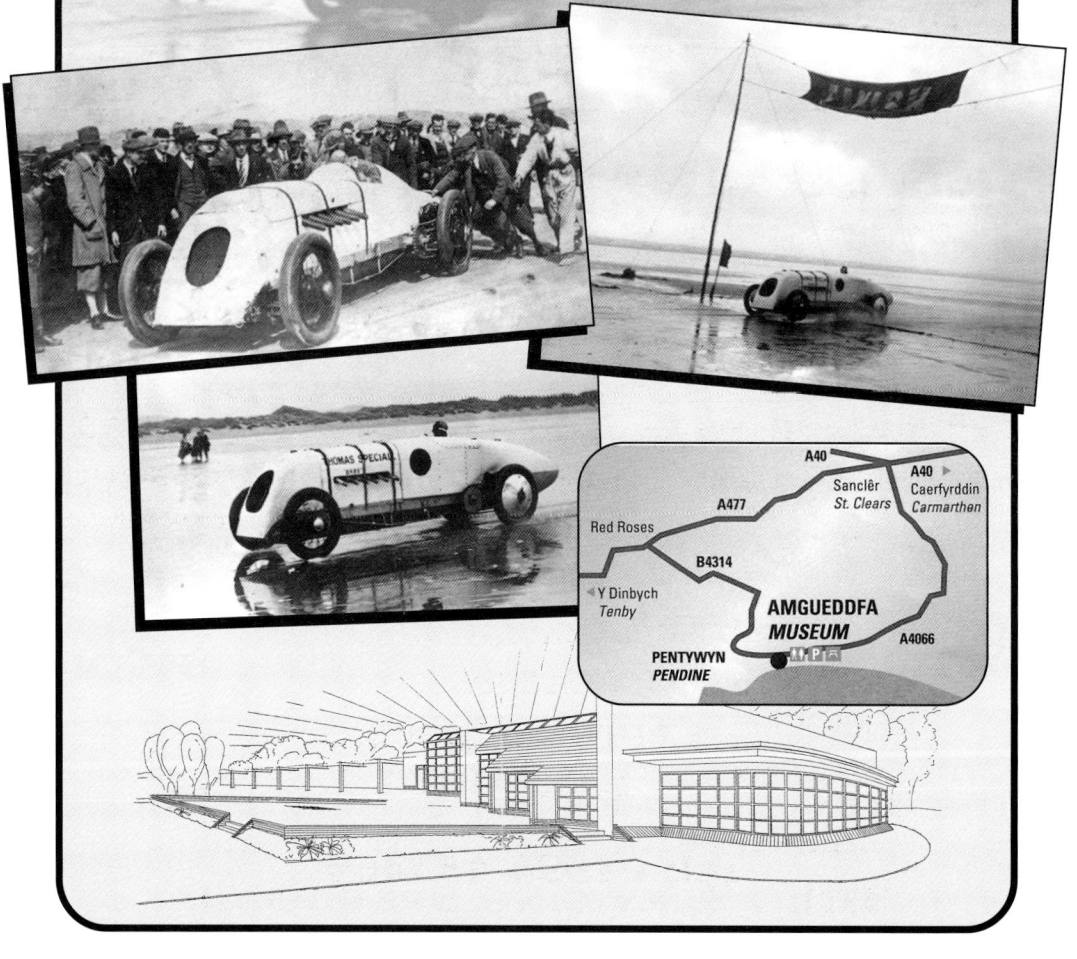

Tywi Damp Proofing Treatments

- Damp Course – Injection
- Wet & Dry Rot
- Condensation Control
- Woodworm
- Specialists in Tanking, Cellars, Basements and Swimming Pools

30 Year Manufacturer Guarantee

Approved contractors for **Sovereign, Crown** and **Mapei** products

Agents for Nuaire Condensation Units

27 ASHGROVE
PONTAMMAN
AMMANFORD

TEL/FAX: 01269 595179
Mobile 07860 456869

THE BEACH HOTEL

PENDINE

Headquarters of land-speed record teams wishes future land-speed record breakers all success

The Beach Hotel,
Pendine,
Carmarthenshire
SA33 4PA

Tel: 01994 453469

MANSEL DAVIES & SON LTD

Local and Long Distance Specialists
Bulk Liquid Specialists, Bulk Transport with Pneumatic Loading and Unloading, Heavy Haulage with Low Loaders

Agricultural Merchants
Suppliers of Ground Limestone, Magnesium Limestone, Slag and Fertiliser with spreading service

Suppliers of Building Materials
Quarry Owners Warehousing & Distribution Facilities

PEMBROKESHIRE FREIGHT LTD (A member of the Mansel Davies Group)

U.K. – Ireland Freight Services

Mansel Davies & Son (Garages) Ltd
Commercial Vehicle Repairs and MOT Preparation
Dept. of Transport Approved Tachograph Centre
Commercial Vehicle & Trailer Rental Service

VOLVO MAIN DEALERS FOR VOLVO TRUCKS

MITSUBISHI MOTORS CANTER

CERTIFICATE No. 956312/Y

Lucas Kienzle DTp Approved Tachograph Agent

LLANFYRNACH PEMBROKESHIRE SA35 0BZ
TEL: 01239 831631   FAX: 01239 831596

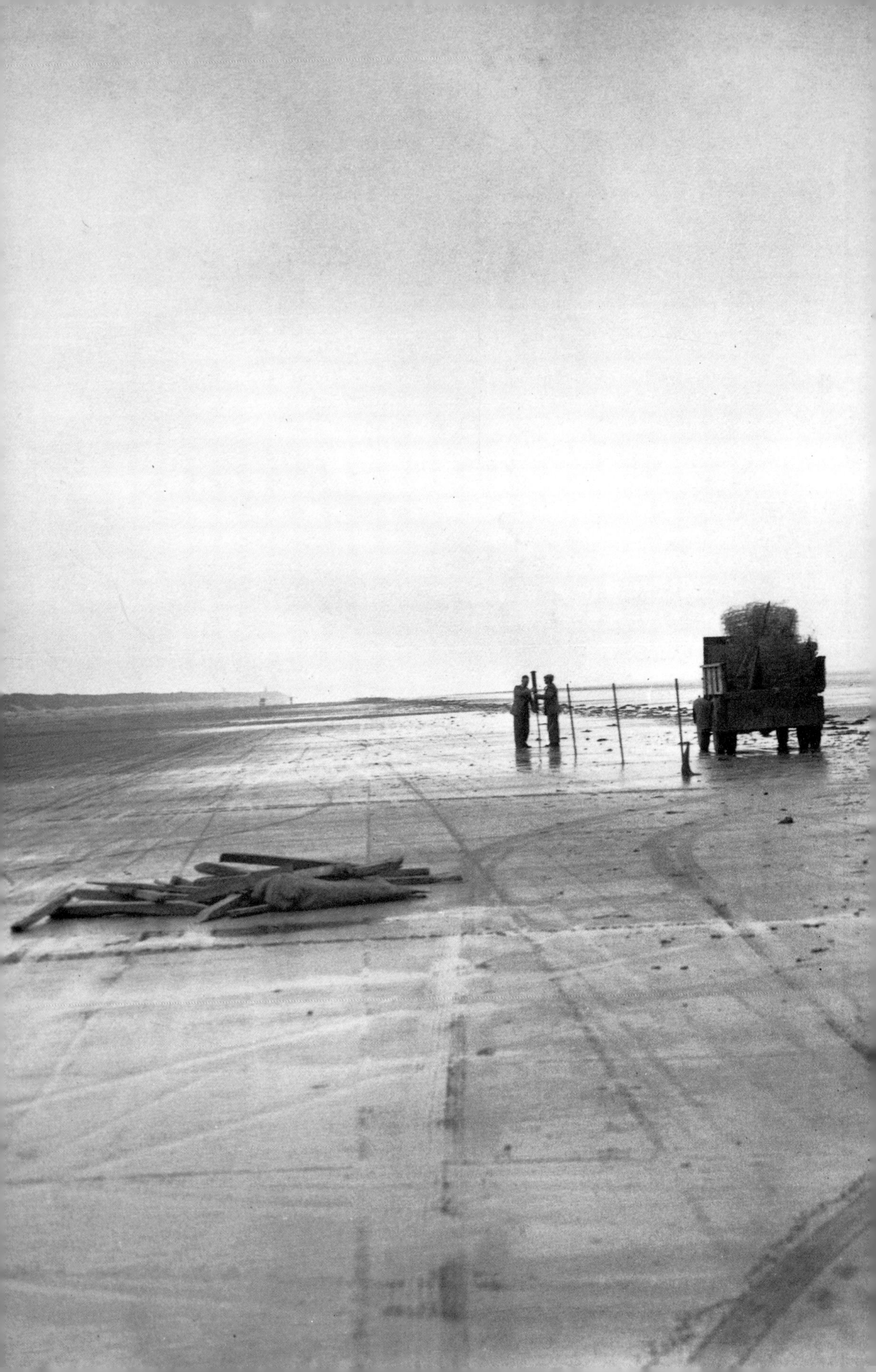